AUSTRALIA

RESEARCH AND DEVELOPMENT POLICY HANDBOOK

VOLUME 1

STRATEGIC INFORMATION, OPPORTUNITIES, CONTACTS

International Business Publications, USA
Washington DC, USA- Australia

AUSTRALIA

RESEARCH AND DEVELOPMENT POLICY HANDBOOK

VOLUME 1 STRATEGIC INFORMATION, OPPORTUNITIES, CONTACTS

UPDATED ANNUALLY

Cover Design: **International Business Publications, USA**

We express our sincere appreciation to all government agencies and international organizations which provided information and other materials for this handbook

2018 Edition Updated Reprint International Business Publications, USA
ISBN 1-4330-6248-8

This handbook provides basic information for starting or/and conducting business in the country. The extraordinary volume of materials covering the topic, prevents us from placing all these materials in this handbook. For more detailed information on issues related to any specific investment and business activity in the country, please contact Global Investment Center, USA
Please acquire the list of our business intelligence and marketing reports and other business publications. We constantly update and expand our business intelligence and marketing materials. Please contact the center for the updated list of reports on over 250 countries.

For additional analytical, business and investment opportunities information, please contact Global Investment & Business Center, USA at (703) 370-8082. Fax: (703) 370-8083. E-mail: ibpusa3@gmail.com Global Business and Investment Info Databank - www.ibpus.com

Printed in the USA

AUSTRALIA

RESEARCH AND DEVELOPMENT POLICY HANDBOOK

VOLUME 1

STRATEGIC , OPPORTUNITIES, CONTACTS

]

TABLE OF CONTENTS

STRATEGIC AND BUSINESS PROFILES

STRATEGIC PROFILE

Capital	Canberra 35°18.48′S 149°7.47′E
Largest city	Sydney
Official languages	None
National language	English
Religion	61.1% Christianity 2.5% Buddhism 2.2% Islam 1.3% Hinduism 1.2% Other religions 22.3% No religion 9.4% Not stated or unclear
Demonym	Australian Aussie (colloquial)
Government	Federal parliamentary constitutional monarchy
• Monarch	Elizabeth II
• Governor-General	Sir Peter Cosgrove
• Prime Minister	Malcolm Turnbull
• Chief Justice	Susan Kiefel
Legislature	Parliament
• Upper house	Senate
• Lower house	House of Representatives
Independence from the United Kingdom	
• Federation, Constitution	1 January 1901
• Statute of Westminster Adoption Act	9 October 1942 (with effect from 3 September 1939)
• Australia Act	3 March 1986
Area	
• Total	7,692,024 km^2 (2,969,907 sq mi) (6th)
Population	
• 2017 estimate	24,352,000 (51st)
• 2011 census	21,507,717
• Density	2.8/km^2 (7.3/sq mi) (236th)
GDP (PPP)	2015 estimate
• Total	$1.137 trillion (19th)
• Per capita	$47,318 (17th)
GDP (nominal)	2015 estimate
• Total	$1.223 trillion (13th)
• Per capita	$51,642 (9th)
Gini	33.6 medium · 19th
HDI	▲ 0.935 very high · 2nd
Currency	Australian dollar (AUD)

Time zone	various (UTC+8 to +10.5)
• Summer (DST)	various (UTC+8 to +11.5)
Date format	dd/mm/yyyy
Drives on the	left
Calling code	+61
ISO 3166 code	AU
Internet TLD	.au

Australia officially the **Commonwealth of Australia**, is a country comprising the mainland of the Australian continent, the island of Tasmania, and numerous smaller islands. It is the world's sixth-largest country by total area. Neighbouring countries include Indonesia, East Timor and Papua New Guinea to the north; the Solomon Islands and Vanuatu to the north-east; and New Zealand to the south-east.

For at least 40,000 years before the first British settlement in the late 18th century, Australia was inhabited by indigenous Australians, who spoke languages grouped into roughly 250 language groups. After the European discovery of the continent by Dutch explorers in 1606, Australia's eastern half was claimed by Great Britain in 1770 and initially settled through penal transportation to the colony of New South Wales from 26 January 1788. The population grew steadily in subsequent decades; the continent was explored and an additional five self-governing Crown Colonies were established.

On 1 January 1901, the six colonies federated, forming the Commonwealth of Australia. Since Federation, Australia has maintained a stable liberal democratic political system that functions as a federal parliamentary democracy and constitutional monarchy comprising six states and several territories. The population of 23.6 million is highly urbanised and heavily concentrated in the eastern states and on the coast.

Australia is a developed country and one of the wealthiest in the world, with the world's 12th-largest economy. In 2012 Australia had the world's fifth-highest per capita income, Australia's military expenditure is the world's 13th-largest. With the second-highest human development index globally, Australia ranks highly in many international comparisons of national performance, such as quality of life, health, education, economic freedom, and the protection of civil liberties and political rights. Australia is a member of the United Nations, G20, Commonwealth of Nations, ANZUS, Organisation for Economic Co-operation and Development (OECD), World Trade Organization, Asia-Pacific Economic Cooperation, and the Pacific Islands Forum.

GEOGRAPHY

Location: Oceania, continent between the Indian Ocean and the South Pacific Ocean
Geographic coordinates: 27 00 S, 133 00 E
Map references: Oceania
Area:
total: 7,686,850 sq km
land: 7,617,930 sq km
water: 68,920 sq km
note: includes Lord Howe Island and Macquarie Island

Area—comparative: slightly smaller than the USLand boundaries: 0 km

Coastline: 25,760 km
Maritime claims:

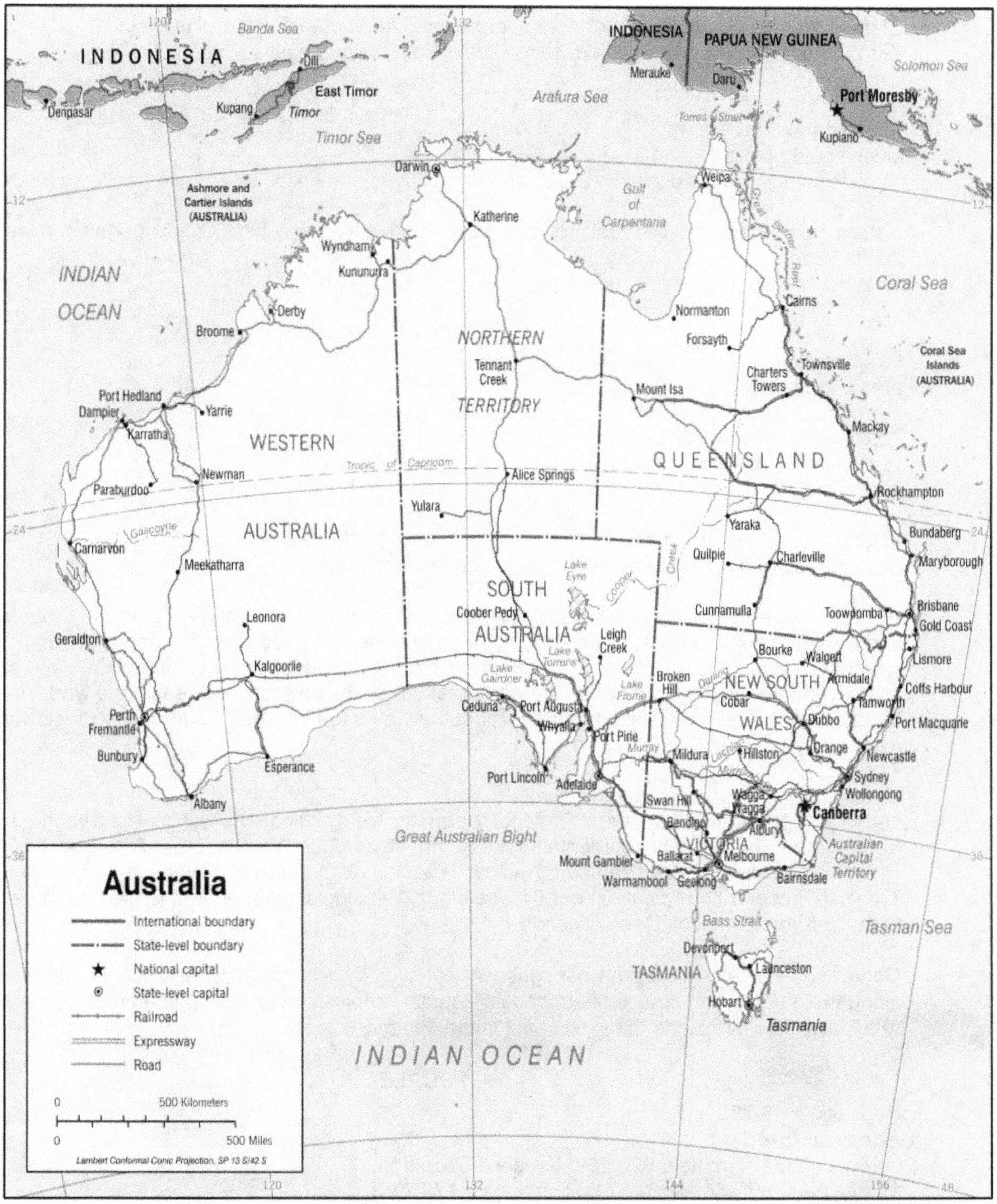

contiguous zone: 24 nm
continental shelf: 200 nm or to the edge of the continental margin
exclusive economic zone: 200 nm
territorial sea: 12 nm

Climate: generally arid to semiarid; temperate in south and east; tropical in north
Terrain: mostly low plateau with deserts; fertile plain in southeast

Elevation extremes:
lowest point: Lake Eyre -15 m
highest point: Mount Kosciusko 2,229 m

Natural resources: bauxite, coal, iron ore, copper, tin, silver, uranium, nickel, tungsten, mineral sands, lead,
zinc, diamonds, natural gas, petroleum

Land use:
arable land: 6%
permanent crops: 0%
permanent pastures: 54%
forests and woodland: 19%
other: 21%

Irrigated land: 21,070 sq km
Natural hazards: cyclones along the coast; severe droughts

Environment—current issues: soil erosion from overgrazing, industrial development, urbanization, and poor farming practices; soil salinity rising due to the use of poor quality water; desertification; clearing for agricultural purposes threatens the natural habitat of many unique animal and plant species; the Great Barrier Reef off the northeast coast, the largest coral reef in the world, is threatened by increased shipping and its popularity as a tourist site; limited natural fresh water resources

Environment—international agreements:
party to: Antarctic-Environmental Protocol, Antarctic Treaty, Biodiversity, Climate Change, Endangered Species, Environmental Modification, Hazardous Wastes, Law of the Sea, Marine Dumping, Marine Life Conservation, Nuclear Test Ban, Ozone Layer Protection, Ship Pollution, Tropical Timber 83, Tropical Timber 94, Wetlands, Whaling signed, but not ratified: Climate Change-Kyoto Protocol, Desertification.

Geography—note: world's smallest continent but sixth-largest country; population concentrated along the eastern and southeastern coasts; regular, tropical, invigorating, sea breeze known as "the Doctor" occurs along the west coast in the summer

PEOPLE

Population: 18,783,551
Age structure:
0-14 years: 21% (male 2,023,569; female 1,926,901)
15-64 years: 66% (male 6,317,045; female 6,172,735)
65 years and over: 13% (male 1,022,485; female 1,320,816)

Population growth rate: 0.9%
Birth rate: 13.21 births/1,000 population
Death rate: 6.9 deaths/1,000 population
Net migration rate: 2.66 migrant(s)/1,000 population

Sex ratio:
at birth: 1.06 male(s)/female
under 15 years: 1.05 male(s)/female
15-64 years: 1.02 male(s)/female
65 years and over: 0.77 male(s)/female
total population: 0.99 male(s)/female

Infant mortality rate: 5.11 deaths/1,000 live births

Life expectancy at birth:
total population: 80.14 years
male: 77.22 years
female: 83.23 years

Total fertility rate: 1.81 children born/woman

Nationality:
noun: Australian(s)
adjective: Australian

Ethnic groups: Caucasian 92%, Asian 7%, aboriginal and other 1%
Religions: Anglican 26.1%, Roman Catholic 26%, other Christian 24.3%, non-Christian 11%
Languages: English, native languages
Literacy:
definition: age 15 and over can read and write
total population: 100%
male: 100%
female: 100%

GOVERNMENT

Country name
:
conventional long form:
Commonwealth of Australia
conventional short form:
Australia

Government type:

federal parliamentary democracy and a Commonwealth realm

Capital:

name:
Canberra
geographic coordinates:
35 16 S, 149 08 E
time difference:

UTC+10 (15 hours ahead of Washington, DC, during Standard Time)
daylight saving time:
+1hr, begins first Sunday in October; ends first Sunday in April
note: Australia has three time zones

Administrative divisions:

6 states and 2 territories*; Australian Capital Territory*, New South Wales, Northern Territory*, Queensland, South Australia, Tasmania, Victoria, Western Australia

Dependent areas:

Ashmore and Cartier Islands, Christmas Island, Cocos (Keeling) Islands, Coral Sea Islands, Heard Island and McDonald Islands, Macquarie Island, Norfolk Island

Independence:

1 January 1901 (from the federation of UK colonies)

National holiday:

Australia Day (commemorates the arrival of the First Fleet of Australian settlers), 26 January (1788); ANZAC Day (commemorates the anniversary of the landing of troops of the Australian and New Zealand Army Corps during World War I at Gallipoli, Turkey), 25 April (1915)

Constitution:

9 July 1900; effective 1 January 1901; amended several times, last in 1977; note - a referendum to amend the constitution to reflect the Aboriginal and Torres Strait Islander Peoples Recognition Act 2013 is to be completed by the end of 2015

Legal system:

common law system based on the English model

International law organization participation:

accepts compulsory ICJ jurisdiction with reservations; accepts ICCt jurisdiction

Suffrage:
18 years of age; universal and compulsory

Executive branch:

chief of state: Queen of Australia ELIZABETH II (since 6 February 1952); represented by Governor General Sir Peter COSGROVE (since 28 March 2015)
head of government: Prime Minister Malcolm TURNBULL (since 15 September 2015); Deputy Prime Minister Barnaby JOYCE (since 18 February 2016)
cabinet: Cabinet nominated by the prime minister from among members of Parliament and sworn in by the governor general

elections/appointments: the monarchy is hereditary; governor general appointed by the monarch on the recommendation of the prime minister; following legislative elections, the leader of the majority party or majority coalition is sworn in as prime minister by the governor general

Legislative branch:
description: bicameral Federal Parliament consists of the Senate (76 seats; 12 members from each of the 6 states and 2 each from the 2 mainland territories; members directly elected in multi-seat constituencies by proportional representation vote; members serve 6-year terms with one-half of state membership renewed every 3 years and territory membership renewed every 3 years) and the House of Representatives (150 seats; members directly elected in single-seat constituencies by majority preferential vote; members serve terms of up to 3 years)

elections: Senate - last held on 2 July 2016; House of Representatives - last held on 2 July 2016; this election represents a rare double dissolution where all 226 seats in both the Senate and House of Representatives are up for reelection
election results: Senate - percent of vote by party NA - awaiting final results; seats by party NA - awaiting final results; House of Representatives - percent of vote by party Liberal/National Coalition 42.14%, ALP 34.91%, The Greens 9.93%, Katter's Australian Party 0.55%, Nick Xenophon Team 1.86%, independents 2.85%; seats by party Liberal/National Coalition 77, ALP 68, The Greens 1, Katter's Australian Party 1, Nick Xenophon Team 1, independents 2

Judicial branch:

highest court(s):
High Court of Australia (consists of 7 justices, including the chief justice); note - each of the 6 states, 2 territories, and Norfolk Island has a Supreme Court; the High Court is the final appellate court beyond the state and territory supreme courts
judge selection and term of office:
justices appointed by the governor-general in council for life with mandatory retirement at age 70
subordinate courts:
subordinate courts at the federal level: Federal Court; Federal Magistrates' Courts of Australia; Family Court; subordinate courts at the state and territory level: Local Court - New South Wales; Magistrates' Courts – Victoria, Queensland, South Australia, Western Australia, Tasmania, Northern Territory, Australian Capital Territory; District Courts – New South Wales, Queensland, South Australia, Western Australia; County Court – Victoria; Family Court – Western Australia; Court of Petty Sessions – Norfolk Island

Political parties and leaders:

Australian Greens Party [Richard DI NATALE]
Australian Labor Party [Bill SHORTEN]

Country Liberal Party or CLP [Gary HIGGINS]
Family First Party [Bob DAY]
Katter's Australian Party [Bob KATTER]
Liberal National Party of Queensland or LNP [Timothy NICHOLLS]
Liberal Party [Malcolm TURNBULL]
National Party of Australia [Barnaby JOYCE]
Palmer United Party or PUP [Clive PALMER]
Political pressure groups and leaders:
other: business groups, environmental groups, social groups, trade unions

Political pressure groups and leaders:

other:
business groups, environmental groups, social groups, trade unions

International organization participation:

ADB, ANZUS, APEC, ARF, ASEAN (dialogue partner), Australia Group, BIS, C, CD, CP, EAS, EBRD, EITI (implementing country), FAO, FATF, G-20, IAEA, IBRD, ICAO, ICC (national committees), ICRM, IDA, IEA, IFC, IFRCS, IHO, ILO, IMF, IMO, IMSO, Interpol, IOC, IOM, IPU, ISO, ITSO, ITU, ITUC (NGOs), MIGA, NEA, NSG, OECD, OPCW, OSCE (partner), Pacific Alliance (observer), Paris Club, PCA, PIF, SAARC (observer), SICA (observer), Sparteca, SPC, UN, UN Security Council (temporary), UNCTAD, UNESCO, UNHCR, UNMISS, UNMIT, UNRWA, UNTSO, UNWTO, UPU, WCO, WFTU (NGOs), WHO, WIPO, WMO, WTO, ZC

Diplomatic representation in the US:

chief of mission:
Ambassador Kim Christian BEAZLEY (since 7 February 2010)
chancery:
1601 Massachusetts Avenue NW, Washington, DC 20036
telephone:
(202) 797-3000
FAX:
(202) 797-3168
consulate(s) general:
Atlanta, Chicago, Honolulu, Los Angeles, New York, San Francisco

Diplomatic representation from the US:

chief of mission:
Ambassador John BERRY (since 25 September 2013)
embassy:
Moonah Place, Yarralumla, Canberra, Australian Capital Territory 2600
mailing address:
APO AP 96549
telephone:

[61] (02) 6214-5600
FAX:
[61] (02) 6214-5970
consulate(s) general:
Melbourne, Perth, Sydney

Flag description:

blue with the flag of the UK in the upper hoist-side quadrant and a large seven-pointed star in the lower hoist-side quadrant known as the Commonwealth or Federation Star, representing the federation of the colonies of Australia in 1901; the star depicts one point for each of the six original states and one representing all of Australia's internal and external territories; on the fly half is a representation of the Southern Cross constellation in white with one small, five-pointed star and four larger, seven-pointed stars

National symbol(s):

Southern Cross constellation (five, seven-pointed stars); kangaroo; emu

National anthem:

name:
"Advance Australia Fair"

ECONOMY

Following two decades of continuous growth, low unemployment, contained inflation, very low public debt, and a strong and stable financial system, Australia enters 2016 facing a range of growth constraints, principally driven by a sharp fall in global prices of key export commodities. Demand for resources and energy from Asia and especially China has stalled and sharp drops in current prices have impacted growth.

The services sector is the largest part of the Australian economy, accounting for about 70% of GDP and 75% of jobs. Australia was comparatively unaffected by the global financial crisis as the banking system has remained strong and inflation is under control.

Australia benefited from a dramatic surge in its terms of trade in recent years, although this trend has reversed due to falling global commodity prices. Australia is a significant exporter of natural resources, energy, and food. Australia's abundant and diverse natural resources attract high levels of foreign investment and include extensive reserves of coal, iron, copper, gold, natural gas, uranium, and renewable energy sources. A series of major investments, such as the US$40 billion Gorgon Liquid Natural Gas project, will significantly expand the resources sector.

Australia is an open market with minimal restrictions on imports of goods and services. The process of opening up has increased productivity, stimulated growth, and made the economy more flexible and dynamic. Australia plays an active role in the World Trade Organization, APEC, the G20, and other trade forums. Australia's free trade agreement

(FTA) with China entered into force in 2015, adding to existing FTAs with the Republic of Korea, Japan, Chile, Malaysia, New Zealand, Singapore, Thailand, and the US, and a regional FTA with ASEAN and New Zealand. Australia continues to negotiate bilateral agreements with India and Indonesia, as well as larger agreements with its Pacific neighbors and the Gulf Cooperation Council countries, and an Asia-wide Regional Comprehensive Economic Partnership that includes the ten ASEAN countries and China, Japan, Korea, New Zealand and India. Australia is also working on the Trans-Pacific Partnership Agreement with Brunei, Canada, Chile, Japan, Malaysia, Mexico, New Zealand, Peru, Singapore, the US, and Vietnam.

GDP (purchasing power parity):

$1.189 trillion (2016 est.)
$1.156 trillion (2015 est.)
$1.128 trillion (2015 est.)
note: data are in 2016 dollars
country comparison to the world: 20

GDP (official exchange rate):
$1.257 trillion (2015 est.)

GDP - real growth rate:
2.9% (2016 est.)
2.4% (2015 est.)
2.7% (2015 est.)
country comparison to the world: 102

GDP - per capita (PPP):
$48,800 (2016 est.)
$48,300 (2015 est.)
$47,800 (2015 est.)
note: data are in 2016 dollars
country comparison to the world: 26

Gross national saving:
21.7% of GDP (2016 est.)
22.1% of GDP (2015 est.)
23.7% of GDP (2015 est.)
country comparison to the world: 72

GDP - composition, by end use:
household consumption: 58.5%
government consumption: 18.7%
investment in fixed capital: 24.3%
investment in inventories: 0%
exports of goods and services: 19.4%
imports of goods and services: -20.9% (2016 est.)

GDP - composition, by sector of origin:
agriculture: 3.6%
industry: 28.2%
services: 68.2% (2016 est.)
Agriculture - products:

wheat, barley, sugarcane, fruits; cattle, sheep, poultry
Industries:
mining, industrial and transportation equipment, food processing, chemicals, steel

Industrial production growth rate:
2% (2016 est.)
country comparison to the world: 104

Labor force:
12.63 million (2016 est.)
country comparison to the world: 45

Labor force - by occupation:
agriculture: 3.6%
industry: 21.1%
services: 75.3% (2009 est.)

Unemployment rate:
5.8% (2016 est.)
6.1% (2015 est.)
country comparison to the world: 62

Household income or consumption by percentage share:
lowest 10%: 2%
highest 10%: 25.4% (1994)

Distribution of family income - Gini index:
30.3
35.2 (1994)
country comparison to the world: 120

Budget:
revenues: $420.5 billion
expenditures: $446.4 billion (2016 est.)

Taxes and other revenues:
33.5% of GDP (2016 est.)
country comparison to the world: 65

Budget surplus (+) or deficit (-):
-2.1% of GDP (2016 est.)
country comparison to the world: 70
Public debt:
46.1% of GDP (2016 est.)
44.2% of GDP (2015 est.)
country comparison to the world: 98

Fiscal year:
1 July - 30 June

Inflation rate (consumer prices):
1.4% (2016 est.)
1.5% (2015 est.)

country comparison to the world: 87

Central bank discount rate:
3% (28 February 2013)
4.35% (31 December 2010)
note: this is the Reserve Bank of Australia's "cash rate target," or policy rate
country comparison to the world: 106

Commercial bank prime lending rate:
5.1% (31 December 2016 est.)
5.58% (31 December 2015 est.)
country comparison to the world: 138

Stock of narrow money:
$245.3 billion (31 December 2016 est.)
$223.2 billion (31 December 2015 est.)
country comparison to the world: 18

Stock of broad money:
$1.661 trillion (31 December 2013 est.)
$1.648 trillion (31 December 2012 est.)
country comparison to the world: 11

Stock of domestic credit:
$2.158 trillion (31 December 2016 est.)
$1.986 trillion (31 December 2015 est.)
country comparison to the world: 11

Market value of publicly traded shares:
$1.187 trillion (31 December 2015 est.)
$1.289 trillion (31 December 2015 est.)
$1.366 trillion (31 December 2013 est.)
country comparison to the world: 13

Current account balance:
-$43.85 billion (2016 est.)
-$57.98 billion (2015 est.)
country comparison to the world: 194

Exports:
$184.3 billion (2016 est.)
$188.3 billion (2015 est.)
country comparison to the world: 26

Exports - commodities:
coal, iron ore, gold, meat, wool, alumina, wheat, machinery and transport equipment

Exports - partners:
China 32.2%, Japan 15.9%, South Korea 7.1%, US 5.4%, India 4.2% (2015)
Imports:
$203.1 billion (2016 est.)
$207.7 billion (2015 est.)
country comparison to the world: 21

Imports - commodities:
machinery and transport equipment, computers and office machines, telecommunication equipment and parts; crude oil and petroleum products

Imports - partners:
China 23%, US 11.2%, Japan 7.4%, South Korea 5.5%, Thailand 5.1%, Germany 4.6% (2015)

Reserves of foreign exchange and gold:
$54.3 billion (31 December 2016 est.)
$49.27 billion (31 December 2015 est.)
country comparison to the world: 36

Debt - external:
$1.692 trillion (31 December 2016 est.)
$1.524 trillion (31 December 2015 est.)
country comparison to the world: 12
Stock of direct foreign investment - at home:
$614.5 billion (31 December 2016 est.)
$582.6 billion (31 December 2015 est.)
country comparison to the world: 16

Stock of direct foreign investment - abroad:
$441.9 billion (31 December 2016 est.)
$437.8 billion (31 December 2015 est.)
country comparison to the world: 18

Exchange rates:
Australian dollars (AUD) per US dollar -
1.352 (2016 est.)
1.3291 (2015 est.)
1.3291 (2015 est.)
1.1094 (2013 est.)
0.97 (2012 est.)

ENERGY

Electricity - production:
235 billion kWh (2015 est.)
country comparison to the world: 21

Electricity - consumption:
224 billion kWh (2015 est.)
country comparison to the world: 18

Electricity - exports:
0 kWh (2013 est.)
country comparison to the world: 211

Electricity - imports:
0 kWh (2013 est.)
country comparison to the world: 213

Electricity - installed generating capacity:
67 million kW (2015 est.)
country comparison to the world: 17

Electricity - from fossil fuels:
78.5% of total installed capacity (2012 est.)
country comparison to the world: 95

Electricity - from nuclear fuels:
0% of total installed capacity (2012 est.)
country comparison to the world: 204

Electricity - from hydroelectric plants:
12.7% of total installed capacity (2012 est.)
country comparison to the world: 107

Electricity - from other renewable sources:
7.6% of total installed capacity (2012 est.)
country comparison to the world: 49

Crude oil - production:
322,300 bbl/day (2015 est.)
country comparison to the world: 32

Crude oil - exports:
248,400 bbl/day (2015 est.)
country comparison to the world: 28

Crude oil - imports:
332,800 bbl/day (2015 est.)
country comparison to the world: 26

Crude oil - proved reserves:
1.2 billion bbl (1 January 2016 es)
country comparison to the world: 40
Refined petroleum products - production:
481,800 bbl/day (2015 est.)
country comparison to the world: 37

Refined petroleum products - consumption:
1.116 million bbl/day (2015 est.)
country comparison to the world: 21

Refined petroleum products - exports:
42,730 bbl/day (2015 est.)
country comparison to the world: 60

Refined petroleum products - imports:
546,700 bbl/day (2015 est.)
country comparison to the world: 15

Natural gas - production:
62.64 billion cu m (2015 est.)

country comparison to the world: 15

Natural gas - consumption:
38.51 billion cu m (2015 est.)
country comparison to the world: 25

Natural gas - exports:
31.61 billion cu m (2015 est.)
country comparison to the world: 12

Natural gas - imports:
6.938 billion cu m (2015 est.)
country comparison to the world: 30

Natural gas - proved reserves:
860.8 billion cu m (1 January 2016 es)
country comparison to the world: 26

Carbon dioxide emissions from consumption of energy:
385 million Mt (2013 est.)
country comparison to the world: 18

COMMUNICATIONS

Telephones - fixed lines:
total subscriptions: 9.08 million
subscriptions per 100 inhabitants: 40 (July 2015 est.)
country comparison to the world: 22

Telephones - mobile cellular:
total: 31.77 million
subscriptions per 100 inhabitants: 140 (July 2015 est.)
country comparison to the world: 39

Telephone system:
general assessment: excellent domestic and international service
domestic: domestic satellite system; significant use of radiotelephone in areas of low population density; rapid growth of mobile telephones

international: country code - 61; landing point for the SEA-ME-WE-3 optical telecommunications submarine cable with links to Asia, the Middle East, and Europe; the Southern Cross fiber-optic submarine cable provides links to NZ and the US; satellite earth stations - 10 (2015)

Broadcast media:
the Australian Broadcasting Corporation (ABC) runs multiple national and local radio networks and TV stations, as well as Australia Network, a TV service that broadcasts throughout the Asia-Pacific region and is the main public broadcaster; Special Broadc

Internet country code:
.au

Internet users:
total: 19.238 million

percent of population: 84.6% (July 2015 est.)
country comparison to the world: 28

TRANSPORTATION

National air transport system:
number of registered air carriers: 11
inventory of registered aircraft operated by air carriers: 175
annual passenger traffic on registered air carriers: 69,294,187
annual freight traffic on registered air carriers: 1,887,295,820 mt-km (2015)
Civil aircraft registration country code prefix:
VH (2016)

Airports:
480 (2013)
country comparison to the world: 16

Airports - with paved runways:
total: 349
over 3,047 m: 11
2,438 to 3,047 m: 14
1,524 to 2,437 m: 155
914 to 1,523 m: 155
under 914 m: 14

Airports - with unpaved runways:
total: 131
1,524 to 2,437 m: 16
914 to 1,523 m: 101
under 914 m: 14

Heliports:
1

Pipelines:
condensate/gas 637 km; gas 30,054 km; liquid petroleum gas 240 km; oil 3,609 km; oil/gas/water 110 km; refined products 72 km (2013)

Railways:
total: 36,967.5 km
broad gauge: 3,727 km 1.600-m gauge (372 km electrified)
standard gauge: 18,727 km 1.435-m gauge (650 km electrified)
narrow gauge: 14,513.5 km 1.067-m gauge (2,075.5 km electrified)
country comparison to the world: 7

Roadways:
total: 823,217 km
paved: 356,343 km
unpaved: 466,874 km (2011)
country comparison to the world: 9

Waterways:
2,000 km (mainly used for recreation on Murray and Murray-Darling river systems) (2011)
country comparison to the world: 42

Merchant marine:
total: 41
by type: bulk carrier 8, cargo 7, liquefied gas 4, passenger 6, passenger/cargo 6, petroleum tanker 5, roll on/roll off 5
foreign-owned: 17 (Canada 5, Germany 2, Singapore 2, South Africa 1, UK 5, US 2)
registered in other countries: 25 (Bahamas 1, Dominica 1, Fiji 2, Liberia 1, Netherlands 1, Panama 4, Singapore 12, Tonga 1, UK 1, US 1) (2010)
country comparison to the world: 75

Ports and terminals:
major seaport(s): Brisbane, Cairns, Darwin, Fremantle, Geelong, Gladstone, Hobart, Melbourne, Newcastle, Port Adelaide, Port Kembla, Sydney
dry bulk cargo port(s): Dampier (iron ore), Dalrymple Bay (coal), Hay Point (coal), Port Hedland (iron ore), Port Walcott (iron ore)
container port(s) (TEUs): Brisbane (1,004,983), Melbourne (2,467,967), Sydney (2,028,074)(2011)
LNG terminal(s) (export): Darwin, Karratha, Burrup, Curtis Island

MILITARY

Military branches:
Australian Defense Force (ADF): Australian Army, Royal Australian Navy (includes Naval Aviation Force), Royal Australian Air Force, Joint Operations Command (JOC)

Military service age and obligation:
17 years of age for voluntary military service (with parental consent); no conscription; women allowed to serve in most combat roles, except the Army special forces

Military expenditures:
1.71% of GDP (2012)
1.84% of GDP (2011)
1.71% of GDP (2010)
country comparison to the world: 50

TRANSNATIONAL ISSUES

Disputes - international:
In 2007, Australia and Timor-Leste agreed to a 50-year development zone and revenue sharing arrangement and deferred a maritime boundary; Australia asserts land and maritime claims to Antarctica; Australia's 2004 submission to the Commission on the Limits of the Continental Shelf extends its continental margins over 3.37 million square kilometers, expanding its seabed roughly 30 percent beyond its claimed EEZ; all borders between Indonesia and Australia have been agreed upon bilaterally, but a 1997 treaty that would settle the last of their maritime and EEZ boundary has yet to be ratified by Indonesia's legislature; Indonesian groups challenge Australia's claim to Ashmore Reef; Australia closed parts of the Ashmore and Cartier reserve to Indonesian traditional fishing

Refugees and internally displaced persons:
refugees (country of origin): 7,785 (Afghanistan); 5,201 (Iran)

Illicit drugs:

Tasmania is one of the world's major suppliers of licit opiate products; government maintains strict controls over areas of opium poppy cultivation and output of poppy straw concentrate; major consumer of cocaine and amphetamines

IMPORTANT INFORMATION FOR UNDERSTANDING AUSTRALIA

OFFICIAL NAME: Commonwealth of Australia

Geography
Area: 7.7 million sq. km. (3 million sq. mi.); about the size of the 48 contiguous United States.
Cities: *Capital*--Canberra (pop. 323,000). *Other cities*--Sydney (4.2 million), Melbourne (3.6 million), Brisbane (1.7 million), Perth (1.4 million).
Terrain: Varied, but generally low-lying.
Climate: Relatively dry, ranging from temperate in the south to tropical in the north.

People
Nationality: *Noun and adjective*--Australian(s).
Population: 20.2 million.
Annual population growth rate: 1.1%.
Ethnic groups: European 92%, Asian 6%, Aboriginal 2%.
Religions: Anglican 21%, Roman Catholic 27%, other Christian 20%, other non-Christian 5%, no religion 16% and not stated 12%.
Languages: English.
Education: *Years compulsory*--to age 15 in all states except Tasmania, where it is 16. *Literacy*--over 99%.
Health: *Infant mortality rate*--5/1,000. *Life expectancy*--males 78 yrs., females 83 yrs.
Work force (10.1 million): *Agriculture*--4%; *mining, manufacturing, construction, and utilities*--21%; *services*--70%; *public administration and defense*--5%.

Government
Type: Democratic, federal-state system recognizing British monarch as sovereign.
Constitution: July 9, 1900.
Independence (federation): January 1, 1901.
Branches: Head of state is the governor general, who is appointed by the Queen of Australia (the British Monarch). *Legislative*--bicameral Parliament (76-member Senate, 150-member House of Representatives). The House of Representatives selects as head of government the Prime Minister, who then appoints his cabinet. *Judicial*--independent judiciary. Administrative subdivisions: Six states and two territories.
Political parties: Liberal, Nationals, Australian Labor, Australian Democrats, Australian Greens, and Family First. The Liberal Party and the Nationals form the governing coalition.
Suffrage: Universal and compulsory over 18.
Central government budget: FY 2004-05 $149.86 billion; FY 2005-06 $158.76 billion.
Defense: 1.9% of GDP for FY 2005-06.

PEOPLE

Australia's aboriginal inhabitants, a hunting-gathering people generally referred to as Aboriginals and Torres Straits Islanders, arrived more than 40,000 years ago. Although their technical culture remained static--depending on wood, bone, and stone tools and weapons--their spiritual and social life was highly complex. Most spoke several languages, and confederacies sometimes linked widely scattered tribal groups. Aboriginal population density ranged from one person per square mile along the coasts to one person per 35 square miles in the arid interior. When Capt.

James Cook claimed Australia for Great Britain in 1770, the native population may have numbered 300,000 in as many as 500 tribes speaking many different languages. The aboriginal population currently numbers more than 410,000, representing about 2.2% of the population. Since the end of World War II, the government and the public have made efforts to be more responsive to aboriginal rights and needs.

Immigration has been a key to Australia's development since the beginning of European settlement in 1788. For generations, most settlers came from the British Isles, and the people of Australia are still predominantly of British or Irish origin, with a culture and outlook similar to those of Americans. However, since the end of World War II, the population has more than doubled; non-European immigration, mostly from the Middle East, Asia, and Latin America, has increased significantly since 1960 through an extensive, planned immigration program. From 1945 through 2000, nearly 5.9 million immigrants settled in Australia, and about 80% have remained; nearly two of every seven Australians is foreign-born. Britain and Ireland have been the largest sources of post-war immigrants, followed by Italy, Greece, New Zealand, and the former Yugoslavia.

Australia's humanitarian and refugee admissions of about 12,000 per year are in addition to the normal immigration program. In recent years, refugees from Africa, the Middle East, and Southwest Asia have comprised the largest element in Australia's refugee program.

Although Australia has scarcely more than two people per square kilometer, it is one of the world's most urbanized countries. Less than 15% of the population lives in rural areas.

CULTURAL ACHIEVEMENTS

Much of Australia's culture is derived from European roots, but distinctive Australian features have evolved from the environment, aboriginal culture, and the influence of Australia's neighbors. The vigor and originality of the arts in Australia--films, opera, music, painting, theater, dance, and crafts--are achieving international recognition.

Australian actors such as Nicole Kidman, Rachel Griffiths, Cate Blanchett, Russell Crowe, Geoffrey Rush, Paul Hogan, Hugh Jackman, Heath Ledger, and children's entertainers, The Wiggles, have achieved enormous popularity in the United States. Australian movies and directors such as Peter Weir and Philip Noyes also are well known.

Australia has had a widely respected school of painting since the early days of European settlement, and Australians with international reputations include Sidney Nolan, Russell Drysdale, and Pro Hart and Arthur Boyd. Writers who have achieved world recognition include Thomas Keneally, Colleen McCullough, Nevil Shute, Morris West, Jill Ker Conway, and Nobel Prize winner Patrick White.

AUSTRALIAN STATES

NEW SOUTH WALES

New South Wales (NSW) is in the south east part of the Australian continent. It is the most populous (5.6 million) and heavily industrialized state in Australia above Victoria and below Queensland. New South Wales was the first state to be settled be Europeans, with a highly urbanized population. Sydney, its capital, is the largest city in the nation (population 3.7 million) and one of the world's great seaports. It is also an important international finance center. The year 2000 summer Olympics will be staged in Sydney. The total area of NSW is 802,000 kilometer squared or 10.4 per cent of Australia's total area. This includes Lord Howe, a small island in the Pacific ocean.

NORTHERN TERRITORY

The Northern Territory covers about one-sixth of the continent of Australia. It has an area of 1.35 million square kilometers, equal to the combined areas of France, Spain and Italy, and a coastline of 6200km. About four-fifths of the Territory (1.09 million square kilometers) lies within the tropics. The coastline is generally flat, with a backing of swamps, mangroves and mudflats, rising to a plateau no higher than 450m. In central Australia, the Territory is crossed by the east-west ridges of the Macdonnell Ranges, which reach heights of more than 600m. The well-known monolith, Uluru (Ayers Rock), 348m high, is near the south-west corner of the Territory.

The northern quarter, known colloquially as the Top End, is a distinct region of savannah woodlands and pockets of rainforest. In the north-east, the Arnhem Land plateau rises abruptly from the plain and continues to the coast of the Gulf of Carpentaria. Much of the southern three-quarters of the Territory consists of desert or semi-arid plain.

The main rivers are the Victoria and the Daly, flowing into the Timor Sea; the Adelaide, Mary, South Alligator and East Alligator, flowing into the Arafura Sea; and the Roper and McArthur, flowing into the Gulf of Carpentaria. Inland rivers are dry most of the year and their sporadic flow is lost in the Simpson Desert.

QUEENSLAND

Queensland is Australia's second largest state in area, covering 1,728,000 square kilometers, and the third most populous, with more than 3,000,000 inhabitants 17 per cent of the nation's people.

It occupies 22.5 per cent of the continent in the north east, and has boundaries with New South Wales, South Australia and the Northern Territory. It is bounded by the Gulf of Carpentaria, Torres Strait and the Coral Sea in the north, and the South Pacific Ocean in the east. The total coastline is 5,200km.

The area of Queensland equals the combined areas of France, Germany, Italy, continental Spain and Belgium; or one fifth of the United States; or nearly five times the area of Japan or Britain. From north to south its greatest distance is 2,100km and from east to west 1,450km. About 54 per cent of the state lies within the tropics.

Brisbane, the capital, is in the south eastern corner of the state. The Brisbane statistical division in 1991 had a population of 1,327,000.

Queensland is a state of contrasts. The landscape varies from mountain ranges to extensive plains, tropical forests to deserts, and coral reef islands to deep, clear lakes. It has vast natural resources and is rich in mineral deposits.

SOUTH AUSTRALIA

South Australia has boundaries on the west, north and east with all mainland States, and on the south is flanked by the Southern Ocean. It has a total area of 984,377 square kilometers squared, representing one eighth of the Australian continent. More than 50 per cent is pastoral land, with 6.5 per cent of the state designated as national parks and wildlife reserves. Most of the population lives in the southern coastal zones below the 32nd parallel.

South Australia's inland area is largely covered by plains, sand and gibber deserts. The coastline has a south easterlynorth westerly trend, interrupted by two major indentations, Spencer Gulf between Eyre and Yorke peninsulas, and Gulf St. Vincent between Yorke Peninsula and the Fleurieu Peninsula. To the south of Gulf St. Vincent is Kangaroo Island, about 480km in circumference. It is the largest of the 100 or so islands on the South Australian coastline.

The most important mountains are the Mt. Lofty Flinders Ranges system, which extends north about 800km from Cape Jervis to the northern end of Lake Torrens. In the south, the Mt. Lofty Ranges are of comparatively low altitude, the highest peak being Mt. Lofty at 727m. To the north, the Flinders Ranges are of greater height, with St. Mary's Peak the highest point at 1,166m. The Flinders Ranges contain unusual basins, of which Wilpena Pound is the best known.

The Murray River, which drains about one seventh of Australia, enters the sea in South Australia and is the state's only major river. For 216km to Overland Corner, the river occupies a wide valley, then passes through a narrow, steep sided valley to Lake Alexandrina and Lake Albert at its heavily silted mouth.

Surrounding the northern Flinders Ranges is a series of vast lakes which fill only after heavy rain, normally appearing as shallow depressions with salt or clay encrusted surfaces. The largest of these, Lake Eyre, is 15m below sea level. Lake Eyre is fed by intermittent rivers flowing from the northeast, creating one of the largest areas of internal drainage in the world. Lakes Gardiner, Frome and Torrens are to the south of Lake Eyre.

TASMANIA

Tasmania, the smallest of Australia's six states, is an island lying south of the south east corner of the Australian mainland. Roughly triangular in shape, the main island is surrounded by smaller islands, the most important of which are King, Flinders and Bruny islands.

Including these smaller islands, the State has a total area of 68,331 square kilometers and is separated from the Australian mainland by Bass Strait, a shallow sea with an average width of 240km.

Tasmania, or Van Diemen's Land as it was originally known, is the second oldest of the Australian colonies. The capital, Hobart, near the mouth of the Derwent River on the south east coast, was established in 1803. Early in its history, Hobart was a major whaling port and ship building center, but more recently the city has come to function as the main administrative and commercial center of the State.

Tasmania's population of 456,600 is divided almost equally between the north and the south. About 40 per cent of Tasmanians live in and around Hobart (pop 47,270). The population pattern has resulted from geographical, historical and commercial factors which have led to the development of a number of relatively large centers on the island's north coast. These serve as centers for the agricultural and industrial activities typical of the region and include Launceston (pop 63,430), Devonport (pop 25,500) and Burnie (pop 21,300).

VICTORIA

Victoria, which lies in the southeast corner of Australia, has a population of 4.4 million. Most of the state's people live in Melbourne (3.1 million), the nation's largest city after Sydney. Other important urban centers include Geelong; the inland cities of Ballarat and Bendigo; the industrial towns of the Latrobe Valley, east of Melbourne; Wodonga and Shepparton.

WESTERN AUSTRALIA

Perth, capital of the State of Western Australia, is closer to Singapore and Thailand than it is to Sydney, on Australia's east coast. Because of their closer proximity to Asia, Western Australians realized before many other Australians that Australia's economic and commercial future must be closely interlinked with that of Asia. Western Australia has been in the forefront of the country's trade push into Asia.

Trade, cross investment, joint ventures, government links and personal contacts through education, tourism and immigration constantly reinforce good relations between Western Australia and neighboring Asian nations.

Indonesia, Malaysia and Singapore are the nearest of these. Japan is Western Australia's major export market and the state shares a time zone and strong commercial links with China, Hong Kong and Taiwan. Trade with Korea continues to grow and local businesses are developing links with Thailand and Vietnam.

HISTORY

Australia was uninhabited until stone-culture peoples arrived, perhaps by boat across the waters separating the island from the Indonesia archipelago more than 40,000 years ago. Portuguese, Spanish, Dutch, and English explorers observed the island before 1770, when Captain Cook explored the east coast and claimed it for Great Britain (three American colonists were crew members aboard Cook's ship, the Endeavour).

On January 26, 1788 (now celebrated as Australia Day), the First Fleet under Capt. Arthur Phillip landed at Sydney, and formal proclamation of the establishment of the Colony of New South Wales followed on February 7. Many but by no means all of the first settlers were convicts, many condemned for offenses that today would often be thought trivial. The mid-19th century saw the beginning of government policies to emancipate convicts and assist the immigration of free persons. The discovery of gold in 1851 led to increased population, wealth, and trade.

The six colonies that now constitute the states of the Australian Commonwealth were established in the following order: New South Wales, 1788; Tasmania, 1825; Western Australia, 1830; South Australia, 1836; Victoria, 1851; and Queensland, 1859. Settlement had preceded these dates in most cases. Discussions between Australian and British representatives led to adoption by the British Government of an act to constitute the Commonwealth of Australia in 1900. Since Federation, the Commonwealth Government has established two self-governing territories: the Northern Territory, 1978; and the Australian Capital Territory (where the national capital, Canberra, is located), 1989.

The first federal Parliament was opened at Melbourne in May 1901 by the Duke of York (later King George V). In May 1927, the seat of government was transferred to Canberra, a planned city designed by an American, Walter Burley Griffin. The first session of Parliament in that city was opened by another Duke of York (later King George VI). Australia passed the Statute of Westminster Adoption Act on October 9, 1942, which officially established Australia's complete autonomy in both internal and external affairs. Its passage formalized a situation that had existed for years. The Australia Act (1986) eliminated the last vestiges of British legal authority.

GOVERNMENT

The Commonwealth government was created with a Constitution patterned partly on the U.S. Constitution, although it does not include a "bill of rights." The powers of the Commonwealth are specifically defined in the Constitution, and the residual powers remain with the states.

Australia is an independent nation within the Commonwealth. Queen Elizabeth II is the head of state and since 1973 has been officially styled "Queen of Australia." The Queen is represented throughout Australia by a governor general and in each state by a governor.

The federal Parliament is bicameral, consisting of a 76-member Senate and a 150-member House of Representatives. Twelve senators from each state are elected for 6-year terms, with half elected every 3 years. Each territory has two senators who are elected for 3-year terms. The members of the House of Representatives are allocated among the states and territories roughly in proportion to population. In ordinary legislation, the two chambers have coordinate powers, but all proposals for appropriating revenue or imposing taxes must be introduced in the House of Representatives. Under the prevailing Westminster parliamentary system, the leader of the political party or coalition of parties that wins a majority of the seats in the House of Representatives is named prime minister. The prime minister and the cabinet wield actual power and are responsible to the Parliament, of which they must be elected members. General elections are held at least once every 3 years; the last general election was in October 2004.

Each state is headed by a premier, who is the leader of the party with a majority or a working minority in the lower house of the state legislature. Australia's two self-governing territories have political systems similar to those of the states. The Territories are headed by Chief Ministers who are the leader of the party with a majority or a working minority in the territories' legislature.

At the apex of the court system is the High Court of Australia. It has general appellate jurisdiction over all other federal and state courts and possesses the power of constitutional review.

PRINCIPAL GOVERNMENT OFFICIALS

Following the federal election of 2 July 2016 Prime Minister Malcolm Turnbull announced a new federal Ministry on Monday 18 July 2016 which was sworn in the following day. The cabinet comprises:

Portfolio	Minister	Chamber	Since	Party
Prime Minister	 Malcolm Turnbull	House	2015	LPA (Leader of the Liberal Party)
Deputy Prime Minister Minister for Agriculture and Water Resources	Barnaby Joyce	House	2016 2013	NATS (Leader of the Nationals)
Minister for Foreign Affairs	Julie Bishop	House	2013	LPA (Deputy Leader of the

				Liberal Party)
Minister for Trade and Investment	Steven Ciobo	House	2016	LNP
Attorney-General also Vice-President of the Executive Council also Leader of the Government in the Senate	George Brandis	Senate	2013, 2015	LNP
Treasurer	Scott Morrison	House	2015	LPA
Minister for Revenue and Financial Services	Kelly O'Dwyer	House	2015	LPA
Minister for Regional Development Minister for Regional Communications Minister for Rural Health Minister for Local Government and Territories	Fiona Nash	Senate	2016	NATS (Deputy Leader of the Nationals)
Minister for Finance Special Minister of State	Mathias Cormann	Senate	2013	LPA
Minister for Infrastructure and Transport	Darren Chester	House	2016	NATS
Minister for Defence Industry	Christopher Pyne	House	2015	LPA
Minister for the Environment and Energy	Josh Frydenberg	House	2015	LPA
Minister for Immigration and Border Protection	Peter Dutton	House	2015	LNP
Minister for Industry, Innovation and Science	Arthur Sinodinos	Senate	2015	LPA
Minister for Resources and Northern Australia	Matthew Canavan	Senate	2016	LNP
Minister for Health Minister for Sport	Greg Hunt	House	2013	LPA
Minister for Indigenous Health Minister for Aged Care	Ken Wyatt	House	2017	LPA
Minister for Defence	Marise Payne	Senate	2015	LPA
Minister for Communications Also, Minister for the Arts	Mitch Fifield	Senate	2015	LPA
Minister for Employment Also, Minister for Women Also, Minister Assisting the Prime Minister for the Public Service	Michaelia Cash	Senate	2015	LPA
Minister for Social Services	Christian Porter	House	2015	LPA
Minister for Education and Training	Simon Birmingham	Senate	2015	LPA
Minister for Indigenous Affairs also Leader of the Nationals in the Senate	Nigel Scullion	Senate	2013	CLP

Australia maintains an embassy in the United States at 1601 Massachusetts Avenue NW, Washington, DC 20036 (tel. 202-797-3000), and consulates general in New York (212-351-6500), San Francisco (415-536-1970), Honolulu (808-524-5050), Los Angeles (310-229-4800), Chicago (312-419-1480) and Atlanta (404-760-3400).

ECONOMY

Rank	12th (nominal) / 17th (PPP)
Currency	Australian dollar (A$ or AUD)
Fiscal year	1 July – 30 June
Trade organisations	APEC, WTO and OECD
	Statistics
GDP	$1.525 trillion
GDP growth	2.5%
GDP per capita	$67,722 (5th, nominal; 10th, PPP)
GDP by sector	agriculture: 4%, industry: 27.3%, services: 68.8% (2012 est.)
Inflation (CPI)	2.7%
Gini coefficient	0.331
Labour force	12.15 million
Labour force by occupation	agriculture: 3.6%, industry: 21.1%, services: 75%
Unemployment	6.0%
Main industries	mining, industrial and transportation equipment, food processing, chemicals, steel
Ease-of-doing-business rank	10th
	External
Exports	$258.8 billion
Export goods	coal, iron ore, gold, meat, wool, alumina, wheat, machinery and transport equipment
Main export partners	China 29.5% Japan 19.3% South Korea 8.0% India 4.9%
Imports	$239.7 billion
Import goods	machinery and transport equipment, computers and office machines, telecommunication equipment and parts; crude oil and petroleum products
Main import partners	China 18.2% United States 11.6% Japan 7.8% Singapore 5.9% Germany 4.6% Thailand 4.2% South Korea 4.0%
FDI stock	$329.1 billion
Gross external debt	$1.497 trillion
	Public finances
Public debt	29.3% of GDP
Budget deficit	$12.3 billion
Revenues	$376.1 billion

Expenses	$376.3 billion
Economic aid	donor: ODA, $7.7 billion
Credit rating	Standard & Poor's: AAA (Domestic) AAA (Foreign) AAA (T&C Assessment) Outlook: Stable Moody's: Aaa Outlook: Stable Fitch: AAA Outlook: Stable
Foreign reserves	$41.212 billion

The **economy of Australia** is one of the largest capitalist economies in the world with a GDP of US$1.5 trillion as of 2013. Australia's total wealth is 6.4 trillion dollars. In 2012, it was the 12th largest national economy by nominal GDP and the 17th-largest measured by PPP-adjusted GDP, about 1.7% of the world economy. Australia is the 19th-largest importer and 19th-largest exporter. The Reserve Bank of Australia publishes forecasts of the economy quarterly.

The Australian economy is dominated by its service sector, comprising 68% of GDP. The mining sector represents 10% of GDP; the "mining-related economy" represents 9% of GDP – the total mining sector is 19% of GDP. Economic growth is largely dependent on the mining sector and agricultural sector with the products to be exported mainly to the East Asian market.

The Australian Securities Exchange in Sydney is the largest stock exchange in Australia and in the South Pacific and ranks 9th in the world in terms of market capitalisation. Australia is home to some of the largest companies in the world, including but not limited to, BHP Billiton, National Australia Bank, Commonwealth Bank, Rio Tinto Group, ANZ, Westpac, Telstra, Macquarie Bank, Woolworths and AMP – which also are the 10 largest companies in Australia. The Australian Financial Review is associated with economic-liberalism of the economy of Australia. The Australian dollar is the currency of the Commonwealth of Australia and its territories, including Christmas Island, Cocos (Keeling) Islands, and Norfolk Island. It is also the official currency of the independent Pacific Island nations of Kiribati, Nauru and Tuvalu.

Australia is a member of the APEC, G20, OECD and WTO. The country has also entered into free trade agreements with ASEAN, Chile, New Zealand, Japan and the United States. The ANZCERTA agreement with New Zealand has greatly increased integration with the New Zealand economy and in 2011 there was a plan to form an Australasian Single Economic Market by 2015

Australia's advanced market economy is dominated by its services sector (71% of GDP), yet it is the agricultural and mining sectors (8% of GDP combined) that account for the bulk (52%) of Australia's goods and services exports. Australia's comparative advantage in primary products is a reflection of the natural wealth of the Australian continent and its small domestic market; 20 million people occupy a continent the size of the contiguous United States. The relative size of the manufacturing sector has been declining for several decades, and now accounts for around 10% of GDP.

Australia commenced a basic reorientation of its economy in the 1980s and has transformed itself from an inward looking, import-substitution country to an internationally competitive, export-oriented one. Key reforms included unilaterally reducing high tariffs and other protective barriers; floating the Australian dollar exchange rate; deregulating the financial services sector, including liberalizing access for foreign bank branches; making efforts to restructure the highly centralized system of industrial relations and labor bargaining; better integrating the state economies into a national federal system; improving and standardizing the national infrastructure; privatizing many government-owned services and public utilities; and fundamentally reforming the taxation system, including introducing a broad-based Goods and Services Tax (GST).

The ultimate goal is for Australia to become a competitive producer and exporter, not just of traditional farm and mineral commodities, but also of a diversified mix of high value-added manufactured products, services, and technologies. Australia was one of the OECD's fastest-growing economies throughout the 1990s, a performance that owed much to the economic reform program. Despite a transient slowdown in late 2000, it has been 14 years since Australia experienced a recession and economic growth remains robust. Economic growth should be just under 3% in 2005, although the persistent strength of the Australian dollar and infrastructure bottlenecks could constrain export growth.

The Australia – U.S. Free Trade Agreement (AUSFTA) entered into force on January 1, 2005. The AUSFTA marks the first FTA the U.S. has concluded with a developed economy since the U.S.-Canada FTA in 1988. Australia has also completed FTAs with Singapore and Thailand and is pursuing similar Agreements in the region. A burgeoning trade relationship marked by ongoing, multi-billion dollar resource export contracts has driven FTA negotiations with China. Parallel efforts are underway with Malaysia and ASEAN.

FOREIGN RELATIONS

Australia has been active participant in international affairs since World War I and has fought beside the United States and other Allies in every significant conflict to the present day. In 1944, it concluded an agreement with New Zealand dealing with the security, welfare, and advancement of the people of the independent territories of the Pacific (the ANZAC pact). After the war, Australia played a role in the Far Eastern Commission in Japan and supported Indonesian independence during that country's revolt against the Dutch (1945-49). Australia was one of the founders of both the United Nations and the South Pacific Commission (1947), and in 1950, it proposed the Colombo Plan to assist developing countries in Asia. In addition to contributing to UN forces in Korea--it was the first country to announce it would do so after the United States--Australia sent troops to assist in putting down the communist revolt in Malaya in 1948-60 and later to combat the Indonesian-supported invasion of Sarawak in 1963-65. The U.S., Australia and New Zealand signed the ANZUS Treaty in 1951, which remains Australia's only formal security treaty alliance. Australia also sent troops to assist South Vietnamese and U.S. forces in Vietnam and joined coalition forces in the Persian Gulf conflict in 1991, in Afghanistan in 2002, and in Iraq in 2003.

Australia has been active in the Australia-New Zealand-U.K. agreement and the Five-Power Defense Arrangements--successive arrangements with Britain and New Zealand to ensure the security of Singapore and Malaysia.

One of the drafters of the UN Charter, Australia has given firm support to the United Nations and its specialized agencies. It was a member of the Security Council in 1986-87, a member of the Economic and Social Council for 1986-89, and a member of the UN Human Rights Commission for 1994-96 and 2003-2005. Australia takes a prominent part in many other UN activities, including peacekeeping, nonproliferation and disarmament negotiations, and narcotics control. Australia also is active in meetings of the Commonwealth Regional Heads of Government and the

Pacific Islands Forum, and has been a leader in the Cairns Group--countries pressing for agricultural trade reform in World Trade Organization (WTO) negotiations -- and in the APEC forum.

Australia has devoted particular attention to relations between developed and developing nations, with emphasis on the ten countries of the Association of South East Asian Nations (ASEAN) and the island states of the South Pacific. Australia is an active participant in the ASEAN Regional Forum (ARF), which promotes regional cooperation on security issues. In September 1999, acting under a UN Security Council mandate, Australia led an international coalition to restore order in East Timor upon Indonesia's withdrawal from that territory. In 2003, Australia led a regional mission to restore law and order in Solomon Islands.

Australia provided over $1.6 billion ($A2.1 billion) as official development assistance in FY 2004-05. The Australian aid program is currently concentrated in Southeast Asia (Papua New Guinea is the largest-single recipient) and the Pacific Islands. In 2004, Australia commenced a 5-year $0.8 billion ($A1.1 billion) Enhanced Cooperation Program (ECP), which involved government officials working alongside their PNG counterparts. The future of the program was called into question in 2005, however, when ECP immunity provisions for Australian officials were successfully challenged in the PNG high court. Selected aid flows are allocated to Africa, South Asia, and reconstruction in Afghanistan and Iraq. Contributions to multilateral organizations and other expenses account for about one-third of the foreign assistance budget.

ANZUS AND DEFENSE

The Australia, New Zealand, United States (ANZUS) security treaty was concluded at San Francisco on September 1, 1951, and entered into force on April 29, 1952. The treaty bound the signatories to recognize that an armed attack in the Pacific area on any of them would endanger the peace and safety of the others. It committed them to consult in the event of a threat and, in the event of attack, to meet the common danger in accordance with their respective constitutional processes. The three nations also pledged to maintain and develop individual and collective capabilities to resist attack.

In 1985, the nature of the ANZUS alliance changed after the Government of New Zealand refused access to its ports by nuclear-weapons-capable and nuclear-powered ships of the U.S. Navy. The United States suspended defense obligations to New Zealand, and annual bilateral meetings between the U.S. Secretary of State and the Australian Foreign Minister replaced annual meetings of the ANZUS Council of Foreign Ministers. The first bilateral meeting was held in Canberra in 1985. At the second, in San Francisco in 1986, the United States and Australia announced that the United States was suspending its treaty security obligations to New Zealand pending the restoration of port access. Subsequent bilateral Australia-U.S. Ministerial (AUSMIN) meetings have alternated between Australia and the United States. The 16th AUSMIN meeting took place in Washington on July 7, 2004.

The U.S.-Australia alliance under the ANZUS Treaty remains in full force. Defense ministers of one or both nations have joined the annual ministerial meetings, which are supplemented by consultations between the U.S. Combatant Commander, Pacific and the Australian Chief of Defense Force. There also are regular civilian and military consultations between the two governments at lower levels.

ANZUS has no integrated defense structure or dedicated forces. However, in fulfillment of ANZUS obligations, Australia and the United States conduct a variety of joint activities. These include military exercises ranging from naval and landing exercises at the task-group level to battalion-level special forces training, assigning officers to each other's armed services, and standardizing, where possible, equipment and operational doctrine. The two countries also operate joint defense facilities in Australia.

Following the terrorist attacks on the United States on September 11, 2004, Australian Prime Minister Howard invoked the ANZUS Treaty for the first time on September 14, 2004. Australia was one of the earliest participants in Operation Enduring Freedom. Australian Defense Forces participated in coalition military action against Iraq in Operation Iraqi Freedom. Australian military and civilian specialists are participating in the training of Iraqi security forces and the reconstruction of Iraq. Australian Special Forces are redeploying to Afghanistan to help provide security in time for the country's September 18, 2005 elections.

After a review in 2000 of Australia's future defense needs, the government made a commitment to increase defense spending by an average of 3% a year for the next 10 years. The Australian Defense Force numbers about 52,000 active duty personnel. The Royal Australian Navy's front-line fleet currently includes 12 frigates, including 4 of the Adelaide class and 7 Australian-built ANZAC class, with 1 more to be delivered by 2006. The last of six submarines of the new, indigenous Collins class was commissioned in March 2003. An upgraded version of the US Navy's Arleigh Burke-class destroyer will be the Australian Navy's air warfare destroyer after the August 2005 selection of American firm Gibbs and Cox as the preferred designer for the $4.6 billion project. In August 2004, Australia selected the Aegis Combat Control System for its three air warfare destroyers, which will start coming into service in 2013. The F/A-18 fighter, built in Australia under license from the U.S. manufacturer, is the principal combat aircraft of the Royal Australian Air Force, backed by the U.S.-built F-111 strike aircraft. In October 2002, Australia became a Level III partner in the U.S.-led Joint Strike Fighter (JSF) program. Both of their current fighters are scheduled to exit service by 2012 when they will be replaced by up to 100 JSF aircraft. Boeing will provide the Commonwealth of Australia's Royal Australian Air Force (RAAF) with an Airborne Early Warning and Control (AEW&C) system based on the Next-Generation 737-700 aircraft as the airborne platform. The first two aircraft are planned to be in service by late 2006, with four more due for delivery by 2008. Recent U.S. sales to the Royal Australian Army include the M1A1 AIM tank, as well as Hellfire and JAVELIN munitions.

U.S.-AUSTRALIAN RELATIONS

The World War II experience, similarities in culture and historical background, and shared democratic values have made U.S. relations with Australia exceptionally strong and close. Ties linking the two nations cover the entire spectrum of international relations--from commercial, cultural, and environmental contacts to political and defense cooperation. Two-way trade reached $30.1 billion in 2004. More than 400,000 Americans have visited Australia in a single year.

Traditional friendship is reinforced by the wide range of common interests and similar views on most major international questions. For example, both countries sent military forces to the Persian Gulf in support of UN Security Council resolutions relating to Iraq's occupation of Kuwait; both attach high priority to controlling and eventually eliminating chemical weapons, other weapons of mass destruction, and anti-personnel landmines; and both work closely on global environmental issues such as slowing climate change and preserving coral reefs. The Australian Government and opposition share the view that Australia's security depends on firm ties with the United States, and the ANZUS Treaty enjoys broad bipartisan support. Recent Presidential visits to Australia (in 1991, 1996 and 2003) and Australian Prime Ministerial visits to the United States (in 1995, 1997, 1999, 2004, 2002, 2003, 2004, and 2005) have underscored the strength and closeness of the alliance.

The bilateral Australia-U.S. Free Trade Agreement (AUSFTA) entered into force on January 1, 2005. This comprehensive agreement, only the second FTA the U.S. had negotiated with a developed nation, substantially liberalizes an already vibrant trade and investment relationship. The AUSFTA also creates a range of ongoing working groups and committees designed to explore further trade reform in the bilateral context.

Both countries share a commitment to liberalizing global trade. They work together very closely in the World Trade Organization (WTO), and both are active members of the Asia-Pacific Economic Cooperation (APEC) forum.

A number of U.S. institutions conduct scientific activities in Australia because of its geographical position, large land mass, advanced technology, and, above all, the ready cooperation of its government and scientists. Under an agreement dating back to 1960 and since renewed, the U.S. National Aeronautics and Space Administration (NASA) maintains in Australia one of its largest and most important program outside the United States, including a number of tracking facilities vital to the U.S. space program. Indicative of the broadranging U.S.-Australian cooperation on other global issues, a Mutual Legal Assistance Treaty (MLAT) was concluded in 1997, enhancing already close bilateral cooperation on legal and counter-narcotics issues. In 2004, the U.S. and Australia signed a new tax treaty and a bilateral social security agreement.

Principal U.S. Officials
Ambassador--John Berry
Deputy Chief of Mission--Daniel A. Clune
Consular Affairs Coordinator--Suzanne Lawrence (resident in Sydney)
Economic Counselor--Edgard Kagan (arrival August 2007)
Political Counselor--James F. Cole
Management Counselor--Grace Stettenbauer
Public Affairs Counselor--Scott Weinhold
Defense and Air Attaché--Col Andrew Britschgi, USAF
Agricultural Counselor--Kathleen Wainio
Senior Commercial Officer--Keith Kirkham, acting (resident in Sydney)

The U.S. Embassy in Australia is located at Moonah Place, Yarralumla, Canberra, Australian Capital Territory 2600 (tel. (02) 6-214-5600; fax 6-214-5970). Consulates General are in Sydney (tel. 2-9373-9200; fax 2-9373-9125); Melbourne (tel. 3-9526-5900; fax 3-9510-4646; and Perth (tel. 9-202-1224; fax. 9-231-9444).

TRAVEL AND BUSINESS INFORMATION

The U.S. Department of State's Consular Information Program provides Consular Information Sheets, Travel Warnings, and Public Announcements.

Consular Information Sheets exist for all countries and include information on entry requirements, currency regulations, health conditions, areas of instability, crime and security, political disturbances, and the addresses of the U.S. posts in the country.

Travel Warnings are issued when the State Department recommends that Americans avoid travel to a certain country. **Public Announcements** are issued as a means to disseminate information quickly about terrorist threats and other relatively short-term conditions overseas that pose significant risks to the security of American travelers. Free copies of this information are available by calling the Bureau of Consular Affairs at 202-647-5225 or via the fax-on-demand system: 202-647-3000. Consular Information Sheets and Travel Warnings also are available on the Consular Affairs Internet home page: http://travel.state.gov. Consular Affairs Tips for Travelers publication series, which contain information on obtaining passports and planning a safe trip abroad, are on the Internet and hard copies can be purchased from the Superintendent of Documents, U.S. Government Printing Office, telephone: 202-512-1800; fax 202-512-2250.

Emergency information concerning Americans traveling abroad may be obtained from the Office of Overseas Citizens Services at (202) 647-5225. For after-hours emergencies, Sundays and holidays, call 202-647-4000.

The National Passport Information Center (NPIC) is the U.S. Department of State's single, centralized public contact center for U.S. passport information. Telephone: 1-877-4USA-PPT (1-877-487-2778). Customer service representatives and operators for TDD/TTY are available Monday-Friday, 8:00 a.m. to 8:00 p.m., Eastern Time, excluding federal holidays.

Travelers can check the latest health information with the U.S. Centers for Disease Control and Prevention in Atlanta, Georgia. A hotline at 877-FYI-TRIP (877-394-8747) and a web site at http://www.cdc.gov/travel/index.htm give the most recent health advisories, immunization recommendations or requirements, and advice on food and drinking water safety for regions and countries. A booklet entitled Health Information for International Travel (HHS publication number CDC-95-8280) is available from the U.S. Government Printing Office, Washington, DC 20402, tel. (202) 512-1800.

USTRALIAN STATES

NEW SOUTH WALES

New South Wales (NSW) is in the south east part of the Australian continent. It is the most populous (5.6 million) and heavily industrialized state in Australia above Victoria and below Queensland. New South Wales was the first state to be settled be Europeans, with a highly urbanized population. Sydney, its capital, is the largest city in the nation (population 3.7 million) and one of the world's great seaports. It is also an important international finance center. The year 2000 summer Olympics will be staged in Sydney. The total area of NSW is 802,000 kilometer squared or 10.4 per cent of Australia's total area. This includes Lord Howe, a small island in the Pacific ocean.

NORTHERN TERRITORY

The Northern Territory covers about one-sixth of the continent of Australia. It has an area of 1.35 million square kilometers, equal to the combined areas of France, Spain and Italy, and a coastline of 6200km. About four-fifths of the Territory (1.09 million square kilometers) lies within the tropics. The coastline is generally flat, with a backing of swamps, mangroves and mudflats, rising to a plateau no higher than 450m. In central Australia, the Territory is crossed by the east-west ridges of the Macdonnell Ranges, which reach heights of more than 600m. The well-known monolith, Uluru (Ayers Rock), 348m high, is near the south-west corner of the Territory.

The northern quarter, known colloquially as the Top End, is a distinct region of savannah woodlands and pockets of rainforest. In the north-east, the Arnhem Land plateau rises abruptly from the plain and continues to the coast of the Gulf of Carpentaria. Much of the southern three-quarters of the Territory consists of desert or semi-arid plain.

The main rivers are the Victoria and the Daly, flowing into the Timor Sea; the Adelaide, Mary, South Alligator and East Alligator, flowing into the Arafura Sea; and the Roper and McArthur, flowing into the Gulf of Carpentaria. Inland rivers are dry most of the year and their sporadic flow is lost in the Simpson Desert.

QUEENSLAND

Queensland is Australia's second largest state in area, covering 1,728,000 square kilometers, and the third most populous, with more than 3,000,000 inhabitants 17 per cent of the nation's people.

It occupies 22.5 per cent of the continent in the north east, and has boundaries with New South Wales, South Australia and the Northern Territory. It is bounded by the Gulf of Carpentaria, Torres Strait and the Coral Sea in the north, and the South Pacific Ocean in the east. The total coastline is 5,200km.

The area of Queensland equals the combined areas of France, Germany, Italy, continental Spain and Belgium; or one fifth of the United States; or nearly five times the area of Japan or Britain. From north to south its greatest distance is 2,100km and from east to west 1,450km. About 54 per cent of the state lies within the tropics.

Brisbane, the capital, is in the south eastern corner of the state. The Brisbane statistical division in 1991 had a population of 1,327,000.

Queensland is a state of contrasts. The landscape varies from mountain ranges to extensive plains, tropical forests to deserts, and coral reef islands to deep, clear lakes. It has vast natural resources and is rich in mineral deposits.

SOUTH AUSTRALIA

South Australia has boundaries on the west, north and east with all mainland States, and on the south is flanked by the Southern Ocean. It has a total area of 984,377 square kilometers squared, representing one eighth of the Australian continent. More than 50 per cent is pastoral land, with 6.5 per cent of the state designated as national parks and wildlife reserves. Most of the population lives in the southern coastal zones below the 32nd parallel.

South Australia's inland area is largely covered by plains, sand and gibber deserts. The coastline has a south easterlynorth westerly trend, interrupted by two major indentations, Spencer Gulf between Eyre and Yorke peninsulas, and Gulf St. Vincent between Yorke Peninsula and the Fleurieu Peninsula. To the south of Gulf St. Vincent is Kangaroo Island, about 480km in circumference. It is the largest of the 100 or so islands on the South Australian coastline.

The most important mountains are the Mt. Lofty Flinders Ranges system, which extends north about 800km from Cape Jervis to the northern end of Lake Torrens. In the south, the Mt. Lofty Ranges are of comparatively low altitude, the highest peak being Mt. Lofty at 727m. To the north, the Flinders Ranges are of greater height, with St. Mary's Peak the highest point at 1,166m. The Flinders Ranges contain unusual basins, of which Wilpena Pound is the best known.

The Murray River, which drains about one seventh of Australia, enters the sea in South Australia and is the state's only major river. For 216km to Overland Corner, the river occupies a wide valley, then passes through a narrow, steep sided valley to Lake Alexandrina and Lake Albert at its heavily silted mouth.

Surrounding the northern Flinders Ranges is a series of vast lakes which fill only after heavy rain, normally appearing as shallow depressions with salt or clay encrusted surfaces. The largest of these, Lake Eyre, is 15m below sea level. Lake Eyre is fed by intermittent rivers flowing from the northeast, creating one of the largest areas of internal drainage in the world. Lakes Gardiner, Frome and Torrens are to the south of Lake Eyre.

TASMANIA

Tasmania, the smallest of Australia's six states, is an island lying south of the south east corner of the Australian mainland. Roughly triangular in shape, the main island is surrounded by smaller islands, the most important of which are King, Flinders and Bruny islands.

Including these smaller islands, the State has a total area of 68,331 square kilometers and is separated from the Australian mainland by Bass Strait, a shallow sea with an average width of 240km.

Tasmania, or Van Diemen's Land as it was originally known, is the second oldest of the Australian colonies. The capital, Hobart, near the mouth of the Derwent River on the south east coast, was established in 1803. Early in its history, Hobart was a major whaling port and ship building center, but more recently the city has come to function as the main administrative and commercial center of the State.

Tasmania's population of 456,600 is divided almost equally between the north and the south. About 40 per cent of Tasmanians live in and around Hobart (pop 47,270). The population pattern has resulted from geographical, historical and commercial factors which have led to the development of a number of relatively large centers on the island's north coast. These serve as centers for the agricultural and industrial activities typical of the region and include Launceston (pop 63,430), Devonport (pop 25,500) and Burnie (pop 21,300).

VICTORIA

Victoria, which lies in the southeast corner of Australia, has a population of 4.4 million. Most of the state's people live in Melbourne (3.1 million), the nation's largest city after Sydney. Other important urban centers include Geelong; the inland cities of Ballarat and Bendigo; the industrial towns of the Latrobe Valley, east of Melbourne; Wodonga and Shepparton.

WESTERN AUSTRALIA

Perth, capital of the State of Western Australia, is closer to Singapore and Thailand than it is to Sydney, on Australia's east coast. Because of their closer proximity to Asia, Western Australians realized before many other Australians that Australia's economic and commercial future must be closely interlinked with that of Asia. Western Australia has been in the forefront of the country's trade push into Asia.

Trade, cross investment, joint ventures, government links and personal contacts through education, tourism and immigration constantly reinforce good relations between Western Australia and neighboring Asian nations.

Indonesia, Malaysia and Singapore are the nearest of these. Japan is Western Australia's major export market and the state shares a time zone and strong commercial links with China, Hong Kong and Taiwan. Trade with Korea continues to grow and local businesses are developing links with Thailand and Vietnam.

RESEARCH AND INNOVATION IN AUSTRALIA: STRATEGIC INFORMATION

DEPARTMENT OF INNOVATION, INDUSTRY, SCIENCE AND RESEARCH: IMPORTANT INFORMATION AND CONTACTS

SENATOR THE HON KIM CARR
Minister for Innovation, Industry, Science and Research

Department of Innovation Hotline: 1800 024 095
International: +61 2 6213 6000
Facsimile: +61 2 6213 7000
Email: enquiries@innovation.gov.au

Postal address:
GPO Box 9839
CANBERRA ACT 2601

Street address:
Industry House
10 Binara Street
CANBERRA ACT 2601

Telephone: +61 2 6213 6000
Facsimile: +61 2 6213 7000
Toll Free: 1800 024 095
Website: http://www.innovation.gov.au

AUSINDUSTRY

Hotline: 13 28 46
Email: hotline@ausindustry.gov.au
Website: http://www.ausindustry.gov.au

AUSINDUSTRY STATE/TERRITORY OFFICES

For assistance on AusIndustry programs or general enquiries for information, call the **AusIndustry Hotline** on **13 28 46** in the first instance (for the cost of a local call from anywhere in Australia) or email: **hotline@ausindustry.gov.au**.

If you require information about the Department of Innovation, Industry, Science and Research, please visit **Connect with Innovation** or call **1800 024 095**.

AusIndustry's State/Territory office reception hours are **8.30 am to 5.00 pm**, Monday to Friday, public holidays excluded. See below the list of AusIndustry Regional Offices.

State / Territory	Street address	Postal address	Phone/fax/email
National Office	Industry House 10 Binara Street CANBERRA ACT 2601	GPO Box 9839 CANBERRA ACT 2601	Ph: 13 28 46 Fax: 1300 554 132 email: hotline@ausindustry.gov.au
NSW State Office	Level 5 341 George Street SYDNEY NSW 2000	GPO Box 9839 SYDNEY NSW 2001	Ph: 02 9226 6000 Fax: 02 9226 6002 or 02 9226 6001 email: ainsw@innovation.gov.au
VIC State Office	9th Floor KPMG House 161 Collins Street MELBOURNE VIC 3000	GPO Box 85 MELBOURNE VIC 3001	Ph: 03 9268 7555 Fax: 03 9268 7599 email: aivic@innovation.gov.au
QLD State Office	Level 12 100 Creek Street BRISBANE QLD 4000	GPO Box 9839 BRISBANE QLD 4001	Ph: 07 3227 4700 Fax: 07 3227 4730 email: aiqld@innovation.gov.au
SA/NT State Office	11th Floor Terrace Towers 178 North Terrace ADELAIDE SA 5000	GPO Box 9839 ADELAIDE SA 5001	Ph: 08 8406 4700 Fax: 08 8406 4717 email: aisa@innovation.gov.au
TAS State Office	4th Floor AMP Building 86 Collins Street HOBART TAS 7000	GPO Box 9839 HOBART TAS 7001	Ph: 03 6230 9900 Fax: 03 6230 9901 email: aitas@innovation.gov.au
WA State Office	Level 25 St Martins Tower 44 St Georges Terrace PERTH WA 6000	GPO Box 9839 PERTH WA 6848	Ph: 08 9287 3500 Fax: 08 9287 3511 email: aiwa@innovation.gov.au
ACT and Region Office View Area Map	Industry House 10 Binara Street CANBERRA ACT 2601	GPO Box 9839 CANBERRA ACT 2601	Ph: 13 28 46 Fax: 02 6213 7644 email: aiact@innovation.gov.au

COMMERCIALISATION AUSTRALIA

http://www.commercialisationaustralia.gov.au

ENTERPRISE CONNECT

Enterprise Connect Hotline between the hours of 9.00am and 5.00pm (AEST) on 131 791 (Australian callers only) or email enterpriseconnect@innovation.gov.au.

NATIONAL MEASUREMENT INSTITUTE

Website: http://www.measurement.gov.au

AUSTRALIAN ASTRONOMICAL OBSERVATORY

Website: http://www.aao.gov.au

IP AUSTRALIA NATIONAL OFFICE

Street Address:
Ground Floor Discovery House
47 Bowes St, Phillip

Postal Address:
PO Box 200
Woden ACT 2606

Telephone: 1300 651 010 (Australian callers)
+61 2 6283 2211 (for international callers only)
Facsimile: +61 2 6283 7999
Website: http://www.ipaustralia.gov.au
Email: assist@ipaustralia.gov.au

AUSTRALIAN BUSINESS NUMBERS

- Department of Innovation, Industry, Science and Research: 74 599 608 295
- IP Australia: 38 113 072 755

FREEDOM OF INFORMATION

Applications for access to Departmental documents are made under section 15 of the Freedom of Information (FOI) Act. Requests should be directed to FOI@innovation.gov.au clearly stating that access is being sought under the *Freedom of Information Act 1982* with a clear description of the documents being requested.

Attached is the official statement (57.5KB) as at 1 February 2010. The documents specified in this statement are available to the public for inspection and purchase from the Department.

The FOI Coordinator is located in the legal section of the Corporate Strategy Branch and deals with enquiries and applications for all Departmental areas, including AusIndustry. The contact details for the FOI Coordinator are:

FOI Coordinator
Corporate Strategy Branch
Innovation, Industry, Science and Research
GPO Box 9839
CANBERRA ACT 2601

Telephone: 02 6213 7742
Facsimile: 02 6290 8557
Email: FOI@innovation.gov.au

NATIONAL RESEARCH POLICY AND PRIORITIES

Government announced a number of initiatives foreshadowed in their election platform. The major initiative was a set of Programs aimed at research and innovation related to climate change and funded at A$1.9 billion over four years, including:

- Green Car Innovation Fund (A$500 million over five years) to assist the Australian automotive industry to develop and manufacture low emission vehicles.
- National Clean Coal Fund (A$500 million over eight years) to support the development of clean coal and advanced fossil fuel technology, including CO2 sequestration.
- Renewable Energy Fund (A$500 million over seven years) through competitive grants of between $10 million and $75 million to develop, commercialise and deploy renewable energy, including ethanol.
- Clean Business Australia (A$ 240 million) to assist business to develop more energy and water efficient products and processes
- Energy Innovation Fund (A$150 million over four years) to support the development of clean energy technologies

Enterprise Connect consists of a national network of five manufacturing hubs - including one in Melbourne - and five "innovation centres" focused on the themes of mining technology, remote enterprise, innovative regions, creative industries and clean energy. However, some of these initiatives were funded by redirecting funds from existing Programs. In particular, the Commercial Ready Program was cut. This Program, funded at about A$160m per annum supported commercialization projects, particularly in new ventures.

INNOVATION REVIEW

On 22 January 2008, the Minister for Innovation, Industry, Science and Research, Senator Kim Carr, announced a wide ranging review of Australia's national innovation system to be conducted by an expert panel chaired by Dr Terry Cutler. The review recognises the vital role innovation plays in boosting productivity and international competitiveness and is the first step in implementation of the Rudd Government's commitment to fostering innovation across the economy. The Panel was asked to:

- identify gaps and weaknesses in the innovation system and develop proposals to address them. In particular, it will:
- identify a set of principles to underpin the role and participation of the public sector in innovation.
- develop a set of national innovation priorities to complement the national research priorities,
- identify regulatory and other barriers to innovation and recommend ways to minimise these.
- examine the scope for simplifying and reducing program duplication
- consider the appropriateness, effectiveness and efficiency of the Research and Development (R&D) Tax Concession Scheme in promoting innovation and make recommendations to improve innovation outcomes.

- Consider ways to improve the governance of the national innovation system to support higher expectations of government agencies and industry.

As part of the Innovation Review, a review of the Cooperative Research Centres (CRC) Program was conducted. However, this review was undertaken by a panel chaired by Prof Mary O'Kane. The review examined the overall strategic direction of CRCs, looking at a wide range of issues, including governance and Program design issues, the level and length of funding needed to support the program's objectives, as well as its overall scope and effectiveness.

The CRC review Collaborating for a Purpose, was released in July 2008. It reaffirmed the value of a program designed to support large scale pre-competitive/pre-application research cooperation focused on the needs of end users. However, it recognized the evolution of the program and of the external environment had led to a reduced effectiveness. The review recommended the continuation of the program with increased funding but with substantially greater flexibility in such parameters as the life span of centres (previously fixed at 7, but ranges from 4 to 10 proposed) and structure and governance. The review proposed that humanities and social sciences researchers and topics, and service sector users, be explicitly included in the scope of the program, and that international collaboration be more strongly encouraged. The guidelines for the 2009 selection round for new centres incorporates many of these proposals for greater flexibility.
The reviews received several hundred submissions, organized several public forums and met with major interest groups.

The overall report of the Review of the National Innovation System Venturous Australia, was released in September 2008. The report makes 72 recommendations that range across the components of an effective system, focusing on innovation in business, strengthening people and skills, excellence in national research, information and market design, and taxation. The report is widely seen as a working blueprint to reposition Australia's innovation system. The recommendations indicate the concern of the review panel to refocus innovation policy to reflect a greater focus on innovation capability and effective innovation systems: "Today, innovation is more than just research and development and technology. It is also about improving the capacity of firms to modify technologies and services in response to customer demand. Having a competitive economy depends upon the capacity of businesses to embrace innovation and use it to capitalise on new markets and to satisfy changing customer demands," – Chair of the Review, Dr Terrry Cutler.

The first major recommendation is: Support business innovation as an explicit priority for Australia's innovation policy by incorporating the following objectives into programs aimed at building business innovation capacity:

- assist the generation and absorption of business knowledge by private firms;
- help private firms to secure returns and to appropriate value from undertaking inherently uncertain innovative business activities;
- foster the capacity for innovation at the company level in response to market and customer demands;
- facilitate economically useful connections between firms and other institutions for knowledge transfer and capability building;
- extend the global reach and market access of Australian firms; and
- increase the managerial, technical and collaboration skills and competencies of private firms.

Review of the Textile, Clothing and Footwear Industry

In their policy platform at the 2007 election the Labor Government of Kevin Rudd made clear their commitment to maintaining a manufacturing sector in Australia. The Minister for Innovation, Industry, Science and Research, Senator Kim Carr, announced a comprehensive review of the

TCF Industry by Professor Roy Green supported by an expert reference group. The review was tasked with developing practical and effective strategies to ensure Australia's TCF industry 'enjoys a vibrant, innovative and competitive future'. The review reported in August 2008, Building Innovative Capacity, and proposed a policy framework to support firms to move to higher value added products through greater innovation and collaboration. It recommended a shift in focus away from structural adjustment measures toward 'a new focus on building innovative capability at the level of the enterprise and the workplace', through a A$250 million over five years TCF Innovation Assistance Package. Included in the package is support for a TCF Innovation Council to guide ongoing policy development.

Review of the Automobile Industry
The Minister for Innovation, Industry, Science and Research, also announced in February 2008 a comprehensive review of Australia's automotive industry to be conducted by Mr Steve Bracks, a previous Premier of the major manufacturing State, Victoria. The establishment of the review recognises the importance of the automotive sector in terms of regional employment, as a key sector in skill development and in demand with a systemic role in the wider manufacturing sector, and as a major exporter of high value added manufactures. The final report of the review was released in August 2008 In response to this review, and recognizing the many challenges of adjustment that the industry faces, the Government announced a major new sectoral Program

INNOVATION AGENDA TO 2020

The Government has outlined its innovation agenda for Australia over the next decade in *Powering Ideas: An Innovation Agenda for the 21st Century*, supported by a $3.1 billion boost in funding over the next four years.

The Budget package includes more support for world class university research, a Super Science Initiative focusing on national research strengths, a new Research and Development Tax Credit and other measures to boost business innovation. Innovation is vital to accelerating economic recovery in the short term and opening up new pathways to prosperity in the long term.

Innovation can help us create a better Australia – a fairer, richer and greener nation that is equipped to meet the challenges and grasp the opportunities of the 21st century. It can give us new industries, high-wage jobs, safer communities, and a better quality of life.

Investing in innovation today is critical to addressing the collapse in productivity growth over the last decade, keeping our existing industries competitive and nurturing emerging industries based on new technologies.

Powering Ideas outlines a vision for a national innovation system in 2020 in which:

- The **Australian Government** clearly articulates its national priorities and aspirations to make the best use of resources, drive change and provide benchmarks against which to measure success.
- **Universities and research organisations** attract the best and brightest minds to conduct world-class research, fuelling the innovation system with new knowledge and ideas.
- **Businesses of all sizes and in all sectors** embrace innovation as the pathway to greater competitiveness, supported by government policies that minimise barriers and maximise opportunities for the commercialisation of new ideas and new technologies.

- **Government and community sectors** consciously seek to improve policy development and service delivery through innovation.
- **Researchers, businesses and governments work collaboratively** to secure value from commercial innovation and to address national and global challenges.

Australia can do better in building innovation skills, supporting research to create new knowledge, increasing business innovation and boosting collaboration. The Government's vision is supported by specific policy ambitions, including:

- increasing the number of Australian research groups performing at world-class levels;
- boosting international research collaboration by Australian universities;
- significantly increasing the number of students completing higher degrees by research over the next decade;
- doubling the level of collaboration between Australian businesses, universities and publicly-funded research agencies;
- a 25 per cent increase in the proportion of businesses engaging in innovation; and
- continued improvement in the number of businesses investing in R&D.

The Government's Innovation Agenda sets out a framework of National Innovation Priorities and details concrete actions to help it achieve its policy ambitions.

The Government's targeted investment in innovation capacity in this Budget will boost Australia's research and innovation capacity at a critical time and directly support the Government's longer term vision and policy ambitions by:

- reforming university research funding arrangements and boosting investment, with a focus on excellence and transparency, and increased support for postgraduate research students;
- investing in infrastructure and fellowships to ensure Australia stays ahead of the game in the three priority science fields of marine and climate, space and astronomy, and future industries – each reflecting Australia's research strengths and helping to address challenges like climate change, rising health costs, and increasing global economic competition; and
- boosting business research and delivering better outcomes for the nation by: replacing the R&D Tax Concession with a new, simpler R&D Tax Credit; and taking an innovative approach to the commercialisation of research through the Commonwealth Commercialisation Institute.

Powering Ideas also outlines a range of actions that the Government has already taken to boost Australia's innovation system, as well as new proposals to improve innovation within the Government and to reform the governance of the system.

This Agenda and the Government's specific Budget measures respond to the key findings and recommendations from the Review of the National Innovation System, conducted in 2008 by an expert group chaired by Dr Terry Cutler. They also address the outcomes of a range of other reviews, including Professor Mary O'Kane's review of the Cooperative Research Centres Program.

INNOVATION TAX INCENTIVES

R&D TAX CONCESSION

Status: Applications are received based on individual company reporting periods.

Companies wishing to make an application for registration for the R&D Tax Concession under section 39J of the IR&D Act 1986 for the income year ending on 30 June 2010 must do so by 30 April 2011.

Companies wishing to make an application for registration for the R&D Tax Concession under section 39J of the IR&D Act 1986 for the income year ending on 31 December 2010 should do so by 31 October 2011.

Electronic applications must be lodged by midnight local time. Hard copy (paper-based) applications must be received by 5.00pm local time.

Description: R&D Tax Concession is a broad-based, market driven Tax Concession which allows companies to deduct up to 125% of qualifying expenditure incurred on R&D activities when lodging their corporate tax return. A 175% Incremental (Premium) Tax Concession and R&D Tax Offset are also available in certain circumstances.

Contact: Should you have an inquiry about the R&D Tax Concession or the R&D Tax Incentive contact the **AusIndustry Hotline** on **13 28 46** or emailHotline@AusIndustry.gov.au.

R&D TAX CREDIT

Status: On 12 May 2009 the Government announced it will replace the existing R&D Tax Concession with a new R&D Tax Credit. The Bills to establish the R&D Tax Credit were introduced into Parliament on 30 September 2010 and have been amended to address a number of concerns raised by stakeholders during consultations and as part of the Senate Economics Legislation Committee report of 15 June 2010. The Bills before Parliament propose that the R&D Tax Credit will apply to income years starting on or after 1 July 2010.

Description: The new R&D Tax Credit is to be a broad-based and market driven incentive package. The two core components of the package are:

- a 45 per cent refundable tax credit (the equivalent to a 150 per cent concession) for eligible entities with an aggregated turnover of less than $20 million per annum;
- a non-refundable 40 per cent R&D tax credit (the equivalent of a 133 per cent deduction) for all other eligible entities.

To accompany this change of rates and delivery mechanism is to be a clearer and better targeted definition of eligible 'R&D activities' that will ensure the incentive is available in circumstances consistent with the underlying rationale for government intervention and that it delivers value for money for taxpayers.

The new R&D tax incentive, the R&D Tax Credit, is contained in the *Tax Laws Amendment (Research and Development) Bill 2010* and the *Income Tax Rates Amendment (Research and Development) Bill 2010*, which are available on the Parliament of Australia website.

An interim measure demonstrating the Government's increased support for eligible small companies, prior to the introduction of the R&D Tax Credit, increased the R&D expenditure cap for the R&D Tax Concession Offset from $1 million to $2 million for income years starting on or after 1 July 2009.

INNOVATION SYSTEM MANAGEMENT

Innovation plays a key role in driving productivity and broader prosperity. This raises questions of governance in the innovation system. National government has an important role in providing leadership, but it shares the system with other public and private players and must frame its activities against this wider picture.

This chapter examines how the national government might best execute its particular strategic role within the innovation system and, in so doing, mobilise and coordinate the efforts of the many parties with an interest in the community's innovation-fuelled prosperity.

Government possesses a unique ability to influence and view the overall innovation system. As well as its direct role in supporting innovation in both the public and private sectors, government also plays a key role in structuring those markets within which innovation occurs through regulation of market operations and industry structures. Effective policies are those that facilitate a robust and well-functioning national innovation system which optimises the *flows* of innovation based on the nation's investment in *stocks*.

CRUCIAL GOVERNANCE ROLES WITHIN THE INNOVATION SYSTEM

In examining the role of government in a national innovation system, Ian Marsh posits three crucial governance roles[1]:

This provides a useful framework within which to examine current and possible institutional arrangements.

In considering any governance framework it is important to note that:

- The innovation agenda does and must touch on the whole range of government concerns and cuts across bureaucratic silos. This invites, and indeed requires, a 'whole of government' approach and framework.
- Specialised roles and functions within the innovation system need to be counterbalanced by the capability to take a helicopter view, and to address and resource cross-cutting, platform issues.
- To date it has been difficult to assemble an overall view of the footprint of innovation in Australia. What is needed is an ability to examine the mix of activities and capabilities as a portfolio, and to coordinate government responses.

Step 1: Leadership

To provide effective national leadership on innovation the government must have clear goals and strategies, and a process for arriving at them. An institutional structure is needed to coordinate

---

1 Marsh, I., *The politics of regional economic strategies*, upublished paper, October 2006.

and focus the role of government within the innovation system.[2] In studying governance of national innovation systems, the OECD has commented on the increasing need for more coherent innovation policy agendas which span ministerial boundaries and encompass a broad range of policy areas.

The OECD study points to a range of barriers to coherence in national innovation systems, including policy silos within government, 'short-termism' in resource allocation, and fragmentation and complexity of innovation resources within government. At a time when globalisation, structural change and 'big' problems such as climate change and energy security are posing new challenges, many countries are finding their innovation policy-making and institutional frameworks ill-equipped for the new paradigm.

> *A common problem for many Governments is that they use yesterday's institutions to meet tomorrow's problems*[3].

To achieve the coherence, flexibility and responsiveness necessary for effective innovation policy, the national government requires a 'central brain' that is well informed, can take the overview and assume strategic leadership. Specifically the issues that such a body should address are:

- the need for, and ability to provide, a 'helicopter' view of the overall innovation ecology of the country;
- the importance of developing consensus and support around strategic directions and priorities for Australian innovation policy;
- the importance of a 'whole of government' perspective on innovation to inform the decision making and resource allocation of central government agencies and to inform inter-jurisdictional decision-making frameworks involving Australia's federal structures; and
- how to achieve co-ordination without centralisation which could lead to an erosion of diversity and an inadequate range of innovation activities.
-

A great number of submissions called for the creation of some peak 'Innovation Council' to fulfil this role.[4] The only current such body is the Prime Minister's Science, Engineering and Innovation Council (PMSEIC). This is a large council, comprising mainly representational membership that works essentially on an issues-based agenda, supported by ad hoc working groups and the Office of the Chief Scientist. As such it is not designed to inform strategic co-ordination and leadership functions across the whole of government.

---

[2] The OECD has noted that innovation policy requires co-ordinated, strategic action involving a number of portfolios – "it builds upon its horizontal role by providing a strategic framework across ministerial and institutional boundaries to ensure innovation and adaptation within the context of sustainable social and economic development". OECD, *Governance of Innovation Systems – Volume 1 a synthesis report*, pp. 19–20. 2005.

[3] *Ibid.* p. 30

[4] E.g. Council for Humanities, Arts and Social Sciences – Submission no. 481; Society for Knowledge Economics - Submission no. 522; CSIRO – Submission no. 217; Marceau, Jane - Submission no. 297; Andrews, Peter - no. 431; Australian Industry Group - Submission no. 265; Innovation Research Network – Submission no. 332; FASTS - Submission no. 549; Innovation Research Universities Australia - Submission no. 95, Business Council of Australia - Submission no. 390.

To provide a broader perspective, and considered advice to national government, the Panel favours replacement of PMSEIC with a new and differently-focused National Innovation Council. Such a council would, like its predecessor, be chaired by the Prime Minister in recognition of the importance and whole-of-government nature of the issues.

NEW NATIONAL INNOVATION COUNCIL

The functions of the National Innovation Council would be:

- custodianship of the proposed national innovation priorities, their application in directing investment and resource allocation decisions, and their evolution and focus over time;
- periodic review of the national innovation investment portfolio;
- promotion of robust linkages across government, and between levels of government, especially with regard to cross-cutting issues and capabilities;
- scanning for emerging opportunities or challenges, and the avoidance of surprises;
- issuing an annual Statement on Innovation, including findings from evaluation reviews conducted in the preceding year;
- identifying and advising on innovation options or opportunities which could be addressed through the government's role in market design, competition policy and pro-active market regulation;
- oversight of national information policies and their particular application to public sector information and information generated by publicly funded activity; and
- appropriate international linkages and relationships that should be pursued.

It is important to be explicit about what functions the Council would *not* perform. The NIC would not:

- administer programs;
- conduct detailed innovation research; or
- conduct evaluation and review of specific programs.

In the interests of effectiveness and transparency, the outcomes of Council deliberations, but not its proceedings, should be published.

The Council needs to be significantly smaller than the current PMSEIC (12 ministerial members plus 19 other members). Members should be appointed primarily on the basis of individual merit, but taking into account their overall experience and links within the sector. The Council should include people with the ability to take a strategic overview and provide advice on the shape of the overall innovation system and the Government's investment in it. It should be outward looking in evaluating the global environment and advising on Australia's priorities for both domestic action and international engagement. The Council should encompass a diversity of views and include key sectors within the innovation system (eg universities, the research sector, business etc). The Council should also include key ministers involved in leading the government's innovation agenda, along with the Chief Scientist.

A useful adjunct to the Council, and a means to broaden the perspectives of Council deliberations, would be the creation of an International Innovation Advisory Panel to the Council, drawing on eminent Australians who live and work abroad. Such a Panel might meet once a year. The establishment of such a Panel would recognise the importance of internationalising Australia's innovation system, and co-opt the participation of key global players from Australia's diaspora of expatriate talent.

AN OFFICE OF INNOVATION ASSESSMENT

The functions proposed for the new National Innovation Council will require the support of a high-level, highly talented secretariat. Such a group, with the skills commensurate with the recommended function of the new Council, does not currently exist, although a partial analogue is provided by the erstwhile Australian Science and Technology Council which was disbanded by a former government in the 1990s. To undertake this role, establishment of an Office of Innovation Assessment is proposed.

This office should be small and nimble, with planned turnover of staff to maintain freshness. It is important that such a group does not develop 'a life of its own' with entrenched positions. A significant proportion of staff should be seconded from other areas of government, including State and Territory governments, and from academia and the private sector.

The Prime Minister's National Innovation Council would function as the 'central brain' of a dynamic national innovation system. It would draw upon, and synthesise, the strategic perspectives from a range of bodies including the network of Industry Innovation Councils,[5] Innovation Australia, the Academies, major industry groups, Universities Australia, other tertiary representative groups and the major public sector research agencies.
This last group represents a key critical mass and capability within the national innovation system. Our major public sector research agencies (including CSIRO, the Defence Science and Technology Organisation (DSTO), ANSTO and AIMS are split across a number of portfolios and together have control of over $1.5 billion annually in government funds for research. There is currently no formal coordination of their activities and, while they do often work collaboratively, this largely happens on an ad hoc basis. Arguably our current research effort lacks co-ordination and is too fragmented for a small country. New research initiatives in a range of climate change related areas could exacerbate the problem.

RESEARCH COORDINATION COUNCIL

In order to more effectively coordinate our national research effort and to provide a source of coordinated advice to the National Innovation Council, a Research Coordination Council should be established. The National Research Infrastructure Committee, suggested in Chapter 5, should be a sub-committee of this Council. In addition to major statutory research bodies, the Council should include other key public sector research bodies that may sit within government departments such as the National Measurement Institute and Geoscience Australia.
The Council should also include the major research funding bodies, ie the ARC and the NHMRC. While they do not directly undertake research, between them they award $1.2 billion annually in research funds, largely to universities and medical research institutes, and they have strong influence over the national research program.

Step 2: Execution

The regulation aspects of the government's role in innovation are covered in Chapter 7. This section deals with governance mechanisms for the delivery and coordination of programs and activities that support innovation. Effective governance and coordination is needed both across Australian Government programs and between Australian Government, State and Territory programs and activities.

[5] The Minister for Innovation, Industry, Science and Research has announced the establishment of Industry Innovation Councils (Councils) later in 2008 covering a number of industry groups. Membership will draw on the knowledge and expertise of innovation leaders from business, unions and professional organisations, science and research agencies, and government (Commonwealth, State and Territory). The Councils will have a role in championing innovation in industry, building stakeholder links and advising the Minister on priority innovation issues.

AUSTRALIAN GOVERNMENT PROGRAMS AND ACTIVITIES

The Australian Government's 2008–09 Science and Innovation Budget Tables show budgeted Commonwealth expenditure on science and innovation for the 2008–09 year as totalling $6.37 billion. Of this, $4.36 billion is to be spent through the Innovation, Industry Science and Research portfolio, while over $2 billion is to be spent by ten other portfolios, the largest being Health and Ageing ($625 million); Defence ($394 million); Resources, Energy and Tourism ($324 million); and Agriculture, Fisheries and Forestry ($259 million).

Within the 11 portfolios there is a multiplicity of agencies that deliver innovation programs including the ARC, NHMRC, Rural Research and Development Corporations, DSTO, Innovation Australia and numerous agencies delivering a growing number of programs related to climate change. Following the 2007 election the new Government created a portfolio for innovation and research, thus, we hope, signalling an intention to bring some much needed coherency into government decision-making on these issues.

Currently each portfolio pursues its research and innovation agenda largely independently. Budget bids, funding allocations and delivery mechanisms are all addressed largely within agency silos. Despite a significant financial contribution to research in the former government's *Backing Australia's Ability* packages, they did not include effective institutional mechanisms to support a coherent whole-of-government approach. Mechanisms such as national research priorities were introduced but achieved only limited impact in ensuring coherence across the national government research effort.

One might ask why the ARC has not enjoyed the level of funding increases over recent years that have flowed to the NHMRC. It is hard to assess whether this was the product of conscious priority-setting rather than more effective lobbying, or a better budget strategy by one group over another. Even more pertinently, one might point to the inconsistency of more than doubling funding for the NHMRC's competitive grant programs while not increasing the funds (which come from a different portfolio) for infrastructure and overheads to support these grants. Such outcomes highlight the lack of an overall strategic approach and of effective coordination.
The coordination challenge is to ensure a whole-of-government innovation framework across agencies. Moves in some areas, like the suggestion for a new policy council over the rural R&D corporations, would facilitate horizontal policy coordination, but wider action is required. There have also been suggestions to more closely align the ARC and the NHMRC with the aim of improving co-ordination and possibly reducing overheads. Centralising all these functions is not realistic. What is important is a coherent framework for these activities, so a consistent application of priorities and policy principles can be proposed by the National Innovation Council and considered by Government.

While it will include key Ministers, the National Innovation Council will be an advisory body to Government. Key decisions will still be taken through the established processes of Cabinet consideration. To ensure that a coherent approach flows through into these decision-making processes the Panel suggests that the Minister for Innovation, Industry, Science and Research should be a joint signatory to any proposal from across government significantly bearing on the national innovation agenda.

DELIVERY OF INDUSTRY PROGRAMS THROUGH INNOVATION AUSTRALIA

The Panel believes that, as far as possible, there should be a bias against any proliferation of new program delivery bodies, and a consolidation where possible. As a general principle, industry-facing programs should be administered within the Department of Innovation, Industry, Science and Research and through Innovation Australia in particular. This would promote a user-centric framework, and enable better bundling of support options around industry or firm needs.[6] What needs to be stressed is that program policy responsibility can still reside with relevant line agencies, as, for example, would be the case with innovation or R&D programs established in connection with climate change or the environment.

Innovation Australia uses an existing Australia-wide network of offices and staff (AusIndustry) which streamlines access and means lower transaction costs for the firm and the government. Just as Centrelink has been established as the pre-eminent whole-of-government delivery agency for assistance to individuals, Innovation Australia, through AusIndustry, should play this role for the business sector.

Commonwealth, State and Territory coordination

A further key challenge to effective governance and coordination is presented by the fragmented approach to innovation policy and programs inherent in our federal system of government. The Panel was asked to examine the scope for simplifying and reducing program duplication and ensuring that any innovation support provided is well-targeted and easy to access. To achieve this it asked the Inter-Governmental Working Group (IWG) to examine all relevant Australian Government and State and Territory innovation programs. (For full report see Annex 9).
The IWG analysed industry innovation programs across Australia to inform the Panel about where support is being directed (see Box 7). It found that 69 percent of programs are delivered by the states and territories but 90 percent of the financial support is provided through Australian Government programs. Furthermore, it was found that most support was directed to research and development and funded by the Australian Government and that State and Territory programs were more tailored to the needs of local constituencies.

Main findings of the Intergovernmental Working Group

- Two hundred and twenty one programs supporting innovation in firms were identified, comprising 31 percent Australian Government and 69 percent State and Territory Governments. Australian Government programs account for 90 percent of the total expenditure for these programs, which is approximately $3.7 billion per annum.
- There is some apparent intra- and inter-jurisdictional overlap in programs but this is neither systemic nor likely to have a significant impact. Many programs are targeted to leverage off other programs.
- Most programs are at the early phases of the research commercialisation chain (R&D and early commercialisation).
- Only 36 percent of the programs have been reviewed. Many programs have unclear and/or unmeasurable KPIs.
- Only 10 percent of Australian Government and 28 percent of State and Territory programs have on-line application processes.

Of particular concern is the relatively low level of program evaluation and the small amount of online access for firms and others seeking access to program advice.

Submissions noted a large number of government innovation programs. This may complicate access, particularly as programs are delivered by a range of government departments. Many

[6] The former Senator George Campbell highlighted the desirability of a greater user focus in his recent comment that we have 'a raft of different products in pigeonholes so your project has to fit the pigeonhole otherwise you don't get the funding. You need to change the approach [and] have the capacity to say to companies: 'We can tailor our support to your product, rather than you tailoring your product to meet our support requirements'." *Sydney Morning Herald*, 23 June 2008

firms, especially SMEs, are not aware of programs for which they may be eligible, or where to find information on options. Application processes are seen as too lengthy, cumbersome and/or expensive when weighed against potential gains.

There was strong support for an integrated, national innovation strategy and a governance platform to manage current issues with the program suite. Some submissions advocated a 'one-stop-shop' approach to providing information on government support, with communication and promotion seen to be an important part of the solution.

The IWG proposed *A Framework of Principles for Innovation Interventions* (See Box 8 and Annex 9) to enhance consistency in approach and support the overall accessibility and efficiency of the suite of interventions across Australia. The underlying intent of the Framework is to maximise the effectiveness of individual and collective actions by governments in support of the development of the National Innovation System. It has a particular focus on ensuring that the suite of interventions reflect and respond to changes in demand-side needs and priorities, and improve coordination and consistency across jurisdictions.

Framework Principles for Innovation Interventions

1. Supports the development and effectiveness of the national innovation system.
2. Reflects and responds to demand-side needs and priorities.
3. Rationale for intervention and role of government is clearly identified.
4. The best placed jurisdiction(s) is/are responsible for design and delivery.
5. Innovation risk is assessed, accepted and incorporated into initiative design.
6. Initiatives are well designed with clarity about:
    - Purpose;
    - Expected outcome;
    - Key performance indicators;
    - Evaluation processes;
    - Return on investment (financial, economic or social); and
    - User/target.
7. Initiatives evaluated for impact on regional/national innovation system.

Strengthening of innovation data collection

Innovation policy development and program design is enhanced by longitudinal data collection to identify the impact of interventions on firms and their growth. The Review process revealed that the available data and research findings on innovation in Australia were a constraint on the ability to analyse the impact of interventions.

The Australian Bureau of Statistics (ABS) should be the key innovation data collection agency and in recent years has increased its collection of data on innovation in Australian business. It has strategies to merge different data sets to enhance its advice — for example, the Business Characteristics Survey which brings together the collection of business characteristics and innovation data. It is critical that data collections are long term and not broken due to funding cuts. It is also important that data collections on innovation by the ABS are able to be compared to those in other countries. Finally, it is important that the data collections are available to policy areas and research institutions to model impacts and thereby enhance interventions.

Step 3: Review

Reporting on innovation

One of the most problematic areas in innovation policy is the development of broadly based and meaningful measures for reporting and monitoring.[7] As a general comment, most traditional measures have focussed on supply-side, input parameters. There is less coverage of firm performance and the diffusion of innovation, or measures to link innovative behaviour with social, economic or environmental impacts. The most difficult to measure aspects of the health of an innovation system are the relative robustness of linkages, relationships and information flows. In many areas qualitative assessments are needed in addition to quantitative ones.

In carrying out its proposed reporting functions, the National Innovation Council should drive hard for improved frameworks for monitoring and reporting and, as set out earlier, should produce an annual Statement on Innovation to report on trends in the national innovation system. On the science and technology front, the US provides exhaustive and illuminating global trend data in the National Science Board's biennial science and technology indicators. The UK has probably made the most progress in developing a balanced scorecard framework for monitoring innovation, and a draft Australian version of this scorecard is at Annex 12. This could be further developed by the Office of Innovation Assessment.

Evaluation and Review functions

Rigorous review processes are important to underpin public and industry confidence in the integrity of programs. Program evaluations should be transparent and undertaken from an independent standpoint.

In its 2007 Report on *Public Support for Science and Innovation,* the Productivity Commission found that:

Governance arrangements relating to business programs need to change. Options include:

- *shifting responsibility for commissioning program evaluations to an independent third party or establishing an inter-departmental working group to oversight such evaluations; and*
- *requiring full public disclosure of the results and recommendations and a timely response on the action to be taken.*[8]

We also note that the Department of Finance and Deregulation has embarked on a process of 'arms length' review of major groups of Commonwealth programs.

The Panel agrees with the principle that evaluations should be published and openly available. The same principles that apply to financial audit and risk management functions should apply to evaluation of innovation programs. Independence is only secured by the review function being at 'arm's length' from the administering body. This does not mean that delivery agencies should not do their own performance evaluation – they should, but these should be supplemented by periodic independent reviews that are publicly released.

In view of work underway on these issues in the Department of Finance and Deregulation, the Panel has not made a specific recommendation as to who should undertake these evaluations, but notes that the Department's responsibility for the Budget would provide an unhelpful conflict or bias.

Performance evaluations should be based on *ex ante* evaluation criteria and the best available evidence base. Where evaluations find inadequate data, it should be a requirement that action is mandated to address data deficiencies.

It is desirable that programs be evaluated not only against their specific policy objectives and program parameters, but also reviewed – within appropriate timeframe intervals – for their continued relative effectiveness compared with complementary or related programs. Review

---

[7] At the Roundtable on Targets and Measurements there was a general agreement about the extent of the difficulties.

[8] Productivity Commission, *Public Support for Science and Innovation*, p. 421. 2007.

processes should be conducted to provide robust feedback loops to both the policy sponsors of programs as well as to the delivery agencies. Robust review processes, together with complementary and ongoing strategic assessment processes, are necessary to support policy innovation and to avoid the moral hazard of capture by vested interests.[9]

Finally, it is important that there be a clear separation between evaluation processes and central government budget processes. Clearly budgetary processes should be informed by, and reflect the outcomes of evaluations but they should not, in principle, stand in the place of evaluations. Apparently arbitrary program terminations undermine industry confidence in policy settings and introduce undesirable levels of uncertainty and risk. Changes with retrospective impacts are particularly undesirable.

In addition to having effective evaluation mechanisms, policy makers need to be well informed about the evolution of the national innovation system and how it compares with those in other countries. The Panel, in conducting this Review, was in many cases constrained by the lack of both data and research findings concerning the Australian innovation system. In other countries this shortcoming has been recognised and independent innovation research centres have been created to undertake research on the innovation system, provide independent advice to government and offer meeting places where private sector practitioners can interact with each other, policymakers and academics.[10] The Panel sees merit in establishing such a centre in Australia. It would develop skilled researchers, comprehensive databases and cutting edge methods for research on both the innovation process, broadly defined, and specialised questions of key national importance.

The Panel proposes a broad agenda for the future of innovation policy in Australia and advocates immediate action to address key needs and opportunities. An effective governance system will be critical in bringing together all the elements into a coherent national approach that maximise the value of public investment in innovation. The institutional framework proposed above is designed to provide the leadership required to ensure effective agenda setting, prioritisation, implementation and policy learning. With a vibrant agenda and strong policy leadership we can truly look forward to an innovative and prosperous future.

INNOVATION IN BUSINESS

"Innovation is critical to Australia's national future. Our prosperity, our economic strength and our ability to compete in the global economy all depend on valuing innovation, harnessing its potential and putting it to work for the benefit of all Australians... In particular, we need to find ways to increase innovation performance across the economy, to ensure business has better access to new ideas and new technologies and to bridge the divide between industry and research...
In today's economy, innovation policy is industry policy."
Senator the Hon Kim Carr, 22 January 2008, announcing the Review of Australia's National Innovation System

FINDING OF INNOVATION

Innovation is more widespread than is often imagined, occurring everyday in the way business enterprises operate, meet the needs of customers, and organise their people

[9] *Ibid*

[10] In the UK, DIUS, in conjunction with the ESRC, TSB and NESTA, has funded the establishment of such a centre and this is regarded by the Brutish Government as a key dimension of their innovation strategy.

and processes. This is not traditional science and research-led innovation. It is the non-technological innovation that occurs and transforms businesses as they engage with their customers and markets.

This market-facing business innovation is often overlooked and undervalued. But if it is ignored, Australia squanders an opportunity to make the productivity gains we need to maintain our prosperity and living standards.

This challenge is well recognised in the UK where the National Endowment for Science, Technology and the Arts produced a blueprint report in October 2006 entitled *The Innovation Gap. Why policy needs to reflect the reality of innovation in the UK.*
Innovation is all-pervasive, frequently found in unlikely places and is rarely based on traditional understandings of linear 'pipeline' research and development.
Another critic of the overemphasis on the linear research-to-commercialisation 'pipeline' model of innovation is UK author and commentator, Charles Leadbeater[11]:
Innovation rarely proceeds down an orderly pipeline from boffin to consumer. Innovation often involves changes to business organisation and consumer behaviour as much as science and technology. Many innovative organisations in the UK have no formal R&D capability: they innovate in the job, often through interaction with clients and markets. Often innovation is highly networked and interactive, involving a wide range of players, not least of the ultimate consumers of products and services...
The realities of business innovation were recognised in the submission to the Review by the Group of Eight:[12]

In the real world most innovation occurs in established firms in existing industries through incremental improvements, involving non-scientific and non-R&D based knowledge such as creative design, marketing, organisational improvement and tooling up.

Gary Banks, Chairman of the Productivity Commission in his 2008 Colin Clark Memorial Lecture[13] also recognises the significance of non-technical innovation:

Innovation is sometimes seen as synonymous with technological advances. But it is far wider than that, encompassing changes to all facets of an enterprise's operations, its relationships with its workers, its suppliers and its customers. According to survey data, only 30 percent of what the ABS defines as 'major innovating firms' actually undertake R&D...It is clear that the heightened pace of change will put a premium on business flexibility and adaptability.

Innovation is all about the firm and what happens in businesses. Businesses are the point where new value is created from innovative activities.
Innovation outcomes are shaped by interactions within and across a dynamic system. But as the key players in converting ideas, knowledge and technology into market competitive goods and services, businesses represent the cornerstone of an innovation-based economy and the main mechanism through which the wide benefits of innovation are diffused.

---

11 Charles Leadbeater, The Ten Habits of Mass Innovation, in: Making Innovation Flourish, National Endowment for Science, Technology and the Arts, November 2006.

12 Group of Eight – Submission no. 372

13 Gary Banks, Industry Policy for a Productive Australia, Productivity Commission, Brisbane, August 2008.

Innovation in business is important because it is the primary driver of competitiveness for firms differentiating their products and services from those of low-cost competitors in globalised and deregulated markets.

That Australian businesses need to collectively improve innovation performance is well recognised. Continuous innovation, or the repeated successful introduction of novel products and services, is the only sustainable strategy for firm survival and progress in rapidly changing and turbulent technological and market circumstances

This is a challenge for all business – not only those in high-technology sectors – that are competing on the basis of quality, specialisation, flexibility, customisation and cost. Innovation in businesses includes the non-technological and non-R&D based innovations that typically characterize services businesses in a knowledge-based economy enabled by the increasing sophistication and ubiquity of advanced ICT connectivity.
New innovation patterns

In addition to recognising the broader dimensions of business innovation, we must appreciate that the active ingredients and patterns of innovation are fundamentally changing.
In a globalised knowledge-based economy, patterns of innovation have evolved and shifted beyond the sole gifted inventor or scientist, or the adept researcher and technologist. They are more diverse and complex than just the picture of the creative entrepreneur with proven commercial acumen.

This more nuanced understanding of the dynamics of innovation and in particular of how value is created to lift productivity and prosperity is well presented in a paper by John Steen, Sam Macaulay and Tim Kastelle.[14]

Steen et al present the evidence of value being created from innovation as a system of forming connections and recombining knowledge and technologies which in turn, drive competitive performance:

Newer models of the innovation process make no ... assumptions about value being inherent in any particular process, idea or technology. Value is created through rearranging and recombining knowledge, people, processes and technologies. This problem-solving and improvisational activity is most clearly seen in project businesses and complex product systems such as wind turbines (for instance Vestas Wind Systems), construction (such as Laing O'Rourke) and management consulting (like Deloitte).

It can also be seen in new Australian ventures such as Beeline. While tractors and global-positioning systems are established technologies, combining these to create planting and harvesting efficiencies in large-scale agribusiness is yet another example of innovation by recombination and connection.

The ways businesses innovate are changing. They are adopting new models of innovation by better integrating a wide range of internal activities – such as marketing, operations and

[14] Steen, J, Macauley, S., and Kastelle, T, Mapping and Managing Networks for Innovation Performance: New Perspectives and New Tools, in The Human Dimension of Innovation, Australian Business Foundation, (to be published 2008).

design – and being more open to external sources of ideas and the possibility of new routes to market.[15] This has meant engaging with a larger number and wider range of collaborators. Henry Chesbrough, one of the popularisers of this trend describes the shift to a more distributed, flexible pattern of operations as a move from 'closed' to 'open' innovation. In this model the innovation process has become increasingly complex. To innovate, firms must involve a greater number of players more closely and intensively to realize the commercial potential of their ideas. Openness has been shown to be beneficial for firm innovativeness and performance.[16] It increases the amount of resources and information available to the firm and the opportunities to recombine previously disconnected ideas.[17]

Contemporary business innovation is characterised by more fluid interactions between internal and external activities, where ideas, people, and resources flow in, around, and out of organisations. The boundaries between internal and external activities and the firm's general operating environment are more permeable, making it important to extract as much knowledge from the external environment as possible. In particular, the lesson from virtually all studies of innovation shows that the miraculous alchemy of innovation occurs close to the customer setting. Increasing user-driven or inspired innovation[18], especially in the service industries which dominate our economy, highlights the absolute importance of innovation policy being driven from a demand-side, market-facing perspective.

The changing nature of innovation was also commented on by Gary Banks, Chairman of the Productivity Commission:

...innovation models are evolving. Gone are the days when most business innovation was conducted within the walls of the company seeking to improve its production processes or bring a new product to the market. New technologies, as distinct from their specific applications, are increasingly being bought and sold, leading to new forms of pricing knowledge. Also, potential users of an innovation are much more likely to involve themselves in its development rather than waiting for it to be brought to market.[19]

SERVICES INNOVATION

Services innovation deserves some particular attention as there is increasing recognition that services, being dominant and pervasive features of advanced economies, are significant contributors to productivity gains, business and employment growth and enhanced prosperity in society at large.

The April 2008 report by the Prime Minister's Science Engineering and Innovation Council (PMSEIC) Working Group on Services Innovation, *Science and technology-led innovation in services for Australian industries* identifies two modes of services innovation:

---

15 Chesbrough, H. W., Open Innovation: The new Imperative for Creating and Profiting from Technology, Harvard Business Press, 2004.

16 Laursen, K. and Salter, A., Open for innovation: the role of openness in explaining innovation performance among UK manufacturing firms, Strategic Management Journal, 27(2) 2006.

17 Fleming, L., Recombinant uncertainty in technical search, Management Science, 42, pp 117-132, 2001; Hargadon A. B.and Sutton, R. I., Technology brokering and innovation in a product development firm, Administrative Science Quarterly, 42, 1997

18 von Hippel, E., Democratising Innovation. The MIT Press, Cambridge, Massachusetts, 2005.

19 Banks, G., Industry Policy for a Productive Australia, Productivity Commission, Brisbane, August 2008.

innovation *in* services industries, where innovation is either applied to an industry regarded as service-based, or results in a new service-based industry such as water monitoring services, internet service providers, or innovative uses of IT and digital imaging by hairdressing businesses; and

innovation *through* services in any organisation or business where the application of a service results in innovation in an industry generally not classified as services, such as the use of sonar, GPS and remote sensing satellites to enhance the location, harvesting and productivity of the fishing industry.

The submission to the Review from the Australian Services Roundtable[20] highlights the distinctive characteristics of services innovation and how it can contribute substantially to driving sustained improvement in Australia's productivity performance.
Innovation in services tends:

To take place specifically at the point of interaction between services provider and the client.
To be driven by client relations more than is the case for innovation in manufacturing. Service companies must maintain a flexible approach to innovation, constantly changing to solve client problems and meet new needs.
To be people-driven as well as laboratory-driven, ie to break the bounds of traditional hierarchy by requiring integrated input from all kinds of operational, organisational, technical and managerial staff as well as researchers.
Not to offer necessary economies of scale, as in manufacturing.
To involve a high level of interaction and interdependence between knowledge providers (such as research organisations) and knowledge users (such as service firms) – to the extent that the term co-innovation has relevance.

To be focused not only on new suites of services but also on new modal delivery methods for those services and on new business models to reach new markets.
Not to take place as a specialised and separately accounted activity located in a separately identified part of a firm but to be inextricably tangled up with everyday creativity and design.
To show evidence of a strong responsiveness to both technological and non-technological inputs, including when provided jointly.

To involve the social as well as the natural sciences.
To involve the creative arts and humanities.
To suffer from inadequate formal or informal access to collaboration opportunities between services providers and the education and R&D community.

The Australian Services Roundtable goes on to argue that services innovation not only makes services firms internationally competitive, but also allows them to be 'enablers' and 'change agents' and thereby the mechanisms through which much innovation takes place in other traditional industries and across the economy.

By examining services innovation, we put the spotlight squarely on those hidden non-technological aspects of business innovation that are the source of competitiveness and productivity. That is, we focus on the demand side or market-pull dimensions of innovation, where value is created by firms transforming their business offerings and capabilities in order to solve customer problems more imaginatively.
This is particularly relevant to innovation in services, where firms differentiate themselves by their intangible assets like the skills of their people, the way they engage and serve their customers, the

[20] Australian Services Roundtable – Submission no. 613

character of the customer experience, the ability to use and re-use knowledge and thereby provide valued solutions for which customers are prepared to pay.

Imperial College's Professor John Bessant has made the point that while there are many elements of similarity between innovation in services and innovation in manufacturing, what distinguishes services innovation is the crucially important role of customers and the way companies respond to their understanding of market and customer demands.[21] Services companies compete and innovate to gain their competitive edge by their skill at relationship management, that is, by intimately understanding their customers and servicing their (sometimes unarticulated) needs. Services innovation is strongly driven by customisation, even individualisation, where discerning customers are not passive but are fully engaged in designing the services that they are purchasing. Close relationships with customers help services companies defend against imitators and low entry barriers.

Services innovation brings to the fore non-technical skills such as teamwork, co-operation, negotiation and communication; together with new areas like social network analysis.

Finally, new patterns of knowledge-intensive business activity round out the picture of the contribution of services innovation to competitive performance and productivity. These shifts in the competitive behaviour of successful Australian firms have been identified as:

new hybrid business offerings that blend products and services for customer problem-solving; complex product systems and project-based activities like airports, stadiums and other infrastructure projects;

proficiency as technology integrators, rather than just either technology producers or users; and competing by distinctive knowledge management or by sustained incremental innovation.[22]
Boosting innovation capabilities in firms

Businesses make decisions about innovation based on their particular competitive positions, available resources and strategic intent. Innovation spending by firms is different to most other investments they make. It tends to be riskier, involve more parts of the firm, usually involves some form of collaboration with external parties and is less amenable to conventional financial and accounting indicators. The aims of innovation projects may evolve over time, leading to different outcomes from those initially expected. IBM's Nic Donofrio, who provided advice to the Review, points out that the innovation process itself is complex and changing in unpredictable ways, and involves new skills, technologies and organisational structures. He points particularly to Web 2.0 technologies increasing social networking and the extent of engagement of users in producing innovations.[23]

In the past however, the overwhelming focus of Australia's innovation policy has been to increase the supply and commercialisation of research, scientific discovery and technological advances. Relatively little attention has been paid to policies for improving the capacity of firms to absorb and apply the products of this increased supply of science and research, nor of understanding

---

[21] PMSEIC Services Innovation Working Group discussions, Melbourne 29 November 2007

[22] CSIRO workshop on Services Innovation, 4 February 2008

[23] This point was also stressed in a presentation to the Review by the Boston Consulting Group, and by Peter Williams of Deloitte in Submission no. 598.

how the needs of markets and customers are served and the productivity effects are secured for the Australian community.

Innovation is not just about initial discovery; it is also about learning – learning by doing, learning by applying technology and equipment and learning by interacting with others. The greatest benefits of innovation are activated when firms create a competitive advantage by perceiving and discovering new and better business offerings that provide a solution someone is prepared to pay for.

It is crucial to understand better how innovation works at the level of the firm and in particular, how firms acquire, absorb and apply knowledge from all sources (from science and research as well as from markets and customers) to provide novel, distinctive and valued business offerings, and continually being able to do this as conditions and circumstances change.

Such business innovation involves competency-building and learning by firms. More than just entrepreneurial flair, it requires proficiency in sustaining the everyday business systems and management competencies to bring products and services to market and continually improving business offerings in response to market changes.
Mark Dodgson of the University of Queensland has identified the broad range of strategic, operational and integrative capabilities required to lead innovative businesses as:

STRATEGIC AND LEADERSHIP COMPETENCIES

ability to respond to changes in the market environment;
clearly communicating strategic intent and articulating the need for change through innovation;
nurturing innovative capacity and creativity throughout the organization;
crystallising the value that innovation can deliver, and being open to alternative business models;
openness to learning from failure; and thinking and acting from a global perspective.

Operational competencies
evaluating innovation opportunities using formal methods for their analysis, valuation and selection, including market research and risk assessment;
identifying the challenges in managing innovative activities, acquiring tools to make processes more systematic, and configuring the resources need to support them;
reducing the cycle time and cost of innovation by simulating, modeling and using virtual and rapid prototyping;

creating value from design;
encouraging employee innovativeness through incentives and rewards;
protecting intellectual property appropriately; and
auditing and measuring innovation performance in a meaningful way, including the option values it creates.

Integrative
collaborating effectively with partners, customers and suppliers in the creation and delivery of innovation;

complying with and developing regulatory frameworks, technical standards and environmental requirements; and
brokering knowledge on innovation across organisational, professional and disciplinary boundaries.

Success rests on deliberate and long-term strategies that support investment in an enterprise's tangible and intangible assets. Most important here are training and skills acquisition, risk management, recruitment, organisational design, technology transfer, sales and marketing proficiency and specific production and managerial capabilities. Innovation thus needs to be understood as neither just new products and technologies, nor creativity and entrepreneurship. The essence of innovation in practice is creating new value by market-facing business transformation.

RESETTING INNOVATION POLICY

The focus of Australia's innovation policy needs to be on the value generated from innovation that supports business engagement with customers and markets, and, in particular, initiatives that foster capabilities for business transformation and problem-solving for customers.

Australia's innovation policy needs to balance investment in increasing the supply of knowledge from science and research with increasing the capacity of Australian enterprises to receive, absorb and take up such knowledge.

An example of this flows from the asymmetry of knowledge. It is not uncommon that two firms could enhance their joint value by combining their ideas and information but do not do so either because they are not aware of the other's knowledge, or the risk involved in revealing their own information to another party is too great. This can be overcome through the use, for example, of trusted intermediaries, a concept that grew out of the open innovation work in the US[24]. The practice is now being exported to other parts of the world in a broadening network of genuine operational innovation. Exposing more firms to this sort of service, and mindset, could have significant value for the nation as well as the firms.

Submissions by the New Zealand Government to the Review[25], particularly a paper by New Zealand Treasury, *Innovation and Productivity: Using Bright Ideas to Work Smarter* make the case for the centrality of the firm to innovation and for framing national innovation policies with this in mind:

Innovating firms are the key institution for translating knowledge into national economic success and ... in order to raise productivity by a significant margin (a country) needs a large number of firms to raise their performance through smart new product offerings, better technology, the use of more skilled workers and improved organisational and human resource practices.

Consequently, the key actions required to make business innovation a priority in Australia's innovation system are three-fold:

to reset Australia's innovation policy to foster a critical mass of Australian firms with the skills and capabilities to make innovation a decisive business strategy;
to provide additional resources to innovation support programs designed to increase the innovation competencies of business enterprises at the point of engagement with customers and markets and to create opportunities for innovation through knowledge-sharing and collaboration; and to better recognise, understand and measure Australia's business innovation performance and the productivity outcomes captured as a result.

---

24 The concept and was first made operational in Australia through the InnovationXchange
25 New Zealand Government - Submission no. 257

The ARC funds research and researchers under the National Competitive Grants Program (NCGP). As part of its commitment to nurturing the creative abilities and skills of Australia's most promising researchers, the NCGP provides:

- support for the highest-quality research leading to the discovery of new ideas and the advancement of knowledge
- financial assistance towards facilities and equipment that researchers need to be internationally competitive
- support for the training and skills development of the next generation of researchers
- incentives for Australia's most talented researchers to work in partnership with leading researchers throughout the national innovation system and internationally, and to form alliances with Australian industry.

The NCGP comprises two main elements - Discovery and Linkage - under which the ARC funds a range of complementary schemes to support researchers at different stages of their careers, build Australia's research capability, expand and enhance research networks and collaborations, and develop centres of research excellence.

A major component of Linkage is the ARC Centres scheme, which brings together leading researchers from around the world to work collaboratively on specific research problems. The Centres scheme is administered independently of the other components of Discovery and Linkage.

Administration of the NCGP is usually scheme-based and across the following inter-disciplinary groupings:

- Biological Sciences and Biotechnology
- Engineering and Environmental Science
- Humanities and Creative Arts
- Mathematics, Information and Communication Sciences
- Physics, Chemistry and Earth Sciences
- Social, Behavioural and Economic Sciences

Funding recommendations are made to the Minister for Innovation, Industry, Science and Research by the CEO following independent and extensive competitive peer review by Australian and international experts.

AUSTRALIA RESEARCH COUNCIL CENTRES OF EXCELLENCE

In 2002, the Australian Research Council (ARC) established the *ARC Centres of Excellence* scheme to create the scale and focus necessary to maintain and develop Australia's international standing in areas of research priority. An initial group of ARC Centres of Excellence commenced operation in 2003. A second selection round was opened for applications in September 2004.

Following a competitive selection process, 11 ARC Centres of Excellence (Centres) were established commencing in 2005. Provision was made for the Centres to be funded for an initial five-year period from mid-2005 to mid-2010 inclusive.

In drafting the Funding Rules for the *ARC Centres of Excellence* scheme, the ARC recognised that innovative research leading to outstanding international recognition takes several years to be fully realised. Accordingly, the *ARC Centres of Excellence Funding Rules for funding commencing in 2005* state that "In the case of exceptional performance by an ARC Centre of Excellence and subject to the availability of funding, the ARC may consider making a recommendation for financial assistance for an additional period of up to five years." Reviews of the 11 ARC Centres of Excellence from the 2005 cohort were undertaken in 2008 to assess their performance with a view to funding a number for an additional three and a half years (to 2013).

OBJECTIVES

The objectives of the *ARC Centres of Excellence* scheme are to:

- undertake highly innovative research at the forefront of developments within areas of national importance, with a scale and a focus leading to outstanding international and national recognition;
- enhance the scale and focus of research in designated National Research Priorities. In 2003, the Australian Government designated the following areas as National Research Priorities for Commonwealth-funded research:
- Research Priority 1: An Environmentally Sustainable Australia
- Research Priority 2: Promoting and Maintaining Good Health
- Research Priority 3: Frontier Technologies for Building and Transforming Australian Industries
- Research Priority 4: Safeguarding Australia;
- promote research that will enhance Australia's future economic, social and cultural wellbeing;
- link existing Australian research strengths and build new capacity for interdisciplinary, collaborative approaches to address the most challenging and significant research problems;
- build Australia's human capacity in a range of research areas by attracting, from within Australia and abroad, researchers of high international standing as well as the most promising research students;
- provide high-quality postgraduate and postdoctoral training environments for the next generation of researchers in innovative and internationally competitive research;
- offer Australian researchers access to world-class infrastructure and equipment, and to key research technologies;
- develop relationships and build new networks with major international Centres and research programs that help achieve global competitiveness and recognition for Australian research; and
- establish Centres of such repute in the wider community that they will serve as points of interaction among higher education institutions, Governments, industry and the private sector generally.

Assessment of the extension proposals for the 2008 Centres reviews was based on the following criteria:

1. Research program and investigators
   i. the creative and innovative nature of the proposed research program;
   ii. the degree to which the Centre will provide coordinated scale and focus of research in the particular field(s) of research during the proposed extension;
   iii. the adequacy of the underlying conceptual framework, design, methods and analyses and their integration into the aims of the research programs during the proposed extension;
   iv. the track records, relative to opportunity, for the Centre researchers, as indicators of their potential to contribute to the Centre's extended research program; and

   v. the commitment of Chief and Partner Investigators to the extended research program.
2. Research training and professional education
   i. the future contribution of the Centre to research training at the Honours, postgraduate and postdoctoral levels; and
   ii. the value of the education and outreach programs in professional and technical training through the extension period.
3. National benefit
   i. the extent to which the Centre will continue to expand Australia's knowledge base and research capability;
   ii. the Centre's potential to continue to enhance innovation in Australia; and
   iii. the Centre's potential to underpin further economic, cultural, environmental or social benefits for Australia during and after the period of the proposed extension.
4. International, national and regional links and networks
   i. the potential of the Centre to build upon its current standing relative to major international centres during the period of the proposed funding extension;
   ii. the potential for further enhancement of international interaction and linkages;
   iii. the potential for further enhancement of links with Australian researchers in universities and other research organisations working in the field(s) of research; and
   iv. the level of commitment and the mechanisms proposed to provide a national and regional intellectual focus for the field(s) of research.
5. End-user links
   i. the adequacy of plans to optimise the participation of end-users in research planning and Centre governance;
   ii. where applicable, the adequacy of plans and strategies for facilitation of technology transfer, including fostering a culture of innovation; and
   iii. the adequacy of organisational arrangements and plans relating to ownership of intellectual property and/or use or commercialisation of research during the proposed extension period.
6. Organisational support
   i. the commitment of the Administering and Collaborating Organisations to provide basic infrastructure, including provision of space, equipment, administrative and technical staff support, telecommunications and computing facilities, library and other key resources, over the proposed extension period; and
   ii. the provision of funding to support the Director and key investigators to execute their research leadership roles over the period of the proposed extension.
7. Governance
   i. the Director's ongoing capacity for leadership, vision, management and strategic planning;
   ii. the adequacy of proposed management arrangements and responsibilities, including the organisational structure of the Centre, its reporting arrangements both internally and externally, its financial systems, and its business and strategic plans which should include milestones for achievement of objectives; and
   iii. the relevance of any proposed revisions to the performance measures (as listed in the Centre's Funding Agreement) to the Centre's objectives and their pertinence for assessing the Centre's performance during the period of the proposed extension.

Table 1: *ARC Centres of Excellence* approved funding extensions

Centre	Amount of additional funding ($2008)	Years of extended funding
ARC Centre of Excellence for Coral Reef Studies	9,800,000	2010-13
ARC Centre of Excellence for Free Radical Chemistry and Biotechnology	9,800,000	2010-13
ARC Centre of Excellence in Plant Energy Biology	9,800,000	2010-13
ARC Centre of Excellence in Ore Deposits	9,450,000	2010-13
ARC Centre of Excellence for Design in Light Metals	8,050,000	2010-13
ARC Centre of Excellence for Coherent X-ray Science	7,700,000	2010-13
ARC Centre of Excellence for Electromaterials Science	7,700,000	2010-13
ARC Centre of Excellence for Creative Industries and Innovation	5,950,000	2010-13
ARC Centre of Excellence in Structural and Functional Microbial Genomics	5,250,000	2010-13*
ARC Centre of Excellence in Vision Science	5,250,000	2010-13*
ARC Centre of Excellence for Antimatter-Matter Studies	3,500,000	2010-13*
Total	82,250,000	

*Funding beyond mid-2010 subject to conditions being met at later review.

Table 2: Funding and numbers requested, approved and success rates for *ARC Centres of Excellence* extensions, by discipline group

Discipline*	Total funding requested over extension period	Approved extension allocation ($2008)	Total approved funding as % of funding requested	Extension proposals received	Extension proposals approved	Success rate %
BSB	36,298,445	30,100,000	82.9	4	4	100
EE	21,621,418	15,750,000	72.8	2	2	100
HCA	5,711,317	5,950,000	104.2	1	1	100
MIC	-	-	-	-	-	-
PCG	34,490,720	30,450,000	88.3	4	4	100
SBE	-	-	-	-	-	-
Total	98,121,899	82,250,000	83.8	11	11	100

*BSB = Biological Sciences and Biotechnology; EE = Engineering and Environmental Sciences; HCA = Humanities and Creative Arts; MIC = Mathematics, Information and Communication Sciences; PCG = Physics, Chemistry and Geoscience; SBE = Social, Behavioural and Economic Sciences

NATIONAL RESEARCH PRIORITIES

All of the Centre extension proposals addressed one or more of the National Research Priority areas, with the primary priority falling into three areas: *An Environmentally Sustainable Australia*, *Promoting and Maintaining Good Health* and *Frontier Technologies for Building and Transforming Australian Industries*, as shown in Table 3.

Table 3: Numbers of proposals and success rates for *ARC Centres of Excellence* extensions by National Research Priority

Priority area	Extension proposals received	Extension proposals approved	Success rate %	Funding approved over extension period ($2008)
An Environmentally Sustainable Australia	2	2	100	19,250,000
Promoting and Maintaining Good Health	2	2	100	15,050,000
Frontier Technologies for Building and Transforming Australian Industries	7	7	100	47,950,000
Safeguarding Australia	-	-	-	-
None selected	-	-	-	-
Total	11	11	100	82,250,000

OUTCOMES BY ORGANISATION

The number of proposals considered and approved, and funding requested and approved, by organisation is shown in Table 4.

Table 4: *ARC Centres of Excellence* extension proposals by Administering Organisation: total requested and approved funding over life of the project

Administering Organisation	Total funding requested over extension period	Approved extension allocation ($2008)	Extension proposals considered	Extension proposals approved for funding	Success rate %
James Cook University	9,790,829	9,800,000	1	1	100
Monash University	19,989,613	13,300,000	2	2	100
Queensland Universitv of	5,711,317	5,950,000	1	1	100

Technology					
The Australian National University	14,180,209	8,750,000	2	2	100
The University of Melbourne	16,941,514	17,500,000	2	2	100
The University of Tasmania	12,243,997	9,450,000	1	1	100
The University of Western Australia	9,473,590	9,800,000	1	1	100
University of Wollongong	9,790,831	7,700,000	1	1	100
Total	98,121,899	82,250,000	11	11	100

SCHEME BUDGET

The allocations from the *ARC Centres of Excellence* budget approved for the Centre extensions are shown in Table 5.

Table 5: Approved allocations for *ARC Centres of Excellence* extensions, for funding commencing in 2010

	2010 (half year)	2011	2012	2013	Total
Total	11,750,000	23,500,000	23,500,000	23,500,000	82,250,000

ARC CENTRE OF EXCELLENCE FOR CORAL REEF STUDIES

Funding: $12m for five years commencing 2005
Centre Director: Prof TP Hughes
Administering Institution: James Cook University

Collaborating or Contributing Organisations:
The Australian National University
The University of Queensland
Stockholm University
University of Delaware
University of Maine
University of Perpignan
Australian Institute of Marine Science CSIRO - Marine Research
Great Barrier Reef Marine Park Authority
Doulgas Shire Council
Great Barrier Reef Research Foundation
Mackay City Council
Mackay-Whitsunday Natural Resource
Management Group
Voyages Hotels and Resorts

The primary goal of this ARC Centre of Excellence is to develop research programs of international significance (through the establishment of new collaborative teams of Australia's leading coral reef researchers) that transcend traditional disciplinary, institutional and geographic boundaries. The aim is to add focus, scale and scope to build an enduring program of innovative research development, leading to world leadership in coral reef science. A key outcome of the ARC Centre of Excellence will be to actively transfer scientific knowledge (through its governance structure) to industry partners and end-users, to increase their capacity and effectiveness and provide tangible benefits to all Australians.

ARC CENTRE OF EXCELLENCE IN STRUCTURAL AND FUNCTIONAL MICROBIAL GENOMICS

Funding: $10m for five years commencing 2005
Centre Director: Prof B Adler
Administering Institution: Monash University

Collaborating or Contributing Organisations:
The University of Sydney
The University of Queensland
CSIRO - Livestock Industries
Australian Proteome Analysis Facility
Victorian Bioinformatics Consortium
Victorian Partnership for Advanced Computing
Department of Primary Industries, Victoria
Australian Genome Research Facility Ltd
Pfizer Australia
Department of Innovation, Industry and
Regional Development, Victoria

Australian primary industry will benefit from a team of experts in microbial genetics, bioinformatics and protein structure and function undertaking integrated studies on microbial genomics that are focused on fundamental biological processes and host/pathogen interactions. Whole genome expression and protein profiling will be used to characterise genes whose expression is altered in the infected host and to analyse genes involved in the control of key cellular processes. The ARC Centre of Excellence in Structural and Functional Microbial Genomics will also determine the shapes of key molecules and their interactions. Practical outcomes will include new veterinary vaccines and the identification of novel antimicrobial targets.

ARC CENTRE OF EXCELLENCE IN DESIGN IN LIGHT METALS

Funding: $10m for five years commencing 2005
Centre Director: Prof B Adler
Administering Institution: Monash University

Collaborating or Contributing Organisations:
The University of Sydney
The University of Queensland
CSIRO - Livestock Industries
Australian Proteome Analysis Facility
Victorian Bioinformatics Consortium
Victorian Partnership for Advanced Computing
Department of Primary Industries, Victoria

Australian Genome Research Facility Ltd
Pfizer Australia
Department of Innovation, Industry and
Regional Development, Victoria

Australian primary industry will benefit from a team of experts in microbial genetics, bioinformatics and protein structure and function undertaking integrated studies on microbial genomics that are focused on fundamental biological processes and host/pathogen interactions. Whole genome expression and protein profiling will be used to characterise genes whose expression is altered in the infected host and to analyse genes involved in the control of key cellular processes. The ARC Centre of Excellence in Structural and Functional Microbial Genomics will also determine the shapes of key molecules and their interactions. Practical outcomes will include new veterinary vaccines and the identification of novel antimicrobial targets.

ARC CENTRE OF EXCELLENCE FOR CREATIVE INDUSTRIES AND INNOVATION

Funding: $7m for five years commencing 2005
Centre Director: Prof SD Cunningham
Research Director: Prof J Hartley
Administering Institution: Queensland University of Technology

Collaborating or Contributing Organisations:
The Australian National University
Swinburne University of Technology
University of Wollongong
Charles Darwin University
Edith Cowan University
Australian Film, Television and Radio School
Australasian CRC for Interaction Design
Australian Film Commission
Department of Communications,
Information Technology and the Arts
The Salvation Army
State Library of Queensland
The Australia Council for the Arts
Australian Museum
National Museum of Australia
Queensland Museum

The ARC Centre of Excellence for Creative Industries and innovation drives the development of Australia's capacity to maximise the national economic and cultural benefits of digital content industries. It integrates research across a range of disciplines to develop new modes of access and distribution for user-led innovation. It will provide integrated, empirically grounded solutions to structural, conceptual and policy problems, during an exciting period when new technologies, end-user activism and semi-professional practices are challenging traditional models of production and consumption in the creative value chain. The Centre's research outcomes across six program areas will improve industry, government, education and creative services in Australia.

ARC CENTRE OF EXCELLENCE IN ANTIMATTER-MATTER STUDIES

Funding: $7m for five years commencing 2005
Research Director: Prof SJ Buckman
Administering Institution: The Australian National University

Collaborating or Contributing Organisations:
The Flinders University of South Australia
Murdoch University
Griffith University
CSIRO - Manufacturing and Infrastructure Technology
The University of Western Australia ANSTO
The Open University
The University of California San Diego
The Lawrence Berkeley National Laboratory
The University of California Davis
Drake University
The University of Nebraska - Lincoln
Tohoku University Japan
The University of Munster

The ARC Centre of Excellence in Antimatter-Matter Studies will develop tools and techniques to lead Australia into a new and exciting area of research in the physical, chemical and biological sciences. Pre-eminent Australian and international scientists will explore antimatter-matter interactions, in fundamental and applied fields, so that Australia maintains an international role in this emerging field. All particles have antiparticles of which the most abundant is the positron, the electron's antiparticle. The positron is the "workshop" for most antimatter studies and we shall use it to characterize nanoscale materials, including gases, polymers, insulators, thin films and surfaces, and to develop novel, nanostructured materials.

ARC CENTRE OF EXCELLENCE IN VISION SCIENCE

Funding: $11m for five years commencing 2005
Centre Director: Prof TD Lamb
Administering Institution: The Australian National University

Collaborating or Contributing Organisations:
The University of Queensland
The University of Western Australia
The University of Sydney
Smith-Kettlewell Eye Research Institute
Emory University
Seeing Machines
CSIRO - ICT Centre
Centre for Information Science, Kokushikan University
University of L'Aquila
Helsinki University of Technology
ObjectiVision
Swiss Federal Institute of Technology (EPFL)
Royal Holloway University of London
Universitaet Bielefeld
Regenera

Vision is our most powerful sense, and blindness is a severe loss, yet increasingly common as the population ages. The ARC Centre of Excellence in Vision Science will explore three themes: the extraordinary sensitivity and adaptability of vision; how vision forms the basis for behaviour; and why vision fails, especially with age. One major outcome will be fundamental understanding of retinal mechanisms and brain algorithms of vision. A second will be the application of this knowledge to the design of autonomous visually guided robots (e.g. flying machines). A third outcome will be understanding of the stability and degeneration of the retina and eye, laying the scientific foundation for diagnosis and therapy in a range of age-related blinding diseases.

ARC CENTRE OF EXCELLENCE IN COHERENT X-RAY SCIENCE

Funding: $9m for five years commencing 2005
Centre Director: Prof KA Nugent
Administering Institution: The University of Melbourne

Collaborating or Contributing Organisations:
La Trobe University
Swinburne University of Technology
Monash University
CSIRO - Health Sciences and Nutrition
CSIRO - Manufacturing and Infrastructure Technology
Australian Synchrotron Research Program
Walter & Eliza Hall Institute of Medical Research
SPring8, Riken
National University of Singapore
Lawrence Livermore National Laboratory
Advanced Photon Source
University of California, Los Angeles
Victorian Department of Innovation,
Industry and Regional Development

X-ray sources are becoming ever brighter, and x-ray lasers will be available in the next ten years. These sources will open up whole new areas of investigation such as the structural determination of proteins not amenable to conventional methods. The ARC Centre of Excellence in Coherent X-ray Science will bring physicists, chemists and biologists together to develop fundamentally new approaches to probing biological structures and processes. It combines world-class expertise in imaging, structural biology, laser science and molecular theory. The project will develop novel high-resolution imaging and probing using the Australian Synchrotron, and ultimately x-ray lasers. An overarching scientific aim of the centre is the determination of the structure of membrane proteins.

ARC CENTRE OF EXCELLENCE FOR FREE RADICAL CHEMISTRY AND BIOTECHNOLOGY

Funding: $12m for five years commencing 2005
Centre Director: Prof CH Schiesser
Administering Institution: The University of Melbourne

Collaborating or Contributing Organisations:
Monash University
The Australian National University
The University of Sydney
Queensland University of Technology

Dulux/Orica Pty Ltd
Carlton United Brewery
Bluescope Steel
The Howard Florey Institute
CSIRO - Molecular Science
Victorian Institute for Chemical Sciences

Free radical chemistry plays a crucial role in important processes that affect the manufacturing industry, the environment, human health and animal health. The aim of the ARC Centre of Excellence for Free Radical Chemistry and Biotechnology is to develop new methods of radical generation and explore new reactions of synthetic significance involving radicals, including novel polymerisation processes. In addition, the increased understanding of free-radical chemistry gained through the research carried out in the Centre will be used to develop new biotechnology initiatives, including pharmaceutical products and antioxidants that will defend against oxidative stress associated with several diseases, as well as the degradation of industrial materials.

ARC CENTRE OF EXCELLENCE IN PLANT ENERGY BIOLOGY

Funding: $12.5m for five years commencing 2005
Centre Director: A/Prof JM Whelan
Administering Institution: The University of Western Australia

Collaborating or Contributing Organisations:
The Australian National University
The University of Sydney

Plants are sources of many essential products, including food, fuels, and vitamins. These products result from energy metabolism in sub-cellular compartments (organelles) called mitochondria, chloroplasts and peroxisomes. The ARC Centre of Excellence in Plant Energy Biology aims to use functional genomic analysis to discover and characterise molecular components and control mechanisms that underpin plant energy metabolism. Knowing the factors that control biogenesis of these organelles will better enable the breeding of plants with specified metabolic traits. Benefits include enhanced control of biomass and yield, water and nutrient efficiency, synthesis of nutrients important for human and animal health, and plants better able to tolerate the environmental stresses of Australia.

ARC CENTRE OF EXCELLENCE IN ORE DEPOSITS

Funding: $15m for five years commencing 2005
Centre Director: Prof RR Large
Administering Institution: University of Tasmania

Collaborating or Contributing Organisations:
The Australian National University
The University of Melbourne
The University of Queensland
University of British Columbia
Johns Hopkins University
Colorado School of Mines
AMIRA International
CSIRO - Exploration & Mining
State Government of Tasmania

Minerals Council of Australia
Anglo American
Anglo Gold Ashanti
Barrick
BHP Billiton
Newcrest Mining Limited
Newmont Mining Corporation
Rio Tinto
Teck Cominco Limited
WMC Resources Ltd
Zinifex Limited

The ARC Centre of Excellence in Ore Deposits will encompass an innovative program of multidisciplinary research in ore deposit location, formation, discovery and recovery. Innovative fundamental research on where ore deposits occur, how they form and their deep earth signatures will give our minerals industry a new scientific framework in which to search for ore. The existing ARC Special Research Centre for Ore Deposit Research has played a pivotal role in Australia's current leadership in mineral exploration-related research. The new ARC Centre of Excellence will build on this success by increasing collaboration and expanding into new research areas critical to the growth of Australia's minerals industry.

ARC CENTRE OF EXCELLENCE FOR ELECTROMATERIALS SCIENCE

Funding: $12m for five years commencing 2005
Research Director: Prof GG Wallace
Administering Institution: University of Wollongong

Collaborating or Contributing Organisations:
Monash University
Bionic Ear Institute
St. Vincent's Health
NSW Department of State and Regional Development

The ARC Centre of Excellence for Electromaterials Science brings together eminent scientists to develop the nano-science and nano-technology related to the movement of electric charge within and between materials. Such processes are fundamentally important to a diverse array of phenomena important in many biological and industrial processes. The exciting new developments in nanoscale materials offer the potential for groundbreaking improvements in charge generation and transfer. However, there is a general lack of understanding of these processes at the nano domain. The new ARC Centre of Excellence will study these processes, develop improved electromaterials and apply these materials in biomedicine, industrial processes, energy harvesting and energy storage.

SPECIAL RESEARCH INITIATIVES

ANZCCART

AUSTRALIAN AND NEW ZEALAND COUNCIL FOR THE CARE OF ANIMALS IN RESEARCH AND TEACHING

The ARC contributes to the operation of ANZCCART. This funding assists ANZCCART to provide leadership in developing community consensus on ethical, social and scientific issues relating to the use of animals in research and teaching. ANZCCART was established as a national forum for effective communication between groups concerned for the care and use of animals in research and teaching. It provides objective ethical and animal welfare advice to biological scientists in Australia and is widely recognised as an important source of information for scientists, animal technicians, members of animal ethics committees and government agencies.

AAO FELLOWSHIP

ANGLO-AUSTRALIAN OBSERVATORY FELLOWSHIP (AAO FELLOWSHIP)

The ARC and the UK Particle Physics and Astronomy Research Council (PPARC) co-fund a research Fellowship administered by the Anglo-Australian Observatory (AAO). As a general rule, one Fellowship is awarded alternately to Australian and to British early career researchers to undertake postdoctoral work at the AAO for a duration of two years with provision for an extension of up to 12 months in exceptional circumstances.

EMBL

EUROPEAN MOLECULAR BIOLOGY LABORATORY

EMBL is the flagship of Europe's molecular biology research, receiving annual funding from its 21 member states to support five research facilities. EMBL's missions are to:

- Perform cutting-edge research in molecular biology
- Offer services to scientists
- Provide advanced training to researchers at all levels
- Develop new technologies and instrumentation
- Actively engage in technology transfer to the benefit of science and society

In March 2008 Australia became an Associate Member of EMBL. As EMBL's first Associate Member, Australian life scientists will have access to state-of-the-art core facilities, technologies, and expertise in Europe. Associate Membership will open new opportunities for Australian scientists to forge collaborations with European research networks and institutions and to access European funding sources.

The ARC and The University of Sydney are supporting Australia's first recipient of an EMBL Group Leader position, Dr Marcus Heister. Dr Heister will spend five years from 2009 at EMBL Heidelberg, and an additional four years from 2014 at The University of Sydney.
The ARC will provide a total of $2.5 million (AUD) covering the five year period from 2009 to 2013.

GROUNDWATER

ARC/NWC CO-FUNDED CENTRE FOR GROUNDWATER RESEARCH AND TRAINING

In 2008 the Australian Research Council (ARC) and the National Water Commission (NWC) will fund a new collaborative research initiative to address the National Research Priority Area of 'An Environmentally Sustainable Australia' through the funding of an *ARC/NWC Co-funded Centre for Groundwater Research and Training* to be awarded under the ARC's *Special Research Initiatives* (SRI) scheme.
The aim of this funding initiative is to support novel, innovative and cross-disciplinary research and training in the field of groundwater. The proposed Centre will provide scale and focus to Australia's groundwater research, building research capacity and providing outcomes of significant national benefit. It will undertake research in all aspects of groundwater and will lead

the training of a new generation of hydrogeologists, groundwater engineers and groundwater managers.

POLICING AND SECURITY

ARC CENTRE OF EXCELLENCE IN POLICING AND SECURITY

Applications for funding for the *ARC Centre of Excellence in Policing and Security* closed on Friday 27 October 2006.
Following a competitive assessment process an *ARC Centre of Excellence in Policing and Security* has been approved to start in 2007.
Unlike most Centres of Excellence, the Centre will be funded under the ARC's *Special Research Initiatives Funding Rules for Funding commencing in 2006.* Applicants should read and understand the entire *Special Research Initiatives Funding Rules for Funding commencing in 2006* and *Call for Proposals* for an *ARC Centre of Excellence in Policing and Security* before submitting an application to the ARC.

RESEARCH IN BIONIC VISION

RESEARCH IN BIONIC VISION SCIENCE AND TECHNOLOGY

In 2009, the Australian Research Council (ARC) will fund a new collaborative research initiative to develop a functional bionic eye through funding to be administered under the ARC's Special Research Initiatives (SRI) scheme. Through its response to the 2020 Summit, the Australian Government has committed funding of $50 million over four years.

The Research in Bionic Vision Science and Technology Initiative will fund one or more proposals to deliver a program of activities that support the development of a functional bionic eye. The successful proposal(s) will be funded on the basis of the excellence of the researchers and the proposed research program, including demonstrated opportunities for collaboration and the potential to produce outcomes of significant health and economic benefit for the Australian community through spin-off innovations and commercialisation.
The Initiative will be underpinned by the undertaking of highly innovative and internationally competitive research, significant collaboration, developing significant health and economic benefits and building Australia's human capacity in the area of bionic vision science.
Applications for funding for the *Research in Bionic Vision Science and Technology Initiative* have now closed.

THINKING SYSTEMS

During 2005 and 2006 the Australian Research Council (ARC) and the National Health and Medical Research Council (NHMRC) collaborated in a funding initiative, the *Thinking Systems* initiative, to address the Australian Government's National Research Priority goals of *Breakthrough Science* and *Frontier Technologies* under the National Research Priority *Frontier Technologies for Building and Transforming Australian Industries.*

The aim of this funding initiative was to support novel, innovative and cross-disciplinary research at some or all of the intersections of neuroscience, genetics, proteomics, cognitive science, artificial intelligence, computer science and information technology which will lead to the generation and application of new knowledge in the development of intelligent machines, robots and information systems and will place Australia at the forefront of this area internationally.

IT AND INTERNET DEVELOPMENTS AND RESEACH

SELECTED IT INDUSRY INNOVATIVE COMPANIES[26]

ATSA DEFENCE SERVICES

ATSA is a dynamic company based in Newcastle, NSW, Australia's largest regional port facility.ATSA provides excellence in support for the world's most advanced electronic systems. Our combination of expertise and innovation delivers integrated support solutions for a range of technological applications.core areas of expertise cover the full life-cycle of all electronic systems, from initial development through to production, including technical support and training.ATSA is more than a high-tech maintenance provider. We have developed close partnerships with Original Equipment Manufacturers such as SAAB Underwater Systems (Sweden), which enables us to provide quality systems engineering solutions to all our clients.currently expanding our suite of products and services.

CONTACT INFORMATION

Name:
Darren Burrowes
Title:
Engineering Manager
Phone:
+61 2 4964 3500
Email:
darren@atsa.com.au
Web:
http://www.atsa.com.au

ADVANTECH AUSTRALIA

System integrators all over the world are constantly developing innovative applications to advance our quality of life.

With a staff of more than 3400 people in 18 countries, Advantech works closely with solution partners to provide complete solutions for a wide array of applications in diverse industries. The company offers products and solutions in three business categories: embedded eplatform, eservices and applied computing and industrial automation.

Advantech's mission is to empower innovations by offering trustworthy products and services. "ePlatform" refers to computing platforms with internet connectivity. It serves as the foundation for all kinds of applications in the connected eWorld.

As Advantech offers not only standard computing platform products, but also value-added customisation services, we thus define Advantech's brand mission as "Trusted ePlatform Services".

Unit 1/3 Southpark Cl

[26] Information provided by the companies listed

Keysborough, VIC, 3173
Australia
37° 59' 11.3316" S, 145° 8' 50.172" E

CONTACT INFORMATION

Name: Santo Gazzo
Title: General Manager
Phone: +61 3 9797 0100
Email: santo.gazzo@advantech.com
Web: http://www.advantech.net.au

ALLIED DATA SYSTEMS PTY LTD

Allied Data Systems has been providing custom-engineered products and systems since 1983. They are in use on Australian, Spanish and US naval vessels as well as a variety of aircraft.

The systems have been tested for compliance to MIL-STD-461 (electromagnetic compatibility), MIL-S-901D & IEC 68-2-27 (shock), MIL-STD-167, MIL-STD-810 & IEC 68-2-6 (vibration), MIL-STD-810 (temperature and humidity). They vary from rugged displays and embedded processing systems for data distributions to internal shipboard communications and training systems such as the "Permission to Trains System" used on the Australian Naval FFG's.

Capabilities include hardware design and manufacture where the company can provide design for embedded computers including microprocessors and "System on a Module".

The company can also undertake software design where it not only provides embedded software using assembler and C/C++ but also the Windows software and drivers.

LOCATION

Unit 30/5 Ponderosa Pde
Warriewood, NSW, 2102
Australia
33° 40' 44.7456" S, 151° 17' 21.354" E

CONTACT INFORMATION

Name: Andrew MacLaurin
Title: Director
Phone: +61 2 9997 8844
Email: andym@allieddata.com.au
Web: http://www.allieddata.com.au

ALTIUM LTD

Altium is a leading developer of electronic product development solutions dedicated to unifying the different disciplines involved in electronics design.

Altium products ensure all electronic engineers, designers, developers, and their organisations, take maximum advantage of emerging design technologies to bring smarter products to market faster and easier.

Founded in 1985, Altium has headquarters in Sydney, Australia, sales offices in the United States, Europe, Japan, China, and resellers in all other major markets.

LOCATION

3 Minna Close
Belrose, NSW, 2085
Australia
33° 42' 11.6676" S, 151° 12' 30.7188" E

CONTACT INFORMATION

Name: Dante Dellagnese
Title: Sales Manager
Phone: +61 2 8986 4400
Email: dante.dellagnese@altium.com.au
Web: http://www.altium.com

APPEN PTY LTD

Appen develops and markets sophisticated computer-based speech and language technology products and services for major international information and communication companies and government organisations.

The company's products cover a wide range of areas including speech recognition, text-to-speech (speech synthesis), phonetic search, machine translation and text applications such as Natural Language Processing. These are developed from the high-end fusion of Appen's computer science and linguistics capabilities.

Appen works in more than 80 languages providing grammar-related tools, powerful investigative software tools, speech and language database products, speech file transcription and annotation services, phonemic lexicons.

It can also provide databases and services for the development of handwriting recognition software in multiple languages as well as speech application development and tuning services.

LOCATION

1 Railway St
Chatswood, NSW, 2067
Australia
33° 47' 48.2136" S, 151° 10' 50.9772" E

CONTACT INFORMATION

Name: Chris Vonwiller
Title: Director
Phone: +61 2 9468 6338
Email: cvonwiller@appen.com.au
Web: http://www.appen.com.au

ARROW ELECTRONICS AUSTRALIA

Arrow Electronics is a global provider of products, services and solutions to industrial and commercial users of electronic components and computer products, with 2007 sales of $16 billion. Headquartered in Melville, New York, Arrow serves as a supply channel partner for approximately 700 suppliers and 140,000 original equipment manufacturers, contract manufacturers and commercial customers through a global network of more than 300 locations in 50 countries and territories.

LOCATION

VIC
Australia

CONTACT INFORMATION

Name: George Kouzeleas
Title: Technical Manager
Phone: +61 3 9574 9300
Email: george.kouzeleas@arrowasia.com
Web: http://www.arrow.com

AUDIO-READ PTY LTD

Audio-Read is an Australian company that has developed the award winning Audio Navigator, a user friendly digital audio player for recreational audio reading.

Audio-Read's objective is to be the audio text service provider of choice for news, information and entertainment services to libraries, people who are blind or vision impaired and all users of recreational audio content. Since our incorporation in 2001, Audio-Read's team of highly qualified engineers have been busy developing scalable and modular solutions for the delivery and playback of digital audio content. Our secure digital delivery system and patented portable Audio Navigator, have received endorsement from companies and organisations from around the world.

Audio-Read can deliver audio books, newspapers and other audio and text to vision impaired and non-vision impaired readers anywhere.

LOCATION

Suite 65, 330 Wattle St
Ultimo, NSW, 2007
Australia
33° 52' 45.3576" S, 151° 11' 46.41" E

CONTACT INFORMATION

Phone: +61 2 9212 5535
Email: info@audio-read.com.au
Web: http://www.audio-read.com.au

BAE SYSTEMS

BAE Systems is the premier global defence and aerospace company delivering a full range of products and services for air, land and naval forces, as well as advanced electronics, information technology solutions and customer support services.

With 97,500 employees worldwide, BAE Systems' sales exceeded £15.7 billion (US$ $31.4 billion) in 2007.

BAE Systems is the world's 3rd largest global defence company and the 6th largest US defence company. It has a staff of more than 97,500 highly skilled people and customers in more than 100 countries.

LOCATION

Taranaki Rd Edinburgh Parks
Edinburgh , SA, 5111
Australia
34° 43' 6.1068" S, 138° 39' 2.6964" E

CONTACT INFORMATION

Name: David Bettison
Title: Hardware Development Manager
Phone: +61 8 8480 8888
Email: david.bettison@baesystems.com
Web: http://www.baesystems.com

BCS INNOVATIONS

BCS Innovations specialises in the development and service of various electronic and software products. The company's expertise spans a range of fields including telecommunications, security, instrumentation and medical devices.

The company's involvement in the product development process can be as little as reporting on the feasibility of a design up to the complete project management of the product design and manufacturing cycle. This includes the design and construction of automatic test systems, as well as providing back to base and field service of various medical devices.

BCS has met the requirements for AS/NZS ISO9001:2000 for Quality Management Systems with SAI Global Certification Services. This registration QEC23112 covers the Quality Management System for consulting, design, project management, prototype manufacture and rework services for customised electronic devices related to industrial, medical, defence and commercial applications.

LOCATION

L2 4 Sirius Rd
Lane Cove, NSW, 2066
Australia
33° 48' 37.6956" S, 151° 8' 45.7908" E

CONTACT INFORMATION

Name: Andy Wyatt
Phone: +61 2 9420 3400

Email: awyatt@bcseng.com.au
Web: http://www.bcsinnovations.com.au

BLACK BOX CONSULTING

Black Box Consulting is the sole Authorised Training Provider for Xilinx FPGA education courses in Australia and New Zealand, using high-quality training materials developed with Xilinx. Training courses include FPGA Architecture, VHDL, Design Tips & Techniques, DSP, and Embedded Processors from fundamental to advanced levels.

Recognising the need for faster design cycles, We also provide consulting services to aid clients through all stages of their FPGA design process, including design flows and techniques, optimisation and timing closure, to assisting on more application specific design requirements. Black Box Consulting use technical experts in their field, drawn from right across the industry. To us, it's not only technical know-how which sets us apart, it's the ability to teach and transfer skills in order to best enable a company and its employees to increase their skills base, reduce their design cycle, and become cost effective, now, and for the future.

LOCATION

Stafford City, QLD, 4053
Australia
27° 24' 34.9992" S, 153° 0' 40.5216" E

CONTACT INFORMATION

Name: Peter Boxall
Title: Managing Director
Phone: +61 7 3137 0905
Email: peter@blackboxconsulting.com.au
Web: http://www.blackboxconsulting.com.au

BOEING AUSTRALIA LTD

Boeing Australia Limited is one of the region's leading aerospace and defence companies delivering both products and services in Australia and overseas, through its staff of over 2,000 people.

Aerospace Support provides maintenance, modifications, upgrades, and through-life support of aerospace platforms and their associated systems. Boeing Services Australia offers a comprehensive suite of training, integrated logistics support and sustainment operations services. Integrated Systems Development delivers precise command, control and communications systems; innovative integrated networked solutions; and state-of-the-art micro and tactical unmanned aerial and ground vehicles to support our defence and commercial customers' transition to future operating environments.

LOCATION

363 Adelaide St
Brisbane, QLD, 4000
Australia
27° 27' 53.6472" S, 153° 1' 46.4844" E

Contact Information

Name: Barry Sutherland
Title: Director Industry Engagement
Phone: +61 7 3306 3492
Email: barry.e.sutherland@boeing.com
Web: http://www.boeing.com.au

BRAEMAC PTY LTD

Braemac is Australia's largest electronic component distributor. Braemac's products include: wireless modules, FPGAs, active, passive, and electromechanical components. Braemac's services include: engineering design, custom FPGA IP creation, in-house cable and connector assembly, system integration, IC programming services, sourcing capabilities, VMI and warehousing.

Braemac's Embedded Products division, Braetec, provides total solutions for the COTS defence, telecom, medical, embedded and industrial market segments. Products include: single board computers (SBCs), panel PCs, LCDs, touch screens and embedded operating systems (RTOS, Secure, DO-178B, real-time Linux). Braetec's services include: operating system support, system design and integration.

Location

1/59-61 Burrows Road
Alexandria, NSW, 2015
Australia
33° 54' 50.3892" S, 151° 11' 13.848" E

Contact Information

Name: Dino Calvisi
Title: Director Phone: +61 2 9550 6600
Email: d.calvisi@braemac.com.au
Web: http://www.braemac.com.au

BRISBANE RESEARCH & DESIGN PTY LTD

BRDC is a privately owned Australian Company that has been providing display solutions in the Racing and Gaming industries for over 15 years. Products designed and produced by BRDC are currently in use throughout the Australian Racing Industry.BRDC is involved in the embedded software and hardware industries. We have particular expertise is in WinCE and embedded Linux.

Location

1/21 Indooroopilly Rd
Taringa, QLD, 4068
Australia
27° 29' 33.6336" S, 152° 59' 25.944" E

Contact Information

Name: John Archbold
Title: CTO

Email: jarchbold@brdcpl.com
Web: http://www.brdcpl.com

CAP-XX (AUSTRALIA) PTY LTD

CAP-XX is a world leader in the design and manufacture of thin, flat super capacitors and power architectures for portable electronic devices. Super capacitors resolve the performance limitations of batteries and other current-limited energy sources, bridging the gap between the peak power demanded by the device and that available from the source.

CAP-XX super capacitors enable manufacturers to make smaller, thinner, longer-running and more feature-rich portables such as cell phones, PDAs, location trackers and medical devices. The company, listed on the Alternative Investment Market (AIM) in London, is based in Sydney, Australia, has additional production facilities in Malaysia, and sales offices in the UK and USA.

LOCATION

NSW
Australia

CONTACT INFORMATION

Name: Pierre Mars
Title: VP Applications Engineering
Phone: +61 2 9420 0690
Email: pierre.mars@cap-xx.com
Web: http://www.cap-xx.com

CENTRE FOR HEALTH INNOVATION

The organisation is a health care specialised centre, set up to test trial and demonstrate technologies for health care rather than development. The Centre has a fully simulated hospital to home environment, which is used routinely for education of clinical staff as well as testing and trialling for health services across Australia. Centre staff have clinical and technical backgrounds and work with closely with a wide range of other clinicians to link them to researchers to ensure that technology designs fit clinical needs.

LOCATION

L4 89 Commercial Road Burnet Tower
Melbourne, VIC, 3004
Australia
37° 50' 44.4624" S, 144° 59' 0.1752" E

CONTACT INFORMATION

Name: Cathie Steele
Title: General Manager
Phone: +61 3 9076 0400
Email: c.steele@alfred.org.au
Web: http://www.healthinnovation.com.au

CISRA (CANON INFORMATION SYSTEMS RESEARCH AUSTRALIA)

CiSRA (Canon Information systems Research Australia) is the Australian R&D Centre for Canon Inc., one of the world's leading providers of cameras, business solutions, and imaging & information technologies.

Established in 1990, CiSRA has grown from a small R&D company into one of Canon's largest R&D Centres outside of Japan. It now has more than 300 staff and an annual turnover of more than A$50 million.

CiSRA's primary focus is the development of fundamental image processing technology, which is embedded in many products across Canon's product range. Together with Canon R&D Centres in Japan, USA, Europe and Asia, CiSRA is a key part of Canon's future product development.

LOCATION

1 Thomas Holt Dr
North Ryde, NSW, 2113
Australia
33° 47' 12.3468" S, 151° 7' 47.8236" E

CONTACT INFORMATION

Name: Jim Metcalfe
Title: Director
Phone: +61 2 9805 2737
Email: jim.metcalfe@cisra.canon.com.au
Web: http://www.cisra.canon.com.au

DEK TECHNOLOGIES PTY LTD

DEK Technologies Pty Ltd began operations in 1999 providing expertise in system architecture, design and support activities for cutting-edge hardware including ASICs (Application Specific Integrated Circuits) and FPGAs (Field Programmable Gate Arrays).

DEK Technologies has established strategic partnerships with many of the world's leading ASIC and FPGA vendors, enabling DEK Technologies to deliver complete ASIC/FPGA end-to-end solutions.In recent years DEK Technologies has expanded its focus to include all phases of the product life cycle including system design, software development and verification, project management and product support.

Today, DEK Technologies comprises a number of engineering and project management offices located in Australia and Sweden. These offices have completed a diverse range of projects and delivered innovative and cost effective solutions to various parts of the world.

LOCATION

VIC
Australia

CONTACT INFORMATION

Name: Robert Bunn

Title: General Manager
Phone: +61 3 9302 8984
Email: robert.bunn@dektech.com.au
Web: http://www.dektech.com.au

FLUFFY SPIDER TECHNOLOGIES

FST has been developing embedded software since 1995. A pioneer in the industry, FST has a background in Real Time Operating Systems and portability both used extensively in defence work.

Between 1995 and 2000 FST translated this fundamental knowledge into producing outstanding solutions for some of Australia's leading process monitoring and control installations (BHP), defence subcontractors (GEC) and later within the emerging mobile telecommunications industry (Vodafone, Optus & Telstra).

FST's deep knowledge of software efficiency coupled with embedded systems and Linux proficiency led them to be contacted by Toshiba Japan's Digital Media Company in 2001, thinking outside of their usual square. To date, FST continues to provide R&D expertise to Toshiba in the field of graphics and embedded Linux.

The FANCYPANTS product suite, initially launched at CommunicAsia 2003 arose from the close collaboration with Toshiba and the identification of a gap in the Embedded Linux Graphics marketplace.

LOCATION

Suite 87 330 Wattle St
Ultimo, NSW, 2007
Australia
33° 52' 45.3576" S, 151° 11' 46.41" E
See map: Google Maps

CONTACT INFORMATION

Name: Robi Karp
Title: CEO
Phone: +61 2 9281 9055
Email: robi@fluffyspider.com
Web: http://www.fluffyspider.com

GPC ELECTRONICS

GPC Electronics is an Electronics Manufacturing Service (EMS) provider that uses an Outsourced Business Management (OBM) approach.

Rather than just provide manufacturing services like traditional EMS providers, we create business solutions by tailoring our capabilities for each customer.

The result is a huge increase in competitiveness that delivers greatly reduced costs and new revenue opportunities. Some customers never need to visit the factory because everything is managed for them.

For over 20 years we have managed and manufactured complex electronics equipment for leading global corporations like Harris-Stratex, Toshiba, Nortel, Alcatel, Siemens, NEC, Thomson, Aastra and others.

We manage the introduction, manufacture and support of complex high volume and high mix products like Microwave Radio Systems, Wireless Equipment (WLAN, GPS etc), Carrier & Enterprise class Telecommunications Equipment and telephones.

LOCATION

NSW
Australia

CONTACT INFORMATION

Name: Andrew Greatbatch
Title: Business Development
Phone: +61 2 4737 6600
Email: andrew.greatbatch@gpc.com.au
Web: http://www.gpc.com.au

GREEN HILLS SOFTWARE

Green Hills Software is the technology leader in high performance compilers, software development tools and real-time operating systems (RTOS) for developers of embedded systems. Green Hills Software has:

- the most reliable RTOS
- the most productive software development environment
- the best optimizing compilers.

In Asia Pacific we focus on providing customised solutions leveraging this technology to help our customers get to market faster with better performing products.

CONTACT INFORMATION

Name: David Cooper
Title: Managing Director
Email: dmc@ghs.com
Web: http://www.ghs.com

IV&V AUSTRALIA PTY LTD

IV&V Australia is a NATA-accredited software testing consultancy which provides value-added software testing and independent verification and validation services to the Australian Technology/IT and Defence industries.

The company has significant experience in testing a wide range of application types for both commercial and government clients, including IT business applications, e-commerce/webs, biomedical applications and mobile applications. It maintains a significant niche in testing embedded device software and their supporting PC applications.

Services offered include reviewing a project's test and development activities, strategic reviews, document and process reviews, requirements tracing, risk management and user acceptance testing.

LOCATION

NSW
Australia

CONTACT INFORMATION

Name:
Rodney Parkin
Title:
Technical Director
Phone:
+61 2 9957 6577
Email:
rodney.parkin@ivvaust.com.au
Web:
http://www.ivvaust.com.au

INDUSTRIAL AUTOMATION SERVICES PTY LTD

Industrial Automation Services (IAS) is a high-technology company specialising in the computer control of industrial processes - with particular interests in the metals industry. Clients include many of the major international steel and aluminium producers and automation suppliers.

The staff of 40 includes engineers, computer scientists and mathematicians with specialist skills in mathematical modelling, real-time computer software engineering and industrial process analysis. These skills, coupled with substantial industrial experience, particularly in the area of metals processing, have enabled IAS to develop an international reputation in control of metal processing plants.

The company is knowledge based as it generates its business by packaging 400 man years of experience in flat metal finishing operations in different ways. These include consulting services, rolling mill performance audits, training courses and, most significantly, in automation systems.

LOCATION

NSW
Australia

CONTACT INFORMATION

Phone:
+61 2 4965 8688
Web:
http://www.indauto.com

INTELLIDESIGN PTY LTD

IntelliDesign is a multidisciplinary electronic design company offering a complete turn-key service, from concept to manufacture.

With in-house expertise in a wide variety of disciplines IntelliDesign is able to create highly integrated and cost-effective solutions, and through their small modern assembly facility, they are able to offer practical product assessment.

IntelliDesign has a dynamic team of skilled managers, engineers, designers and manufacturing technicians, with experience spanning a wide variety of products, from precision medical instruments to mobile wireless communication devices, across a broad range of markets, from hospital operating theatres to aluminium smelters.

IntelliDesign has all the required disciplines for a successful product, including: hardware design, firmware design, software design, industrial design, mechanical design, project management, quality management, printed circuit board assembly, and mechanical assembly.

LOCATION

40 Trinder Road
Ashgrove, QLD, 4060
Australia
27° 27' 11.142" S, 152° 58' 13.9836" E

CONTACT INFORMATION

Name: Chris Bishop
Title: Managing Director
Phone: +61 7 3366 6478
Email: chris@intellidesign.com.au
Web: http://www.intellidesign.com.au

KENT SOFTWARE CONSULTANTS

Kent provides contracting services for embedded software and FPGA design.

We design open source microprocessor designs for FPGAs using VHDL. I also work as a contractor developing real time embedded software using C and C++ and microprocessor based hardware systems.

CONTACT INFORMATION

Name: John Kent
Title: Systems Engineer
Email: jekent@optushome.com.au
Web: http://www.kentsoftware.biz/

LX INNOVATIONS

LX Innovations is an innovative contract electronics design company specializing in the design of embedded systems and wireless technologies. The company works with clients take new product ideas from concept through to production.

LX focuses on hardware, firmware and software development and has a number of strategic alliances with other specialist companies in the areas of industrial design, intellectual property, mechanical engineering, manufacturing and software development. This provides a complete turn-key design service.

The company specialises in the design of wireless and embedded systems and has particular experience in technologies including Bluetooth, ZigBee, GSM, GPS, HSDPA, IrDA, RFiD and WiFi.

LOCATION

NSW
Australia

CONTACT INFORMATION

Name: Simon Blyth
Title: Design Engineer
Phone:
+61 2 9209 4133
Email: simon@lx-innovations.com
Web: http://www.lx-innovations.com.au

M2M CONNECTIVITY

LX Innovations is an innovative contract electronics design company specializing in the design of embedded systems and wireless technologies. The company works with clients take new product ideas from concept through to production.

LX focuses on hardware, firmware and software development and has a number of strategic alliances with other specialist companies in the areas of industrial design, intellectual property, mechanical engineering, manufacturing and software development. This provides a complete turn-key design service.

The company specialises in the design of wireless and embedded systems and has particular experience in technologies including Bluetooth, ZigBee, GSM, GPS, HSDPA, IrDA, RFiD and WiFi.

LOCATION

NSW
Australia

CONTACT INFORMATION

Name: Simon Blyth
Title: Design Engineer
Phone: +61 2 9209 4133
Email: simon@lx-innovations.com
Web: http://www.lx-innovations.com.au

MACHINERY AUTOMATION & ROBOTICS

MAR's dynamic team of engineering professionals service the specific needs of production-critical companies with world-class automation solutions.

The continual evolution of automation and robotics has altered the nature of production processes irrevocably. MAR provides the latest world-leading technology and turnkey automation and robotics solutions to industrial clients looking for a competitive technology edge.

MAR strives to provide clients with an increase in quality and productivity whilst reducing labour costs and maintaining occupational health and safety requirements, drastically affecting the bottom line of that business.

LOCATION

NSW
Australia

CONTACT INFORMATION

Name: Clyde Campbell
Title: CEO
Phone: +61 2 9748 7001
Email: ccampbell@machineryautomation.com.au
Web: http://www.machineryautomation.com.au

MACNAUGHT PTY LTD

Our products include lubrication equipment, flow meters, fluid handling and control. Macnaught designs manufactures and distributes its products world wide.

LOCATION

NSW
Australia

CONTACT INFORMATION

Name: Peter Kerr
Title: Senior Design engineer
Email: peter.kerr@macnaught.com.au
Web: http://www.macnaught.com.au

MICROMAX

Experience counts and Micromax has plenty. We have been providing high-technology electronic products and automation solutions to Australian industry for more than 45 years. We represent many of the most technologically advanced companies in the world with a product line ranging from the most basic on-off sensors to the most sophisticated inspection and control systems. We provide you with advanced automation solutions not available anywhere else.

A high technology product is only as good as the people who support it. Micromax has technical personnel with total combined experience exceeding 400 years. This is an average of more than 16 years of experience per staff member in applying sensors, controls and other high-technology products. This expertise is your assurance that the products we sell are applied effectively and efficiently to your applications.

CONTACT INFORMATION

Name: Antonio Fantasia
Title: Sales Manager
Phone: 1300 36 2626
Email: afantasia@micromax.com.au

Web:
http://www.micromax.com.au

NATIONAL INSTRUMENTS

National Instruments transforms the way engineers and scientists around the world design, prototype, and deploy systems for test, control, and embedded design applications. NI provides open graphical programming software and modular hardware, to customers at more than 25,000 companies annually allowing them to simplify development, increase productivity, and dramatically reduce time to market. From testing next-generation gaming systems to creating breakthrough medical devices, Leveraging PCs and commercial technologies, virtual instrumentation increases productivity and lowers costs for test, control, and design applications through easy-to-integrate software, such as NI LabVIEW, and modular measurement and control hardware for PXI, PCI, USB, and Ethernet.

NI empowers engineers and scientists to continuously develop innovative technologies that impact millions of people. At NI, we are committed to being responsible citizens to our global communities and stakeholders. We achieve this by maintaining a fun and innovative corporate culture, providing tools that inspire and empower engineers and scientists to change the world, working to reduce our environmental footprint, and improving the communities in which we work and live.

LOCATION

NSW
Australia

CONTACT INFORMATION

Name: Mark Phillips
Title: Marketing Manager
Email: mark.phillips@ni.com
Web: http://www.ni.com/oceania

ORBIT AUSTRALIA

Orbit Australia was established in July 1994 and comprises a team of professionals with extensive experience in government, industry and defence consulting.

Orbit Australia can provide end-to-end technology solutions that integrate people, processes and technology which deliver quality and value for the customer. Our objective is to assist clients develop and grow profitable business both in Australia and internationally.

Orbit Australia provides innovative solution using latest encryption and security technologies. All information transferred will be secured and users authenticated.

Orbit Australia participates in the Australian Government's policy to promote science and innovation. It is capitalising on Australia's extensive ICT and Aerospace talent through research, commercialisation, and industry collaboration worldwide. Orbit brings together exceptional people from research and industry to create a centre of excellence that generates national wealth.

LOCATION

NSW
Australia

CONTACT INFORMATION

Name: Jacob Malana
Title: Director
Phone: +61 2 9209 4025
Email: jacob@orbitaustralia.com
Web: http://www.orbitaustralia.com

REDARC ELECTRONICS

Redarc is a privately owned company incorporated in South Australia. Established in 1979, it now employs 60 FTEs. Redarc has broad experience in the research, design, development and manufacture of a range of electronic voltage converters and associated products, inverters, power supplies, battery chargers, turbo timers, glow plug timers and trailer braking products.

Essentially, Redarc's products are attached to any moving vehicle that uses battery power (cars, boats, rail, trucks, mining equipment, bus and emergency vehicles etc). Redarc offers surface mount technology services to defence, medical and mining customers.

The market segments are divided into original equipment manufacturers (OEM) and after-market sales to the wholesale sector.

LOCATION

23 Brodie Road
Lonsdale, SA, 5160
Australia
35° 6' 7.614" S, 138° 30' 32.5296" E

CONTACT INFORMATION

Name: Mr Clinton Smith
Title: Electronics Design Leader
Phone: +61 8 8322 4848
Email: power@redarc.com.au
Web: http://www.redarc.com.au

RF TECHNOLOGIES AUST PTY LTD

RF Technologies is a strategic network of associated companies and industry experts formed to provide strategic services to clients.

Scout Communications, a wholly owned subsidiary of RF Technologies, is a leading developer and producer of HFSSB base and land mobile communications products .

RFT Consulting is the consulting arm of RF Technologies. Through RFT Consulting, we offer expert advice on project management, new product development and rapid proto-typing to a diverse range of clients.

RFTech has vast experience in collaborative design as a design partner in larger projects, to ensure adequate resources are available when required. RFTech partners with larger, external companies when complex mechanical design and large scale production becomes necessary.

LOCATION

QLD
Australia

CONTACT INFORMATION

Name: D.M.(Max) Rose
Title: Chief Executive Officer
Phone: +61 7 3279 7177
Email: maxr@rftech.com.au
Web: http://www.rftech.com.au

REDFERN BROADBAND NETWORKS PTY LTD

Programmable and configurable optical transport platforms for a range of applications. The products developed include the RBNi GigaEdge 8200 and the RBNi GigaEdge 2300. Currently the latest GigaEdge 2300 platform is programmed for multi-protocol optical access network applications between 100Mbit/s and 2.5 Gbit/s. These platforms are certified to ETSI, CE Mark and NEBS level 3 standards, enabling their deployment in Europe, Australia and North American Central Offices owned by Regional Bell Operating Companies. RBN is is the process of making the programmable 2300 platform more widely available for other companies and organisations to use for other applications (not necessarily telecommunications related).

RBN specifies, designs and develops new optical transport and data processing platforms with multiple product variants; manages the manufacture of these products; undertakes final assembly and test of these products; prepares sales presentations and product documentation; supports global partners in the integration of these products into their management systems and the promotion of network solutions based on these products to partner's customers; and also undertakes direct selling and support of these products in Asia Pacific and some North American markets not covered by RBN's global partners. RBN is certified to ISO9001.

LOCATION

NSW
Australia

CONTACT INFORMATION

Name: Ross Halgren
Title: CTO
Email: rhalgren@rbni.com
Web: http://www.rbni.com

REINO INTERNATIONAL

Reino International, a division of Saltbush Parking Services, is the largest paid parking equipment and service provider in Australasia and the USA, with an estimated market share of more than 70 per cent.

On-street parking is our only business and, with a dedicated team of more than 350 specialists, we provide intelligent, award winning parking meters, parking management systems, enforcement devices and software as well as complete turnkey solutions.

Established in 1993, Reino International is an Australian owned and operated company and has experienced strong growth with offices in Sydney, Melbourne, Perth, California, Milwaukee, Arkansas as well as being represented throughout Asia and Europe by a distributor network.

Reino International has an organisational capability that encompasses full design, engineering, manufacturing and servicing capabilities.

LOCATION

NSW
Australia

CONTACT INFORMATION

Name: Samantha Lacey
Title: Program Manager
Phone: +61 2 9432 0500
Email: samantha.lacey@reino.com.au
Web: http://www.reino.com.au

SAGE CONSULTANTS PTY LTD

Sage was incorporated in 1996 to satisfy a market demand to streamline the product development process to have market-ready products faster.

Sage offers a complete product development service from concept right through to manufacture. Sage's end-to-end service allows clients to concentrate on their core competencies and reduce the time to market by outsourcing the development process.

Turning an idea into a mass produced product rolling off a production line is a very risky process when left in inexperienced hands.

By leveraging off over 50 years experience in electronics and product design, Sage alleviates the commercial risks and challenges associated with turning an idea into a finished product in the fastest possible time, of the highest quality and within budget.

LOCATION

Level 1 169 Kelvin Grove Rd
Kelvin Grove, QLD, 4059
Australia
27° 27' 6.7608" S, 153° 0' 41.3352" E

CONTACT INFORMATION

Name: Grant Wensor
Title: BDM
Phone: +61 7 3839 7988
Email: grant.wensor@sageconsultants.com.au

Web: http://www.sageconsultants.com.au

SINCLAIR KNIGHT MERZ

Sinclair Knight Merz (SKM) is an independent professional services consulting group with a team of more than 6,000 people located in major business centres across the globe. An Australian based company, the firm also has offices in Asia, Europe, and the Americas.

SKM has significant resources, financial standing and technical capability, designed to help clients achieve project success. We employ a wide range of professional engineers, planners, architects, economists, scientists, and project managers and have successfully delivered significant projects both within Australia and around the world.

SKM can provide valuable support to embedded systems projects in terms of complementary skills and resources in project management, systems engineering, concept and detailed design, and application validation and verification phases.

LOCATION

NSW
Australia

CONTACT INFORMATION

Name: Tony Strasser
Title: Executive Engineer
Phone: +61 2 9928 2194
Email: tdstrasser@skm.com.au
Web: http://www.skmconsulting.com

SLEEP DIAGNOSTICS

Optalert is a drowsy driver detection system designed to save lives and reduce the trauma of drowsy crashes. Optalert is designed and developed in Australia.

CONTACT INFORMATION

Name: Phillip Schwarze
Title: General Manager Product Development
Email: pschwarze@optalert.com
Web: http://www.optalert.com

TECTONICA AUSTRALIA PTY LTD

Tectonica Australia is a leading engineering company committed to delivering innovative engineering products and services to clients in a wide-range of industry sectors.From contract research and product development through to systems integration and in-house manufacture, Tectonica is focused on delivering projects on time and to budget.

We're a responsive organisation with in-depth engineering knowledge and a broad-range of engineering experiences.Our capabilities are built on a diverse range of skills and the know-how of our professional engineering team and extensive engineering experience.To deliver fit-for-purpose solutions we draw upon our broadly based technical expertise in mechanical, electronic, software and systems engineering.We have a proven track-record in delivering complex projects on-time, to specification and on budget.

CONTACT INFORMATION

Name: David Levy
Title: Business Development Manager
Phone: +61 418 151 006
Email: david.levy@tectonica.net
Web: http://www.tectonica.net

TYCO ELECTRONICS

With a 50-plus year history of leadership, Tyco Electronics is a US$13.0 billion global provider of engineered electronic components for thousands of consumer and industrial products; network solutions and systems for telecommunications and energy markets; undersea telecommunication systems; and wireless systems for critical communications. We design, manufacture and market products for customers in industries ranging from automotive, appliance, aerospace and defense to telecommunications, computers and consumer electronics. Tyco Electronics is an independent, publicly traded company whose common stock is listed on the New York Stock Exchange (NYSE) under the ticker symbol "TEL."

We manufacture nearly 500,000 precision-engineered products - all backed by approximately 92,000 committed employees with a singular commitment to bringing a performance advantage to every technology, product and service we provide.

CONTACT INFORMATION

Name: Matthew Corbett
Title: GIC & Medical Sales Manager
Phone: 1800 008 926
Email: matthew.corbett@tycoelectronics.com
Web: http://www.tycoelectronics.com/

UBIQ TECHNOLOGIES PTY LTD

To be successful, mobile workers must be able to easily access, retrieve and respond to information in the field. Administrators also must be able to distribute, update and synchronize information with confidence using an economical and reliable platform.

With this in mind, Ubiq Technologies has developed the QuokkaPad, a wireless handheld computer with a large 8-inch colour screen. QuokkaPad has been optimised for the mobile office worker and student including access to corporate applications, manuals, sales material, browsing the web, email and many other functions. QuokkaPad can be configured with larger memory and optional biometric access for added security.

LOCATION

SA
Australia

CONTACT INFORMATION

Name: Mike Ottoy
Title: CEO
Phone: +61 8 8415 5170

Email: mike.ottoy@einfosolutions.com
Web: http://www.ubiqtechnologies.com

VISIONSTREAM PTY LTD

Visionstream was established in 1994 as a subsidiary of Telstra to specifically address 'ground breaking' processes and employment models for the efficient installation of the Cable TV and Broadband Network.

In December 1996, Leighton Contractors acquired Visionstream as a wholly owned subsidiary. This acquisition has enabled Leighton to expand into the rapidly growing Australian telecommunication services sector. In June 2000, Leighton also acquired LSE Technology, a wireless solutions company and placed it organisationally with Visionstream.Visionstream now offers a comprehensive suite of capabilities that are required to build and maintain both modern and legacy networks.

Services offered include fixed and mobile networks, carrier exchange works, customer connections, design and construction of Telstra access networks and design and construction of intelligent infrastructure networks (IINs).

LOCATION

NSW
Australia

CONTACT INFORMATION

Name: Daniel Credazzi
Title: Manager
Phone: +61 2 9469 7657
Email: dan.credazzi@visionstream.com.au
Web: http://www.visionstream.com.au

VOICETRONIX

VoiceTronix builds a range of Computer Telephony hardware products. We supply solutions, not just hardware components.For OEM customers this means we have taken the pain out of your custom product development - use our free applications as a starting point to accelerate your product development. End users can now build advanced but affordable telephony systems themselves.offer developers the choice in using their favourite open source application or project. Our CT hardware supports all the leading open source telephony projects including OpenPBX, CT Server, Asterisk and Logger.focus on the ultra-stable Linux operating system. As well as Linux, our hardware runs on Windows and FreeBSD, offering customers the luxury of delivering these solutions on their preferred choice of operating system.provide free high quality support with all purchases. We also offer priority support and customisation services under normal commercial terms.

CONTACT INFORMATION

Name: John Kostogiannis
Title: CEO
Phone: +61 2 9231 4811
Email: john@voicetronix.com

Web: http://www.voicetronix.com

IMPORTANT INFORMATION ON INTERNET DEVELOPMENT AND MANAGEMENT

1. INTRODUCTION

Who steers the Internet? "The Internet, a loosely-organized international collaboration of autonomous, interconnected networks, supports host-to-host communication through voluntary adherence to open protocols and procedures defined by Internet Standards." [1]. While this definition is essentially correct, its emphasis might give the reader the impression that no one is at the helm of the Internet. That conclusion would be wrong. Certain protocols, and the parameters required for their usage, are essential in order to operate on the Internet. A number of bodies have become responsible for those protocol standards and parameters. It can be fairly said that those bodies steer the Internet in a significant sense. This document is a summary of those bodies and their most important characteristics. The bodies belong to three major nexuses. Links, both formal and informal, exist between the nexuses.

Almost all Internet technological standards are developed and set by the group consisting of the Internet Society (ISOC) and the units operating under the auspices of ISOC: the Internet Architecture Board (IAB), the Internet Engineering Steering Group (IESG), the Internet Engineering Task Force (IETF), the Internet Research Steering Group (IRSG), the Internet Research Task Force (IRTF), and the RFC Editor. It is important to note that, while these units are responsible to ISOC, ISOC allows them a large degree of independence in their technical work.

Internet domain names and IP addresses are the province of the Internet Corporation for Assigned Names and Numbers (ICANN) and its Internet Assigned Numbers Authority (IANA).

World Wide Web standards are developed by the World Wide Web Consortium (W3C).

It should be noted that the direction of the Internet's physical network structure is not addressed in this document. That structure is essentially determined by a large number of mainly commercial network operators, ranging from small to intercontinental, that build and join their infrastructures in response to market forces, in order to provide them to subscribers on a paid basis. These networks that form the Internet are linked in a topology similar to that of a large, well-developed highway system.

2. ISOC

ORGANIZATION: In 1991, the large growth of the Internet, including its commercial sector, and the Internet community's need for a formal organization to provide a legal home for the standards bodies of that time (IETF, etc.) led to the formation, under the auspices of the Corporation for National Research Initiatives (CNRI), of the Internet Society. In January 1992, the Internet Society was chartered as a U.S. District of Columbia non-profit corporation.

GOVERNANCE: ISOC is governed by its Board of Trustees.

MEMBERSHIP/COMPOSITION: ISOC welcomes individuals and organizations as members. Individuals in the Internet community have ample opportunity to participate in ISOC and its component bodies.

MISSION/GOALS: ISOC's mission is "To assure the open development, evolution and use of the Internet for the benefit of all people throughout the world." [2]. As one of its most important tasks, it "facilitates open development of standards, protocols, administration and the technical infrastructure of the Internet" [2], and so it is the organizational and legal home for most of the groups that are responsible for developing Internet technical standards.

FUNDING: ISOC is funded mainly from organization member fees.

ASSOCIATED BODIES: IAB, IESG, IETF, IRSG, IRTF, RFC Editor.

3. IETF

ORGANIZATION: The Internet Engineering Task Force (IETF) held its first meeting in 1986. It is a loosely self-organized, large, grass roots technical group consisting of network administrators, designers, researchers, vendors, users, etc. In its broader sense, IETF is used to refer to IETF, IAB, IESG, IRSG, IRTF and RFC Editor as a collective.

GOVERNANCE: The IETF is not a formal body, and has no board of directors. It operates as an activity of ISOC and is responsible to it. For its technical work, it is divided into broad units called areas, each led by the Area Director(s) (ADs). ADs are proposed by the nominating committee (the Nomcom) of the IETF, and appointed by the IAB. The areas are divided into more specialized working groups (WGs), each with chair(s). WG chairs serve at the pleasure of the appropriate AD. IETF has a chair who is proposed by the nominating committee of the IETF, and then appointed by the voting members of the IAB, not including the incumbent IETF chair. The IETF chair is also the chair of IESG. WG and AD decisions are subject to appeal to the IESG.

MEMBERSHIP/COMPOSITION: There is no formal membership. Generally, attendance at IETF meetings and subscription to IETF mailing lists is open to all volunteers. Participants are expected to contribute as individuals, rather than as representatives of companies or organizations.

MISSION/GOALS: The IETF concerns itself with the engineering and architecture of the Internet. It is the principal body that develops, tests and implements new Internet technological standards, including protocols. The IETF proposes standards to the IESG.

FUNDING: The IETF, including its small Secretariat, is largely self-funded via IETF meeting attendance fees. A relatively small percentage of IETF's budget is contributed by ISOC.

ASSOCIATED BODIES: ISOC, IAB, IESG, RFC Editor, ICANN, IANA, W3C.

4. IESG

ORGANIZATION: Formed in 1989, the Internet Engineering Steering Group (IESG) is the management group of the IETF.

GOVERNANCE: The IESG operates as an activity of ISOC and is responsible to it. The IESG is led by the IETF/IESG chair. IESG decisions are subject to appeal to the IAB.

MEMBERSHIP/COMPOSITION: The members are the Area Directors of IETF, the chair of IETF/IESG and a small number of ex-officio and liaison members.

MISSION/GOALS: The IESG vets and approves IETF standards, and generally manages the standards process according to the policies and procedures ratified by the ISOC Trustees. The IESG creates IETF working groups, etc.

FUNDING: The IESG is largely self-funded. ISOC contributes.
ASSOCIATED BODIES: ISOC, IAB, IETF, RFC Editor, IANA.

5. IRTF

ORGANIZATION: Formed in 1989, the Internet Research Task Force (IRTF) is a self-organized research group.

GOVERNANCE: The IRTF is divided into research groups (RGs), each with chair(s). RG chairs may be removed by the IRTF chair, subject to appeal to the IAB. The IAB appoints the chair of the IRTF. The IRTF chair reports to the IAB.

MEMBERSHIP/COMPOSITION: Since RGs are expected to be long-term groups, and to encourage the kind of working relationships such groups may need, membership in RGs may be open or closed, in contrast with IETF WGs, which are always open. Participants are expected to contribute as individuals, rather than as representatives of companies or organizations.

MISSION/GOALS: While the IETF focuses on engineering and standards, the IRTF focuses on research. The IRTF investigates Internet topics that are too uncertain or too advanced to be standardized at the moment. When IRTF produces a specification that is suitable for standardization, it is processed via IETF.

FUNDING: The IRTF is largely self-funded. ISOC contributes.

ASSOCIATED BODIES: ISOC, IAB, IRSG.

6. IRSG

ORGANIZATION: Formed in 1989, the Internet Research Steering Group (IRSG) is the management group of the IRTF.

GOVERNANCE: The IRTF chair leads the IRSG. The IRTF chair reports to the IAB.

MEMBERSHIP/COMPOSITION: The IRSG consists of the chairs of the IRTF research groups, the chair of IRTF, and possibly at-large members from the research community.

MISSION/GOALS: The IRTF chair manages the IRTF in consultation with the IRSG.

FUNDING: The IRSG is largely self-funded. ISOC contributes.

ASSOCIATED BODIES: ISOC, IAB, IRTF.

7. IAB

ORGANIZATION: In June of 1992, the Internet Society chartered the Internet Architecture Board (IAB) as one of its components. The ancestor of the IAB was the Internet Configuration Control

Board (ICCB), a technical advisory group formed by Vint Cerf of DARPA in 1979. The ICCB was replaced by the Internet Advisory Board (IAB) in 1984, which became the Internet Activities Board in 1986, which was chartered as the Internet Architecture Board in June, 1992.

GOVERNANCE: ISOC has jurisdiction over the IAB but allows it a large degree of independence in its operations. With respect to technology, the IAB is considered to be a committee of the IETF.

MEMBERSHIP/COMPOSITION: IAB voting members are proposed by the nominating committee of the IETF, and are then appointed by the ISOC Board of Trustees. The IETF chair, who is chair of IESG as well, is also a voting member. The voting members select one of themselves to serve as chair of IAB. Non-voting members, mainly from associated bodies, also exist. Members serve as individuals, and not as representatives of companies or organizations.

MISSION/GOALS: ISOC mandates the IAB to oversee the architecture of the Internet, including its protocols and other standards. IESG decisions may be appealed to the IAB. IAB rulings are final, with the exception that claims that the IAB proceeded unreasonably may be appealed to the ISOC Board of Trustees. The appointment of an organization as RFC Editor is subject to IAB approval. The IAB claims, on behalf of the IETF, to appoint the organization which is to act as IANA (see sections 9 and 10 below). The IAB appoints the IETF Area Directors and the IETF chair on recommendation of the IETF, as well as the IRTF chair. The IAB advises ISOC's Board, and carries out technical external liaison on behalf of ISOC.

FUNDING: The IAB is largely self-funded. ISOC contributes.

ASSOCIATED BODIES: ISOC, IESG, IETF, IRSG, IRTF, RFC Editor, ICANN, IANA.

8. RFC EDITOR

ORGANIZATION: The RFC document series was initiated by UCLA's Steve Crocker in 1969, and maintained originally at the SRI Network Information Center, then at USC ISI. Jon Postel of USC ISI headed the RFC Editor for decades until his passing in 1998. The RFC Editor is currently a small department operated by USC ISI for ISOC.

GOVERNANCE: ISOC appoints an organization as RFC Editor on the recommendation of IAB. The IAB vets the general policy followed by the RFC Editor.

MEMBERSHIP/COMPOSITION: ISOC appointees.

MISSION/GOALS: The RFC Editor is the organization that edits, manages, publishes and maintains the authoritative archive of the Request For Comments (RFC) documents, which are the Internet's documents of record.

FUNDING: ISOC funds the RFC Editor.

ASSOCIATED BODIES: ISOC, IAB, IESG, IETF, IANA.

9. ICANN

ORGANIZATION: In the late '90s, the U.S. government was completing implementation of its decision to privatize the Internet. The implementation called for the continued operational stability of the Internet, including its Domain Name System. In 1998, the Internet Corporation for Assigned Names and Numbers (ICANN) was chartered as a California non-profit corporation for this purpose. It can be regarded as a technical coordinating and regulatory body.

GOVERNANCE: ICANN is governed by its Board of Directors. The majority of Directors are selected by ICANN's nominating committee. A number of others are appointed by ICANN's supporting organizations. Directors are expected to serve as individuals, not as representatives. The U.S. Department of Commerce gives ICANN authorization to perform the IANA function via a renewable contract which contains a number of reporting requirements. For the more technical aspects of its operations, ICANN and its Board rely on the IETF and the IAB for information and guidance.

MEMBERSHIP/COMPOSITION: ICANN has neither individual nor organizational members in the ordinary sense. Its supporting organizations and advisory committees generally provide a great deal of feedback to the Board on the issues of the day, and ICANN regards them as its constituents. They span the globe and cover a broad range of interests: technical, commercial, governmental, academic and user-oriented. Individuals in the Internet community have some opportunity for participation in ICANN, mainly through its advisory committee structure.

MISSION/GOALS: ICANN's revised articles of incorporation state that "... the Corporation shall, except as limited by Article 5 hereof, pursue the charitable and public purposes of lessening the burdens of government and promoting the global public interest in the operational stability of the Internet by (i) coordinating the assignment of Internet technical parameters as needed to maintain universal connectivity on the Internet; (ii) performing and overseeing functions related to the coordination of the Internet Protocol ("IP") address space; (iii) performing and overseeing functions related to the coordination of the Internet domain name system ("DNS"), including the development of policies for determining the circumstances under which new top-level domains are added to the DNS root system; (iv) overseeing operation of the authoritative Internet DNS root server system; and (v) engaging in any other related lawful activity in furtherance of items (i) through (iv)." [3]. The articles further state that ICANN "shall operate for the benefit of the Internet community as a whole, carrying out its activities in conformity with relevant principles of international law and applicable international conventions and local law and, to the extent appropriate and consistent with these Articles and its Bylaws, through open and transparent processes that enable competition and open entry in Internet-related markets. To this effect, the Corporation shall cooperate as appropriate with relevant international organizations." Among ICANN's most demanding responsibilities are the creation of top-level domains and the (re-)delegation of domain registries.

FUNDING: ICANN is funded mainly from domain name and IP address registries and registrars. Its budget includes funds for a number of staff, headed by a President/CEO and including an Ombudsman.

ASSOCIATED BODIES: IANA, U.S. Department of Commerce, IAB, IETF, W3C.

10. IANA

ORGANIZATION: The tasks that the Internet Assigned Numbers Authority (IANA) performs began in the early '70s. Those and ensuing tasks were performed, and the organization was led, by Jon Postel for decades. Formally, IANA is said to be a service or set of functions. In practical terms, it is a subsidiary organization of ICANN.

GOVERNANCE: In March, 2003, the U.S. Department of Commerce awarded its most recent contract to ICANN to perform the IANA functions. ICANN operates IANA under the authority of the U.S. government. IANA works collegially with the IAB, IESG and IETF in carrying out its mission.

MEMBERSHIP/COMPOSITION: ICANN appointees.

MISSION/GOALS: IANA oversees IP address allocation, manages the DNS (this includes root server system oversight and top-level domain delegation), and coordinates protocol parameter assignment. All Internet domain names and IP addresses are allocated from IANA, either directly or, much more likely, indirectly through IANA's delegation of authority via a worldwide system of Internet registries and registrars. FUNDING: ICANN funds IANA. ASSOCIATED BODIES: ICANN, IAB, IESG, IETF, RFC Editor.

11. W3C

ORGANIZATION: The World Wide Web Consortium (W3C) was founded by Tim Berners-Lee in October, 1994 at MIT in collaboration with the European Organization for Nuclear Research (CERN).

GOVERNANCE: The W3C is a group hosted by MIT in the U.S., the European Research Consortium in Informatics and Mathematics (ERCIM) in Europe, and Keio University in Japan (the Hosts). The W3C is responsible to the Hosts, who maintain a Steering Committee that sets general policy and strategy for W3C from time to time; the majority of the Steering Committee are either from, or appointed by, MIT. W3C calls its technical tasks "Activities", and groups them into broad units called domains. Activities are carried out by Working Group(s) (for technical work), Interest Group(s) (for general work) and Coordination Group(s) (for group coordination). Groups have a chair and consist of member representatives, Team representatives and invited experts. The Team is the Hosts' technical and staff corps that leads Activities and manages the W3C. The Team includes the Director, the Chief Operating Officer, the W3C Chair, W3C Fellows, and others. The Director: has responsibility and authority for overall direction of W3C, is the chief technical architect, chairs the Technical Architecture Group (TAG), appoints group chairs, hears appeals of working group decisions, is appointed by MIT and reports to the Director of MIT's Lab for Computer Sciences. The Chief Operating Officer is responsible for worldwide operations and general management of W3C. The W3C Chair, appointed by MIT, is responsible for member relations and external liaison. The Advisory Committee (AC) is the general assembly of the membership, with one representative from each member; it reviews proposed Activities and recommendations, and suggests future directions for the W3C. The Advisory Board, elected by the Advisory Committee, is the representative council of the membership; its chair is appointed by the Team; it is not a board of directors; it gives guidance to the Team on legal issues, strategy, administration, structures, process, etc., and can do so in between Advisory Committee meetings, which are infrequent.

MEMBERSHIP/COMPOSITION: The W3C is structured, and membership is priced, to have organizations as members. Individuals in the Internet community have limited opportunity for participation in W3C, mainly via those W3C mailing lists that are public.

MISSION/GOALS: "The mission of the World Wide Web Consortium (W3C) is to lead the World Wide Web to its full potential by developing common protocols that promote its evolution and ensure its interoperability." [4]. The W3C develops, tests and implements new Web technological standards ("recommendations" in W3C parlance). The W3C is similar to the IETF in that it develops technological standards, but its focus is more tightly directed, at the Web and associated technologies.

FUNDING: W3C is funded mainly from organization member fees, and some grants. Its budget includes funds for a number of staff and collaborative resources. ASSOCIATED BODIES: IETF, ICANN.

13. REFERENCES

[1] Internet Activities Board, "The Internet Standards Process" - RFC1310, RFC Editor, March 1992.

[2] ISOC, URL http://www.isoc.org/isoc/mission/, February 2005.

[3] ICANN, URL http://www.icann.org/general/articles.htm, February 2005.

[4] W3C, URL http://www.w3c.org/Consortium/Process, February 2005.

14. AUTHOR INFORMATION

Alex Simonelis is a faculty member in the Computer Science Department of Dawson College in Montreal, Canada, and is interested in the Internet, operating systems, programming languages and data structures. Email: asimonelis@dawsoncollege.qc.ca

DOMAIN NAMES

Within the .au domain, there are several second level domains (2LDs). Each serves a specific type of enterprise and the options are outlined below. When it comes to registering a *domain name*, you can choose the 2LD which best suits your purposes.

"OPEN" 2LDS

These 2LDs are known as "open" because they are open to the general public, subject to eligibility criteria.

- **asn.au**
  For incorporated associations, political parties, trade unions, sporting and special interest clubs.
  For registration information, please contact an auDA accredited *registrar.*
- **com.au**
  For commercial entities, such as companies (with ACN as registered through ASIC), and businesses (registered with state governments).
  For registration information, please contact an auDA accredited registrar.
- **net.au**
  For commercial entities, such as companies (with ACN as registered through ASIC), and businesses (registered with state governments).
  For registration information, please contact an auDA accredited registrar.
- **id.au**
  For individuals who are Australian citizens or residents.
  For registration information, please contact an auDA accredited registrar.

- **org.au**
  For charities and non-profit organisations.
  For registration information, please contact an auDA accredited registrar.
- **info.au**
  Not accepting new registrations at this time.
- **conf.au**
  Not accepting new registrations at this time.

"CLOSED" 2LDS

These 2LDs are known as "closed" because they are closed to the general public, and only available to entities within a defined sector.

- **edu.au**
  For educational institutions registered at federal or state level. This domain is managed on behalf of the Australian education sector by the Australian Information and Communications Technology in Education Committee (AICTEC).
  For policy and registration information, please contact Education.au Ltd.
- **gov.au**
  For federal, state and local government bodies. This domain is managed on behalf of the Australian government sector by the Australian Government Information Management Office (AGIMO).
  For policy and registration information, please contact AGIMO .
- **csiro.au**
  For the sole use of the Commonwealth Science and Industry Research Organisation (CSIRO). This domain is managed by CSIRO.
  For policy and registration information, please contact CSIRO.

"COMMUNITY GEOGRAPHIC" 2LDS

These 2LDs are known as "community geographic" 2LDs because they are reserved for use by community groups, and only Australian geographic (place) names may be registered.

- **act.au**
  For community use of geographic names within the Australian Capital Territory. For example, westoncreek.act.au.
- **nsw.au**
  For community use of geographic names within New South Wales. For example, bathurst.nsw.au.
- **nt.au**
  For community use of geographic names within the Northern Territory. For example, wyndham.nt.au.
- **qld.au**
  For community use of geographic names within Queensland. For example, kenilworth.qld.au.
- **sa.au**
  For community use of geographic names within South Australia. For example, maslinbeach.sa.au.
- **tas.au**
  For community use of geographic names within Tasmania. For example, scottsdale.tas.au.
- **vic.au**
  For community use of geographic names within Victoria. For example, ballarat.vic.au.

- **wa.au**
  For community use of geographic names within Western Australia. For example, armadale.wa.au.

DOMAIN RENEWAL, EXPIRY AND DELETION POLICY (2006-07)

Policy No: 2006-07
Publication Date: 19/11/2006
Status: Current

1. BACKGROUND

1.1 This document sets out auDA's policy on the renewal, expiry and deletion of domain names in the open 2LDs (asn.au, com.au, id.au, net.au, org.au) and the community geographic 2LDs (act.au, qld.au, nsw.au, nt.au, sa.au, tas.au, vic,au, wa.au).

1.2 This document does not detail the technical steps required to renew or delete a domain name. This information is contained in the *registry*'s technical procedures manual, which is made available to all auDA accredited *registrar*s.

2. DOMAIN NAME GRACE PERIOD
2.1 There is a 3 calendar day grace period during which a new domain name registration can be deleted, or a renewal cancelled, with immediate effect and the registration/renewal fee will be refunded to the registrar.

3. DOMAIN NAME RENEWAL

3.1 The domain name licence period is fixed at 2 years. This means that when a domain name is registered or renewed, it has a fixed expiry date 2 years from the date of registration of renewal. For example, if a domain name is registered or renewed on 1 January 2007, the expiry date is 1 January 2009.

3.2 Domain names may be renewed a maximum of 90 calendar days before the expiry date, and 30 calendar days after the expiry date (see section 4 below).

4. DOMAIN NAME EXPIRY

4.1 The following procedure applies in the case of domain names that are not renewed on or before the expiry date:

a) domain name is removed from the DNS (ie. no longer works on the Internet);

b) domain name enters “serverUpdateProhibited” and “serverHold” status for 30 calendar days;

c) domain name can be renewed during the 30 calendar day period;

d) after 30 calendar days, domain name is purged from the registry at a random time between 10.30am and 5.00pm AEST (or 11.30am and 6.00pm AEDT) on the next business day.

5. DOMAIN NAME DELETION

5.1 The following procedure applies in the case of domain names that are deleted at the request of the registrant:

a) domain name is removed from the DNS (ie. no longer works on the Internet);

b) domain name enters "pendingDelete" status for 3 calendar days;

c) domain name can be reactivated on the registrant's instruction during the 3 calendar day period;

d) after 3 calendar days, domain name is purged from the registry at a random time between 10.30am and 5.00pm AEST (or 11.30am and 6.00pm AEDT) on the next business day.

5.2 The following procedure applies in the case of domain names that are deleted for breach of an auDA Published Policy (known as "policy deletes"):

a) domain name is removed from the DNS (ie. no longer works on the Internet);

b) domain name enters "serverTransferProhibited", "serverUpdateProhibited" and "pendingDelete" status for 14 calendar days;

c) domain name can be reactivated on auDA's instruction during the 14 calendar day period;

d) after 14 calendar days, domain name is purged from the registry at a random time between 10.30am and 5.00pm AEST (or 11.30am and 6.00pm AEDT) on the next business day.

AUSTRALIAN ICT INDUSTRY AND INNOVATION

In Australia the Internet is now an established feature of life in industry, households, offices and schools. Online participation continues to expand across age and gender groups, albeit at a slower pace than in previous years, reflecting a pattern of consolidation experienced by other global information economy leaders such as the US, Canada and Sweden. This is true also for business online participation, where Australia performs well in terms of Internet access and is ranked among the most connected and active countries in the world.

There are some aspects of Internet activity, however, in which Australia has recently shown a level of growth well above the prevailing pattern of stabilisation recorded in areas such as total Internet access by population and business.

The growth in the uptake of broadband technology in Australia since 2001, for example, has been outstanding, with the percentage of home Internet users using broadband technology growing from 5% in June 2001 to 57% in July 2005.

The reasons for this upward trend include a greater level of market competition and the lower entry prices experienced in Australia, as well as the increasing level of sophistication of Australian Internet users who, through broadband, can perform more complex online activities at a greater speed than that offered by a dial-up connection. Rapid growth in the use of broadband technology is not confined to households and population, with data produced by Sensis in 2005 indicating that the percentage of online Small and Medium Enterprises (SMEs) with a broadband connection increased from 43% in 2004 to 63% in 2005.

Also notable is the substantial increase recorded in terms of the value of e-commerce for Australian business in the last five years.

The Australian Bureau of Statistics (ABS) estimates that Internet income for businesses in Australia increased from $5.1 billion in 1999-2000 to $33 billion in 2003-2004, representing an increase of 55% over a period of 4 years.

The growing economic significance of e-commerce cannot be disputed on the basis that business Internet income in 2003-2004 represented an estimated 4% of Gross Domestic Product (GDP) for the year. For SMEs in particular, rising levels of Internet income were underpinned by strong levels of online activity in areas such Internet banking, placing and receiving orders for goods and services online, and placing and receiving payments online.

Other data presented in the 2005 Current State of Play report include: • 67% of persons aged 14 years and over in Australia used the Internet in April 2005 (up from 54% in September 2001). Online activities performed were:

- buying and selling online (59% of Internet users);
- Internet banking (52%); - paying bills online (39%).
- 74% of total businesses in Australia had Internet access in 2003-2004;
- 57% of home Internet users in July 2005 used broadband technology;
- the percentage of online SMEs with a broadband connection increased from 43% in 2004 to 63% in 2005;
- 39% of home Internet users accessed government websites (up from about 27% in June 2002)

BUSINESS USE OF SELECTED ICTS

The trend for business use of PCs and the Internet is similar to the trend for households shown in the previous graph: faster growth until 2001 followed by a stabilisation period. At June 2004, 85% of all businesses had use of a PC, 74% used the Internet and 25% had a website.
SMEs' use of both PCs and the Internet has marginally increased from 2004 to 2005. PC ownership has increased from 94% to 95% of all SMES. The proportion of all SMEs connected to the Internet has also increased from 86% to 88% in the same period.
The percentage of home Internet users using broadband technology (ISDN excluded) grew from 5% in June 2001 to 57% in July 2005.

- In 2004-05, total revenue in Australia from the production of ICT goods and services was $54.4 billion.[1]
- Sixty per cent of this revenue was from telecommunications services.
- ICT industries in Australia earned a total income of $103.3 billion in 2004–05, ICT specialist firms accounted for 89.1 per cent of this total.[2]
- In 2002-03, ICT gross domestic product (GDP) accounted for 4.6 per cent of Australia's total GDP.

ICT TRADE

Australia's total ICT goods [3] exports in 2005-06 remained relatively steady at $2.17 billion, declining 1.8 per cent from the previous year. This occurred despite an 18 per cent decrease in the value of exports to New Zealand – Australia's largest ICT export market.[4]
Imports of ICT goods approached $17 billion in 2005-06. This compares to $15.5 billion in 2004-05.

Data for 2004-05 indicates that Australia continues to maintain a positive trade balance in computer and information services of $106 million, both imports and exports experienced a slight rise

China remained Australia's largest source of imports, increasing by 26 per cent from 2004-05 levels. While software remains a small portion of Chinese imports to Australia, the value of those imports tripled.

ICT EMPLOYMENT

According to the Australian Bureau of Statistics (ABS) *Labour Force Survey* there were approximately 371 150 people employed in ICT related positions across the economy in August 2006. Nearly 92 per cent of these people were employed full-time.

Males represented 84.5 per cent of ICT employees. Female employees were most represented in the occupations of computing support technicians (26.2 per cent), computing professionals (18.8 per cent) and IT managers (22.7 per cent).[6]

Of the settlers arriving in Australia during 2004-05 who stated an occupation, 5197 were computing professionals, making up 19 per cent of the total professionals arriving in that period.

ICT RESEARCH AND DEVELOPMENT

Total ICT research and development (R&D) expenditure in Australia is nearly $3 billion[7] per annum, accounting for approximately 25 per cent of gross expenditure[8] on R&D.

Organisations outside the ICT business sector[9] are responsible for more than half of all ICT R&D expenditure. These organisations are using ICT R&D to economically develop their businesses and to achieve other social, environmental and defence goals.

Australian ICT R&D expenditure is concentrated in the research field of information, computing and communication sciences, accounting for approximately 74 per cent of private and 77 per cent of public expenditure, respectively.

ABS data is used with permission from the Australian Bureau of Statistics (www.abs.gov.au).

ICT INDUSTRY PROFILE

In 2004-05, ICT income was $87 billion, which represented 84.2 per cent of the $103.3 billion total income generated by Australian ICT industries accordingthe Australian Bureau of Statistics (ABS) survey of ICT industries. Industries with the highest ICT income included telecommunications services ($34.9 billion), computer wholesaling ($20.7 billion) and computer consultancy services ($19.5 billion).[10]

Total revenue from the Australian production of ICT goods and services in 2004-05 was $54.4 billion.[11] The value of production cannot be compared with previous years due to changes to the basis for compiling data for this survey.

Figure 1: ICT industry revenue ($ billion) from the production of ICT goods and services, 2004-05 (Total: $54.4 billion)

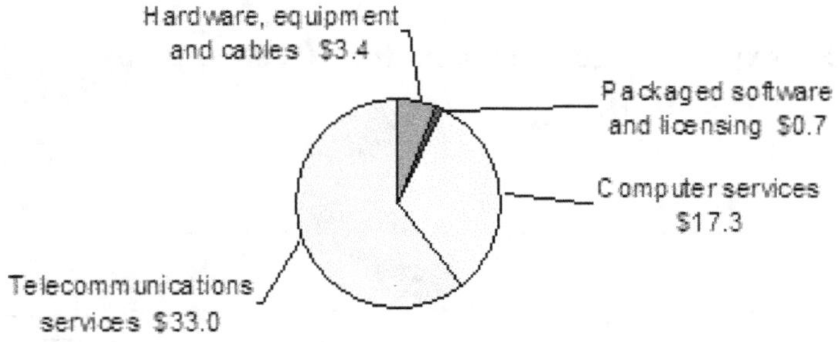

Source: ABS, *Information and Communication Technology, Australia,* 2004-05. Cat. 8126.0

ICT gross domestic product (GDP) represents the total market value of ICT products produced in Australia after deducting the cost of goods and services used in the process of production. According to the ABS ICT Satellite Account, ICT accounted for $36.2 billion or 4.6 per cent of total GDP in 2002-03.[12] ICT GDP in 2002-03 contained several ICT related activities such as wholesale trade ($5.2 billion), telecommunication services ($16.5 billion), computer services ($9.8 billion) and ICT related activity in other industries ($4 billion).

ICT TRADE

Figure 2: Total ICT goods - imports and exports (1995 to 2006)

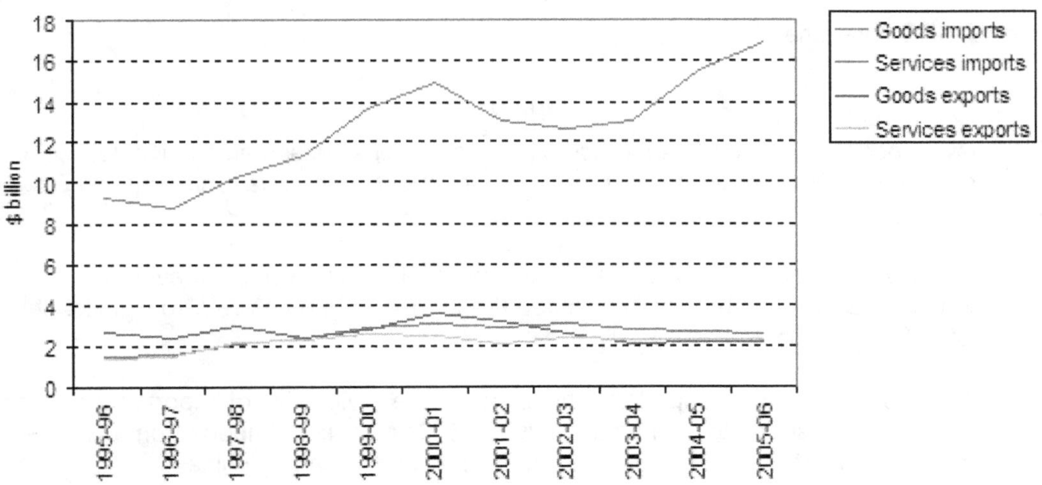

Source: STARS database

EXPORTS

Exports of Australian ICT goods stabilised in 2004-05 ($2.21 billion) and 2005-06 ($2.17 billion) following a period of decline commencing in 2001-02. Notably this occurred despite an 18 per cent decrease in exports to New Zealand which is Australia's major ICT export market. This decline in exports to New Zealand was offset by expansion of many minor export markets for Australia, for example Spain, Chile and Fiji, which reflects an increasingly diverse global ICT market.

Figure 3: ICT goods - exports by selected countries (1993 to 2006)

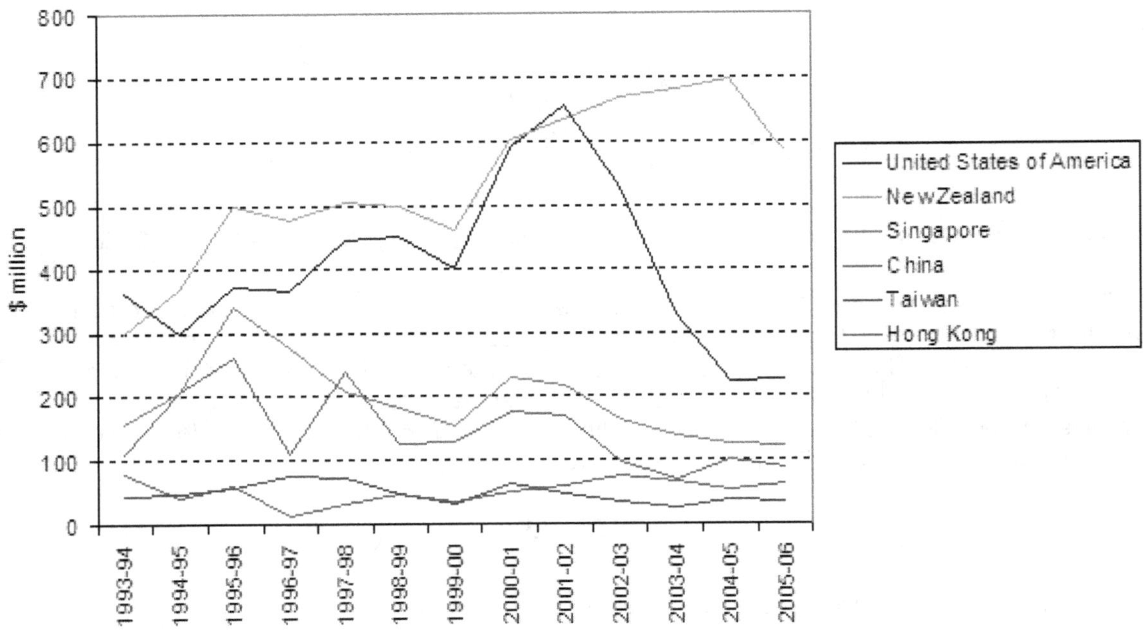

Source: STARS database[13]

IMPORTS

2005-06 saw imports of ICT goods approach $17 billion as businesses and individuals continued to invest in ICT capability in response to broader economic growth. This represents an 8 per cent increase on the previous year.

Organisation for Economic Co-operation and Development data shows that developed nations such as the United States of America, the United Kingdom and France are also significant importers of ICT equipment.

The greatest trend in Australian imports continues to be the prolific rise of imports from China. A further 26 per cent was added to their value in 2005-06. The value of imports from China is now greater than those imported from North America, Europe and Japan combined.

Figure 4: ICT goods - imports by selected countries (1993 to 2006)

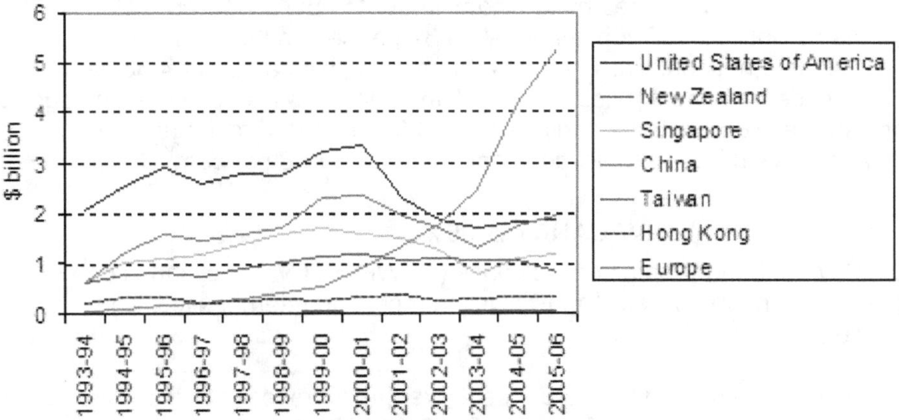

Source: STARS database

ICT EMPLOYMENT

According to the the ABS survey of ICT industries, there were 274 132 people employed by Australia's ICT industries at the end of June 2005. ICT specialist businesses accounted for 89.1 per cent of this employment (244 238 people). The ICT business groupings employing the most people were computer services (41.1 per cent), telecommunications services (27.1 per cent), and wholesale trade (24.6 per cent).

From a different perspective, the ABS *Labour Force Survey*, reported that there were approximately 371 150 people employed in ICT related positions across the economy in August 2006. This consisted of approximately 253 850 people in direct ICT roles (including IT managers, computing professionals and computing support technicians) and 117 300 in 'engineering and trades' occupations. 91.8 per cent of these people were employed full-time.

Of these ICT employees, 84.5 per cent were male. Female employees were most represented in the occupations of computing support technicians (26.2 per cent), computing professionals (18.8 per cent) and IT managers (22.7 per cent In general, females were more poorly represented in the engineering and trades related occupations.

People under 30 years of age make up 27.7 per cent of all ICT employees, and are most represented in the occupations of computing support technicians (44.4 per cent), electronic and office equipment tradespersons (38.0 per cent), and computing professionals (28.4 per cent).[16]

MIGRATION

Of the settlers arriving in Australia during 2004-05 who stated an occupation, 5197 were computing professionals, making up 19 per cent of the total professionals arriving in that period. While the total number of professionals settling has increased by 78 per cent over the past 10 years from 1995-96 to 2004-05, the number of computing professionals settling has increased by 339 per cent over the same period. In 2004-05 computing professionals represented over 8.8 per cent of settlers.

ICT LABOUR DEMAND

Olivier Job Index

The Olivier Internet Job Index is a regular survey of recruitment advertising levels around Australia, which includes ICT and non-ICT industry sectors. The Information Technology and

Telecommunications (IT&T) and Multimedia, Internet and Graphic Design sectors represented 11.62 per cent of total employment measured by the index in September 2006.
The index reports that the number of IT&T jobs grew by 43.37 per cent in the 12 months to September 2006 compared to a national average of 34.06 per cent, with a further 4.58 per cent (seasonally adjusted) increase from the previous month. The largest IT&T employment categories represented were software development and engineering (30.06 per cent), management and sales (19.74 per cent) and networks communications and security (11.88 per cent).[18]

ICT VACANCY INDEX

The Department of Employment and Workplace Relations (DEWR) ICT vacancy index draws data from job advertisements on three Australian ICT online recruiting Internet sites. This provides a measure of demand for ICT skills.

The DEWR ICT vacancy index decreased by 0.6 per cent over the four weeks to mid October 2006, 23.9 per cent higher than in October 2005. Since 2002 the ICT vacancy index has demonstrated a clear upward trend, rising by over 200 per cent to 304.9 (November 2002 = 100). DEWR's broader skilled vacancies index rose by 1.2 per cent in October 2006, and is 1.5 per cent higher than in October 2005.[19]

ICT RESEARCH AND DEVELOPMENT

Expenditure by the Australian private sector significantly outweighs public sector expenditure on ICT research and development (R&D). In 2002-03 business accounted for 86 per cent of total ICT R&D expenditure. The Australian Government accounted for seven per cent and the higher education sector seven per cent.

ICT is a significant component of private sector R&D. It accounted for 36-43 per cent of annual private sector R&D expenditure over the last three years

Organisations outside the ICT business sector[21] are responsible for more than half of all ICT R&D expenditure. This ICT R&D is conducted to achieve business goals outside the ICT business sector. For instance, ICT R&D accounts for 98 per cent of the finance and insurance sector's R&D expenditure and is focused on the development of commercial services[22].

Table 1: Business sector ICT R&D expenditure, 2003-04 financial year

Sector	Contribution to ICT R&D expenditure (per cent)
ICT sector	45
Finance and insurance	23
Manufacturing[23]	10
Communication services[24]	9
Property and business services[25]	8
Wholesale trade[26]	3
Other[27]	2

Source: Extracted from business R&D data purchased from the Australian Bureau of Statistics (ABS) by the Department of Communications, Information Technology and the Arts.
The public sector conducts ICT R&D for a variety of reasons. Only 15 per cent of public ICT R&D is focused on the development of new product offerings and services for the ICT business

sector[28]. The remaining 85 per cent of public ICT R&D is focused on achieving other economic, defence, environmental and social goals.

Australian ICT R&D expenditure is concentrated in the research field of information, computing and communication sciences, accounting for approximately 74 per cent of business and 77 per cent of public expenditure.

Table 2: Business and public sector ICT R&D		
Field of research	Contribution to public sector ICT R&D (per cent)	Contribution to business sector ICT R&D (per cent)
Information, computing and communications sciences[29]	77	74
Communication technologies	13	14
Electrical and electronic engineering	9.5	11
Computer hardware	0.5	1

Source: Extracted from R&D data purchased from the ABS for 2003-04 (business) and 2002-03 (public).

GLOSSARY

.au second level domains
: eg, www.yourbusinessname.com.au - the letters after the name and before the .au

2LD
: Second Level Domain eg, www.yourbusinessname.com.au, the letters after the name and before the .au (www.auda.org.au/domains/)

ABN
: Australian Business Number

ACCC
: Australian Competition & Consumer Commission (www.accc.gov.au)

ACN
: Australian Company Number - for more information go to www.asic.gov.au/asic/asic.nsf

APTLD
: Asia-Pacific Top Level Domain Association (www.aptld.org/)

ASIC
: Australian Securities and Investments Commission (www.asic.gov.au/asic/asic.nsf)

AUNIC
: Australian Network Information Centre (www.aunic.net/)

ccTLD
: Country Code Top Level Domain

Computers
: Basically a database, it's a location on the internet that has the software to accept domain name queries and translate the domain names into IP addresses.

DNS
: Domain Name System domain name - internet address, eg, www.yourbusinessname.com.au

domain name
: internet address, eg, www.yourbusinessname.com.au

gTLD
: Generic Top Level Domain hosting/webhosting - a location (a server somewhere, connected to the internet) which houses your internet address

ICANN
: Internet Corporation for Assigned Names and Numbers (www.icann.org/)

ISP
    Internet Service Provider
Registrant
    Someone who holds, is applying for, or renewing, a domain name licence
Registrar
    auDA-accredited companies who handle domain name licence applications and renewals. The list of auDA-accredited registrars can be found at www.auda.org.au/registrars/
Registry
    The database of domain names registered in each 2LD. For more information go to www.auda.org.au/registry/
Reseller
    Non-accredited companies who handle domain name licence applications and renewals.
Transfers
    Change of Registrar of Record
WHOIS
    A search tool to find contact details for domain names. For more information go to www.auda.org.au/whois/ . To use WHOIS, go to www.mywebname.com.au

STRATEGIC INFORMATION AND REGULATIONS

INTERNET CONTENT REGULATION

The legislative basis for the regulatory regime for online content is the *Broadcasting Services Amendment (Online Services) Act 1999*. This legislation was preceded by a number of reports from the Australian Broadcasting Authority (ABA) and parliamentary committees.

The Senate Select Committee on Community Standards Relevant to the Supply of Services Utilising Electronic Technologies, *Report on Regulation of Computer On-Line Services* is in three parts. *Part 1* (September 1995) described the proceedings of a public seminar convened by the Committee to examine the computer industry's concerns about regulatory proposals. *Part 2* (November 1995) examined the nature of online services and outlined regulatory options. *Part 3* (June 1997) looked at regulatory measures, filtering devices and overseas developments.

The Senate Select Committee on Information Technologies report on the *Broadcasting Services Amendment (Online Services) Bill 1999* (May 1999) examined the regulatory regime for online content that the Bill would introduce. The Committee is currently conducting a review of the regulatory regime.

The Australian Broadcasting Authority (ABA) is responsible for administering the Commonwealth's Internet censorship regime. The ABA web page 'Online services content regulation' provides an overview of the scheme, together with details on :

- the complaints mechanism under the scheme;
- community education programs;
- research studies on online service regulation, attitudes to the Internet, and technological developments;
- Internet Codes of Practice;
- Information about the scheme for ISPs and Internet hosts;
- International liaison on Internet content regulation.

The Australian Family's Guide to the Internet was established by the Commonwealth Government to provide:

- information about filtering software and special 'safe zones' that children can use;
- guides for avoiding 'stranger danger' and advice against giving out personal details; and
- links to sites for children of all ages, covering homework tips, research material and amusement.

Electronic Frontiers Australia is an organisation with the objective of changing laws which restrict free speech or impede the community's access to information. It maintains a detailed page on Internet regulation in Australia, with information on Commonwealth and State activities. Another page with a similar point of view is Regulating the Net (maintained by Roger Clarke).

INTERNET GAMBLING

The Australian Institute of Criminology (AIC) paper, Internet Gambling (June 1998) examines the policy options concerning this issue. Papers for the Conference on "Gambling, Technology and Society: Regulatory Challenges for the 21st Century" (May 1998) convened by the AIC in conjunction with the Australian Institute for Gambling Research are also available from this page. The Senate Select Committee on Information Technologies has conducted an inquiry into online gambling. A copy of the report, *Netbets: a Review of Online Gambling in Australia* (March 2000), can be obtained here. The report recommends that no further online gambling licences be issued until after the introduction of a range of consumer protection measures.

The Productivity Commission's Inquiry into Australia's Gambling Industries Final Report (December 1999) has a substantial chapter on policies for Internet gambling.
A number of overseas reports on Internet gambling are also available online. They include Internet Gaming and South Africa: Implications, Costs and Opportunities (August 1999) and the work of the US National Gambling Impact Study Commission.

Show Hand Gaming News is a magazine site reporting on gambling developments (online and land based) in Australasia and Asia. It includes online gambling statistics and reports on gaming regulation.

INTERNET COMMERCE

Access to a large range of news releases, policy documents and reports concerning Internet commerce in Australia can be obtained from the Department of Communications, Information Technology and the Arts (DCITA).

The DCITA report, Australia's e-commerce report card (1999) gives the policy framework for e-commerce and describes those areas in which the Commonwealth is partnering industry and other governments to increase the use of e-commerce by Australian business. Some key State and Territory e-commerce activities are also briefly outlined.

The National Office for the Information Economy (NOIE) develops and coordinates Commonwealth policy with regard to electronic commerce in Australia. Useful NOIE sites and documents include:

- a quarterly information economy statistical report;
- the report, E-commerce Beyond 2000, which makes forecasts on the impact of e-commerce on the Australian economy;

The DCITA, in conjunction with the NOIE and the Commonwealth Treasury have produced "Shopping on the Internet - Facts for Consumers", a series of papers dealing with some of issues involved with online purchasing. The papers are as follows:

- #1: What are the benefits and risks of shopping online?
- #2: What type of information should I look for in a Website?
- #3: How safe is it to use my credit card?
- #4: Do I have to pay sales tax or duties on imported goods?
- #5: What happens to my personal information?
- #6: What if something goes wrong with my purchase?
- #7: Banking on the Internet

The Australian Electronic Business Network is a Government initiative supported by industry to foster awareness of electronic commerce among small to medium enterprises.

The Joint Committee of Public Accounts and Audit report, Internet Commerce To buy or not to buy? (May 1998) focussed on the impact on Australian small to medium businesses, the implications for the tax system, the Customs screen free limit, and privacy issues.
E-commerce today is an independent magazine containing news and analysis on developments in electronic commerce in Australia.

PRIVACY AND THE INTERNET

On the 12 April the Government introduced the Privacy Amendment (Private Sector) Bill 2000. The Bill seeks to establish a national scheme for the appropriate collection and usage of personal information by the private sector.

The Australian Privacy Commissioner maintains a web page on IT and Internet Issues which provides access to:

- guidelines for workplace e-mail and web browsing;
- guidelines for Commonwealth government sites; and
- advice on the protection of privacy.

Roger Clarke's Current Developments in Internet Privacy paper is a detailed analysis of the Australian situation. It argues that regulatory and organisational responses to the privacy threats created by the Internet have been seriously inadequate. The paper contains many links to other papers and sites of interest.

Other relevant documents include:

- the Australian Communications Industry Forum (ACIF) industry code on the Protection of Personal Information of Customers of Telecommunications Providers;
- the Privacy Commissioner's National Principles for the Fair Handling of Personal Information (January 1999);
- the Internet Industry Association's Code of Practice.

INTERNET STATISTICS

The Australian Bureau of Statistics (ABS) produces a number of publications that deal with Internet usage in Australia. It should be noted that the ABS only provides a summary of the main features of each publication online.

- *Use of the Internet by Householders, Australia* provides details of the number of households with Internet access, the frequency of use, characteristics of users and commercial use by householders. This is a quarterly survey conducted in February, May, August and November each year.

- *Household Use of Information Technology, Australia 1998* consolidates the quarterly Internet usage data on an annual basis, and also includes information on household expenditure and usage of computers and other information technology.
- *Business Use of Information Technology, Australia 1997-98* (October 1999) contains data on the number of businesses with Internet access and web sites, purpose of Internet usage and expenditure on information technology.
- *Government Use of Information Technology, Australia 1997-98* (December 1999) has details on use, employment and expenditure by Federal, State and local government.
- *Use of Information Technology on Farms, Australia 1998-99*, Preliminary (December 1999) provides statistics on the use of computers and the Internet by primary producers.
- *Telecommunications Services 1996-97* (January 1999) includes information on the number, income, assets and employment of Internet service providers. This survey was conducted to provide a benchmark so that the impact of deregulation (which occurred in July 1997) could be assessed.

Statistics on current Australian Internet usage are also available from www.consult Pty Ltd, a research and consulting group which also produces reports on Internet shopping and banking. However, only the most basic data is made available without cost.

International indicators of Internet usage and development are available from the OECD. These include a graphical analysis by domain and language, as well as Internet infrastructure indicators. The OECD also produces a wide range of policy papers on telecommunications, a number of which deal with Internet developments.

The Internet Domain Survey sponsored by the Internet Software Consortium provides statistics on the number of hosts on the Internet. The January 2000 survey indicated that there were 72 398 092 Internet hosts, of which 1 090 468 were in the .au domain.

Statistics on Internet commerce in Australia are available from the NOIE web site, in particular their Current State of Play page (a quarterly summary of statistical and other data) and their report, stats. electronic commerce in australia (April 1998).

INTERNET RATINGS/CHARTS

Several Australian organisations have developed methodologies for ranking the most popular sites with Australian Internet users. These sites survey the proxy servers or logs of a sample of Internet service providers (ISPs) to estimate which sites are most visited by Australians. However, it should be noted that Internet ratings are in their infancy and that significant methodological difficulties still exist. The charts should be used as guides to the more popular web sites, rather than as definitive indicators of relative usage.

Where did we go in Australia? provides weekly charts of web sites most visited by Australians, including:

- the top 500 Australian web sites;
- the top 100 (Australian and overseas) web sites;
- the top five Australian web publishers;
- the most popular web sites by category;
- statistics and information on domain registrations.

Top 100 charts the relative popularity of web sites amongst Australians across more than 70 categories. Information available from the site includes the following:

- weekly charts of the top 100 Australian and global sites;
- a detailed category breakdown of the most popular sites;
- a domain name watch;
- news, analysis and a search facility.

AC Neilsen/Net Ratings are also developing a global Internet research service but there are no statistics on Australian usage available from their Australian site at this time. The US site provides some free data on US usage. A similar situation exists with Media Metrix: the global site offers extensive ratings and statistics on Internet usage, but the Australian site requires a subscription to obtain local data.

Another source of global information is CyberAtlas, which contains reports on commercial usage, ratings and other statistics (including Australian data). Nua Internet Surveys also provides access to a wide range of news stories, surveys and charts. The GVU WWW User Surveys site provides details of ten Internet user surveys conducted since 1994.

OTHER SITES OF INTEREST

The web magazine australia.internet.com provides news, information and analyses on Internet developments in Australia.

The Australian ISP List provides details on Australian Internet access providers. Access and hosting prices, network details and descriptions of consultancy and other services offered are given for over nine hundred ISPs.

The Australian Internet Awards acknowledge and celebrate Australian talent and expertise on the Internet. Awards are given in a range of categories, with the winners being selected by an independent panel of judges. There is also an award for Most Popular Australian Web Site that is determined by votes from the public. The Awards commenced in 1996.

The Internet Industry Association (IIA) is the Australian national industry body for Internet commerce, content and connectivity. The IIA web site provides access to a wide range information concerning Australia and the Internet, including:

- press releases, seminar proceedings, articles and policy statements;
- the IIA Code of Practice, as well as guides to online content for ISPs and Internet users; and,
- reports on the activities of IIA taskforces on Internet issues.

The Internet Society of Australia is the Australian chapter of the Internet Society (ISOC). ISOC has more than 150 organisational and 6,000 individual members in over 100 countries. It addresses issues that confront the future of the Internet, and is the organisational home for the groups responsible for Internet infrastructure standards, including the Internet Engineering Task Force and the Internet Architecture Board. Both the Australian and the international ISOC web sites contain extensive material on Internet news and issues.

The Asia Pacific Network Information Centre (APNIC) is one of three regional Internet registries responsible for providing allocation and registration services which support the global operation of the Internet. The other two registries are in Europe and the United States. APNIC is a non-profit organisation comprising ISPs, national Internet registries and network information centres. APNIC serves over sixty countries and territories in the Asia-Pacific region. The APNIC secretariat is located in Brisbane. The APNIC web site provides access to a large number of documents, although most are of a technical nature.

STRATEGIC, LAWS AND REGULATIONS AFFECTING ICT INTERNET AND DEVELOPMENT[27]

- **Commonwealth**
  - Copyright Amendment (Digital Agenda) Act 2000 (Cth)
    An Act to amend the Copyright Act 1968, and for related purposes.
  - Electronic Transactions Act 1999 (Cth)
    An Act to facilitate electronic transactions, and for other purposes.
  - Electronic Transactions Bill 1999 (Cth)
    Text of the Bill and Exlanatory Memorandum.
  - Electronic Transactions Regulations 2000 (Cth)
    Statutory Rules 2000 No. 19 as amended made under the Electronic Transactions Act 1999
  - Spam Act 2003 (Cth)
    An Act about spam, and for related purposes.
- **New South Wales**
  - Electronic Transactions Act 2000 (NSW)
    An Act to facilitate electronic transactions, and for other purposes.
  - Electronic Transactions Regulations 2000 (NSW)
    This Regulation is made under the Electronic Transactions Act 2000, including sections 7, 12 and 15 (the general regulation-making power) and the definition of court in section 14A (1).
- **Northern Territory**
  - Electronic Transactions Act 2000 (NT)
    An Act to facilitate electronic transactions, and for other purposes.
  - Electronic Transactions Regulations (Northern Territory) Regulations
    Regulations under the Electronic Transactions (Northern Territory)Act 2000
- **Queensland**
  - Electronic Transactions (Queensland) Act 2001 (Qld)
    An Act to facilitate electronic transactions, and for other purposes.
- **South Australia**
  - Electronic Transactions Act 2000 (SA)
    An Act to facilitate electronic transactions; and for other purposes.
  - Electronic Transactions Regulations 2002 (SA)
    Regulations made under the Electronic Transactions Act 2000 (SA)
- **Tasmania**
  - Electronic Transactions Act 2000 (TAS)
    An Act to facilitate electronic transactions and for other purposes.
  - Electronic Transactions Regulations 2001 (TAS)
    Regulations made under the Electronic Transactions Act 2000 (TAS)
- **Victoria**
  - Electronic Transactions (Victoria) Act 2000 (VIC)
    An Act to facilitate electronic transactions and for other purposes.
  - Electronic Transactions (Victoria) Regulations 2000
    Regulations under the Electronic Transactions (Victoria) Act 2000 (VIC)
  - Transfer of Land (Electronic Transactions) Act 2004 (Vic)
    The main purposes of this Act are:(a) to amend the Transfer of Land Act 1958 (i) to provide for the lodgement and registration of electronic instruments; and to

[27] Please contact IBP USA at IBPUSA@comcast.net for texts of specific laws and regulations

empower the Registrar to require verification of identity before registering an instrument under that Act.

VISION FOR 2010

Australia will maintain its position as a leader in e-government, demonstrating how effective use of technology transforms government into a more efficient and client-oriented sector of the economy.

Through effective use of technology, the government will improve its structures and processes. Online, electronic and voice-based services will be fully integrated into government service delivery. Electronic delivery will underpin all other delivery channels, ensuring a consistent base to all activities and providing consistent service no matter how government is approached.

MEETING USERS' NEEDS

Government will be regarded as approachable. Government information services will be easy to understand and locate and interacting with government will be quick and straightforward. It will be easy for people to pinpoint the service or information they need, regardless of how and where they initially approach government: every door will be the right door when approaching government. Regardless of which door is chosen, at most only one onwards referral will be needed.

People will be able to choose from a range of service delivery modes, but will prefer the added convenience and functionality of online, electronic and voice-based channels, which they will use frequently. The government will continue to ensure that people with a disability can access government information and services with ease.

Authentication and personal or business information will need to be provided only once through a simplified government sign-on, to access government information and services and for ongoing interactions, transactions and updates. This will be a single sign-on, except where circumstances require otherwise.

It will be possible to group diverse transactions and complete them at the same time, without navigating the underlying structure and complexity of government. People will be able to interact with many areas of government without needing to understand exactly which agencies deliver which services.

Privacy and security rights will be paramount in all service delivery channels offered by government, and will underpin the implementation of this strategy. People will manage the integrity of and access to their own personal details. Anyone unable to do this will be able to nominate agents to manage personal details on their behalf.

The government will increasingly manage its programs and relations with stakeholders electronically, providing organisations and businesses with the same benefits and options of interacting electronically with the Australian Government as citizens will experience – both Australian citizens and those of other countries who need to interact with the Australian Government.

Connected service delivery will amalgamate the requirements of government. This integration, combined with online and electronic service delivery, over time will reduce the cost of interacting with government and in particular will reduce the paper burden on citizens, businesses and organisations, including community organisations.

In each year from 2006 to 2010, in support of program outcomes, the government will send ten per cent fewer letters – either paper or electronic – to citizens. By 2010, the government will have halved the number of forms that must be filled in. The nature of forms will also change. Rather than numerous static forms, either electronic or paper, dynamic forms will be available from a single entry point where users can automatically enter required details already held by other government agencies, complete their details electronically, and trace the resulting actions online.

CONNECTED SERVICE DELIVERY

Connected government will become a reality and will drive reform of government business processes.
Government will present a consistent and unified face regardless of whether approaches are made in person, over the telephone, using the Internet or any other form of technology. This consistency will address the common frustration associated with trying to understand government structures to find the right agency. The government will match private sector best practice for electronic interactions. This consistency will extend to non-government entities delivering government services. For example, the burden for business will be reduced by increasingly embedding government processes in the natural systems being used by the business community.

Figure 1: Connected Government - Client's View

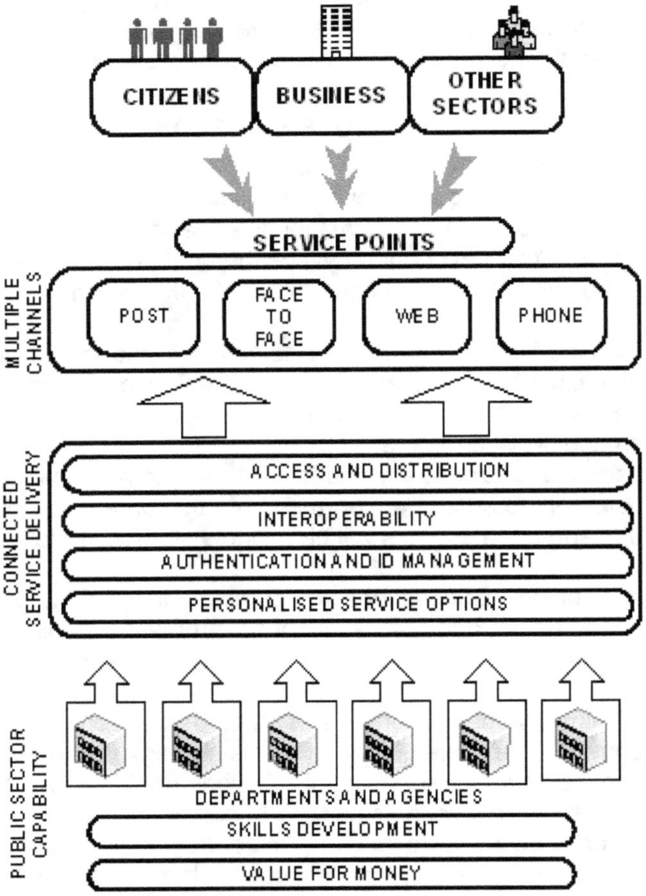

The government will use the opportunities presented by connected government and technology to improve its business processes. It will reform poorly designed and redundant processes and reduce duplication by standardising similar processes across agencies and, where possible, combine those processes. Agencies will operate in a collaborative, connected manner, rather than in isolation from each other.
The considerable benefits from a more connected approach include more agile service delivery and the ability to quickly redeploy services to different sites, including temporary locations. For example, Centrelink can deploy family applications into Medicare Australia shopfronts thanks to the modular design of its systems.
Government's ability to respond to emergencies will also be enhanced. All the parties that need to respond to an emergency situation will be linked and operating under a common framework. For

example, the Immigration and Multicultural Affairs, Human Services, and Foreign Affairs departments could share the same information models and emergency information systems. Connected government using new technology also offers new ways to think about policy and delivery. Recent whole of government policies such as *Australians Working Together* and *Welfare to Work* reflect the opportunities provided by information and service connectivity. They illustrate how government can provide a seamless service to people progressing through different stages of initiatives that cross several agencies. As connected government expands and a whole of government approach to systems is adopted, more opportunities like these will arise.

VALUE FOR MONEY

A more connected approach to service delivery means more efficient government. Greater use of online, electronic and voice-based service delivery will reduce costs. For example:

- less double handling and fewer errors in initial transactions mean less work down the track to identify and make corrections
- more informed users require less assistance and can be served more quickly
- systems where people maintain their own personal details reduce this direct cost for taxpayers as well as reducing the costs associated with using out-of-date information.

In addition to these service delivery cost reductions, the government's overall use of information technology will be much more efficient. More targeted and strategic investments in technology will see less duplication and more common underlying business processes across different government agencies. Processes will be simpler and more integrated. Projects will be better managed, with reduced cost and time overruns.

Connected government will provide public sector infrastructure better able to deal with outages and disruptions. Much of the necessary infrastructure to ensure business continuity will be a natural by-product of the planning required for connected government. Common standards and extensive connections across government agencies will support shared processing capability and multiple delivery pathways for dealing with outages. Connected government will also enable processing loads to be shared across agencies, reducing the need for redundant capacity to manage peaks.

Connected government will provide greater opportunities for agencies to share and re-use technology, reducing overall infrastructure costs. Electronic delivery also serves the government's environmental objectives by helping to reduce paper and energy consumption and greenhouse gas emissions.

PUBLIC SECTOR CAPABILITY

The public sector will have the necessary capabilities to deliver on this vision. From 2006, capabilities will be assessed and any gaps or deficiencies addressed, in areas such as public sector ICT skills and recruitment, ICT business practices, ICT procurement processes, knowledge management, project management and delivery, and in accountability and legislative arrangements as they relate to supporting online and electronic service delivery.

TABLE 1: Progress towards the vision—indicative intermediate and final outcomes

	Current situation: 2005–06	Initial phase: 2006 – 2008	Final phase: 2008 – 2010
Meeting users' needs	The government has moved towards a client-focussed service delivery agenda. Government information is readily available online, and an increasing number of	People will only need to tell government once. They will be able to update their details once and make the update available to other agencies, under privacy safeguards.	Government services will be widely available through participating private sector providers. People will be able to choose who they contact for government services.

	services are also available electronically. australia.gov.au provides a convenient interface to government, but transactions with government are still agency-based, and not available through all channels. People often still need to understand how government is structured.	safeguards. Every door will be the right door when approaching government. australia.gov.au will be the central access point to government, providing basic personal accounts. The capacity to interact with government through other providers will be introduced.	services. Fully functional personalised accounts will be available. Significantly simplified sign-on to government will be available. This will be a single sign-on, except where circumstances require otherwise.
Connected service delivery	A few fully connected services are available. For example, *e-tax* enables individuals to automatically enter account information from selected other government agencies into their electronic tax return.	High priority common infrastructure required for the final phase will be identified and planned. Building connected government will have commenced from selected agency services, or 'pathway projects'. The number of connected services will be increasing. Agency systems will be designed so that services from different agencies, and selected private sector service providers, can be bundled seamlessly.	Connected government will be fully established. People will be able to package together different services from different agencies. Private sector providers will be able to package government services with their own.
Value for money	Agencies make independent investment decisions, with little re-use of systems developed by other agencies. More information is needed on the efficiency of government technology investment.	A robust ICT investment framework will be established, including online guidance and tools for ICT strategic planning, business case development, and project management. Project management will be improved through Gateway™ reviews. A repository for re-use of government systems will have been established.	ICT investment will be well planned and managed, delivering the responsiveness and value for money required by government. Government investments in technology will have clear benefits and returns. There will be widespread re-use of agency systems.
Public sector capability	Achievements and progress to date in the area of e-government indicate that there is a substantial	A capability stocktake will be completed to identify strengths, weaknesses and gaps.	The public sector will have addressed all gaps in capability, and will be widely recognised as an exemplar in capability

	reservoir of capability in the public service, but this reservoir of capability is not yet fully scoped and understood.	Actions to address skills shortages and imbalances will be well underway.	development. There will be a 'virtuous circle' between capability and implementation of this strategy, with each reinforcing the other—with capability and skills enhanced as various aspects of the strategy are achieved.

STRATEGIC PRIORITIES

The government has identified four strategic priorities to guide agencies over the next five years:

- meeting users' needs
- establishing connected service delivery
- achieving value for money
- enhancing public sector capability.

MEETING USERS' NEEDS

AGIMO's comprehensive June 2005 report, *Australia's Use of and Satisfaction with E-government Services (Australia's Use)* found relatively high satisfaction levels with current government online services. However, it also revealed low expectations of what can be achieved online, and showed that other channels, such as face-to-face, are still preferred for transactions which are considered more complex or ambiguous.

In response, this strategic priority outlines actions designed to improve people's satisfaction when dealing with government and accessing government services.

Australia's Use also found that there is no such thing as 'a typical government user'. The number and diversity of users will increase, and this strategy outlines how the government will address this increasing diversity.

SECURITY AND PRIVACY

Building trust and confidence has been a consistent theme of the government's e-government strategies. Respecting and protecting the privacy and information security of citizens, businesses and community and other organisations will underpin all e-government activities. As part of the government's wider set of initiatives to promote a culture of security in relation to e-commerce, AGIMO, in conjunction with the Privacy Commissioner and relevant security agencies, will assist government agencies to understand and implement the government's own legislation and requirements for security and privacy. This will lead to even better protection of people's personal information.

MEASURING USER NEEDS AND PREFERENCES

The government will develop a consistent and coordinated approach for agencies to measure the use of and satisfaction with their services. Not only will agencies be better able to respond to user needs, a consistent approach across government will also allow an aggregate picture of use and satisfaction levels, enabling a whole of government approach to meeting the needs of users. The needs of specific groups, such as the disabled, can be better identified and addressed. Government policy development and implementation will be better informed. AGIMO will complement agency-based measurements with annual overall measurements of the use of and satisfaction with e-government services.

THE AUSTRALIAN GOVERNMENT ENTRY POINT

The government will review and consolidate its websites, so that it is easier for people to find what they want. A simpler, more streamlined government online presence will be easier to promote, enhancing awareness and use. The principal entry point to the Australian Government will be australia.gov.au, incorporating publications.gov.au and directory.gov.au. Other major government entry points will be integrated more tightly to australia.gov.au, to further streamline the government's online presence and make it easier to use. The security arrangements for australia.gov.au will be enhanced to match its more prominent role.

USER ACCOUNTS AND PERSONALISED SERVICES

The government will provide individual, personalised accounts through australia.gov.au. All users—citizens, citizens of other countries who need to interact with the Australian Government, businesses and organisations—will only need to update details once, with the option for the update to be made automatically across other government agencies. They will also be able to change their government-registered details when interacting with participating non-government service providers.

User accounts will address the growing diversity of people interacting with government. Each will be able to construct a personalised view of government highlighting the services and information most relevant to their needs.

VISIBLE AND TRACEABLE SERVICES

It will be possible to track government transactions in real time. Users will be provided with immediate receipts for transactions which cannot be completed straight away. As part of the reform of government business processes, many more transactions will be completed electronically at the time of commencement than is possible using traditional means.

INCREASING USER AWARENESS OF SERVICE DELIVERY OPTIONS

The Australian Government will promote its electronic service delivery options more prominently, so it is easier to find and access government services. AGIMO will work closely with agencies such as the Department of Human Services, the Department of Employment and Workplace Relations, the Department of Industry, Tourism and Resources, the Department of Health and Ageing, the Department of Education, Science and Training, the Australian Taxation Office and others to increase user awareness. Despite efforts to date including creating facilities such as australia.gov.au, *Australia's Use* found a lack of awareness about services available over the Internet. This is a significant barrier to greater e-government uptake and indicates the need to consolidate and more effectively promote government online services.

ONLINE ENGAGEMENT WITH GOVERNMENT

The government will set principles for online engagement to support a consistent experience for everyone engaging with Australian governments electronically. The entry point at australia.gov.au will also provide consolidated information about government online consultation and engagement initiatives and how to take advantage of them.

AGIMO will work with government agencies to enhance their understanding and uptake of online engagement, including developing guidelines and better practice guides.

ACTIONS:

INITIAL PHASE 2006 – 2008:

- Continue to measure overall use and satisfaction with government services annually.
- Develop a consistent and coordinated approach by agencies to measuring the use of and satisfaction with their services.
- Develop australia.gov.au as the principal Australian Government entry point, including a consolidated entry point to government online engagement initiatives.
- Review and consolidate the number of the government's own websites.
- Provide users with basic individual government service accounts.
- Enable users to track incomplete transactions.
- Promote the government's service delivery options more prominently.
- Establish principles for online engagement, plus practical guidelines and better practice guides.
- Introduce access to government services through selected non-government providers.
- Introduction of limited capacity for users to opt to have their government-registered details updated automatically when they interact with selected non-government service providers.

FINAL PHASE 2008 – 2010:

- Provide users with fully-functional government service accounts which they can personalise.
- Widespread access to government services through participating non-government providers.
- Users able to opt to have their government-registered details updated automatically when they interact with participating non-government service providers.

ACHIEVING VALUE FOR MONEY

This strategic priority outlines how government will improve its ICT investments to gain better value for money. A stronger focus on efficiency will ensure more targeted ICT investment that contributes to and drives reform of government business processes, particularly through re-use and sharing of existing investments across agencies.

A ROBUST INVESTMENT FRAMEWORK

The government will develop a robust ICT investment framework, improving the quality of:

- ICT strategic planning
- project development and management
- procurement
- evaluation.

The ICT investment framework will be used by AGIMO and other agencies to ensure that ICT investment across government is well planned and managed, and will deliver the responsiveness and value for money required by government. The framework will identify duplicate proposals, and opportunities for collaboration between agencies, contributing to the reform of government business processes.

The framework will guide agencies on business case development, applying the Australian Government Demand and Value Assessment Methodology (DAM/VAM) to a broader range of ICT projects.

The framework will encourage good practice and consistency in ICT strategic planning, by providing access to good practice tools and methodologies. Business cases will be assessed against a good practice review guide to ensure projects are appropriately planned and avoid common causes of project failures.

A mechanism to gather and analyse strategic and procurement plans of agencies that are major investors in ICT will also be included in the framework. This will forecast significant future pressure on the Federal Budget and on the ICT skills market, and help to prioritise whole of government strategic directions and capability development.

The framework will include tools to improve planning and managing that will help achieve measurable benefits and outcomes, including a performance indicator library and resources for designing evaluation strategies. Central reviews of business cases by AGIMO will focus on planning to measure and manage performance and on delivering outcomes.

PROJECT MANAGEMENT CAPABILITY

The Australian Government will introduce a new project management process known as *Gateway*™ to improve the delivery of major projects.

Gateway™ is a project assurance methodology originally implemented by the United Kingdom's Office of Government Commerce in 2000, and has been used in Victoria since 2003. *Gateway*™ involves short, sharp reviews at critical points throughout a project's life, conducted by reviewers not associated with the project. In this way, it provides an arm's length assessment of the project against its specified objectives and identifies any areas that may require corrective action.

Information technology projects valued over $10 million and procurement or infrastructure projects valued over $20 million will be assessed for risk. Where the risk warrants it, the *Gateway*™ methodology will be applied to those projects. To support agencies and to facilitate the reviews, a small *Gateway*™ unit has been established in the Department of Finance and Administration. The unit will develop detailed advice for agencies on the application of *Gateway*™. Reviews will commence in 2006–07 with all projects assessed as medium or high risk, and over the financial thresholds, subject to *Gateway*™ from 2008–09.

The government will also encourage the establishment of Project Management Offices in government agencies, to improve project management skills and capability in the Australian Public Service.

INTER AND INTRA-AGENCY RE-USE AND SHARING OF SYSTEMS

The adoption of common, standardised, modular business processes by government agencies is intended to eliminate or change duplicated, redundant and inefficient processes. This will require the re-use and sharing of existing systems.

A repository will be established so that agencies can discover, publish and re-use information, business processes and systems in a trusted environment. One possible repository, GovDex, is being trialled by selected government agencies.

ACTIONS:

INITIAL PHASE 2006 – 2008:

- Develop and implement a robust ICT investment framework, including online guidance and tools for ICT strategic planning, business case development, and project management, benefits realisation and evaluation.
- Establish a government-wide approach to project management, involving independent peer reviews for major government projects, including ICT projects.

- Encourage the establishment of Project Management Offices in agencies.
- Implement a repository of business and technical systems implementation, including a catalogue of design solutions, to encourage re-use of existing systems.

FINAL PHASE 2008 – 2010:

- Adopt common business processes across government agencies.

ENHANCING PUBLIC SECTOR CAPABILITY

Successful implementation of this strategy will depend on the Australian Public Service having the necessary capability. This strategy outlines how government will enhance the capability of the public sector.

SERVICE CAPABILITY AND MATURITY

The government will measure the extent to which it has the necessary capabilities to deliver the vision, and will assess the maturity of these capabilities, using the *Delivering Australian Government Services—Service Capability Model*, which lists the elements of the government's service delivery capability. This stocktake will identify strengths and address any revealed gaps and weaknesses in capability and maturity.The stocktake will cover the following service delivery requirements:

- people
- business processes
- business continuity
- physical facilities (non-ICT)
- information and communication technologies
- knowledge and information management
- accountability and governance.

This model provides an agreed language to describe, build and improve all those things that enable an agency to deliver efficient and effective services. It will be applied across government to ensure online service delivery is enabled by the maturity of departments' and agencies' capabilities.

SKILLS DEVELOPMENT

There is increasing recognition in government and industry of the need to ensure Australia has the ICT skills that it requires. The government will increase the ICT skill level of its employees as part of the process of building agencies' service delivery capability and maturity.
Particular emphasis will be placed on raising the level of information technology literacy amongst executives and senior executives. In addition to ICT-specific skills, including technical interoperability and information architecture expertise, skills will be required in a wide range of areas, such as business processes, project management, and security.
Some skills strategies are included here. For example, the ICT investment framework will broaden and deepen the skills base, as will *Gateway™*. In addition, a systematic process to address recruitment and retention is already being implemented to strengthen skills. AGIMO has partnered with the Australian Public Service Commission (APSC) and other agencies through the Chief Information Officer Committee, to coordinate the newly established working group of the Committee, the *ICT Professional and Skills Development Group*.
In support of skills development, the government will be a leader in using ICT to design and build more efficient and effective work processes, for example enabling greater and better use of

telework (that is, working in locations independent of the central employer or contractor, using ICT to facilitate communications).

ICT PROCUREMENT

The government will develop procurement plans at the agency and whole of government levels, to promote more strategic and targeted decisions about ICT procurement. An increased preparedness by agencies to collaborate on ICT procurement and systems will help obtain the best prices and deliver improved efficiency and effectiveness.
Industry will also have an important role in improving public sector ICT procurement. In developing its procurement plans, the government will consult fully with industry to draw on private sector expertise.

APS EMPLOYEE IDENTITY MANAGEMENT

The government will develop a secure identity management framework for government employees and for its contractors, enabling government to streamline access and better account for its own staff. Government security will be enhanced while making it easier for people to move across organisational boundaries and into new organisational arrangements.

3.4.5 ENABLE THE LEGISLATIVE FRAMEWORK WHERE NECESSARY

The government will identify, review and remove any legislative barriers to connected government. The reasons for such barriers will vary and new ways of overcoming them will be found, for example offering connected services while respecting privacy by enabling people using technology to manage their own privacy.

ACTIONS:

INITIAL PHASE 2006 – 2008:

- Conduct a stocktake of the extent to which the government has the necessary capabilities to deliver the vision, and assess the maturities of these capabilities.
- Strengthen skills through a systematic process to address recruitment and retention.
- Develop procurement plans which promote good ICT procurement decisions by agencies.
- Implement a secure identity management framework for all government employees.
- Review and address legislative barriers to connected government.

FINAL PHASE 2008 – 2010:

- All gaps in capacity will have been addressed.
- Public sector capability is reinforced by achievements under the strategy.

IMPLEMENTING THE STRATEGY

USING INNOVATIVE TECHNOLOGY

The government will continue to be an informed user of new and emerging technologies.

EXPLOIT EMERGING MOBILE TECHNOLOGY

Mobile devices are one technology with a sufficient level of maturity and immediate potential application. Close to 75 per cent of people in Australia have a mobile phone or other wireless device, and around the same number have access to personal computers (*The Current State of Play November 2005* and *Information Economy Index 2004*, Department of Communications, Information Technology and the Arts).

AGIMO will work with government agencies to identify best practice applications of mobile technologies from a whole of government perspective, including areas such as emergency response and law enforcement, education, health care and teleworking opportunities.

SMART CARDS

The term 'smart card' has been used to describe a class of credit card-sized chip devices with varying capabilities such as stored-value cards, contact-less cards and integrated circuit cards (ICC). These differ in functionality, both from each other and from the more familiar magnetic-stripe cards. The ICC (more commonly known as the 'chip card' or 'smart card') provides a toolbox of enhanced capabilities for functions such as access control, payment, information storage, management tools and multiple applications. Smart card technology will allow people to access multiple government services more securely, either in-person or online, essentially by providing them with their own miniature computer.

The Australian Government, through AGIMO, is developing a smart cards framework for how government agencies can use smart card technology. The primary objectives are to assist Australian Government agencies who want to implement multi-application smart card technology and ensure interoperability through agreed standards.

Establishing an interoperable multi-application smart card environment across the Australian public sector requires agencies to support and commit to the following principles:

- interoperability
- open government system framework
- open standards
- choice and flexibility.

The framework will be part of the blueprint for connected government, discussed in section 3.2, and in more detail in Appendix A.

The states and territories will be consulted through the Cross Jurisdictional Chief Information Officers Committee of the Online and Communications Council to ensure smart card interoperability across all levels of government.

DEVELOP EXISTING INNOVATIVE INFRASTRUCTURE

The government will develop and extend its existing substantial investment in innovative technology and infrastructure that supports connected government. For example, FedLink is a system that allows for transactions to be conducted and information exchanged over the Internet in a way that is secure and protects privacy. The government is committed to enhancing this infrastructure through tools such as those that attach and recognise email security classifications.

ASSESS OTHER EMERGING INNOVATIVE TECHNOLOGY

The Australian Government will continue to monitor emerging technologies and their implementation within government, such as has already occurred with voice over internet protocol (VoIP) and natural speech recognition technology. The whole of government opportunities (and risks) these technologies present will be identified, and their potential will be harvested as they move into mainstream practice.

The principles that will underpin the government's approach to technology are:

- technology change will be incremental rather than revolutionary, yet the net effect of these increments will enable far-reaching changes for agencies

- information technology will become ubiquitous, with mobile connectivity widely available, and intelligence embedded in almost all objects
- as the information technology industry becomes increasingly standardised and new technologies become commodities, web services will be a common feature of all business systems, leading to them becoming interoperable
- consistent implementation of open standards by agencies will be essential to realise the potential of standardised and commoditised web services
- new technologies will need a level of demonstrated maturity for widespread adoption in government
- government will continually assess all emerging technologies for their potential whole of government application to electronic service delivery.

PARTNERING WITH INDUSTRY

The government will maintain an effective dialogue with industry. This will keep industry informed of progress towards the government's vision for 2010. Government will also draw on industry expertise through a series of regular industry forums, by including industry in public sector forums for departments and agencies, and through industry consultation on procurement plans outlined in section 3.4.3.

The government will explore with industry the potential for providing access to government's common, standardised, modular business processes (discussed in sections 3.2 and 3.3.3), so that industry can be better informed of emerging government system and technology requirements. Increasingly, industry will be able to meet the standardised business requirements of government in off-the-shelf product offerings.

The government will develop a set of model contracts to replace the existing Government Information Technology Contract (GITC) arrangements. These new model contracts will be developed to apply to a range of information technology procurement circumstances, and will be more targeted than the existing GITC arrangements. The government is also implementing new arrangements to cap liability in the majority of ICT contracts and to encourage commercial use and exploitation of intellectual property (IP) from government procurement.

MANAGING THE VISION

GOVERNANCE STRUCTURES

The government will maintain and strengthen its existing ICT governance structures, through which its agencies are able to collaborate in the implementation of this strategy, and participate in joint decision-making. AGIMO has overall coordination responsibility for the use of ICT within government. AGIMO reports to the Special Minister of State.

AGIMO is supported by, and supports, the Information Management Strategy Committee (IMSC), the Chief Information Officer Committee (CIOC), the Cross Jurisdictional Chief Information Officer Committee (CJCIOC), and the Online and Communications Council (OCC). These whole of government forums have been central to progress to date, and the government remains committed to them. They ensure that ICT-related decisions reflect the impact and benefits across government rather than just on individual agencies, and that there is collaboration with the states and territories on the implementation of this Australian Government strategy.

Figure 2: GOVERNANCE MODEL FOR GOVERNMENT ICT

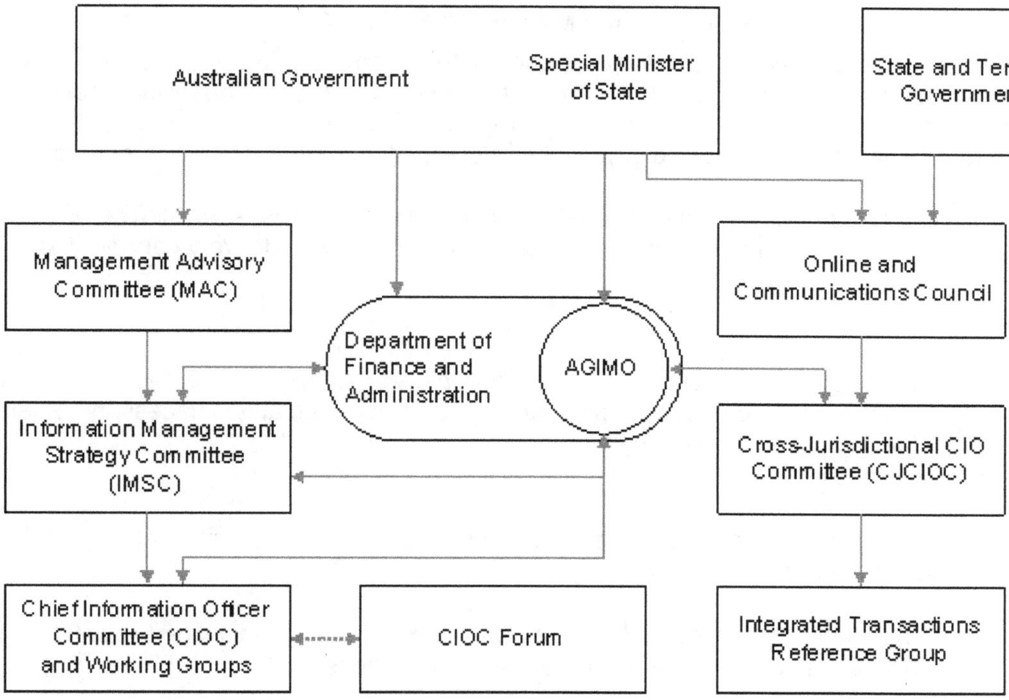

INTERNATIONAL CONTEXT

The government is committed to working collaboratively with other countries to share experiences in the design and implementation of electronic service delivery, both bilaterally and multilaterally. Australia is a strong supporter of the e-government project at the Organisation for Economic Cooperation and Development (OECD), and participates in a range of other relevant multilateral forums, including the Asia-Pacific Economic Cooperation (APEC). Australia also nurtures bilateral cooperation with comparable countries whose experiences most closely parallel our own.

MEASURING THE IMPACT

DEVELOP A SET OF SERVICE DELIVERY METRICS

In implementing its vision, the government will build on previous achievements in measuring and tracking progress.
The government will develop service delivery metrics based on the strategic priorities in this strategy, namely:

- user satisfaction levels
- the level of connected government
- value for money
- improvements in public sector capability.

The metrics will be designed to guide progress towards the vision, as well as function as a reporting and accountability tool.

A SERVICE ORIENTED ARCHITECTURE

CAPABILITY AND MATURITY STOCKTAKE

In parallel with the development of the cross-agency SOA, a comprehensive assessment of the government's service delivery capability and maturity will be undertaken. Capability is defined as 'the sum of all those things that enable an organisation to deliver services'. The capability stocktake will identify opportunities and gaps to be addressed as part of the implementation of the cross-agency SOA.

The stocktake will reflect the *Delivering Australian Government Services—Service Delivery Capability Model*, which lists the elements of the government's service delivery capability as:

- people
  - the organisation's people and their collective skills, experience, tacit knowledge, culture, attitudes, relationships, and needs and expectations necessary to deliver the organisation's services
- business processes
  - the documented practices and processes that underpin service delivery
- business continuity
  - the plans, processes and facilities which enable the organisation to continue to deliver its services, despite unforeseen disruptions
- facilities and equipment
  - the physical facilities and (non-ICT) equipment required to enable service delivery
- information and communication technologies
  - the systems for the communication, capture, classification, storage, management, retrieval and dissemination of knowledge
- knowledge and information management
  - knowledge and information relevant to the responsibilities of the organisation which is applied in delivering services
- accountability and governance
  - the framework to determine accountability and governance for all aspects of service delivery.

This model provides an agreed language to describe, build and improve all those things that enable an agency to deliver efficient and effective services. It will be applied across government to ensure online service delivery is enabled by the maturity of departments' and agencies' capabilities.

The capability inventory will be informed by assembling an inventory of Business Plans and ICT Strategic Plans for key service delivery departments and agencies.

PATHWAY PROJECTS

The government will use the cross-agency SOA and the capability stocktake to identify pathway projects. This project-based approach will be more flexible, less risky and will deliver tangible results sooner than attempting a complete 'design and build' approach for the whole of government.

Pathway projects will be selected to drive strategic investments which fill gaps identified by the capability and maturity model. They will provide a well defined route towards the model architecture, by using selected government services and agencies to develop, implement, test and broaden key parts of the cross-agency SOA.

As far as possible, existing services and facilities will be used as the basis of pathway projects. The projects highlighted under the list of possible components of the cross-agency SOA are therefore prime candidates for pathway projects. Other possible pathway projects include:

- a 'straight-through' service built around a set of related organisational or individual life events. Such a service would prove the concept and define the architecture for future like services
- a 'one-time update' service, in which a person would be able to change a piece of information common to multiple agencies. Change of address is often raised as a candidate, but this may have entitlement implications which would make it too complex for an initial pathway project
- a 'no wrong door' project where a service from one agency can be accessed in some way from one, some, or perhaps all, service delivery channels of several other agencies
- a 'data-vault' project, comprising a user-managed data-vault for personal information that the user can make available to specified agencies as the single source of update. Links with the Business Entry Point's Transaction Manager tool would need to be explored
- a 'generic web-service' project, which could be used by all agencies requiring that service. This could lead to the specification of standard web services as commodities and the building of a common architecture to enhance connectivity.

Each of these projects would be designed to be scaled up, in terms of adding more agencies and services, and interlinked at some stage of their development.

POLICY AND REGULATORY FRAMEWORKS FOR COMMUNICATIONS SERVICES[28]

Description

The Department assists the Government to develop and maintain policy and regulatory frameworks to support a competitive communications sector deliver innovative, diverse broadcasting and telecommunications services. Policy advice is also directed towards enabling all Australians to access a diverse range of communications services, and towards providing adequate consumer safeguards.

The Department deals with intellectual property issues related to the communications sector, to achieve an appropriate balance between ownership and access. Many issues arise from the development of digital technologies and new opportunities provided by the Internet for creating, exploiting and accessing copyright material.

Summary of major activities, significant issues and developments for Output 2.1

- The Department worked on the Broadcasting Services Amendment (Digital Television and Datacasting) Bill 2000 and the Datacasting Charge (Imposition) Amendment Bill 2000. Both were passed by the Parliament by June 2000, as scheduled.

[28] Department of Communications, Information Technology and the Arts Report

- The Department assisted the Government to finalise an assistance package of up to $260 million over 13 years under the Regional Equalisation Plan, designed to assist regional commercial television broadcasters introduce digital television.
- Amendments were made to the *Broadcasting Services Act 1992* (BSA) including an anti-hoarding regime for certain television broadcasting rights; out-of-area reception of satellite commercial broadcasting services; increased sponsorship limits for community broadcasters and measures to enforce Australian drama expenditure requirements on subscription television. Amendments to the BSA were also introduced to ensure that national interest considerations are taken into account in licensing international broadcasting services.
- The ABC and SBS were assisted in seeking Government funding for capital, distribution and transmission costs associated with the introduction of digital television.
- A review of the telecommunications Universal Service Obligation was completed.
- The Telecommunications (Consumer Protection and Service Standards) Amendment Bill (No.2) 2000 (the Bill), which provides for the replacement of Part 2 of the *Telecommunications (Consumer Protection and Service Standards) Act 1999*, was introduced and is awaiting debate. Part 2 establishes the universal service regime for telecommunications. The Bill builds on recent amendments made to Part 2 by the *Telecommunications (Consumer Protection and Service Standards) Amendment Act (No. 1) 2000*, which was passed.
- Policy advice was provided on the Telstra 2 sale process.
- Legislative amendments were introduced into Parliament to encourage increased competition in the postal sector.
- Policy advice was provided on radiofrequency spectrum licence auctions.
- The Department prepared a price control determination capping Telstra□s standard untimed local call price at 22 cents, including GST.
- On 19 March 2000, the Minister for Communications, Information Technology and the Arts established the independent Telecommunications Service Inquiry to report on the adequacy of service levels across Australia. The Department is providing secretariat support to the Inquiry, which is expected to report by 30 September 2000.
- The Copyright Amendment (Digital Agenda) Bill 1999, which was passed by the House of Representatives in June 2000, updates the Copyright Act for the digital environment and other new communications technologies. As far as possible, the new framework will replicate the balance struck in the print environment between the rights of copyright owners and copyright users.
- The Senate Legal and Constitutional Legislation Committee recommended in August 1999 that the Copyright Amendment (Importation of Sound Recordings) Bill 1999 should be passed without amendment; it is now awaiting Parliamentary debate. The Bill proposes an extension of existing parallel importation provisions for sound recordings to include CDs which contain video and/or software enhancements.
- The *Copyright Amendment (Computer Programs) Act 1999*, which received assent in August 1999, creates an exception to copyright infringement by allowing software engineers to decompile computer hardware and software and make back-up copies in limited circumstances so they can make interoperable software, correct errors, and test the security of information systems.
- *The Digital Environment* CD-ROM, produced through the New Technologies Working Party, was completed and distributed nationally.
- The Department convened Round Table discussions on statutory deposit of electronic material with Government agencies, copyright collecting societies and publishers.

Performance information: Output 2.1

Ministerial satisfaction with quality and timeliness of advice and draft legislation.
The Minister for Communications, Information Technology and the Arts has expressed satisfaction with the timeliness and quality of advice and draft legislation on the broadcasting and telecommunications regulatory frameworks.

Successful introduction of digital television by January 2001.
The *Broadcasting Services Amendment (Digital Television and Datacasting) Act 2000* and the *Datacasting Charge (Imposition) Amendment Act 2000* were passed by the Parliament on 30 June 2000. This legislation puts in place the framework for introducing digital television and datacasting in Australia from 1 January 2001.
The Government agreed to provide funding to the national broadcasters for the actual costs associated with digital transmission and distribution, as well as matching expenditure by the ABC on digital television capital equipment, and funding in full the remaining costs to SBS of digital television capital equipment. The funding commitment provided was consistent with the national broadcasters□ requirement to commence digital transmission by January 2001.
Improved access to communication services in regional Australia.
Broadcasting
A significant amount of work completed during the year was aimed at improving television broadcasting services, particularly for viewers in regional Australia. This work included legislative measures to:

- encourage additional commercial television services in under served regional markets with a total population of more than 1.8 million;
- allow the Australian Broadcasting Authority (ABA) to approve out-of-area direct-to-home reception of satellite commercial broadcasting services, to overcome areas of poor terrestrial reception. This offers improved television reception in regional Australia. To June 2000, some 300 applications had been approved by the ABA; and
- require pay TV operators to obtain ABA approval of any proposals to include significant □look alike□ metropolitan prime time programming on their services.

In addition, funding to be provided under the Regional Equalisation Plan□agreed to by the Government in the 2000□01 Budget□will assist the roll-out of digital television and datacasting services to viewers in regional and remote Australia.
The *Broadcasting Services Amendment (Digital Television and Datacasting) Act 2000* puts in place a framework for the development of new datacasting services in regional Australia, providing a wide range of information, education, transactional and other services.
A total of 35 additional community radio licences were granted by the ABA during the reporting period, all in regional and remote areas.
Access to television services for communities in rural and regional Australia will also be improved through schemes under the Television Fund to offer television retransmission equipment subsidies, and subsidised access to National Transmission Network sites for the □Self-Help□ retransmission of commercial, ABC and SBS television services. In addition, SBS extensions will reach over 1.2 million people in regional Australia.
Telecommunications
Improvements to the Customer Service Guarantee (CSG) will decrease the amount of time allowed for telecommunications service providers to repair faults and provide new connections, before penalties are imposed.

Price control arrangements have contributed to the Government□s policy of promoting equitable pricing of basic telecommunications services, especially to low bill users, and users in rural areas where competition is less established than in metropolitan areas.

The Department□s website is being redeveloped to ensure that information relevant to regional, rural and remote telecommunications users is easily accessed and useful.

In considering spectrum matters, the Department ensured that the potential impact on regional areas was explicitly addressed, in particular the impact on existing services. In terms of what competition limits, if any, might be imposed in a particular spectrum auction, the Government endeavoured to enhance competition, in particular facilitating the entry of new competitors in regional and metropolitan markets.
In conjunction with legislative amendments, the continuation and improvement of the Universal Service Obligation (USO) contributes to ensuring equitable access to telecommunication services.

The rollout, implementation and enhancement of the Digital Data Service Obligation was undertaken to ensure equitable access to high-speed data services.

Improvements in price, quality, type and spread of communication services.
In accordance with the Government□s commitment to improvements in the telecommunications regulatory framework, the Department facilitated:

- the introduction of postal reform legislation into Parliament in April 2000, to promote opportunities for competition in the postal services market, with the objective of improving the quality and range of services to customers;
- legislation to meet the Government□s scheduled date of 18 October 1999 for issuing the second tranche of Telstra shares, and developing accompanying changes to the telecommunications regulatory framework;
- the Telecommunications (Low-impact Facilities) Determination 1997 Amendment No. 1 of 1999, which was issued in August 1999 to clarify the operation of a number of the provisions of the determination;
- the *Telecommunications (Consumer Protection and Service Standards) Amendment Act 2000* to include provisions that streamlined the carrier levy payment schedule/arrangements;
- a new Part 9A into the *Telecommunications (Consumer Protection and Service Standards) Act 1999* to regulate telephone sex services;
- the Telstra Carrier Charges□Price Control Arrangements, Notification and Disallowance Determination, which came into effect on 28 June 2000, to implement the Government□s commitment that Telstra□s standard price for untimed local calls would not rise with the GST and that Telstra would not recoup the cost through other price changes; and
- the Customer Service Guarantee (CSG) Direction No. 1 of 1999, which required the Australian Communications Authority (ACA) to develop a new CSG standard. The standard will come into effect in early July 2000, and will build on and strengthen the one that operated from 1 January 1998. The new standard decreases the amount of time telecommunications service providers are allowed to take to repair faults and provide new connections. It provides better scrutiny of claims made by telephone companies that they are exempt from the CSG, and also removes the option of all-day appointments. The new standard is intended to lead to improved quality of services to consumers.

Policy advice on the price-based allocation of spectrum was developed to encourage competition in telecommunications services and to improve the availability, quality and range of services. The auction of 1.8 GHz spectrum, conducted by the ACA, raised $1.327 billion, creating the environment for increased competition in the mobile phone market.
The Department:

- maintained an active interest in electromagnetic energy (EME) emission issues after responsibility for these matters was transferred in 1998 to the Australian Radiation Protection and Nuclear Safety Agency (ARPANSA) in the Health Portfolio;
- monitored the transition from the AMPS analog mobile phone network to Telstra□s CDMA digital network, which is expected to provide coverage to an estimated 500 000 additional Australians who could not access AMPS; and
- developed a proposal for the Online Council of Commonwealth and State Ministers to prepare case studies on innovative market models for the delivery of enhanced telecommunications services to regional, rural and remote Australia. The case studies will be published in various formats and included in a tool kit for groups interested in undertaking similar telecommunications enhancement initiatives in their region.

***Policy advice and review of Government reforms through the* Copyright Act 1968.**
The Department provided policy advice and facilitated Government copyright reforms in the following areas:

- the Copyright Amendment (Digital Agenda) Bill 1999 was introduced into the House of Representatives in September 1999, referred to the Standing Committee on Legal and Constitutional Affairs and then returned to the House of Representatives for debate. The Department prepared briefings for introduction and debate in the Senate and consideration by the Senate Committee;
- a draft Cabinet Submission and briefings were provided on parallel importation of computer software products, and parallel importation of books (with the Attorney-General□s Department);
- briefings were provided to the Minister for Communications, Information Technology and the Arts and the Senate Committee considering the extension of existing parallel importation provisions for □enhanced□ CDs, under the Copyright Amendment (Importation of Sound Recordings) Bill 1999;
- the *Copyright Amendment (Computer Programs) Act 1999*, addressing Year 2000 issues and reproduction for study, back-up, interoperability, error correction and security testing was passed as non-controversial legislation through both Houses of Parliament with Ministerial briefing on progress at all stages. The legislation has attracted considerable support from Parliament, industry bodies and the community;
- the Department chaired and provided the secretariat for the New Technologies Working Party (NTWP), which completed and distributed the CD-ROM *The Digital Environment*. Ministers were briefed on progress and issues. The NTWP also held discussions and reported to the Cultural Ministers Council and its Standing Committee;
- submissions were provided to:
- the Intellectual Property and Competition Review Committee;
- the House of Representatives Standing Committee Inquiry into Copyright Enforcement;
- the Copyright Law Review Committee Inquiry into the Jurisdiction and Procedures of the Copyright Tribunal; and
- a Government response was developed, with the Attorney-General□s Department, to the report of the House of Representatives Standing Committee on Legal and Constitutional Affairs *Don□t Stop the Music!* and to the *Review of Australian Copyright Collecting Societies* by consultant, Shane Simpson.

In accordance with* the Broadcasting Services Act 1992*, completion by 1 January 2000 of statutory reviews into regulation of digital television broadcasting and the regional equalisation plan for facilitating introduction of digital television services in regional areas.

Reviews required by the *Broadcasting Services Act 1992* were finalised and tabled in Parliament in May 2000. The reviews examined whether amendments should be made to laws of the Commonwealth in relation to:

- convergence between broadcasting services and other services;
- retransmission of commercial digital free-to-air television services on pay TV;
- ways to ensure that under served regional licence areas are provided with up to the same number of commercial television services as metropolitan areas;
- national and commercial broadcasters providing enhanced programs;
- multichannelling by the ABC and SBS in relation to certain types of programs;
- the scope of datacasting services; and
- standards relating to HDTV and captioning.

All but one of the reports of the statutory reviews required under s. 59 of Schedule 4 of the *Broadcasting Services Act 1992* have been tabled.

The remaining report concerns the regulatory arrangements that should apply to allocation of broadcasting spectrum for datacasting services and community television. The Minister for Communications, Information Technology and the Arts will finalise the review and table the report in Parliament when the ABA□s digital channel plans have progressed further, and the quantum of spectrum available for datacasting is clearer.

Extensive analysis and advice was provided in the development of options for the Government on assistance under the Regional Equalisation Plan. Outcomes were announced in the 2000□01 Budget.

Development of amendments to the* Broadcasting Services Act 1992 *and associated legislation in relation to the outcome of the digital television statutory review.
The Broadcasting Services Amendment (Digital Television and Datacasting) Bill 2000 and the Datacasting Charge (Imposition) Amendment Bill 2000 were introduced into the Parliament in May 2000, reflecting policy decisions taken by the Government in response to the statutory reviews on digital television and datacasting. The Bills were examined by the Senate Committee on Environment, Communications Information Technology and the Arts, and debated and amended in the Senate in late June 2000. They were passed by the House of Representatives on 30 June 2000.

Policy advice on digital television reviews; digital television planning and implementation; introduction of radio services; access to broadcasting services; digitisation of national broadcasters; digital transmission of national television and digital industry development; and regulation of content.
The Department provided policy advice on television and radio broadcasting issues including:

- the anti-hoarding regime, out of area direct-to-home access to satellite commercial television services in black spot reception areas, and protection of regional free-to-air services from □look alike□ metropolitan networks programming on regional pay TV services;
- imposition of a three-year surcharge on licence fees paid by commercial television broadcasters to assist the costs of digital television spectrum planning;
- formulation of the *Regional Equalisation Plan*, specifying Commonwealth support measures to assist regional commercial television broadcasters with their conversion to digital broadcasting;

- issues relating to high-power open narrowcasters and the apparent hoarding of low-power open narrowcasting services;
- ABA licence area plans for metropolitan radio services including the draft and final plans for Sydney and Melbourne and the draft plan for Brisbane; and
- work and conclusions of the Digital Radio Planning and Steering Committee and its Technical Working Group.

Frequency and timing of meetings relating to policy development and implementation.
Amendments to the *Broadcasting Services Act 1992* were developed with extensive and regular industry consultation, including consultations on specific issues and inviting industry comment on draft legislative amendments.

The Digital Radio Planning and Steering Committee, the main consultative forum for implementing digital radio, met twice during 1999□2000. Its sub-committee□the Technical Working Group, which was formed to advance technical planning for digital radio services□and a committee subgroup on multiplex issues, each met once.

The Department assisted the Government with extensive consultation during reviews associated with the development of the digital television legislation and in relation to the legislation itself. This consultation involved issuing discussion and options papers, and consideration and discussion of stakeholder input, on the issues raised in these papers.
In the telecommunications area, the Department:

- chaired the Online Council Regional Communications Working Group, comprising Commonwealth and State representatives working together to communicate Government initiatives concerning regional telecommunications;
- consulted with industry and the public on reforms to the universal service regime;
- participated in the Regional Summit held in October 1999 and provided resources to the secretariat for progressing Summit outcomes;
- attended the Universal Postal Union (UPU) Congress in Beijing;
- attended the UPU Council of Administration High Level Group in Berne;
- attended meetings to progress the reform of INTELSAT in Penang in October 1999 and in Kuala Lumpur in June 2000;
- consulted with industry, Australia Post and relevant Government agencies while developing the Postal Services Legislation Amendment Bill;
- liaised with the ACA about implementing Mobile Number Portability, Local Number Portability and Local Rate and Freephone Number Portability;
- monitored and reported on industry preparedness for the transition to the Year 2000;
- participated in the Law Enforcement Advisory Committee meetings;
- consulted with the education sector to review Australian Vice Chancellors□ Committee (AVCC) exemption from carrier licence obligations;
- liaised with Treasury about establishing terms of reference of the 12 month-long review of Part XIB of the *Trade Practices Act 1997* to be conducted by the Productivity Commission;
- liaised with the ACA and the Australian Competition and Consumer Commission (ACCC) to provide advice on the 2000□01 program of spectrum auctions;
- organised a public Regional Communications Forum in November 1999;
- met with Telstra to discuss regulatory and shareholder issues;
- consulted with regulatory agencies and stakeholders about the implementation of the new legislative controls on telephone sex services;
- undertook ongoing liaison with industry representatives to ensure the Department was fully aware of new products, services and strategies;

- consulted with State and Territory Governments, and invited industry and public comment on the proposed approach for the tender to provide untimed local calls, and untimed Internet access in remote Australia; and
- participated on an inter-departmental committee, chaired by ARPANSA, in relation to potential health effects from electromagnetic emissions.

The Department will make submissions to relevant reviews by other agencies or Parliamentary committees.
The Department provided a submission to the Racing Radio Inquiry□conducted by the House of Representatives Communications, Transport and the Arts Committee□into the ABC□s decision to discontinue racing radio services in regional Australia in August 1999. The Department has also provided additional information to the committee on request.

The Department appeared before the Senate Committee on Environment, Communications Information Technology and the Arts about its review of the Broadcasting Services Amendment (Digital Television and Datacasting) Bill 2000, and the Datacasting Charge (Imposition) Amendment Bill 2000.

The Postal Services Legislation Amendment Bill was introduced into Parliament in April 2000 and referred to the Senate Environment, Communications, Information Technology and the Arts Legislation Committee. The Department prepared a submission and appeared before the committee.

A submission was made to the Joint Committee on Public Accounts and Audit inquiry into Corporate Governance and Accountability Arrangements for Government Business Enterprises. Submissions and responses to parliamentary inquiries, Senate committees and others also included:

- Jobs for the Regions;
- Pregnant and Productive;
- Time Running Out;
- Islands to Islands;
- Regional Australia Forum;
- USO Amendment Bill; and
- Digital Data Service Obligation amendments.

Establish review into the telecommunications competition regime under the* Trade Practices Act 1974 *in 2000.

In June 2000, the Government announced the terms of reference for a 12-month Productivity Commission Review of Part XIB of the *Trade Practices Act 1974* (TPA) that deals with anti-competitive conduct within the telecommunications industry. The review will examine interconnection and access issues (Part XIC TPA). It will also assist in determining whether the telecommunications regulatory regime is effective and if the benefits of competition regulation are being delivered to customers.

Completion of the review into telecommunications Universal Service Obligation (USO) funding arrangements to enable any new legislation provisions to take effect from 1 July 2000.
A review of the USO arrangements was completed during the year, and Government decisions in response to the Department□s report were announced on 23 March 2000. Legislative amendments to implement initial priority actions were drafted and passed by Parliament in the

first half of 2000. A second Bill containing further comprehensive amendments to implement the new USO regime was introduced in June 2000. As an outcome of the review, new Telstra Net Universal Service Costs (NUSC) were determined for 1998□99, 1999□2000 in March 2000.

Implementation of the Government's response to Telecommunications Interception Review Recommendations by 1 January 2000.

In conjunction with the Attorney-General□s Department, the Department provided advice on a possible Government response to the *Telecommunications Interception Review* by the ACA. The Government is expected to consider its response to the review in 2000□01.

Advice on the development and implementation of policies for the competitive selection of telecommunications universal service providers.

In response to policy proposals developed by the Department during 1999□2000, the Government took a number of decisions about the future of the USO arrangements. For example, the Government agreed to trial the introduction of competition in providing universal services, and committed to seek tenders for the provision of universal service and untimed local calls in Telstra□s Extended Zones. These decisions were announced on 23 March 2000. Legislative amendments to implement the decisions were passed with other changes to USO funding arrangements. A discussion paper on the selection of areas for the first USO pilots was released in May 2000.

Implementation of the Government□s policies on reform of the postal industry following the National Competition Commission (NCC) report, through legislation to take effect from 1 July 2000.

The Postal Services Legislation Amendment Bill, introduced into Parliament in April 2000, implements a number of decisions made by the Government in response to the NCC report.

Implementation of the Government□s response to the review of the* Radiocommunications Act 1992 *with any legislative changes to take effect from 1 July 2000.

The review required an evaluation of the appropriateness, effectiveness and efficiency of the present legislative framework for using the radiofrequency spectrum. It took account of comments received on a public discussion paper and had particular regard for the needs of small business, community groups and individual users. A draft report has been prepared for consideration by the Minister for Communications, Information Technology and the Arts.

Advice on telecommunications consumer and competition policy, telecommunications industry development, communications infrastructure and services, radiocommunications licensing and spectrum management, satellites, postal policy, and Government Business Enterprise (GBE) governance.

The Department provided advice to the Minister on a wide range of Government Business Enterprise governance issues.

On the Telstra 2 (T2) sale, the Department provided input and comment during the drafting of the Australian and United States offer documents, fulfilled its due diligence obligations, and provided regular input to the T2 Due Diligence Committee on matters leading up to the sale. The Minister was briefed on matters debated during the sale process and other sale-related issues affecting the policy responsibilities of the Portfolio.
Advice was provided on:

- the framework for spectrum auctions (1.8GHz, 3.4GHz and 27GHz);
- the Federal Court challenge in regard to the validity of ACCC Declarations;

- the ACCC declarations made under Part XIC of the *Trade Practices Act 1974*; and
- the ACA□s quarterly reports on carrier quality of service, suggesting ways of improving performance.

The Department examined a series of telecommunications specific foreign investment proposals. Part 5, Schedule 1, of the *Telecommunications Act 1997* was reviewed. The Department provided advice in relation to the interaction between the privacy aspects of *the Telecommunications Act 1997* and the Government□s new Privacy Act Amendment Bill.

The Government appointed members of the Telecommunications Service Inquiry□Mr Tim Besley AO, Mr Ray Braithwaite and Ms Jane Bennett.

The Inquiry secretariat, drawn primarily from the Department, with additional staff provided by the Department of Transport and Regional Services and the ACA, analysed telecommunications service levels, new infrastructure developments, new technologies, competition developments, Networking the Nation and social bonus funding, and new market models, including analysing submissions to the Inquiry. It also established and administered three consultancy studies.

The secretariat arranged briefing from key stakeholders; arranged advertising of the Inquiry and invitations for submissions; arranged round table consultations with submitters to the Inquiry in all States and Territories (by 30 June consultations had been held in Perth, Brisbane, Sydney and Melbourne, and about ten regional centres, particularly in Western Australia and Queensland); and arranged visits to remote communities and State-wide videoconferences.

OUTPUT 2.2GOVERNMENT INITIATIVES WHICH SUPPORT THE DEVELOPMENT OF INNOVATIVE INFORMATION INDUSTRIES.

Description

The Department develops policies and administers programs which foster world competitive information industries. It provides assistance and advice to encourage innovation and growth among Australian enterprises, particularly small to medium firms. The Department also encourages international investment in Australia□s information technology and telecommunications (IT&T) industry.

The Department deals with intellectual property issues related to the evolving information economy, with the objective of achieving an appropriate balance between ownership and access. Other issues relate to the management of intellectual property in the public and private sectors.

Summary of major activities, significant issues and developments for Output 2.2

- The Department provided input to the development of a business taxation environment that supports innovation and entrepreneurship, and to improved IT&T trade and investment measures, including developing and implementing the Information Industries Investment Strategy.
- Programs were developed to assist commercialisation of IT&T-related research and development, for example, the Building on IT Strengths (BITS) program and the Software Engineering Quality Centres program, which encourages innovation and technology diffusion in the IT&T sector.
- The Department managed programs to increase the level of investment and activity in the Australian IT&T industry, through leverage from Commonwealth purchasing and outsourcing and through industry development commitments made by telecommunications carriers.
- Management guidelines for intellectual property associated with Government information technology contracts were produced and circulated across Government and industry.

Performance information: Output 2.2

Ministerial satisfaction with quality and timeliness of advice.
The Minister for Communications, Information Technology and the Arts has expressed satisfaction with the timeliness and quality of advice on program design and implementation.

View of key stakeholders, including other government agencies and industry associations.
Industry has provided positive feedback on the administration of the Partnerships for Development program and the development and implementation of the BITS incubator program.
***Policy advice and review of Government reforms through the* Copyright Act 1968.**
Intellectual Property in Information Technology Guidelines
The Department commissioned the Australian Government Solicitor to produce draft management guidelines for intellectual property associated with Government information technology contracts. A draft document, *Commercialisation of Commonwealth Intellectual Property in the field of Information Technology*, was circulated widely and workshops convened to progress consultation with Government agencies and peak information industry representatives. The Guidelines are intended to facilitate and encourage the commercial development of intellectual property (IP) in Commonwealth owned information technology contracts and have been favourably received by Government agencies and peak information industry bodies.
The Department provided policy advice and facilitated Government copyright reforms on a range of further issues reported under Output 2.1.

The Department will make submissions or respond to relevant reviews or Parliamentary Committees.
The Department provided submissions to the:

- House of Representatives Standing Committee on Legal and Constitutional Affairs Inquiry into Copyright Enforcement; and
- Intellectual Property and Competition Review Committee.

The Department responded to the Copyright Law Review Committee Inquiry into the Jurisdiction and Procedures of the Copyright Tribunal.
Ministerial briefings on the intellectual property-related outcomes of the National Innovation Summit were provided, and the Department is monitoring arising opportunities.

Advice on information industries development in areas including investment attraction, new business formation, exports and trade, emerging opportunities (both technological and business), technology diffusion and innovation.
Business environment

The Department was closely involved in examining options for consideration by Government, as part of the Ralph Review of Business Taxation. The Department examined:

- the way in which the Capital Gains Tax (CGT) regime affects entrepreneurship;
- the willingness of foreign pension funds to invest in Australian venture capital funds;
- the incentives for superannuation funds to invest in Australian venture capital funds;
- the availability of CGT rollover relief for script to script takeover transactions; and
- the competitiveness of Australian taxation provisions for employee share ownership and option schemes.

Trade and Investment Facilitation

The Department has collaborated extensively with Invest Australia and Austrade in developing an *Information Industries Investment Strategy*. Under this strategy a more proactive approach is being taken to promote Australia as an IT&T location and to develop specific investment opportunities. In particular, substantial work is being done to better identify targets for investment attraction.

During 1999-2000, the Department also:

- supported various inwards/outwards trade and investment missions and major conferences. These included the Austrade Silicon Valley e-business Mission and the Asian-Oceanian Computing Industry Organisation□s General Assembly and Symposium 1999 (ASOCIO□99), held in Canberra. ASOCIO□99 was a major international industry event, which was used to promote Australian IT&T industry capability to high profile international delegates;
- established a State/Territory/Commonwealth IT&T Industry Development Forum with the first meeting scheduled in early 2000□01; and
- prepared awareness-raising material, for example a brochure promoting Australia as an IT&T investment location.

Advice to the Office of Asset Sales and Information Technology Outsourcing (OASITO) on the industry development aspects of the selection process for group tenders.

Under the Government□s IT outsourcing process, tenderers are required to offer contractually binding commitments to industry development. OASITO and the Department jointly evaluate tenderers□ industry development bids. The Department is also responsible for monitoring tenderers□ compliance with those commitments.

In 1999□2000, two IT outsourcing contracts were finalised, one with IBM GSA for the Health Group (Department of Health and Aged Care, Health Insurance Commission, and Medibank Private Limited), the other with Ipex ITG, an Australian SME, in relation to the □Group eight□ agencies.

The following table outlines the industry development commitments made under the two new IT outsourcing contracts finalised in 1999-00:

Item	**Total commitment**
Payments to small□medium enterprises	$174.85 million
Australian value add	$365.09 million
Strategic investment	$12.59 million
Export revenue	$140.5 million
Regional employment	174

Across the entire initiative, IT outsourcing contracts finalised to date include commitments of about $280 million dollars of exports or import replacements and approximately 390 new jobs in regional Australia. The contracts ensure that about 30 per cent of the total work is done by Australian SMEs, and that the goods and services to be provided under the contracts will be of approximately 75 per cent Australian Value Added content. The total figures for industry development commitments are projections over the five years of the contract and are subject to change as the scope of the contract varies.

Implementation of Building on IT Strengths program (BITS) and support provided for incubator centres, network testbeds and Tasmanian IT industry development.

BITS aims to build the strength and competitiveness of the Australian information industries sector, including fostering much stronger commercialisation links with R&D organisations and the creation of clusters of innovative IT&T businesses.

BITS incubator program

Program guidelines were released on 29 November 1999, and 47 applications were received by the closing date of 20 January 2000. On 10 April 2000, the Minister for Communications, Information Technology and the Arts announced nine applicants to whom a total of $171 million in funding would be offered subject to negotiation of an acceptable grant deeds. In addition, $5 million funding was set aside for the Northern Territory pending further development of the preferred applicant□s proposal. To date, eight of the incubator centres have signed grant deeds and received an initial payment.

BITS Advanced Networks Element

The Department commissioned a consultancy in October 1999 to assist the Department on the direction of the Australian Advanced Communications Infrastructure Development initiative and examine issues associated with advanced networks. This involved a wide-ranging consultation process with stakeholders, including telecommunications carriers, research organisations, multinational network equipment suppliers, industry associations and State and Territory Governments.

The Department finalised the design of the program on the basis of key issues raised during consultations with key stakeholders and examination of overseas initiatives. The program is expected to be launched in July 2000.

Tasmania

The Intelligent Island (II) Memorandum of Understanding between the Commonwealth and Tasmanian Governments, in relation to the $40 million allocated to II under the BITS program, was signed on 1 March 2000. A Strategic Plan has been developed that identifies key strategies and directions for the program, as well as major elements to be funded. The Commonwealth and Tasmanian Governments approved the Strategic Plan in late June 2000.

In addition, the Launceston Broadband Project (LBP) is underway. The Commonwealth is providing $15 million for this project, which is designed to introduce the Launceston community to new online applications through limited market trials and early deployment of new products. The LBP Grant Deed was signed between the Department and Telstra on 14 June 2000 and the initial Commonwealth payment has been made.

Finalisation of agreement on Commonwealth Technology Port and level of funding provided.

The Federation Fund Grant Deed between the Department and the Docklands Authority, for the development of the Commonwealth Technology Port in Melbourne, was signed on 10 May 2000. The first payment of $3 million has been made. The Docklands Authority has finalised and released bid proposal documentation to the short-listed parties and completed the majority of trunk infrastructure works to the Comtechport precinct.

Funding support provided under the continuing technology and innovations programs, i.e. software quality, and testing and conformance.

Software Engineering Quality Centres (SEQC) program

The objective of the program is to diffuse improved software development processes to the Australian software development industry, through activities undertaken by Software Engineering Australia (SEA). It supports the operations of SEA, by providing a grant-in-aid to SEA (National), which provides services in each State and the ACT.

Funding of around $11 million has already been provided to SEA, under both the SEQC program, and earlier under the Technology Support Centres program. A further $14 million has been committed to 30 June 2003 to enable SEA to improve the quality and technological sophistication of software development and acquisition in Australia.

Testing and Conformance Infrastructure program

The program was established to provide grants to develop testing, trialing and demonstration facilities to improve the competitiveness of the information and communication industries and their capacity to export.

Four projects were funded in the first grant round, totalling $228 000. Two of these were for a study on the current capabilities and future testing requirements of the electronics and software industries. Others were to establish a facility to provide international traceability for measurements of low frequency electromagnetic signals by test equipment and to evaluate the feasibility of establishing a Smart Card Certification Facility in Australia. An additional $239 500 was provided to two more projects in the second round, which closed on 20 March 2000. The two most recent grants funded a healthcare-messaging laboratory centred at the University of Ballarat and a broadband telecommunications test and measurement facility in Melbourne.

High Performance Computing and Communications Technology Diffusion Centres program

The Technology Support Centres program provided almost $3 million to establish two centres to encourage the transfer of high performance computing technologies from the academic/research environment into Australian industry.

Centres were developed at the Brisbane Technology Park and at the Australian Technology Park in Sydney. The two centres have conducted numerous awareness seminars and short courses in high performance computing applications. Between them, the two centres were involved in 71 collaborative projects that gave 69 different companies a hands-on introduction to high performance computing.

Level of industry development commitments made under the Partnership for Development program, Endorsed Supplier Arrangement, major Government purchases over $10 million, and IT outsourcing.

Under the Partnerships for Development (PfD) program, IT&T companies that wish to sell IT equipment and services to the Government are required to develop a business plan outlining their industry development activities, sales to the Australian Government and their global strategies.

The PfD program continued to play a major role in developing Australian IT&T industries, with more than $16 billion of industry development activity (including more than $3.3 billion in R&D, around $12 billion in direct and facilitated exports and approximately $1 billion in strategic investment) reported since the program began in 1987. The program also continued to facilitate a two-way exchange between PfD companies and Federal, State and Territory government officials as well as helping to build strategic alliances between Australian SMEs and the partner companies.

During the year one company was deemed non-compliant (Simoco Pacific) and three voluntarily exited the program (Annabelle Bits, Attachment Australia and Fulcrum Technologies). As a result of company mergers, the PfD Agreements of six partner companies were taken over by other partners (Data General Australia, Memorex Telex, Newbridge Networks, Sequent Computer Systems, Sterling Software and Tektronix Australia).

On 30 September 1999, the Minister announced enhancements to the PfD program designed to streamline its operations and absorb the former Fixed Term Arrangements scheme. At 30 June 2000, there were some 80 companies in the program.

The following significant industry development commitments arose from the two IT Outsourcing contracts finalised during the 1999□2000 financial year:

- $356 million of products and services will be sourced and developed within Australia;
- $170 million of work will flow to small and medium enterprises;
- 300 new jobs will be generated out of new business initiatives□of these, 174 will be located in regional Australia;
- $137 million in exports; and
- $8 million in strategic investments.

***Level of industry development activity by carriers licensed under the* Telecommunications Act 1997.**
Each telecommunications carrier is required to have a current industry development plan (IDP) approved by the Minister for Communications, Information Technology and the Arts.
The carriers foreshadowed total investment of more than $16 billion during the life of their IDPs.
At 30 June 2000, there were 45 licensed telecommunications carriers operating networks and providing services to each of the major capital cities and many regional centres in Australia.
Carrier outcomes reported for 1998□99 (the last reporting year) included:

- $6 billion of capital investment□this brings the total since IDPs commenced on 1 July 1997 to $11.1 billion;
- $430 million in research and development□this amount included Telstra□s record R&D spending of $337 million, with particular focus on Internet and the data environment, broadband services, mobility services and systems and personalised services. Total R&D expenditure since 1 July 1997 is $790 million with carriers undertaking R&D projects in Internet and e-commerce applications; broadband services; billing systems; switch management software; and GSM and CDMA network systems;
- $200 million in exports□mostly undertaken by the carrier□s strategic partners as a result of their relationship with the carriers. Export in the past two years have totalled $830 million, and several carriers are developing substantial international and export sales strategies which are planned to come to fruition over the next few years; and
- $210 million in training expenditure□total direct employment by the carriers at June 1999 was 64 000, and at least another 5 000 positions were maintained within supplier companies specifically to meet carrier requirements.

Finalisation of Telecommunications Carrier Industry Development Plans (IDPs) for companies wishing to participate in the Australian carrier market.
The Minister approved 24 new carrier IDPs in 1999□2000.

OUTPUT 2.3PROGRAMS WHICH PROMOTE ACCESS TO COMMUNICATIONS SERVICES.

Description
Departmental programs aim to increase access to, and promote use of, communications services by people in regional, rural and remote areas of Australia. Through their demand-driven, community-based approach, they support new and enhanced services, at the same time as encouraging competitive commercial supply wherever feasible. This has been enhanced through funding from the further sale of Telstra for social bonus programs ($670 million over five years), including the $120 million Television Fund.
Summary of major activities, significant issues and developments for Output 2.3

- The $120-million Television Fund was implemented, comprising the Television Black Spots program ($35 million); Second Remote Commercial Subsidy ($5 million); Regional Communications Partnership ($5 million); SBS New Media Unit ($2 million); and SBS extensions ($70 million) and program administration costs ($3 million).
- The Government fulfilled its pre-election commitments to community broadcasting, providing increased indexed funding to the sector of $1.5 million per year for three years from 1996□97. This funding has been extended for a further three years.
- The Networking the Nation program enhanced telecommunications in regional, rural and remote Australia by funding improvements to the type, quality and price of telecommunication services.
- The Department progressed the implementation of social bonus programs including untimed local call access to the extended zone of remote Australia ($150 million), Internet points of presence ($36 million), Isolated Islands program ($20 million), Building

Additional Rural Networks (BARN) ($70 million), the Local Government Fund ($45 million), extended mobile phones ($3 million), mobile phones on highways ($25 million), and connecting Tasmanian schools ($15 million).

- The Department established an internal coordination briefing system for these and other social bonus programs managed in several different areas.
- Work continued towards helping people with disabilities gain effective access to online information services.
- *Networking the Nation Online* was implemented to provide online access for applicants.
- The Department provided advice on financial grants to consumer bodies for research into telecommunication issues.

Performance information: Output 2.3

Programs deliver improved communications services in regional Australia.

All elements of the Television Fund are designed to improve access to television services in Australia by providing fully-funded services (SBS television extensions); assistance for communities to establish self-help retransmission services (television Black Spots program, second remote commercial television subsidy and the Regional Communications Partnership self-help subsidy scheme); and through assistance to enhance the range of text and audio programs available online (SBS New Media Unit).

Commercial Broadcasters in Declared Remote Areas were funded for the difference between the concessional transmission fees paid to the National Transmission Agency (NTA) and the commercial fees paid to the new owner of the National Transmission Network. Commercial Broadcasters in Declared Remote Areas were supplemented by the Government at a cost of $97 559 in 1999□00 for the increase in their transmission costs, to ensure broadcasting services to remote areas are maintained at current levels.

Radio for the Print Handicapped (RPH) received $358 332 in 1999□2000 for all station transmission costs.

The Networking the Nation (NTN) program aims to improve the type, quality and price of telecommunication services to communities in regional, rural and remote parts of Australia. A total of 174 new projects totalling $90.3 million were approved in 1999□2000, providing a range of communications services to meet community needs across regional Australia.

In 1999□2000, *Networking the Nation Online* was implemented□providing online access for applicants to register and apply for funding, and for the secretariat to assess applications and manage grants online. NTN is one of the first grants programs in the Commonwealth to implement a full online system. It will be used as a model for other areas within the Department and possibly the broader public sector.

In late April 2000, State and Territory Governments presented an update of their regional communications strategies and priorities to the NTN Board. The Board found the presentations valuable in considering how project applications fit within these strategies and priorities.

The NTN Board visited the Eyre Peninsula region, South Australia, in October 1999 to observe projects funded through the program. The visit increased the Board□s understanding of the needs of communities in the region and the telecommunications issues facing rural, regional and remote Australia more generally.

A number of projects funded under the NTN program have now reached a stage where information and experience can be shared with other communities now developing strategies and projects to address their communications needs.

New social bonus programs funded from the sale of a further 16.6 per cent of Telstra implemented.

In December 1999, the Minister for Communications, Information Technology and the Arts launched guidelines for funding under the social bonus initiatives (realised through the sale of the second tranche of Telstra) which are designed to enhance telecommunications infrastructure and services in rural, regional and remote Australia Applications for the first round of funding from these initiatives closed in early March 2000. (These programs are listed in the major activities of this output.)

High quality applications and advice to the NTN Board and high level of satisfaction by the NTN Board of departmental recommendations.

The NTN Board met for two funding rounds and four other meetings during 1999□2000. The Board approved 174 new projects and a total of $90.3 million, including $35.3 million from the social bonus initiatives. This brings the number of projects approved to 409 and the amount of funding approved to $197.4 million since the inception of the program.

The very high proportion of recommendations accepted by the NTN Board demonstrates the level of satisfaction with the secretariat□s advice.

Grant deeds with the Community Broadcasting Foundation (CBF) Limited, to support the community broadcasting sector, signed by 30 June 2000.

A draft grant deed was provided to the CBF for circulation and comment, with the final deed expected to be signed early in the new financial year.

The launch of the Community Broadcasting Australian Music Channel by June 2000.

A total of $1.5 million is being provided through the CBF over a three-year period as part of the Commonwealth□s Contemporary Music Package. A key objective of the initiative is to make Australian music more readily available to audiences through community radio stations.

The Department consulted widely with the community broadcasting sector and the music industry when developing the project. In November 1999, the CBF Board established a Contemporary Music Project Committee (CMPC) to oversee the development and implementation of the project. The launch of the Music Channel is on track to take place in November 2000.

Improving access to, and reception of, analog television services in metropolitan, regional and rural areas.

A two-thirds subsidy has been provided under the Second Remote Commercial Television Subsidy Scheme for decoders and transmitters. A total of 42 organisations have been funded for 72 retransmission sites to the tune of $489 790.

The Television Black Spots program was announced on 21 June 2000 and will make retransmission services by communities more affordable by providing funding towards the purchase of relevant equipment.

SBS television extensions will provide 1.2 million regional viewers with access to its analog television service, involving 36 transmission areas and/or 78 sites.

The Regional Communications Partnership (RCP) self-help subsidy scheme will make access to National Transmission Network sites operated by ntl Australia Ltd affordable for communities in regional and remote areas wishing to fund an expansion in the range of analog services they receive. SBS has received money following the sale of the National Transmission Network to ntl, to shift its main transmission site to Artarmon to improve analog television reception in Sydney.

Cooma Technology and Call Centre grant finalised under appropriate deed of agreement by 30 September 1999.

The deed of agreement was signed on 20 September 1999 for the multi-purpose Cooma Technology and Call Centre, which provides call centre operations and selected industry advisory assistance to the Cooma region.

NTN funding rounds announced in November 1999 and May 2000. AccessAbility round announced in September 1999; project grants administered in accordance with deeds.

In October 1999 the Minister for Communications, Information Technology and the Arts, announced the second (and final) round of grants under the AccessAbility program. Fourteen projects valued at $1.44 million successfully sought funding. The program aims to improve access to the Internet and online services for people with disabilities. NTN funding rounds were announced on 1 December 1999 and 31 May 2000. All project grants were administered in accordance with deeds.

Funding round for the telecommunications consumer representation and social policy research program completed in May 2000.

In July 1999, the Minister also awarded grants to consumer representation bodies totalling $630 000.
On 10 February 2000, the Minister announced grants totalling $157 824 for telecommunications research.

OUTPUT 2.4RESEARCH, ADVICE AND INFORMATION ON COMMUNICATIONS AND INFORMATION TECHNOLOGY ISSUES.

Description
The aim of this output is to ensure that Ministers, the Department and a range of Government agencies are provided with sound and timely economic, technical and statistical advice to support policy.

The Department consults with stakeholders to ensure that its advice takes account of industry developments and community concerns. It also assists industry to better understand Government objectives and policies. A targeted program of research and statistics-gathering by the Department□s Communication Research Unit (CRU) ensures that the economic and technical implications of policy options are identified and explained.

The CRU also provides a targeted program of fee-for-service consultancies for Government bodies within the communications sector, which assists in benchmarking the quality and timeliness of research and statistics activities.

Summary of major activities, significant issues and developments for Output 2.4

- The Department□s CRU has significantly improved its capability for providing timely statistical data through the development of a compendium of statistics.
- An electronic version of this compendium was placed on the Department□s Intranet to provide access for all areas of the Department and the Ministers□ offices. Training courses were provided on its use.
- The Department□s library was officially opened in August 1999. Since then it has introduced a range of reference services (including electronic desk-based services) aimed at providing best- practice library services to the Department.

Performance information: Output 2.4
Continuing client satisfaction with timely, professional sound and relevant advice, briefing material and statistical information provided. Satisfaction of clients with the quality and timeliness of fee-for-service work, as evidenced by further contracts and written feedback.
The CRU sought extensive feedback on services provided to the Department and the Ministers□ offices. Feedback has been highly positive, especially on the provision of statistical information and the usefulness of DATALINK, an online database.
Written advice has been received from fee-for-service clients. These clients have expressed overall satisfaction with quality and timeliness, and major clients□the ACA and the ACCC□have awarded further contracts to the CRU. Suggestions have been made on how to improve future work and as a result, research for new contracts will significantly extend previous analysis.

Preparation of advice and reports on a range of topics relevant to policy development in the Portfolio. For example, estimates of bandwidth demand and supply, improving digital TV services provided to non-metropolitan areas and technical advice on digital broadcasting.

The CRU provided advice on a range of topics for the Department, including an analysis of the cost of upgrading non-metropolitan television stations to digital services. This also involved managing a consultancy on behalf of the Department. The results of this work were fed directly into Government policy considerations.

A model of bandwidth demand and supply was developed for the National Bandwidth Inquiry, and incorporated into the Inquiry□s final report.
A major review was completed on the Department□s requirements for technical advice and more cost effective means were identified and implemented.
One of two papers prepared for the 1999 Communications Research Forum received a special commendation. The CRU has also been invited to submit articles to policy and research journals.
The Department□s library was officially opened and a range of services, including online research services, developed for use by all areas of the Department and the offices of the Ministers and Parliamentary Secretary.

Provision of statistics on the communications, information technology and the arts industry sectors to assist in monitoring developments in the sectors.

An electronic Department-wide compendium of useful statistics for the portfolio was developed and placed on the Department□s Intranet. The CRU regularly collected statistical information, including a quarterly Internet-based survey of prices charged for a range of services by major telecommunications carriers.
The CRU handled a large number of requests for statistical advice, and input to briefs from all areas of the Department and the Ministers□ offices. There was a major increase in demand for statistical information as the CRU□s capabilities improved.
Undertaking fee-for-service consultancies for a range of Government agencies on topics of relevance to the Portfolio.
The CRU undertook fee-for-service consultancies for the ACA, ACCC and the ABA. Work for the ACA and ACCC were repeat contracts to help these agencies meet legislative reporting requirements under the *Trade Practices Act 1974* and the *Telecommunications Act 1997.*

DOING IT BUSINESS WITH AUSTRALIAN GOVERNMENT: FAQS

AGENCIES

WHY SHOULD AN AGENCY USE THE ICT MANAGEMENT CONSULTANTS MULTI USE LIST?

Looking for specialist skills or a streamlined procurement process?
Australian Government agencies' investments in ICT are often complex and costly. Projects have to integrate with existing legacy systems, new and emerging business systems within and across agencies, jurisdictions and the private sector. ICT management consultants on the multi use list can assist agencies to establish and/or improve:

- their strategic approach to ICT investment;
- ICT business case analysis and option development;
- corporate and project governance of ICT;
- all aspects of project management from methodology through to outcome evaluation; and
- ICT benchmarking.

The ICT Management Consultants multi use list provides a streamlined procurement process for agencies. Once the appropriate category is identified, an agency may shortlist and select tender from the multi use list to establish an agency specific panel, or to undertake a single procurement. By knowing the maximum number of suppliers which will respond to the tender, agencies can plan resources involved in the tender evaluation.

WHY INCLUDE INTENDED PROCUREMENTS IN YOUR AGENCY ANNUAL PROCUREMENT PLAN.

The intention of Annual Procurement Plans is to draw business' early attention to potential procurement opportunities. Annual Procurement Plans are published by each agency on AusTender by 1 July each year. The Commonwealth Procurement Guidelines (8.32) advise that an agency may establish a time limit that is less than 25 days but no less than 10 days:

> *"a. where the agency has published details of the procurement in an Annual Procurement Plan on AusTender, at least 30 days and not more than 12 months in advance, and these details include a description of the procurement, the estimated timing of the approach to the market, and the procedure to obtain request documentation."*

Agencies must ensure that such notice will give potential suppliers sufficient time to complete the application process for the multi use list. For more information on Annual Procurement Plans, see *Preparing and Maintaining an Annual Procurement Plan*, part of the Good Procurement Practice series published by the Department of Finance and Administration or contact your CFO unit.

HOW DO I USE THE ICT MANAGEMENT CONSULTANTS MULTI USE LIST?

For information on how agencies can use the ICT Management Consultants multi use list please click here.

SUPPLIERS

DOES BEING ON THE MULTI USE LIST GUARANTEE GOVERNMENT CONTRACTS?

No. Agencies may use the information provided by suppliers and published on the multi use list to shortlist agencies for a select tender process. The tender process will be conducted in accordance with the Commonwealth Procurement Guidelines and agency specific Chief Executive Instructions.

Suppliers should ensure that their information relating to their capabilities and experience for the relevant service category, is accurate, current and succinct.

HOW AND WHEN CAN I APPLY?

The ICT Management Consultant multi use list will operate for 2 years from 22 October 2007. The Department of Finance and Administration (through AGIMO) may elect to extend the multi use list for a further year. Applications can be submitted at any time during that period. Additions and amendments to the multi use list will be made as soon as practicable after evaluation.

The Request for Application is available online. Applicants must articulate their organisational capability and experience in the provision of the identified services, as part of the Conditions for Participation. Organisations that have submitted a Request for Application and have satisfied the Conditions for Participation will be included on the ICT MCL as soon as practicable.

The information provided by successful applicants (pre-qualified suppliers) will be available for access by all agencies and the public through the AGIMO website.

To start an application please click on Request For Application Online Form.

HOW IS MY APPLICATION ASSESSED?

All applications will be assessed by AGIMO and a cross agency Evaluation Committee. All suppliers that meet the minimum conditions for participation will be included. A supplier may be accepted for one or more of the service categories applied for.

WHEN IS THE ICT MANAGEMENT CONSULTANTS MULTI USE LIST UPDATED?

The list is updated as soon as practicable after each evaluation round or as suppliers update their details.

HOW AND WHEN SHOULD I UPDATE MY INFORMATION?

To update supplier details, including contact information, please send an email to ictinvestmentframe@finance.gov.au.

To correct typographical errors, please send an email - containing the content for the entire field - to ictinvestmentframe@finance.gov.au. This will be used to cut and past over your existing information. *Note: if the content substance is amended, AGIMO will have the application reassessed.*

HOW DO I APPLY FOR A FURTHER ONE OR MORE CATEGORIES?

This applies to current ICT Management Consultant multi use list suppliers seeking inclusion for additional categories. It also includes situations where a supplier updates or refines original data provided to AGIMO.

1. Download the online Request for Application form - noting "Subsequent Application".
2. Complete Organisation Name and ensure contact information is current.
3. Complete all Supplier's Statement fields which have either changed or are new offers of service.
4. Complete Supplier's Declaration and submit for evaluation.

AGIMO will refer the new category content to the Evaluation Committee for assessment. On approval, the online multi use list will be updated.

ICT MANAGEMENT CONSULTANCY SERVICE DESCRIPTIONS

STRATEGIC PLANNING

This refers to the development and implementation of the planning process and documentation, examining how ICT should be used to achieve and support the organisation's overall business strategy and objectives.

CORPORATE GOVERNANCE OF ICT

This refers to the structure and processes an organisation uses to direct, evaluate and monitor its portfolio of ICT investments and their performance.
It could cover: the design and implementation of the governance structure; roles and responsibilities; quality assurance; risk management and change management policies and processes; stakeholder engagement mechanisms; and measurements to assess the effectiveness of the governance processes.
Applicants should note that Australian Standard 8015-2005: *Corporate governance of information and communication technology*, provides guiding principles on the effective, efficient, and ethical use of ICT within an organisation.

ORGANISATIONAL PROJECT MANAGEMENT MATURITY ASSESSMENT

This refers to the assessment of an organisation's current project management practices, the level of organisational effectiveness and the development of a roadmap to improve an organisation's overall performance.
There is a range of industry standards, methodologies and best practice in organisational project management maturity assessment tools. Some commonly referred examples are:

- Capability Maturity Model – Integration (CMMI) of the Carnegie Mellon University and Software Engineering Institute, USA;
- Portfolio, Programme and Project Management Maturity Model (P3M3) of the Office of Government Commerce, UK Government;
- Organisational Project Management Maturity Model (OPM3) of the Project Management Institute, USA.

PROJECT AND PORTFOLIO MANAGEMENT

This refers to the processes and tools used to support the ICT governance process at corporate and/or project levels and could include the:

- Establishment of a centralised body to provide project management support and services, often referred to as a PMO (Project or Programme or Portfolio Management Office depending on its functions and roles); and
- Evaluation, selection and/or implementation of industry standard enterprise project and portfolio management software tools.

PROJECT GOVERNANCE

Project Governance can be seen as a discipline under Corporate Governance. It refers to the design and implementation of processes, structures and communications that need to exist for a successful project.

BUSINESS CASE ANALYSIS AND DEVELOPMENT

This refers to the analysis work required to provide an understanding and knowledge of a project's values and options. The analysis could examine the values, feasibility, performance, risks and costing of the various options. Such analysis work is important for the development of a business case.
AGIMO has developed an ICT Business Case Guide and Tools to help agencies develop business cases with comprehensive cost benefit analysis and more detailed project planning.

PROJECT MANAGEMENT METHODOLOGY

This refers to the evaluation, selection, development, and/or implementation of appropriate project management methodology, procedures, templates, and the associated skill transfer and training.
Note the use of industry standards, methodologies and best practice in project management. Some commonly referred examples are Prince2 and Project Management Body of Knowledge (PMBOK).

PROJECT OUTCOME EVALUATION AND BENEFIT REALISATION MANAGEMENT

Refers to the development and implementation of organisational processes and procedures to identify, monitor, track and harvest the realisation of project benefits.

ICT BENCHMARKING

This refers to the analysis and reporting of ICT spending on hardware, software, outsourcing, personnel, and in various technology areas, against industry trends.
The benchmarking analysis could be used to provide quality assurance of the costings of a project business case and/or ICT spending performance at the organisational level.

GOVERNMENT ICT GOVERNANCE COMMITTEES

SECRETARIES' COMMITTEE ON ICT

The Secretaries' Committee on ICT (SCICT) is a strategic, decision-making committee for whole-of-government ICT use by the Australian Government. The SCICT's agenda is informed and supported by both the Business Process Transformation Committee (BPTC) and the Chief Information Officer Committee (CIOC).

The SCICT was established in place of the Information Management Strategy Committee (IMSC) in June 2006 as a strategic, decision-making committee, to drive whole of government approaches relating to the use of ICT across government.

The SCICT was created to enable a strategic and focused approach to implement the e-Government strategy, to improve efficiency in the Government's use and investment in ICT, and to use ICT to reduce 'red tape' or duplication in government, for citizens and business.

The SCICT comprises members at the Secretary or CEO level and is chaired by Dr Ian Watt, the Secretary of the Department of Finance and Administration. The agencies represented on the SCICT include:

- Attorney-General's Department
- Australian Customs Service
- Department of Education, Science and Training
- Department of Finance and Administration
- Department of Human Services

- Department of Industry, Tourism and Resources
- Department of the Prime Minister and Cabinet

BUSINESS PROCESS TRANSFORMATION COMMITTEE (BPTC)

The Business Process Transformation Committee (BPTC) oversees the reform of government business processes.
Government business processes is a key part of the implementation of the 2006 e-Government Strategy: *Responsive Government: A New Agenda.* The BPTC is a companion body to the CIOC, and provides assistance and technical advice to help to coordinate business process improvement initiatives.
The BPTC comprises members at deputy secretary level or equivalent and is chaired by Ms Ann Steward, the Australian Government Chief Information Officer, AGIMO, Department of Finance and Administration. The agencies represented on the BPTC include:

- Australian Bureau of Statistics
- Australian Public Service Commission
- Australian Taxation Office
- Centrelink
- Department of Defence
- Department of Education, Science and Training
- Department of Finance and Administration
- Department of Immigration and Citizenship
- Department of Industry, Tourism and Resources
- Department of the Prime Minister and Cabinet

CHIEF INFORMATION OFFICER COMMITTEE (CIOC)

Reporting to the SCICT, the CIOC addresses the priorities determined by the SCICT, provide 'thought leadership' in the ICT arena, identify strategic issues, and is a forum for exchange of information between agencies.
The CIOC develops options for adoption and implementation of ICT at agency or whole-of-government level, and is supported by issue-specific working groups.
The CIOC comprises 13 members and is chaired by Ms Ann Steward, the Australian Government Chief Information Officer, AGIMO, Department of Finance and Administration.
The agencies represented on the CIOC include:

- Attorney-General's Department
- Australian Bureau of Statistics
- Australian Taxation Office
- Centrelink
- Defence Signals Directorate
- Department of Communications, Information Technology and the Arts
- Department of Defence
- Department of Education, Science and Training
- Department of Finance and Administration
- Department of Foreign Affairs and Trade
- Department of Industry, Tourism and Resources
- Department of the Prime Minister and Cabinet
- CIO Forum Representative

SECRETARIES' COMMITTEE ON ICT

The Secretaries' Committee on ICT (SCICT) is a strategic, decision-making committee for whole of government ICT use by the Australian Government. The SCICT's agenda is informed and supported by both the Business Process Transformation Committee (BPTC) and the Chief Information Officer Committee (CIOC).

The SCICT was established in place of the Information Management Strategy Committee (IMSC) in June 2006 as a strategic, decision-making committee, to drive whole of government approaches relating to the use of ICT across government.

The SCICT was created to enable a strategic and focused approach to implement the e-Government strategy, to improve efficiency in the Government's use and investment in ICT, and to use ICT to reduce 'red tape' or duplication in government, for citizens and business.

The SCICT comprises seven members at the Secretary or CEO level and is chaired by Dr Ian Watt, the Secretary of the Department of Finance and Administration. The agencies represented on the SCICT include:

- Attorney-General's Department
- Australian Customs Service
- Department of Education, Science and Training
- Department of Finance and Administration
- Department of Human Services
- Department of Industry, Tourism and Resources
- Department of the Prime Minister and Cabinet

BUSINESS PROCESS TRANSFORMATION COMMITTEE

The new governance arrangements included the creation of the Business Process Transformation Committee (BPTC), to oversee the reform of government business processes, and the refocusing of the CIOC.

Government business processes is a key part of the implementation of the 2006 e-Government Strategy: *Responsive Government: A New Agenda.* The BPTC is a companion body to the CIOC, which will provide assistance and technical advice to help to coordinate business process improvement initiatives.

The BPTC comprises members at deputy secretary level or equivalent and is chaired by Ms Ann Steward, the Australian Government Chief Information Officer, Australian Government Information Management Office (AGIMO), Department of Finance and Administration. The agencies represented on the BPTC include:

- Australian Bureau of Statistics
- Australian Public Service Commission
- Australian Taxation Office
- Centrelink
- Department of Defence
- Department of Education, Science and Training
- Department of Finance and Administration
- Department of Immigration and Multicultural Affairs
- Department of Industry, Tourism and Resources
- Department of the Prime Minister and Cabinet

CHIEF INFORMATION OFFICER COMMITTEE

Reporting to the SCICT, the CIOC will address the priorities determined by the SCICT, provide 'thought leadership' in the ICT arena, identify strategic issues, and be a forum for exchange of information between agencies.

The CIOC will also develop options for adoption and implementation of ICT at agency or whole-of-government level, and be supported by issue-specific working group.
The CIOC comprises 13 members and is chaired by Ms Ann Steward, the Australian Government Chief Information Officer, AGIMO, Department of Finance and Administration. The agencies represented on the CIOC include:

- Attorney-General's Department
- Australian Bureau of Statistics
- Australian Taxation Office
- Centrelink
- Defence Signals Directorate
- Department of Communications, Information Technology and the Arts
- Department of Defence
- Department of Education, Science and Training
- Department of Finance and Administration
- Department of Foreign Affairs and Trade
- Department of Industry, Tourism and Resources
- Department of the Prime Minister and Cabinet
- CIO Forum Representative

AUTOMATED ASSISTANCE IN ADMINISTRATIVE DECISION MAKING (AAADM) WORKING GROUP

Reporting to the BPTC, the Automated Assistance in Administration Decision Making (AAADM) working group was established to give effect to Principle 25 of the Administrative Review Council Report No 46: Automated Assistance in Administrative Decision Making (the Report). The Report contains 27 best practice principles for ensuring that decision making undertaken with the assistance of expert systems is consistent with the administrative law values of lawfulness, fairness, rationality, openness and efficiency.

The AAADM working group comprises 15 members and is chaired by Ms Ann Steward, the Australian Government Chief Information Officer, AGIMO, Department of Finance and Administration. The membership is drawn from agencies that have experience or interest in the use of automated systems for administrative decision making. The agencies represented on the AAADM working group include:

- Administrative Review Council
- Attorney General's Department
- Australian Customs Service
- Australian National Audit Office
- Australian Taxation Office
- Centrelink
- Department of Families, Community Services and Indigenous Affairs
- Department of Finance and Administration
- Department of Foreign Affairs and Trade
- Department of Health and Ageing
- Department of Human Services

- Department of Immigration and Citizenship
- Department of Veterans Affairs
- Medicare Australia
- Office of the Commonwealth Ombudsman

CONTACT DETAILS

Mr Phillip Lynch
Director, SCICT Secretariat
Australian Government Information Management Office
Department of Finance and Administration
Ph: [+61] 02 6215 1627
Email: phillip.lynch@finance.gov.au

FOR FURTHER INFORMATION ON THE AAADM WORKING GROUP, PLEASE CONTACT:

Service Delivery Operations Branch
Australian Government Information Management Office
Department of Finance and Administration
Ph: [+61] 02 6215 1569
Email: aaadm@finance.gov.au

DEPARTMENT OF COMMUNICATIONS, INFORMATION TECHNOLOGY AND THE ARTS

Enquiries: (02) 6271 1000
Fax: (02) 6271 1901
Website Link
Postal Address:
GPO Box 2154,
Canberra ACT 2601
Location:
38 Sydney Ave,
Forrest ACT 2603

Function:
The Department provides strategic advice and professional support across a wide range of policy areas including: the arts and cultural development; broadcasting and online regulation; information and communications technology; post and telecommunications; and sport. The Department also administers legislation; regulations; grants and incentives to industry and the wider community; and supports advisory councils and committees. In world forums, the Department looks at ways to maximise Australia's opportunities in global markets and on related international treaties and agreements

BROADCASTING, ICT, REGIONAL STRATEGY & CORPORATE

Name: Mr Abul Rizvi
Phone (02) 6271 7022
Role: Deputy Secretary
Email abul.rizvi@dcita.gov.au

REGIONAL STRATEGY, ICT AND RESEARCH

Name: Dr Beverly Hart
Phone (02) 6271 1701
Fax (02) 6271 7042

Role: Assistant Secretary
Email beverly.hart@dcita.gov.au
Location Burns Centre, 28 National Circuit, Forrest ACT 2603
Postal Address GPO Box 2154, Canberra ACT 2601

ICT STRATEGY

Provides analysis and advice on long term trends affecting the role of the portfolio and the strategic implications for the Department. Key areas include longer term issues relating to ICT research and the development of advanced communications infrastructure. Key activities include: research and analysis on key elements of the information economy, including evolving industry and market structures, technological change and its impact on the economy; and implementation of programs which support ICT-oriented and enabled research, including NICTA and the Advanced Networks Program.

Name: Mr Tom Dale
Phone (02) 6271 1099
Fax (02) 6271 7042
Role: Assistant Secretary
Email tom.dale@dcita.gov.au
Location Burns Centre, 28 National Circuit, Forrest ACT 2603
Postal Address GPO Box 2154, Canberra ACT 2601
Name: Ms Louise Jackson
Phone (02) 6271 7098
Fax (02) 6271 7042
Role: Executive Assistant
Email louise.jackson@dcita.gov.au

ICT OPPORTUNITIES

ICT Incubators; COMICTA (Committee for Marketing ICT Australia); ICT Procurement Policies; Intelligent Island (Tasmania) programs; ICT trade issues; and ITOL (Information Technology Online).

INDUSTRY STRUCTURE AND INITIATIVES SECTION

ICT Innovation and R&D policy; ICT industry initiatives, including skills and telework; ICT industry analysis
Name: Mr Scean Kearns
Phone (02) 6271 1719

STRATEGIC ANALYSIS SECTION

Portfolio strategic environment; DCITA strategic priorities; Technology Scanning; National ICT Priorities; Future ICT platforms and convergence; Communications benchmarking and analysis; Future of the Internet Project.
Name: Mr David Jansen
Phone (02) 6271 1667

TELECOMMUNICATIONS SERVICES MARKET

The telecommunications services market in Australia is significant, contributing more than 5% to Australia's GDP. It is a sophisticated and developed market, yet offers opportunity for growth in certain sub-sectors. Generally, there are opportunities in the areas of broadband access, data communications services and content provision.

The telecommunications industry in Australia has boomed over the past 5 years and is anticipated to continue to grow strongly. The telecommunications services market for business and residential consumers in Australia is predicted by one prominent industry commentator to reach A$37 billion (US$18.5 billion, assuming a constant exchange rate) in revenues by 2005. In 2000, revenues reached A$30 billion (US$17.1 billion), following industry growth rates of 15% a year.

Growth is anticipated to slow somewhat in 2004, due to the effects of the broad economic downturn, and also the unfavorable climate for telecommunications companies following stock market falls over the past year. However, there are some areas predicted to maintain high growth. Broadband services is one of these. Although subscriber numbers at the present are low, overall growth in the number of broadband connections is expected to gain considerable speed during 2002-2005. This would make Australia one of the fastest growing countries for broadband access. Revenue from broadband services alone is expected to reach A$15-20 billion (US$7-10 billion, assuming a constant exchange rate) by 2010.

As a consequence of the growth in broadband, it is anticipated that data communications services will also experience increasing demand. This segment has already been growing at around 30% per annum.

The Australian market is receptive to US companies and services, but it is a competitive one. There are many local and global players active in the sector. US companies must be prepared to invest significant time and energy in entering the market, developing relationships with local partners where necessary.

Telecommunications services (as far as this report is concerned) include:

- Fixed telephone services;
- Mobile services;
- Data services (incl. on-line services, value-added voice services, voicemail, e-mail);
- Broadband services (incl. high-speed Internet, interactive services);
- Interactive television, games, digital TV;
- Content providers; and
- Mobile commerce (or M-commerce).

(Sources: Paul Budde Communications and BIS Shrapnel report for ACCC on Telecommunications Infrastructure - available at www.accc.gov.au)

MARKET OVERVIEW

A) REGULATORY ENVIRONMENT

The Australian telecommunications industry was fully deregulated in 1997. The industry has since gone from essentially 2 carriers initially to 70 in 2004, all offering a menu of services.

There are two statutory authorities regulating the telecommunications industry. The Australian Communications Authority (ACA) regulates the technical side of the industry, handling standards, performance monitoring and spectrum. The ACA is the licensing body for telecommunications carriers.

The Australian Competition and Consumer Commission (ACCC) is the economic regulator for the telecommunications industry, handling pricing, encouraging competition and ensuring the best outcome for consumers.

A carrier license authorizes the operation of specified facilities (called 'network units') to supply telecommunications services to the public. Carriers are obliged to meet a number of specified requirements, including contributing toward the cost of universal service provision, fulfillment of industry development plans and compliance with the telecommunications access regime (under conditions of the license). However, it is not necessary to have a carrier license to provide the public with some carriage services (such as phone or Internet access), or content services (such as an electronic newspaper or pay television). Service provider licenses with appropriate conditions will cover these activities, and the existing legislation provides some general rules.

There are other pieces of legislation that may affect the provision of telecommunications services or convergent communications services. This legislation includes acts covering broadcasting, including digital broadcasting; Internet content; and privacy.

B) INFRASTRUCTURE

Investment in telecommunications infrastructure has been steady and there has recently been strong growth in the provision of Internet and on-line services. Considerable investment has been made in new networks, both fiber and cable. Australia is now well-serviced by fiber networks within and between major cities: in fact, it is the predominant technology supporting over 95% of the "backbone" networks. There are 13 carriers which have deployed or are deploying fiber optic infrastructure local area networks, with 2 or more in addition to Telstra's network in each of the following major cities: Melbourne, Sydney, Brisbane, Adelaide and Perth.

While the majority of infrastructure development has been in the more lucrative metropolitan areas, rural communities are increasingly being wired up. Companies such as Austar, Neighborhood Cable and Heartland are focusing on the installation of local networks in rural areas. Often, these networks involve satellite or microwave technologies. Some rural communities have been selected to trial projects involving fiber to the home, and others have taken advantage of other infrastructure development to roll-out telecommunications (i.e., the expansion of gas mains into rural Victoria and New South Wales allowing enterprising carriers to lay fiber in the gas main trenches). Australia's capital city, Canberra, with a population of 400,000, has recently been part of a project run by TransACT to wire the entire city with fiber. Content providers will then negotiate with TransACT to deliver content to Canberrans.

Planned investment in xDSL infrastructure between 2004 and 2003 is estimated at a minimum of A$1.9 billion. (ACCC figures).

Internationally, there are links by optic cable to the USA, Asia and Europe, with considerable capacity. Major cables include Southern Cross, the Australia-Japan cable, Tasman, and the SEA-ME-WE3 cable.

As of 2004, there are more than 70 carriers operating in the market, from effectively 2 prior to deregulation. Major players include the former monopoly carrier Telstra, as well as Optus, AAPT and Primus Telecommunications. The competitive dynamic in the domestic market changed in 2004 with the collapse of One.Tel and the takeover of Optus by SingTel (Singapore's incumbent monopoly). Competition in the long distance market and price regulation in the local call market has led to consumers enjoying falling prices. One.Tel was aggressive in offering low prices (and causing the rest of the industry to match some of them) and it is now expected that prices will not fall much further in the near term.

In August 2000, the unbundling of the local loop presented opportunities for other providers to initiate services to the residential market. ADSL has been a major service, but this has not been without difficulties. There have been criticisms levelled at Telstra for the slow roll-out of ADSL at the exchanges, as well as for high pricing and poor quality of service. One year after the unbundling of the local loop, there are only 346,000 subscribers to broadband, about two-thirds of which are ADSL subscribers. Some new carriers have attempted to bypass the "last mile" access problems by introducing other technologies, such as broadband wireless (LMDS and MMDS technologies), satellite and laser. Market opportunity in the local access market in Australia is sizeable (A$6bn), representing about 60% of total fixed telephone revenues. Being the incumbent, Telstra has 90% of the access market, followed by Optus with 6%. (Source: BIS Shrapnel report).

In the mobile arena, the major mobile carriers are Telstra, Optus, Vodafone and Hutchison Telecommunications, operating under the Orange brand. Each of these carriers operates their own network: Telstra (GSM and CDMA networks), Optus (GSM), Vodafone (GSM) and Orange (CDMA). Other carriers lease time on the networks, and the larger players include AAPT/Cellular One and Virgin Mobile. One.Tel was in the process of building their own network when the company collapsed. At the time of this report, the One.Tel network was yet to be sold.

A recent round of auctions offering spectrum suitable for 3G (third generation) mobile applications generated strong competition, with two new companies being introduced into the Australian market: CKW Wireless Pty Ltd and 3G Investments Pty Ltd. These two companies are subsidiaries of U.S. technology firms ArrayComm and Qualcomm, respectively.

3G Investments plans to deploy a cdma2000 network for commercialization, when the spectrum becomes available in October 2002. ArrayComm's subsidiary, CKW Wireless, intends to promote its technology, I-Burst, and focus on the data capabilities of 3G, rather than voice. Although the I-Burst technology is still in development, it is anticipated that, by October 2002, products will be commercially available.

Australia has three major pay TV operators. In metropolitan areas, the competitors are Foxtel (owned by a consortium comprising News Corp, Telstra and Publishing & Broadcasting Limited) and OptusVision (owned by Optus), and in regional areas, Austar (owned by United GlobalCom - NASDAQ: UCOMA). Austar and Foxtel have an agreement not to compete in the same markets. Both Foxtel and OptusVision offer broadband access through their hybrid fiber coaxial cable. In the meantime, Austar is making inroads offering satellite TV and broadband connections to their rural and regional customers.

Australia's broadband cable networks currently operate using analog technologies. Digitization will occur in the near future. However, there is still doubt over whether "open access" to these digital platforms will eventuate (whether through market forces or government intervention). This may determine the extent to which opportunities for content providers and equipment suppliers (including set-top boxes) materialize.

C) Market Factors

Australia offers a great opportunity for US companies to expand. It is a sophisticated market, with high uptake of new technologies. Relative geographic isolation has meant that Australians are high users of telecommunications services and eager to exploit services.

Australia can also provide an ideal platform from which to enter other Asian markets. The major cities of Sydney, Melbourne, Brisbane, Adelaide and Perth are home to many regional headquarters. Hobart, the capital of the island state of Tasmania, has become a call center mecca, with many large companies taking advantage of a skilled workforce and low business costs. Furthermore, Australia has many cultural similarities with the US, ensuring that Americans generally find it an easy place to do business. In addition, there is political and economic stability, with a transparent business and legal environment.

However, US companies must be mindful of the relative small size of the Australian domestic market. With a population of 19 million, it is less than one-tenth the population of the US. Companies wishing to supply to the market must adapt expectations to the realities of a market of 19 million people (over a land mass approximately the same size as continental USA). This impacts on such aspects of business as order sizes and distribution practices, and companies should also be attuned to local market parameters such as standards, voltage, and metric weights and measures.

D) Statistical Data

Australia's State of Play

Australian GDP, 2000	A$640 billion (US$377 billion)
Population	19 million
Growth rate 2004 (estimate)	2.5%
Growth rate 2002 (forecast)	3.0%
Telecommunications revenue 2000	A$30 billion (US$17.1 billion)*
Telecommunications revenue 2004	A$32 billion (estimate) (US$16 billion)
Fixed line subscribers	10.7 million
Penetration households	96%
Mobile phone subscribers	10.8 million (as of June 2004)
Number of ISPs	Approximately 700
Internet subscribers	3.92 million
Points of Presence	2,394
Australians adults accessing Internet	50%
At home	33%
At work	25%
Other sites	22%
Australians aged 5-14 years accessing Internet	47%
Households with PCs	56%
Households online	37%

Broadband subscribers	estimated at 346,000 by end 2004

TELECOMMUNICATIONS SERVICES REVENUES

	1996	1997	1998	1999	2000
TELECOMMUNICATIONS SERVICES REVENUES	A$18.3bn	A$20.0bn	A$22.5bn	A$26bn	A$30bn
Services Revenues (by market)					
Local telephone services	A$3.3bn	A$4.0bn	A$4.5bn	A$4.7bn	A$5bn
Long distance telephone services	A$4.3bn	A$4.5bn	A$4.7bn	A$4.9bn	A$5bn-A$5.5bn
International call services	A$1.6bn	A$2.0bn	A$2.2bn	A$2.4bn	A$2.5bn
Cellular services	A$3.3bn	A$4.0bn	A$5.4bn	A$6.5bn	A$7.2bn
Paging services	A$0.1bn	A$0.1bn	A$0.1bn	A$0.1bn	A$0.1bn
Value-added services	A$3.0bn	A$3.0bn	A$5.1bn	A$6.0bn	A$7-A$7.5bn
Services Revenues (by service)					
Fixed voice	A$10.0bn	A$10.2bn	A$10.8bn	A$11.2bn	A$12.0bn
Mobile	A$3.32bn	A$4.0bn	A$5.4bn	A$6.5bn	A$7.2bn
Data	A$2.7bn	A$3.2bn	A$4.2bn	A$5.3bn	A$7.0bn
US dollar exchange rate	A$1=US$0.78	A$1=US$0.73	A$1=US$0.62	A$1=US$0.64	A$1=US$0.57

Source: Figures provided in BIS Shrapnel report for ACCC on Telecommunications Infrastructure

MARKET TRENDS

The telecommunications services industry has exhibited a number of trends since deregulation. Telstra remains the dominant market player, although market share has been diminishing over the past few years, particularly in the data communications area. This has been dominated by new competitors to the industry, which have been able to harness new technologies in the development of their networks and services, and are not encumbered by their historical network architecture.

2004 has seen some significant movement in the fortunes of some of the new entrants to the carrier market. Companies such as Davnet and UeComm, along with some other smaller carriers have experienced lower revenue growth during late 2000 and into 2004, disenchantment with the telecommunications sector by investors (and, hence, plummeting stock prices), and consequently have suffered larger than expected financial losses. The industry was shaken by the collapse of carrier One.Tel in July. Also significantly impacting the local market was the takeover of Cable and Wireless Optus by Singapore's major carrier, SingTel. It is anticipated that there will be further rationalization in the market in the near to medium term.

Overall, the market for telecommunications services is anticipated to grow strongly over the next 10 years. Predicted annual growth rates range at around 10% per annum. The global economic slowdown may have some impact on these levels, however the Australian economy has continued to grow during 2004 and is expected to grow at about 3% during 2002. One aspect affecting the local market for US products has been the ongoing strength of the US dollar relative to the Australian dollar. This has been causing US-made products to look uncompetitive price-wise, when compared with technology from Asia, and to some extent Europe.

BROADBAND ACCESS

Trends in services include the inexorable progression toward greater broadband access. Access to broadband by Australian consumers has been slow, blamed for the most part on stalling by Telstra in terms of providing access, high prices, and a lack of competitive offerings. The Australian Government has also come under fire for not actively promoting the issue. Many industry commentators believe Australia is now several years behind other countries in providing broadband access to its consumers, particularly the USA, Korea and Singapore. It is estimated that there will be 350,000 broadband subscribers by the end of 2004, two-thirds of which are cable subscribers, according to IDC Australia. Another industry research agency, the Gartner Group, estimates that less than 0.5% of the Australian population are broadband subscribers.

However, the level of subscription to broadband services is predicted to grow quickly from 2002-2005. IDC Australia estimates that by end 2002, there will be 3.75 million narrowband subscribers versus 786,000 broadband. By 2004, the trend will be shifting to broadband, with 4 million narrowband and 2.9 million broadband subscribers. The balance between cable subscribers and ADSL is predicted to swing strongly in ADSL's favor, with 3.6 million DSL subscribers versus 800,000 cable subscribers in 2005.
(Source: Figures quoted in Australian Financial Review Special Report on Broadband, August 15, 2004.)

BUNDLING OF SERVICES

Carriers are attempting to bundle services together to maintain their market share and customer numbers. Optus has been quick to market packages handling local and international calls, mobile services, pay TV access and broadband access via cable. These packages sometimes offer considerable discounts to consumers. Telstra, while bundling telephony services, has been unable to include broadband access and pay TV, due to disagreements with its Foxtel joint venture partners.

MOBILE COMMUNICATIONS

The introduction this month (September 2004) of mobile number portability is also expected to impact on the mobile phone industry and churn levels. Until now, Australia's consumers have had to change their mobile phone number if they wanted to change provider, with potentially considerable costs for business. This has meant many have stayed with their original provider, even if they could get better deals elsewhere. Expected implications of the introduction of number portability are increased competition between the carriers for the lucrative corporate customers and a probable shift away from the dominant player, Telstra, to the other carriers. Many small-to-medium sized companies are anticipated to change providers now that they can change and keep their current number with no fear of financial loss.

There are now nearly 10 million mobile phone subscribers in a population of 19 million. WAP services are increasing in popularity, although most people are still waiting for the "killer application". WAP content is still considered fairly dismal, with major content including weather, sports results, financial and stock market updates, jokes and the like. SMS texting has experienced strong growth, due to the low pricing of messaging, and it is estimated that more than two million messages are being sent daily. Hutchison Telecommunications, which markets its services under the "Orange" brand, have committed to building a 3G network in Australia, although services are yet to actually be announced. Hutchison's 3G network is expected to be operational by 2003.

M-commerce (or mobile commerce) is starting to make an appearance, although uptake levels are reported as being lower than other Asian countries. At this stage, the majority of Australians are yet to use technologies allowing access to the Internet and other interactive content while on the move. However, applications and technologies are being reported in the trade press, and conferences and workshops are introducing this subsector to the broader Australian industry. As technologies and services are progressively introduced, m-commerce will take a greater share of telecommunications services.

INTERNET USAGE

Internet usage in Australia is reasonably high, with more than 50% of Australian adults regularly accessing the Internet at home or work. There are approximately 700 Internet Service Providers (ISPs) operating in Australia. A number of local and global players offer web hosting services to Australian companies.

The Australian Government has been committed to supplying information, services and undertaking its own operations on-line through its "Government Online" strategy. This strategy was outlined in 1997. As of March 2004, 93% of Commonwealth agencies will meet the online service commitment as outlined by the Prime Minister. Consequently, the Australian Government has actively encouraged the use of e-commerce amongst the Australian community and regularly tracks progress through the "Current State of Play" series, available on-line at www.noie.gov.au.

DIGITAL TELEVISION

Digital TV began transmission in Australia in January 2004. The Australian Government has given 2008 as the target date for analog transmissions to cease. In introducing digital TV, the Australian Government controversially granted the three existing commercial terrestrial TV networks in Australia the capacity to transmit digital TV -- gratis. An added incentive that the existing networks received (to promote the uptake of digital TV) came in the guise of a Government concession restricting competition -- barring the entry of any other commercial TV operator until at least 2006. The standard adopted by Australia differs from those adopted in Europe and the USA. Under provisions set out by legislation, television stations will be required to broadcast in three formats: HDTV, SDTV and analog. By 2002, TV companies will be required by to transmit 20 hours of HDTV per week, as well as continuing to broadcast SDTV signals at all times.

COMPETITION

The Australian telecommunications services market is extremely competitive in the provision of services to the business market. Companies wishing to enter this market must be prepared to invest significant time and money into their efforts. Marketing is crucial in gaining market share.

The marketing strategies of service providers targeting the residential market have focused on differentiating their product offerings from Telstra by price and service quality.

IBIS industry researchers estimate that the level of imports in the telecommunications services market is low. Imports currently generate less than 5% of the industry's domestic demand. (Source: IBIS report, "Communications Services in Australia," available at www.ibisworld.com.au.)

Major carriers include:

Name	**Major Services Include:**	**Target**	**Revenues***
Telstra	-fixed line telephony -mobile communications -Internet -data services -directory services -pay TV via Foxtel joint venture	Business, residential and wholesale	A$18.9 billion (year ending June 30, 2004)
Optus	-long distance telephony -local telephony -mobile communications -business network services -Internet -pay TV via OptusVision	High value business and residential customers	A$5.2 billion (year ending June 30, 2004)
AAPT	-mobile telephony -satellite communications -data services	Corporate and government sectors	A$941 million (year ending June 30, 2000. 2004 figures N/A)
Primus	-data services -mobile telephony -Internet	Residential; medium and large business	Estimated at approximately A$600-800 million (calendar year 2004)
Vodafone	-mobile telephony -data services	Universal	N/A but estimated at A$1.1 billion for calendar year 2000
Hutchison	-mobile telephony -paging, messaging -long distance telephony -ISP	SME and residential market	A$404.7 million (for calendar year 2000)
PowerTel	-data services -Internet (narrowband and broadband) -voice services, including local and international	Australian corporate and wholesale market	A$37.5 million (for calendar year 2000)

*Exchange rates applicable are:
2000 – A$1=US$0.57; and
2004 – A$1=US$0.50.

END USERS

The major end users in the Australian market are business, residential and government customers. Government represents a substantial user group as government spending with estimates at around 10-15% of total revenues.

Since deregulation and the introduction of competition, end users have received a steady flow of price reductions on telecommunications services. The introduction of competition caused the tariffs for long-distance calls to fall significantly. The cost of local calls has also fallen, however, this has been driven by regulation on the incumbent carrier, Telstra rather than by competition. The price of wholesale bandwidth has also decreased, particularly on the Melbourne/Canberra/Sydney/Brisbane routes. This is due to increased competition, as there are now four major "backbone" networks operating on these routes. Australian consumers enjoy untimed local calls. As a consequence, Internet access rates also benefit.

SALES PROSPECTS

Areas expected to provide future opportunities are:

- Provision of ADSL services and associated equipment, particularly those targeted to the home consumer, small-to-medium enterprises and home offices. Equipment may provide access to the Internet and also facilitate other services to the home.
- Provision of security services, such as firewalls and other protection from hacker attacks, given the greater uptake of Internet over time and the "permanently on" nature of broadband access.
- M-Commerce and mobile Internet data services: provision of equipment, content for phones, personal digital assistants (PDAs) etc.
- Content and infrastructure for broadband applications, such as interactive TV, games and video-on-demand.

MARKET ACCESS

As mentioned above, entry into the Australian telecommunications sector is fully deregulated. Companies are freely able to begin operations. The Australian dollar is fully convertible and the financial markets are well serviced by Australian and global players.

For information on licensing and certification, please visit the Australian Communications Authority website at www.aca.gov.au. The Australian Competition and Consumer Commission provides information on economic regulation of telecommunications at www.accc.gov.au.

US companies wishing to investigate the Australian market for their telecommunications products or services can contact the US Commercial Service in Australia:

Ms. Elly Bartak
Commercial Specialist - Telecommunications
US Commercial Service
American Consulate General - Melbourne
E-mail: elly.bartak@mail.doc.gov or melbourne.office.box@mail.doc.gov

Website: www.csaustralia.org
Fax: 61-3-9510-4660

IMPORTANT CONTACTS

AUSTRALIAN GOVERNMENT SUPPORT FOR THE ICT SECTOR

Business Entry Point - Online Government resource for Australian business. A centralised access to a range of Australian, State and Local Government resources. www.business.gov.au
Grantslink - Online database of sources of Australian Government funding and application forms. www.grantslink.gov.au

AusIndustry - Provides a range of assistance to industry, including grants, loans, R&D tax concessions, duty concessions and support for investment by venture capital firms. www.ausindustry.gov.au

Austrade - Provide export programs and services that are designed to reduce the time, cost and risk involved in accessing international markets: www.austrade.gov.au/IT and www.myexportcoach.gov.au

INDUSTRIAL ASSOCIATIONS

Australian Direct Marketing Association (ADMA) represents over 500 Australian organisations involved in information-based marketing.
www.adma.com.au
Australian Computer Society (ACS) is the professional body representing ICT professionals.
www.acs.org.au
Australian Electrical and Electronic Manufacturers Association (AEEMA) represents Australia's ICT, electronics and electrical manufacturing industries.
www.aeema.asn.au
Australian Electronic Business Network (AUSe.NET) is a national, not-for-profit organisation that encourages small business awareness and adoption of electronic commerce.
www.ecommerceadvantage.com.au/ausenet.htm
Australian Information Industry Association (AIIA) represents the ICT industry in policy issues and encourages productivity among its members.
www.aiia.com.au
Internet Industry Association (IIA) provides policy input to government and advocacy on a range of business and regulatory issues.
www.iia.net.au
Australian Interactive Media Industry Association (AIMIA) represents Australian creators and developers of digital media.
www.aimia.com.au
Communication Alliance (incorporating the former Australian Communications Industry Forum and the Service Providers Association Inc) provides a national and unified forum for the Australian communications industry .
www.commsalliance.com.au/
Engineers Australia is the national forum for the advancement of engineering and the professional development of members.
www.engineersaustralia.org.au
Standards Australia is the peak, non-government standards body in Australia and promotes excellence through the Australian Design Awards.
www.standards.org.au

IMPORTANT INTERNET AND RESEARCH BUSINESS CONTACTS

SUPPORT AGENCIES AND BODIES

Australian eCommerce Network

AeCN is a professional networking group based in Melbourne. Their main activity is industry information seminars, which we hold on an occasional basis, addressing topics of contemporay interest and/or strategic significance.

Type	E-business support agencies and bodies
Topics	Support agencies and bodies
Address	GPO Box 1240L
Suburb	Melbourne
State	Vic
Postcode	3001
Email	mail@aecn.org
Website	http://www.aecn.org
Geographical Coverage	Victoria

Canberra Business Advisory Service

Provides small and medium sized enterprises (SMEs) support in establishment, operation and development of their business in the Canberra Region.

Type	E-business support agencies and bodies
Topics	E-business support contacts
Address	Mungga-iri House Suite 6, 18 Napier Close
Suburb	Deakin
State	ACT
Postcode	2600
Phone	+61 2 6260 5000
Fax	+61 2 6282 5288
Email	help@canbas.com.au
Website	http://www.canbas.com.au
Date	2002
Geographical Coverage	ACT

EAN Australia

EAN Australia is non-profit organisation that locally administers the global multi-industry system of identification and communication for products, services, assets and locations - the EANUCC system.

Type	E-business support agencies and bodies
Topics	E-business support contacts Reference Sources
Phone	1300 366 033
Website	http://www.ean.com.au
Date	2003

Electronic Commerce Association of Central Victoria

Provides support, information & networking opportunities for business people, especially in the

Type	E-business support agencies and bodies
Topics	E-business support contacts
Address	P.O. Box 1229
Suburb	Bendigo
State	VIC
Postcode	3552
Email	jmann@britafe.vic.edu.au
Website	http://www.ecomcv.asn.au/
Date	2003
Geographical Coverage	Victoria

Internet Industry Association

IIA provides policy input to government and advocacy on a range of business and regulatory

Type	E-business support agencies and bodies
Topics	Support agencies and bodies
Author Owner	Internet Industry Association (IIA)
Address	PO Box 3986
Suburb	Manuka
State	ACT
Postcode	2603
Phone	+61 2 6232 6900
Fax	+61 2 6232 6513
Email	info@iia.net.au
Website	http://www.iia.net.au/default.htm
Date	2003

Small Business Development Corporation's e-Com entry point

Small Business Development Corporation's e-Com entry point

A website for small business about doing business electronically. Covers information from e-commerce start up issues to electronic selling. SBDC provides small business in WA with information to make informed decisions about applying e-commerce. SBDC have a selection of physical resources available at their offices in Perth.

Type	E-business support agencies and bodies
Topics	Building your e-business E-business support contacts Managing your e-business Planning your e-business Support agencies and bodies
Author Owner	Small Business Development Corporation (WA)
Address	553 Hay St
Suburb	Perth
State	WA
Postcode	6000
Phone	1300 366 837 (within WA), 1800 199 125 (country callers within WA) +61 8 9220 0222
Email	e-com@sbdc.com.au
Website	http://www.sbdc.com.au/drilldown/drilldown.asp?refid=7
Date	2002
Geographical Coverage	Western Australia

Small Business Website

Provides information, business tools, case studies and a forum for discussion on issues affecting small business, including e-business.

Type	E-business support agencies and bodies
Topics	E-business support contacts Support agencies and bodies
Author Owner	NSW Dept of State & Regional Development
Phone	1300 134 359 (within NSW) +61 2 9338 6666
Email	first@business.nsw.gov.au
Website	http://www.smallbiz.nsw.gov.au
Date	2002
Geographical Coverage	New South Wales

Sydney Business Enterprise Centre

Offers practical assistance and confidential advice to small business.

Type	E-business support agencies and bodies

Topics	E-business support contacts Support agencies and bodies
Address	Level 11 418a Elizabeth St
Suburb	Surry Hills
State	NSW
Postcode	2010
Phone	+61 2 9282 6977
Fax	+61 2 9281 2546
Email	sydneybec@sydneybec.com.au
Website	http://www.sydneybec.com.au
Date	2002
Geographical Coverage	New South Wales

Tasmanian Electronic Commerce Centre Pty Ltd

TECC describes itself as a bridge between the IT industry and traditional business, as well as a trusted deliverer of Government programs.

Type	E-business support agencies and bodies
Topics	E-business support contacts
Address	Head Office 42-48 St John St
Suburb	Launceston
State	TAS
Postcode	7250
Phone	1800 249 105 (within Tasmania),+61 3 6336 7777
Fax	+61 3 6331 0660
Email	info@tecc.com.au
Website	
Date	2002
Geographical Coverage	Tasmania

PRIVATE SUPPORT PROVIDERS

This resource assists small South Australian businesses take their first steps into doing e-business. It includes a searchable directory of South Australian companies who provide services in the area of e-business.

Type	E-business support providers (private)
Topics	E-business support contacts
Author Owner	IT Council of South Australia
Website	http://www.ebusiness.on.net/
Date	2003
Geographical Coverage	South Australia

eDIRECT

eDIRECT is a directory of Northern Territory Information, Communication and Technology(ICT) businesses.

Type	E-business support providers (private)
Topics	E-business support contacts
Author Owner	NT Dept of Business Industry & Resource Development
Website	http://notes.nt.gov.au/dib/edirect.nsf
Date	2002
Geographical Coverage	Northern Territory

Queensland ICT Product & Services Guide

This Guide profiles Queensland ICT companies, highlighting their capabilities, products and services.

Type	E-business support providers (private)
Topics	E-business support contacts
Author Owner	QLD Dept of Innovation & Information Economy, Information Industries Board
Website	http://www.iib.qld.gov.au/guide/
Geographical Coverage	Queensland

Tasmanian IT / EC Register

A register of information technology and electronic commerce providers to assist Tasmanian companies realise their electronic commerce plans.

Type	E-business support providers (private)
Topics	E-business support contacts
Author Owner	Tasmanian Electronic Commerce Centre Pty Ltd
Website	http://www.tecc.com.au/tecc/registry/search.asp
Date	2002
Geographical Coverage	Tasmania

VicIT : a directory of Victorian IT companies

VicIT is a directory of Victorian IT companies. It has been developed by the Victorian Government for businesses seeking information about Victorian IT companies. This is a useful resource for anyone looking for IT support in Victoria.

Type	E-business support providers (private)

Topics	E-business support contacts
Author Owner	Multimedia Victoria
Website	http://www.vicit.com.au/
Date	2002
Geographical Coverage	Victoria

GOVERNMENT ASSISTANCE

ebizSA

ebizSA is a unique program specifically developed to help South Australian small-to-medium-sized enterprises (SMEs) exploit today's Internet technologies-to use those technologies to offer better, faster, more cost-effective service, streamline their business systems and processes, and compete successfully locally, nationally and internationally.

Type	Government assistance and grant programs, training and e-business skills development workshops, seminars and e-business work placement programs.
Topics	E-business support contacts Support agencies and bodies Building your e-business Managing your e-business Planning your e-business
Phone Email:	(08) 8303 2133 ivor.hay@state.sa.gov.au
Website	http://www.ebiz.sa.gov.au
Date	2004
Geographical Coverage	South Australia

Ecommerce: information on how your business can take advantage of ecommerce opportunities

This site provides information including case studies and factsheets on using e-business and e-commerce strategies.

Type	Government assistance and grant programs
Topics	Building your e-business E-business support contacts Managing your e-business Planning your e-business Support agencies and bodies
Author Owner	Qld Dept of State Development
Phone	13 26 50 (within Queensland)
Website	http://www.sdi.qld.gov.au/dsdweb/v3/guis/templates/content/gui_cue_cntnhtml.cfm?id=48
Date	2002
Geographical	Queensland

Coverage

Industry TechLink

This service allows small and medium size enterprise owners to talk to a technology consultant who can help them, identify their technology needs and improve their profits. This is a free service and is available nationally Monday through Friday from 9:00 am - 4:00 pm. For faster service, have your ABN number ready when you call.

Type	Government assistance and grant programs
Topics	E-business support contacts Support agencies and bodies
Author Owner	Ausindustry
Phone	1800 111 485
Email	enquiries@industrytechlink.com.au
Website	http://www.industrytechlink.com.au/
Date	2003

Multimedia Victoria

Multimedia Victoria (MMV) is the agency responsible for implementing the State Government's information and communication technology policy, "Connecting Victoria".

Type	Government assistance and grant programs
Topics	E-business support contacts Support agencies and bodies
Address	Level 10 55 Collins St
Suburb	Melbourne
State	Vic
Postcode	3000
Phone	+61 3 9651 9868
Fax	+61 3 9651 8031
Email	queries@mmv.vic.gov.au
Website	http://www.mmv.vic.gov.au
Date	2003
Geographical Coverage	Victoria

Victorian Business Line

Business Access is responsible for fostering the growth of Victoria's small business sector. It provides information, assistance and referral service for small business.

Type	Government assistance and grant programs
Topics	E-business support contacts

	Support agencies and bodies
Author Owner	Business Access Victoria
Phone	13 22 15
Fax	03 9651 9725
Email	businessaccess@iird.vic.gov.au
Website	http://www.businessaccess.vic.gov.au
Date	2003
Geographical Coverage	Victoria

Victorian eCommerce Info Centre

This website is designed to assist users understand the possible applications of e-commerce for their business, explain the benefits and risks, list steps for getting on the Web, and provide tips for a successful eCommerce implementation.

Type	Government assistance and grant programs
Topics	E-business support contacts Support agencies and bodies
Email	enquiries@ecommerce.vic.gov.au
Website	http://www.ecommerce.vic.gov.au
Date	2002
Geographical Coverage	Victoria

West Australian E-commerce Centre

This site provides information to assist with e-commerce initiatives including e-commerce news, events, ca studies, e-commerce guides and explanations.

Type	Government assistance and grant programs
Topics	E-business support contacts Support agencies and bodies
Author Owner	WA Dept of Industry & Technology
Address	Dumas House 2 Havelock St
Suburb	West Perth
State	WA
Postcode	6005
Phone	+61 8 9222 5673 (direct line to E-commerce Centre)
Fax	+61 8 9222 5055
Email	ecommercecentre@indtech.wa.gov.au
Website	http://www.doir.wa.gov.au/businessandindustry/CA668192841A4F74BF0605D7F3367D39.a
Date	2003
Geographical Coverage	Western Australia

Information Technology Online (ITOL) Funding Program

An Australian Government funding program administered by the Department of Communications, Information Technology and the Arts (DCITA) designed to accelerate the national adoption of e-business solutions, especially by small to medium enterprises (SMEs), across a broad range of industry sectors and geographic regions.

Type	Government assistance and grant programs
Topics	Government agencies and bodies Support agencies and bodies
Author Owner	DCITA
Publisher	DCITA
Organisation Name	DCITA
Website	http://www.dcita.gov.au/communications_for_business
Date	2003
Geographical Coverage	Australia

PRINTED AND ELECTRONIC INFORMATION

Australia.gov.au - The entry point to Australian government services

Australia.gov.au provides access to a range of websites, specifically built to provide access to relevant government services and information without the need to know which government agency to go to.

Type	Printed and electronic information
Topics	Reference sources
Author Owner	National Office for the Information Economy
Website	http://www.australia.gov.au/

Australian Tax Office - Dealing Electronically

The website enables you to deal electronically with the ATO.

Type Printed and electronic information
Topics Managing your e-business
Reference sources
Website http://www.ato.gov.au/esd/esd_main.htm

Exporting online

Provides information about having an effective website and online communication.

Type Printed and electronic information
Topics Managing your e-business
Planning your e-business
Reference sources
Author Owner Austrade
Website http://www.austrade.gov.au/australia/layout/0,,0_S2-1_CLNTXID009-2_-3_PWB1142402-4_-5_-6_-7_,00.html
Date 2003

Internet Tool Kit

This page provides access to the ACA Internet Tool Kit. The Tool Kit is an information portal designed to help you choose the best value mobile, Internet and fixed line products and services to meet your unique needs.

Type Printed and electronic information
Topics Reference sources
Author Owner Australian Communications and Media Authority
Phone 1800 35 11 35 (free call) to a print or CD-ROM version of the Toolkit
Email consumer.awareness1@aca.gov.au.
Website http://www.toolkit.aca.gov.au/internet/index.htm

e-business @ work: an Australian overview

Provides information for small and medium enterprises looking to develop or expand an e-business strategy.

Type Printed and electronic information
Topics Managing your e-business
Reference sources
Author Owner Pauline Farrell, Elizabeth Bradbury and Julia Durovic
Publisher Frenchs Forest, NSW: Pearson Education Australia
Website ISBN: 1740093135

Australian e-business guide. 2nd ed.

Contains information, tools, resources and references to aid business advisers and small to medium businesses in adopting and operating e-business. This is an annual publication.

Type Printed and electronic information
Topics Legal issues
Maintaining your e-business systems
Marketing
Reference sources
Security
Author Owner CCH Australia
Publisher North Ryde, NSW: CCH Australia
Website ISBN: 1864686375

Marketing for e-business in Australia

Addresses marketing and business principles for e-business.

Type Printed and electronic information
Topics Marketing
Reference sources
Author Owner Lynne H de Weaver
Publisher Frenchs Forest, NSW : Pearson Education Australia
Website ISBN: 1740095529

How to win more work with e-business

Type Printed and electronic information
Topics Building your e-business
Managing your e-business
Planning your e-business
Security
Author Owner NIEF - National Infrastructure and Engineering Forum Inc
Publisher Dept. Industry Tourism and Resources
Phone +61 2 9231 0764
Fax +61 2 9231 0765
Email info@nief.com.au

Website http://www.nief.com.au

our brisbane.com - Get your business online
Provides an 'e-journey' audit as a way of working out how much your business is using the opportunities available via the Internet.

Type Printed and electronic information
Topics Building your e-business
Planning your e-business
Reference sources
Author Owner Brisbane City Council
Address GPO Box 1434
Suburb Brisbane
State Qld
Postcode 4001
Fax +61 7 3403 7433
Email obsales@team.ourbrisbane.com
Website http://www.ourbrisbane.com/ourwebstarter/guide.htm
Date 2003
Geographical Coverage Queensland

E-biz: commerce on the net
A video available for purchase through the ABC Video Program Sales. A web site is also available http://www.abc.net.au/ebiz.
A six part television series about doing business on the Internet, includes case studies. It has been designed as a "starter kit" for small business who are thinking of conducting some aspect of their business online.

Type Printed and electronic information
Topics Building your e-business
Managing your e-business
Planning your e-business
Reference sources
Author Owner Australian Broadcasting Corporation
Website http://www.abc.net.au/ebiz/

E-business start-up: the complete guide to launching your internet and digital enterprise
Provides information about starting an e-business.

Type Printed and electronic information
Topics Building your e-business
Planning your e-business
Reference sources
Author Owner Philip Treleaven and Charles Birch
Publisher Elsternwick, Vic: Wrightbooks
Website ISBN: 1876627719

Measuring the success of your website: a customer-centric approach to website management
Explains how to monitor the experience of visitors to your website and evaluate the site in terms of the business objectives.

Type Printed and electronic information
Topics Evaluating your e-business
Reference sources
Author Owner Hurol Inan
Publisher Frenchs Forest, NSW: Pearson Education Australia

Website ISBN: 1740096487

OZeculture: eBusiness for the cultural sector

This site has an e-business manaual, website agreement and business plan templates. This was originally a national training program in 2001 to assist cultural organisations develop e-Business strategies.

Type Printed and electronic information
Topics Planning your e-business
Reference sources
Author Owner Commonwealth Dept of Communications, Information Technology and the Arts (DCITA)
Website http://www.cultureandrecreation.gov.au/ebusinessguide/

The rural and regional guide to e-commerce

Further details are available at http://www.rirdc.gov.au/farmersguide/RRGTEdefault.htm. Introduces e-commerce from a rural and regional perspective.

Type Printed and electronic information
Topics Building your e-business
E-commerce on your website
Marketing
Planning your e-business
Reference sources
Author Owner Robert Parker & Franco Papandrea
Publisher Barton ACT: Rural Industries Research & Development Corp.
Address PO Box 4776
Suburb Kingston
State ACT
Postcode 2600
Phone +61 2 6272 4819
Fax +61 2 6272 5877
Website ISBN: 0642584028

ShopSafe

The ShopSafe website demonstrates how online shopping works and what to look out for. There are quizzes to see how much you have learned.

Type Printed and electronic information
Topics E-commerce on your website
Reference sources
Security
Author Owner Consumer Affairs Victoria
Publisher Melbourne: Communications Branch, Consumer Affairs Victoria, Vic. Dept of Justice
Website http://www.consumer.vic.gov.au/shopsafe/index.html
Date 2002
Geographical Coverage

Opportunity Wales eCommerce website

This site contains a range of articles written by the eCommerce Centre of Excellence. They cover a wide spectrum of topics addressing business and technical issues.

Type Printed and electronic information
Topics International sites
Website http://www.opportunitywales.co.uk/0-0-0/2-0-0.htm

NZ ecommerce
This website is a gateway to the information about e-commerce available in New Zealand.
Type Printed and electronic information
Topics International sites
Email info@nzecommerce.co.nz
Website http://www.biz.org.nz/public/section.aspx?sectionid=37

Hong Kong Digital 21: E-commerce web site
"Digital 21" web site is a dedicated channel through which the Hong Kong Government disseminate information about the "Digital 21" IT Strategy. It is a joint effort of the Commerce, Industry and Technology Bureau, the Information Technology Services Department, and other government bureaux and departments. It is updated on a regular basis.
Type Printed and electronic information
Topics International sites
Author Owner Hong Kong Special Administrative Region Government
Email webmaster@digital21.gov.hk
Website http://www.info.gov.hk/digital21/eng/ecommerce/intro.html

Canada's ebiz.enable
ebiz.enable is a Candian site designed specifically for small and medium-sized businesses (SMEs). It has a number of on-line resources that allows you to explore e-business problems and solutions.
Type Printed and electronic information
Topics International sites
Author Owner Industry Canada
Email strategis@ic.gc.ca
Website http://strategis.ic.gc.ca/epic/internet/inee-ef.nsf/vwGeneratedInterE/Home

Practical advice for business – E-commerce
The Businesslink.gov.uk website is a truly “joined-up” government website, drawing on the expertise of numerous key government bodies that deal with business. It offers jargon-free advice, plus information and support on the use of technology for small and medium-sized business (SMEs).
Type Printed and electronic information
Topics International sites
Author Owner UK Dept of Trade and Industry (Small Business Service)
Website:http://www.businesslink.gov.uk/bdotg/action/layer?r.l1=1073861197&r.s=tl&topicId=1073866263

STRATEGIC INFORMATION FOR CONDUCTING BUSINESS[29]

INFRASTRUCTURE

Geographically, Australia is similar in size to the continental U.S. Despite its small population and relatively large landmass, it has a well-developed capital infrastructure, including nationwide air, road, rail, port and telecommunications networks comparable to other OECD countries. The Asian economic downturn did not affect infrastructure development in Australia to any measurable extent.

Privatization and corporatization of Government-owned facilities and services has been high on Australian state and federal government agendas since the early 90's, and the sale and/or lease of public facilities and utilities continues to progress at a steady and determined pace.

A significant proportion of large projects being undertaken in Australia is as a result of infrastructure developments and privatization of facilities formerly run by federal, state and local governments. Demand for further infrastructure development is due to population growth, changing demographic patterns, increased environmental awareness, and a cumulative obsolescence of existing infrastructure facilities. Reforms in the ownership and management of public utilities, such as electricity, natural gas and telecommunications, are resulting in a more competitive supply and distribution infrastructure. In Sydney, for example, the 2000 Olympic Games contributed to a sense of urgency to establish a transport infrastructure capable of meeting the needs of a city highly dependent on inbound tourism, but which has been slow to develop an efficient urban road system.

The private sector has accepted the privatization challenge and is now engaged in nationwide infrastructure creation, upgrade and maintenance. An open market in the airline industry has reduced the cost of air travel, improved passenger service and encouraged competitors to challenge traditional rivals, Ansett and Qantas. Australia's airports, with few exceptions (one of which is Sydney's Kingsford Smith), have been sold to private consortia on long-term leases. The federal government's waterfront reform policies, after a bitter feud with the maritime union, have begun to show improvements in efficiency and work practices. It is now moving ahead with plans to sell rail assets, and is showing determination to sell off a further third of its telecommunications carrier, Telstra.

AIR TRANSPORT

Air transport is used extensively within Australia, which, including its territories, has around 280 licensed airports. The major international gateways, of which there are nine, include Sydney, Melbourne, Brisbane, Perth and Cairns. The majority of all airports are owned and operated by local and state governments, private companies and the Department of Defense. International passenger and cargo flights are frequent and reliable.

Air is used extensively for lighter cargo, small high-value items, and for urgent needs. Domestic airlines carry about 200,000 tons of cargo per annum. An extensive network of air cargo operators, including major international companies, offers a full range of cargo services, processing of documentation relating to importation and clearance of goods, and follow-on-

[29] This section based in part on the materials of the US Department of Commerce and the US State Department

delivery to regional centers. Australia is serviced by most of the world's major air carriers, feeding into a well-established domestic network covering the trunk commuter routes. An active regional airline service links regional centers with the capital cities. Almost all of Australia's airports have been privatized, and now operate on a commercial, profit-oriented basis, competing for passenger and freight revenue. Australia's major airport, Sydney's Kingsford Smith, is in the process of being sold by the Federal Government, which should be completed by the end of 2004. The aviation industry is unregulated, and is dominated by long-time carriers Qantas and Ansett. Virgin Blue is operating on a limited service basis and is exerting a moderating influence on fares for air transport users.

Australia is a member of the International Civil Aviation Organization and is represented on the Air Navigation Commission. It has full treaty air service agreements with forty countries. Within Australia, Airservices Australia manages air traffic control over Australia's eleven percent of the earth's surface, and the Civil Aviation Safety Authority is responsible for ensuring aviation safety.

During 2004, the commercial airline industry is undergoing a period of rapid change and consolidation, with the forging of new alliances and shareholding transfers. It is unlikely that stability will return to the industry until at least 2002.

Road/Rail Transport

With its huge land mass, small population and limited tax base, the extensiveness of Australia's modern national, state and local road system is quite remarkable. Road funding continues to feature prominently in both State and Federal Government budgets, with the voting public demanding high quality roads. Australia's road transport industry is relatively efficient and approaches world best practice. The majority of interstate goods transport is by road.

A 24,000-mile network of railroads competes with road transport. Rail transport is the preferred mode to Perth, in Western Australia, for the transportation of freight from Eastern ports, and for the bulk transport of Australia's mineral exports. Traditionally, rail transport has lagged behind international best practice. In the last century, before Federation of the States into the Commonwealth, each state government established its own (differing) gauge railway to encourage its own industries, with cargo having to be transferred at state boundaries.

The completion of the first standard-gauge rail line from Brisbane to Perth (via Sydney, Melbourne and Adelaide) in June, 1995, heralded a new era in rail freight transport and the prospect of an efficient, truly national rail transportation system. The ability to track a coal train from Queensland to South Australia was a symbolic step in Australia's reform agenda. In 1999, a major rail line from Adelaide to Darwin was announced, with a completion date of 2003.

The mid-1990s also saw every rail administration in Australia substantially restructured, with most becoming corporatized entities. In August 1997, the Federal Government sold Australian National Railways (AN), which operated various freight and passenger operations. In January 1999, the Victorian State Government privatized its freight business, V/Line Freight, and franchised its passenger rail and suburban tram networks. In October 2000, Western Australia's freight business was sold and, at the time of writing, the Federal Government was planning to sell the National Rail Corporation, an interstate freight business.

Sea Transport

Australia is a trade-dependent country, with the fifth-largest shipping task in the world. It trades with around 200 countries, moving approximately half a billion tons of cargo per annum. In volume terms, ninety-nine percent of its imports arrive by sea and ninety-six percent of its exports leave by waterborne transport. It is serviced by major shipping lines transporting goods worldwide, to and from the major ports of Melbourne, Sydney, Brisbane, Adelaide and Fremantle. Ninety-five percent of the trade volume is carried by non-Australian flagged vessels.

Australia has modern, deep-water ports. New South Wales and Queensland account for 58 percent of all ships registered in Australia (8,246 total), the majority of which are used for non-commercial purposes. The major Australian trading fleet is comprised of 62 ships of 2,000 tons or over, two-thirds of which operate on coastal routes, moving around 60 million tons of cargo annually. Interstate trade accounts for nearly two-thirds of coastal freight, although in recent years this proportion has shown a steady decline. The majority of cargo shipped between Australian ports is comprised of bulk commodities.

The government business enterprise responsible for maritime safety in Australian waters (including regulatory issues, the navigational aids network, maritime search and rescue, pollution prevention and clean up, and registration) is the Australian Maritime Safety Authority (AMSA). AMSA is funded mostly by levies on the shipping industry.

TELECOMMUNICATIONS

Australia's telecommunications infrastructure is as sophisticated and modern as any in the world, with a fully digitalized network. The main telephone lines are mostly land-based and penetrate about 96 percent of all households. In a population of 19 million, there are almost 10 million mobile phone subscribers, more than 3.9 million Internet subscribers, and over 9 million Internet users in Australia.

Australia's telecommunications industry was fully deregulated on July 1, 1997. There are now more than 70 carriers registered with the Australian Communications Authority, compared to two prior to deregulation. The new carriers, often former service providers, are generally reliant upon leasing network capacity from Telstra, although some have developed their own switching and network capability, particularly on the eastern seaboard and for overseas call markets. Aside from Telstra, the most significant carriers include Optus, Primus, AAPT (owned by Telecom NZ), Orange and Vodafone. All carriers, excluding Telstra (with 51 percent Government ownership), are private.

The influx of smaller carriers into the telephony market has acted as one of the major developments in producing important competitive results in the deregulated market. The Australian Competition and Consumer Commission (ACCC) released, in June 2004, a summary of the effects of increased competition on pricing to consumers. The average price of telecommunications purchased has fallen by 17.5% in real terms over the past four years (between 1996/97 and 1999/2000).

Telstra, the former monopoly carrier, is the dominant provider of Australia's land-based telephony service. This network has nearly 10 million connections and an annual growth rate of five percent. Telstra still dominates the telecommunications environment, although its market share has dropped significantly in recent years. Optus Communications, the second largest carrier, provides its own switching capability, but primarily uses the Telstra trunk and local loops. It has developed a broadband network (alongside the Telstra broadband network) to collectively "pass" some 4 million homes.

Mobile phone services are well-established in Australia, which has one of the highest user rates in the world. The current number of mobile phone subscribers is just under 10 million. Mobile phone services are provided using the two major technologies: GSM and Code Division Multiple Access (CDMA). Telstra, Optus and Vodafone each operate separate GSM mobile networks.

CDMA services are provided by Telstra, Orange and AAPT. Hutchison Telecommunications, under the brand name Orange, has 120,000 subscribers on their Orange One CDMA network. The fate of the network built by failed carrier One.Tel, which went into receivership in June 2004, is yet to be decided. Telstra's share of the mobile phone market is around 48% with Optus at 33% and at Vodafone 18%.

Hutchison Telecommunications (Orange) has announced the development of a 3G network across Australia, covering the greater metropolitan areas of Sydney, Brisbane, Adelaide, Perth and Melbourne. It is anticipated that services will be available on this network from early 2003.

Australian communications technology is historically European-based, due to Australia's historical links with the U.K., and to Swedish company Ericsson's early (1928) establishment in Australia. Land-based telephony operates according to European E1 standards, but differ somewhat to create a uniquely Australian version. However, since newer technologies or protocols are largely U.S.-developed, U.S.-made products are also in high demand.

Telstra, Optus and Vodafone have already purchased, or are committed to purchasing network infrastructure and equipment, following massive development of their networks during the past 3-5 years. Infrastructure has been established for digital mobile technology and the digitalization of land-based networks. Carriers are required under the Telecommunications Act of 1997 to submit and follow Industry Development Plans, listing companies they have negotiated with for the supply of infrastructure and equipment.

ENERGY

The fuel presently used for power generation in Australia is mainly coal (black and brown). Overall, natural gas consumption is predicted to grow by 30 percent to 2014-15. Capital investment in generation is estimated to have cost US$25 billion to date, and the value of the predicted infrastructure for the expansion of generation capacity is estimated to be US$15 billion.

The deregulation of both the electricity and natural gas industries has led to more competition and energy efficiency in both sectors. Australia's energy consumption is expected to grow by 14 percent by the year 2010. The energy market is now fully competitive and contestable for electricity generation by the year 2002, and approximately 70 percent of electricity and gas utilities are owned by U.S. companies.

With regard to raw materials, international economists have nominated the Australasian region as the powerhouse of the next century. The region already has an abundance of natural resources and development in the oil and gas sector is set to play a major role on the world stage. It is estimated that more than US$95 billion will be invested in new petroleum development in the Australasian region over the next ten years.

The oil and gas industry continues to make a major contribution to the Australian economy. The annual value of oil and gas production in Australia is approximately US$15 billion. There are plans for US$30 billion of oil and related projects to be studied in Australia over the next five years. One of the largest projects is the development of significant oil discoveries worth (to date) approximately US$9 billion in the Timor Sea (off the coast of Darwin), and a multi-billion dollar expansion plan for the US$12 billion Northwest Shelf LNG project in Western Australia.

Current electricity generation in Australia is around 45,000 MW and is expected to grow to 55,000 MW by the year 2010. This new generation capacity of 10,000 MW is expected to come from plants in the development stage for 3,400 MW, with the remaining 5,600 MW coming from plants being proposed. Many of these projects will be using clean coal technologies and other renewable energy methods of generation, such as co-generation, combined gas-cycle plants, wind, solar and biomass. This will improve efficiencies over the present generation methods, such as coal.

WATER AND SEWERAGE

Average annual expenditure on new capital works and renewal works for urban water supply and sewerage treatment is on the order of US$522 million. Expenditure on reticulation (the transport of water via pipes, sewers, etc. accounts for 50 percent of capital works. Investment in water treatment facilities accounts for 30 percent and expenditure on bulk storage is approximately 20 percent.

Australia's water supply and sewerage treatment infrastructure is well-established, and systems are being expanded to meet demand generated by industrialization and urbanization. Water authorities are the main purchasers and users of goods and services in this sector, while private industry is the most effective developer and marketer of new technology.

In response to public concern and demand, the industry is moving from an emphasis on the supply of water toward a greater focus on resource usage, the quality of the water supplied to consumers, and pollution control. There are also significant concerns regarding the protection of the environment, particularly with regard to discharges of wastewater.

Between 0.5 and 6 percent of the population currently receive water of unsatisfactory quality and there is growing impetus to achieve the high quality found in major urban supplies. While some technologies for water treatment and sewerage systems are well established, this sector is now subject to significant technological change as the sewage to be treated becomes chemically more complex due to pollutants, and as more stringent standards are imposed on effluent discharges to protect the recipient land or water body.

National responsibility for water and environmental matters falls under the Department of Primary Industries and Energy (DPIE) and the Environment Protection Agency (EPA), respectively. Design, construction, management and maintenance of water and wastewater treatment facilities, however, are primarily shared between state authorities, boards, county councils, local government councils, and private interests. The roles of these parties vary from State to State.

CONSTRUCTION

Some 80 percent of all engineering construction work in Australia is classified as infrastructure and includes roads, railways, dams, bridges, major pipelines, electricity, telecommunications, mining, and heavy industry. A recent survey by a leading Australian project developer and economic forecaster estimated the value of engineering construction work for the year ended June 30, 2004 at US$5.7 billion (down 11 percent on 1999-00), with US$5.8 billion forecast for 2004-02.

According to leading industry forecaster BIS Shrapnel, the extraordinary near-decade long boom in engineering construction has come to a temporary halt. The reason for the decline is that the biggest and most attractive projects for private investment have largely been done. Most state and territory infrastructure construction programs launched in the late 1990s have been completed and new government projects have not been brought forward fast enough to replace them. However, construction activity is expected to soar once again in June 2004-June 2005 and exceed US$10.8 billion, before peaking in 2006 at a level well above the previous peak of the late 1990s.

BIS Shrapnel warns that the current decline should not cause alarm, as in reality the decline represents only a small proportion of the increases experienced during the last eight years. Several sectors will in fact remain strong and even strengthen, among them mining and heavy industry construction. The rail, pipeline, and harbor sectors will perform strongly, as will water storage supply.

INTERNET ACCESS

Internet access is affordable and ubiquitous in Australia. Access rates are falling constantly, and at the current exchange rate, subscribers can find unlimited access plans (downloads and time) from any of the major carriers from US$10/month for 56K lines.

In Australia, local telephone calls are charged at a flat rate.

According to a recent survey conducted by the Australian Bureau of Statistics (ABS), as of the September quarter 2000 there were 718 Internet Service Providers (ISP's), supplying Internet access to 3.8 million active subscribers in the local market. Of the 718 ISPs operating in the Australian market, there are a large number of small ISPs (377 small ISPs, with between 101-1,000 subscribers), and a small number of large ISPs, which have the largest share of subscribers (8 very large ISPs, with more than 100,000 subscribers, provide Internet access to 60 percent of total subscribers). Some of the principal ISPs in the local market include: Telstra Big Pond, Optus, MCI Worldcom (UUNet), Primus and AAPT.

Most household subscribers access the Internet on 56K modems. The major telecommunications carriers, Telstra and Optus, offer attractive bundling deals with cable television and Internet access, but unfortunately, these services are only offered in select suburbs of the major capital cities, and both carriers have no plans to roll out new cable in underserviced areas.

Telstra has recently introduced ADSL technology to the major Australian cities. It has been reported that there are approximately 200,000 subscribers to this US$50/month service, but it has been plagued with intermittent faults. It will take Telstra at least six months to iron out all the bugs in its ADSL Internet access technology.

INVESTMENT IN BROADBAND TECHNOLOGY

The future of Australian communications has never been so exciting and challenging, as the nation embraces the advent of number portability, digital technology, greater mobility, and demands for new and innovative services requiring the use of broadband spectrum.

Since deregulation of the telecommunications industry in 1997, there has been a great surge in the development of broadband infrastructure. A number of telecommunications carriers have invested in fiber optic access networks, including Telstra, Optus, AAPT, MCI WorldCom and PowerTel. Generally speaking, these networks parallel the most heavily used of Telstra's infrastructure (between capital cities).

The Australian Government has been actively pursuing development of technologies as part of its general push for Australia to become an information economy, particularly in rural and regional areas. Through "Networking the Nation", the Commonwealth has provided more than US$250 million in grants to encourage the development of information services to regional and rural Australia and overcome the "Digital Divide" between the cities and remote areas.

Interestingly, some smaller Australian towns will have access to broadband services sooner, and of better quality, than customers in the capital cities. For example, Cooma (NSW) will shortly have a fiber optic network, due to an agreement between their local ISP and Australian Gas Light Company (AGL), which is installing gas mains through out the town. The ISP negotiated an agreement to install fiber alongside the mains, which will now provide consumers with 100 mbit/sec access, free telephony between customers, and other services. This agreement is likely to benefit other rural towns as AGL rolls out gas mains. A major project being conducted by TransACT Communications in the national capital, Canberra, is wiring up the entire city with fiber. This network is open to all service providers and will offer full telephone service, a permanent high-speed Internet connection, and a wide range of video and television services.

Australia lags somewhat behind the U.S. in terms of broadband access for both corporate and residential customers. XDSL technologies became available to consumers in August 2000, following the unbundling of the local loop. However, there are still some teething problems with this service, nearly one year after its introduction: pricing, delivery quality and ease of access have all been cited as problems. In addition, Telstra has come under fire for its wholesale pricing of DSL to competitors, which is higher than the retail pricing to consumers buying the service from Telstra.

Inequality of access to services between regional and metropolitan consumers has been modified somewhat by the introduction of satellite services. Telstra and Optus both offer a range of broadband services, including DSL, satellite and cable. Regional consumers are now able to access satellite services, as are those metropolitan consumers who either live near exchanges not fitted with DSL or away from the cable route. Level of income now seems the major cause of inequity in access to services, rather than metropolitan/regional issues.

Hutchinson Telecommunications, under the brand name Orange, operates a wireless telephony network called Orange One. They have also just announced the development of their 3G network, estimated to cost around US$500 million and to be operational in 2003. This network will cover the greater metropolitan areas of Sydney, Brisbane, Adelaide, Perth and Melbourne.

The main types of broadband infrastructure in place are:

a) "Fiber to the Curb (FTTC)" architecture;

b) "Hybrid Fiber Coax", an FTTC architecture deployed by Telstra and Optus for cable TV and data services;

c) xDSL technologies, available through a number of providers;

d) Wireless broadband access, including microwave (LMDS and MMDS), infrared and laser, which is being implemented in metropolitan/capital city environments; and

e) Satellite, which is offered by both Telstra and Optus, for corporate, residential and military customers to provide TV, Internet, telephony and data transmission.

E-COMMERCE

As mentioned in the previous section, Australia has been implementing a range of broadband technologies that can be used in commercial applications. Many of these services are available to "Small Office Home Office" (SOHO) customers, who are usually small business owners.

The Australian Government, like its U.S. counterpart, is encouraging its citizens to become literate in the on-line environment. To ensure that regional and rural locations do not miss out, the "Networking the Nation" Commonwealth-funded grants system is providing funding to encourage e-commerce in these areas. This funding is providing infrastructure and capacity, as well as support and training for businesses. Some state governments also provide funding to businesses to develop a web presence. This is particularly aimed at small business.

Australia has more than 690 ISPs servicing 3.92 million subscribers. More than 85% of these subscribers are households. In terms of business connections, 361,000 businesses were connected to the Internet. Of these:

- 36% use the internet for banking and financial services;
- 28% use the internet for selling-related acts; and
- 24% use the internet for procurement.

In 2000, the National Office of the Information Economy further reported that of those businesses with websites:
- 95 percent use the website to promote products and services;
- 65 percent use the website for customer services;
- 54 percent use the website to receive online orders; and
- 41 percent use the website for online advertising to promote their own business.

STATE SUMMARIES

NEW SOUTH WALES

New South Wales, Australia's most populous state, has the most sophisticated and diverse economy in Australia. Its capital, Sydney, is the nation's only 'global city', and a major financial center in the Asia-Pacific region. NSW Gross State Product grew by 3.7% in real terms in 1999-2000, representing 36% of the national economy, larger than each of the national economies of Thailand, Singapore, Malaysia, the Philippines and New Zealand.

Sydney is a strong financial center in the region, home to the Reserve Bank of Australia, the Australian Stock Exchange and the Sydney Futures Exchange. It is also the head office location for 40 of Australia's 51 banks, which includes 34 of 38 foreign banks in Australia. The State accounts for almost one-third of the total Australian workforce and more than 45% of all employees in the finance and insurance sector. NSW also employs more than one-third of the national workforce in the transport, communications and property and business services sectors. NSW continues to attract the largest number of regional headquarters of multinational companies in Australia, mostly in the information technology, communications and finance sectors. Fifty percent of the top 500 companies in Australia have also chosen to locate in NSW.

NSW and Sydney are the major entry points to Australia, with Sydney Airport providing the bulk of air freight and business air passenger activity. NSW is also well-serviced with efficient, cost-effective port facilities, as well as with other land transport networks. The cost of telecommunications services, real estate, transport and energy are (globally) very competitive.

The State is a major consumer and user of modern technology products, and is at the forefront of developments in knowledge-based industries. It has the largest number of adults of any state accessing computers and the Internet.

NSW is the base for 45.8% of Australia's finance and insurance industry, 40.7% of its property and business services (including IT) industry, and 35% of its communications industry. NSW also accounts for 38.6% and 36.3%, respectively, of national output in the 'lifestyle' industries – accommodation, cafes and restaurants, and cultural and recreational services.

There was US$8 billion in new private investment in NSW in 1999-2000, accounting for more than one third of the national total.

VICTORIA

Victoria boasts a significant and prosperous history in the finance and banking sectors. Today, the capital of Victoria, Melbourne, stands as one of Australia's leading industrial centers. The Victorian Gross State Product (GSP) in 1999 totaled US$79.5 billion, with exports increasing by an annual average growth rate of 8.7 percent over the past six years. Victoria accounts for 34 percent of the nation's manufacturing and 26 percent of Australia's Gross Domestic Product (GDP).

With a solid manufacturing base and strong food and agricultural sectors, Victoria has a competitive advantage in numerous industries, including food, textiles, clothing and footwear, automotive, information technology, scientific, biotechnology, communications, health, and business services. The capital of Victoria, Melbourne, is Australia's leading center for biotechnology in the Asia-Pacific region. Agriculture and food provide over 35 percent of the State's export income. Increasingly a large export earner, the automotive sector in Victoria achieved exports of vehicles and automotive parts totaling US$636 million. The Port of Melbourne, the largest port in the country, handles 39 percent of Australia's container trade.

The Australian headquarters of the seven of the top twenty U.S. *Fortune 500* companies are based in Melbourne. Well-known U.S. companies that have established regional headquarters in Victoria include Campbell's, Ford, GE Capital, Gillette, Monsanto, Hewlett-Packard, and many others.

In the State of Victoria, the Labour Party, which is comparable to the Democratic Party in the United States, currently holds power. The Australian Labor Party (ALP) is Australia's oldest political party, formed nationally in 1901 and given its present name in 1918. The Labour Party of Victoria is led by Victoria's 45th Premier, the Honorable Stephen Bracks.

As a result of the Victorian Government's responsible approach to financial management, Victoria has exceptionally low debt levels, is in a strong fiscal position, has a balanced budget, and boasts a triple-A credit rating. In Victoria, public debt has decreased significantly since 1992.

Victoria has Australia's largest industrial concentration of information technology, scientific, and medical facilities, as well as a highly-skilled workforce. Approximately 50 percent of the Victorian workforce holds post high school qualifications, with over 67,000 people holding postgraduate degrees, the highest concentration in Australia. The 2004-02 state budget positions Victoria as a world leader in innovation, science, and technology, with a massive funding injection for science, technology, research, education, and skills development.

Victoria features the nation's largest concentration of research institutions. The State of Victoria accounts for 35 percent of Australia's total business research and development (R&D) and 70 percent of Australian expenditure is on communications R&D. Victoria is the home to 63 of Australia's 185 dedicated biotechnology companies, accounting for one-third of the national total. The State of Victoria is committed to science, technology and innovation, as reflected in the recent announcement for construction of a synchrotron (the first in Australia) and the development of *Bio 21*, a biotechnology precinct in central Melbourne.

QUEENSLAND

The rapid growth experienced by Queensland in recent years slowed considerably during 2000/2004. The moderation in growth is due mainly to weak conditions in domestic housing and business investment, where there has been a decline in equipment and machinery investment. During the same period, the retail sector maintained steady but solid growth. The relatively low Australian dollar against major currencies, higher oil prices, lower business activity due to the effect of the GST on the construction sector, and a weaker U.S. economy are reported to have exerted downward pressure on growth over the past twelve months. The low Australian dollar, however, has assisted exports in more recent months, coupled with increases in world commodity prices, although the agricultural contribution to the State's exports has been blunted by poor weather and reduced demand.

The Queensland government, boosted by an election victory, continues to support business development, arguably more than any other Australian State. Boasting Australia's lowest state taxes and debt levels, it not only recognizes and welcomes foreign investors as major contributors to the State's economic development, but also aggressively seeks new investment through high-level visits and missions.

Queensland is Australia's most decentralized state, having the largest rail network and more deepwater ports than the rest of Australia combined. It is a resource-rich state, and its ports are the closest to the Asia-Pacific region, with which it has a strong trading relationship. Major export earners for the state include coal, meat, non-ferrous metals and crude minerals. Business and investment opportunities occur in these traditional industries, supplemented by recent growth in communications services, biotechnology, information technology and leisure industries.

Queensland has two fully-operational international airports. A third, Coolangatta, servicing the Gold Coast, is undergoing a ten-year development and management plan, including runway and terminal upgrading, to bring it up to international standards by 2010. The area surrounding Surfers Paradise on the Gold Coast has become Australia's third largest city, yet has no downtown. Innovative fiber-optic technology is creating a virtual downtown in this, the fastest-growing area of Australia

Japan is the major destination for Queensland merchandise exports, the United States being the third largest. Very strong growth has been experienced in both markets in recent months, supporting optimistic views that the economy will return to traditional strong growth during 2004/2002.

WESTERN AUSTRALIA

Western Australia continues to be an important engine for the growth of Australia's industry, trade and investment. WA covers the resource-rich western third of Australia. It is a major world source of a wide range of commodities and is rapidly expanding into the manufacturing and services sectors. The state covers 2.5 million square kilometers and has a population of 1.8 million and a highly-educated workforce of 850,000.

In 1999/2000, Western Australia's gross state product (GSP) totaled A$66.5 billion and accounted for 11 percent of the national economy. Over the last decade, Western Australia's annual rate of growth has averaged 4.9 percent, compared to the national average of 4.1 percent over the same period. These growth rates compare favorably with the OECD average of 2.3 percent since 1990/91. In 2000 WA attracted 12.5 percent of all new private capital investment in Australia. About one-third of all Australian private investment projects committed or being considered in 2000 were in Western Australia, worth an estimated A$26 billion over five years.

Western Australia is a global supplier of minerals and energy, with output totaling A$21.3 billion in 1999/2000. Oil, gas and liquefied natural gas (LNG) comprised 36 percent of output. Iron ore was the state's largest mineral output at A$3.7 billion. Western Australia provides 25 percent of Australia's exports. The state produces 40 percent of the world's diamonds; 44 percent of its zircon; 22 percent of its alumna; 13 percent of its iron ore; and 9 percent of its gold, nickel and LNG.

The services sector, which accounts for about 70 percent of the state's economic activity, is also highly competitive. Western Australian businesses have expertise in healthcare, education, building and construction, communications, environmental management, tourism, business services and resources engineering. The capital city, Perth, has become a preferred location for international companies choosing a regional base for Southeast Asia, especially in industries servicing the oil and gas sectors. Finally, Perth receives more sunshine per day, on average, than any other Australian capital city.

SOUTH AUSTRALIA

South Australia has a land area of 590,863 sq. mi., slightly larger than that of the state of Alaska, and a population of just 1.5 million, the majority of which resides in the capital, Adelaide. Its extensive plains, mild winter and warm summer make the land highly suitable for agriculture, which dominates the economy. Electrical equipment and appliance manufacturing (including automotive and defense industries), together with mining, represent other major sectors of the South Australian economy.

Agricultural products contribute around A$3.3 billion (US$1.7 billion) to the South Australian economy each year. South Australia is Australia's largest grape grower, producing around 40% of the national crop, and a leading producer of wheat and barley.

South Australia is at the center of Australia's defense industry. Facilities include the Defense Science and Technology Organization complex in Adelaide, the Port Adelaide construction site for conventionally-powered submarines and the Woomera Rocket Range test and evaluation facility. South Australia is also a leading producer of passenger motor vehicles and automotive parts. The automotive industry is the state's largest employer. In the minerals and energy sector, South Australia has one of the world's largest lead/zinc smelters. It also has one of the largest copper/uranium sites in the world, and its on-shore oil and gas resources are among the most significant in Australia. The state is also developing strengths in niche industries, such as aquaculture, water management and environmental services.

South Australia produces about A$42 billion (US$22 billion) in Gross State Product, representing approximately 7% of Australia's Gross National Product. The economy has performed moderately well over the course of the 2000/01 financial year, growing at around 2.5%. Unemployment is down from 8.5% in 2000 to 7.4% in 2004 and exports are booming, rising by 8% in 2000, to a record A$6.732 billion (US$3.5 billion). In addition, South Australia's substantial public debt has been significantly reduced by the sale of the state's A$5.3 billion (US$2.8 billion) electricity industry. This, in turn, will significantly improve South Australia's ability to invest in infrastructure. Several recently commenced infrastructure projects, the Adelaide to Darwin Railway, Pelican Point Power Station, Adelaide Airport runway extension project and Port River Expressway, are expected to improve the efficiency of South Australia's key industries and access to export markets. However, the lingering effect of the interstate migration from South Australia, which occurred during the economic recession of the early 1990s, and the state's low rate of population increase, represent a permanent cap on substantial economic growth.

Despite these difficulties, there are commercial opportunities in South Australia. The government is well disposed towards business and the workforce is well educated and highly skilled. Moreover, skilled labor is available at a lower premium than in Australia's eastern states. Real estate and office space is similarly cheaper and gas and electricity are competitively priced. South Australia is well served by east-west rail and road transport, a domestic airport and an international container port. South Australia's natural endowments in agriculture and minerals are significant. Potential business opportunities lie in light and heavy industries, agriculture and agribusiness, acquaculture and information technology.

NORTHERN TERRITORY

The Northern Territory (NT) covers 1.3 million square kilometers of Australia. This is just under twice the size of the State of Texas (equivalent to 677,000 square kilometers). In such a vast area, there is a population of just 190,000, which is about 1% of the total Australian population. The Northern Territory produces 10% of the nation's exports. Darwin is the capital and is a young and vibrant city, with all the modern conveniences and sound infrastructure. The second largest city of NT is Alice Springs, located 1,500 kilometers south of Darwin in Central Australia. The Northern Territory is rich in natural resources, which are being developed by the private sector along with the support of the Northern Territory Government. The Government is currently half way through a five-year, A$16 million geophysical survey of the Territory. This data is being produced primarily for mineral and hydrocarbon exploration companies and is aimed at promoting exploration in the Territory.

Average population growth in the Northern Territory from 1996-2000 was 1.7%. The 2000-2004 estimate for unemployment is 5.5%. Gross State Product (GSP) growth for 2002 to 2006 is estimated at 7%--essentially double the rate of Australian GDP growth overall. Finally, NT exports in 1999-2000 were valued at A$2.6 billion, with the estimated value for 2000-2004 coming in at a significantly larger A$4.5 billion.

The Northern Territory is a world-class producer of bauxite, manganese ore, magnesium, gold, diamonds, uranium oxide, and silver-lead-zinc concentrates. Opportunities exist in the extraction of non-metallic minerals. The Territory is set to lead the country in economic growth over the next five years, albeit from a small base, expanding by an estimated 50 percent.

The NT Government has a clear objective of developing Darwin as a multi-modal transport hub between the markets of Southeastern Australia and Asia. Construction of the A$100 million first stage of the East Arm Port was completed in 1999. Work is underway on the A$70 million second stage of this project, which is expected to be completed in late 2003, to coincide with the completion of the Darwin to Alice Springs rail link. Work on the A$1.3 billion, 1,500 kilometer rail link started in May 2004 and has a planned completion date of early 2004. Eventually, the rail line will run from Darwin in the north all the way down to the southern port city of Adelaide, given recent approval of funding by Federal, NT, South Australian, and private-sector sources.

The shift in Australia's oil industry focus to the north and northwest of Australia has ensured a continuing presence of oil and gas infrastructure and services in the Territory--including engineering, transportation and communications. Mining and manufacturing are important users of natural gas, which will lead to the demand for further infrastructure.

The Timor Sea oil and gas deposits have led to the following outcomes:

- Agreement between major oil and gas companies on principles for bringing Timor Sea gas ashore at Darwin. This will involve the construction of about 500 kilometers of sub-marine pipeline.

- The announcement of the sale of significant quantities of Timor Sea LNG to a large U.S. energy supply company, for use in Southern California and Mexico's Baja Peninsula.

- Announcement by two major producers that Darwin is their preferred site for methanol plants.

- Commencement of preliminary work on the construction of gas pipelines from Darwin to domestic Australian markets in Southeastern Australia.

- The establishment within the new East Arm Port industrial precinct of a range of service and support companies to the offshore oil and gas industry.

- An allocation of funds in the NT Government's 2004-2002 budget for the development of petrochemical industrial precincts at Wickham Point and Glyde Point, near Darwin.

The Northern Territory's traditional industries are showing strong growth also. The tourism industry has averaged 7% growth over the last seven years and experienced 11% growth in 2000. This represents 1.4 million tourists to the eco-tourism region at Uluru (Ayers Rock), as well as Kakadu National Park. The NT Government and the tourism industry have developed a master plan that positions the industry toward 2005. This plan carries a range of investment opportunities in infrastructure and others areas of the tourism industry.

The cattle industry in NT is also booming. In 2000, the Northern Territory exported 300,000 head of live cattle to Southeast Asia--mainly to the Philippines and Indonesia.

Business in the Northern Territory enjoys state-of-the-art facilities and infrastructure, at competitive costs. The Territory features modern social and industrial infrastructure, a supply of skilled labor, a sophisticated telecommunications network, modern hospitals, an extensive road network, an international airport, and reliable water and power supplies.

TASMANIA

Many Tasmanians are optimistic, despite an 8.5 percent unemployment rate and an economy that continues behind most other Australian states. The State Government is seeking to combine innovative agricultural and manufacturing techniques with Tasmania's natural beauty and environmental cleanliness. Recent and ongoing economic developments include pyrethrum, a plant which produces a natural pesticide; a booming aquaculture industry; further development of Tasmania's high-speed ferry industry (the State is home of Incat, one of the world's largest manufacturers of high-speed ferries); tourism; and the State's plan to dramatically increase its energy supply by simultaneously facilitating a gas pipeline and an electricity cable to mainland Australia.

Investment is welcome, but only on Tasmania's terms. While Tasmania's Green Party no longer has the balance of power in the Legislative Assembly and the State is actively pursuing economic development, Tasmanians have not abandoned their "green" sentiments. Officials and private citizens alike, including senior economic development officers, have made it clear that investors will have to meet various environmental and quality of life standards for projects in the State.

Due to a lack of sites outside of *World Heritage* areas, Tasmania is no longer able to develop new hydroelectric power plants to offer low-cost power. As a result, the State is actively seeking to develop additional sources of supply--specifically a gas pipeline and the high-capacity "Basslink" electricity cable--both traveling to and from Victoria. Government officials think that these projects will attract new investment and jobs for Tasmanians by providing a new competitive source of energy and allowing the State to purchase power from the mainland when prices are low, conversely selling it back when prices are high. The gas pipeline is being developed by the U.S. company, Duke Energy International. The project is well advanced and is expected to be completed by mid-2002. Furthermore, wind power is also being explored in Tasmania--one official noted recently that he expects wind turbines to eventually produce up to 20 percent of the State's power.

Tasmanians generally believe that the current Labor Government is performing well and will have no trouble winning the next election, which will take place during 2002. As a result, the opposition Liberal Party is reportedly adopting a long-term strategy of rebuilding its leadership, with a goal of regaining power in 2006.

In the most recent State Budget the Government announced a reduction in payroll tax rates and an increase in the general exemption threshold so that employers with 50 employees pay less in taxes than any other Australian State.

AUSTRALIAN CAPITAL TERRITORY

Canberra, Australia's capital city, is located in the Australian Capital Territory (ACT). There are over 13,000 businesses in the ACT, employing 55 percent of the ACT's workforce. Canberra's workforce is more computer-literate and highly-educated than any other workforce in Australia with, on average, 51 percent having university qualifications, compared to 42 percent nationally. Canberra is a city with a growing business center and is located between the major markets of Sydney and Melbourne.

Canberra's strengths include:

- excellent communications and advanced technology and transport infrastructure;
- world-class education and research facilities;
- young, highly-skilled and educated workforce;
- sophisticated and flexible tertiary industry sector; and
- headquarters of several hundred significant national associations.

Canberra is a city of the future, with industries taking advantage of the National Capital's access to R& D institutions, world-class communications infrastructure, and a highly educated workforce. Competitive operating costs, combined with lower than average private-sector labor costs, make Canberra an attractive business destination.

Canberra has developed a leading edge in the following major industries and services:

- Information Technology & Telecommunications;
- Advanced Technology Manufacturing & Defense-Related Services;
- Environment Management Technology & Services;
- Call Centers;
- Information & Business Services;
- Light Manufacturing & Assembly; and
- Agribusiness.

The ACT has a highly competitive and internationally-focused information industries sector. With estimated spending power of approximately US$1 billion per year, national and international companies are attracted to Canberra to compete for, and service, the Australian Government's large IT&T contracts. Canberra is often described as having been transformed from a public sector town to a city of entrepreneurs. Multinational companies doing business in the ACT include Hewlett-Packard, NEC, British Aerospace, Fujitsu, Unisys, Oracle and Intec.

Canberra is recognized as an environmental city, with the highest recycling rate in Australia, and is capitalizing on emerging "green" industries. There are currently over 100 businesses operating in the environment management industry.

Canberra also has a world-renowned research base and is home to Australian National University (ANU), the Commonwealth Scientific and Industrial Research Organization (CSIRO), the University of Canberra (which specializes in telecommunications research), and the Australian Defence Force Academy (ADFA).

INVESTMENT AND BUSINESS CLIMATE

OPENNESS TO FOREIGN INVESTMENT

1. ENCOURAGING FOREIGN DIRECT INVESTMENT CONSISTENT WITH NATIONAL GOALS

The Australian Government welcomes foreign investment and the United States is the country's largest source of foreign capital. Total U.S. investment in Australia, including both direct and portfolio investment, exceeds US$80 billion. Australia's policy, as first enunciated by former Treasurer John Dawkins in the introduction to a 1992 pamphlet entitled "Australia's Foreign Investment Policy, a Guide for Investors" is:

"to encourage foreign direct investment consistent with the needs of the Australian community, including the expansion of private investment, the development of internationally competitive and export-oriented industries and the creation of employment opportunities... Administration of the policy is based on guidelines rather than inflexible rules; it is intended to be practical and non-discriminatory."

Takeovers of domestic firms by foreign investors while occasionally generating nationalistic public reaction when a cultural icon is involved, (as was the case with a biscuit company several years ago), generally are not interfered with. They are treated under the same guidelines as any other foreign investment.

REGULATION IN SOME SECTORS: MEDIA, CIVIL AVIATION, URBAN REAL ESTATE

The Federal Treasury regulates foreign investment with the assistance of the Foreign Investment Review Board (FIRB). The Board screens investment proposals for conformity with Australian law and policy. (See section I below.) Regulation of foreign investment is based on the Foreign Acquisitions and Takeovers Act, 1975 (amended in 1989) and on 1991 regulations issued pursuant to the Act. Foreign investment in three sectors is severely limited:

a. MEDIA The Broadcasting Services Act of 1992 provides that a foreign person may not exercise control of a television license, or have company interests in such a license exceeding 15 percent; and, two or more foreign persons may not have company interests in such a license exceeding 20 percent in the aggregate. Foreign investors are limited to a 20 percent share individually and a 35 percent share in the aggregate, of any subscription TV broadcaster. Foreign investment in mass circulation newspapers is limited. A single foreigner may hold a minor share of 25 percent and unrelated foreign interests may hold an additional 5 percent. Both the cross-media and foreign ownership limitations have proven controversial. Some argue they are becoming obsolete as the distinctions between communications media blur with new developments in information technology.

CIVIL AVIATION

Foreign airlines flying to Australia generally can expect approval to acquire up to 25 percent of the equity in a domestic carrier individually, or up to 40 percent in the aggregate. All other foreign investors (including those that do not operate an airline service to Australia) may acquire up to 100 percent of a domestic carrier, or establish a new aviation business. In the case of Qantas, foreign voting equity is restricted to 49 percent, with individual holdings limited to 25 percent. British Airways currently owns 25 percent of Qantas. c. URBAN REAL ESTATE The purchase of urban real estate by foreign interests is regulated closely. Prior to April 1, 1993, Australia sought to assure 50 percent equity participation by Australians in all such ventures. Where such participation was not available on reasonable terms and conditions, however, applications for up to 100 percent foreign ownership were considered. Effective that date, however, the 50 percent requirement for developed, non-residential, commercial real estate was abolished. All proposals by foreign investors to acquire developed residential real estate are now examined. They normally are not approved except in the cases of foreign companies buying residences for their senior executives living in Australia and foreign nationals temporarily resident in Australia for more than twelve months buying a principal residence for their own use, to be sold upon their departure.

INCENTIVES FOR INVESTMENT

Like the U.S., Australia provides no direct federal tax incentives for investment in the country. Those incentives which are available apply equally to foreign and domestic investors. Examples include:

- research and development tax concessions for companies incorporated in Australia;
- the discretionary grants scheme, which can cover up to 50 percent of research and development tax losses;
- the national procurement development program, which provides grants to underwrite the development of Australian products required by the public sector that have export potential;
- the generic technology scheme, and the advanced manufacturing technology development program, which provide development grants for selected new technologies; and,
- the investment promotion program, which encourages investment in greenfield resource processing projects, and links with global markets.

Each of the state governments has an aggressive investment promotion program and is willing to negotiate investment incentives on a case-by-case basis. They often offer concessionary packages to attract companies to establish themselves in their state.

PREFERENTIAL TARIFF ARRANGEMENTS WITH SOME COUNTRIES

Australia traditionally has accorded a uniform 5 percent tariff preference to developing countries. In addition, it maintains a preferential arrangement with Pacific Forum Islands, and has bilateral trade agreements with Papua New Guinea, New Zealand, Malaysia and Canada. The developing country rate for all but the least developed countries, including the South Pacific Island Territories, is being phased out and will be brought in line with other tariffs in conjunction with Australia's overall program of tariff reduction. Products affected are chemicals, plastics, rubber, textiles, clothing and footwear.

While the 1983 Closer Economic Relations (CER) agreement with New Zealand continues in force, it does not yet include a formal investment agreement.

Investors, both foreign and domestic, operating in export-oriented industries can obtain duty free import privileges on finished goods under certain conditions. This practice is most visible in the automobile industry. Several firms in Australia both manufacture and import vehicles for sale on the domestic market. All four major automotive manufacturers (Ford, GM Holden, Toyota and Mitsubishi) export finished vehicles and/or components. These companies receive, in accordance with the value of their exports, exemption from import duties on the equivalent value of finished vehicles they import for sale here. In effect, they can obtain duty free import privileges not available to competitors without export capability. This import duty exemption is available to all auto importers on a non-discriminatory basis.

EFFICIENT CAPITAL MARKETS AND PORTFOLIO INVESTMENT

Australia has a well-developed and sophisticated financial market regulated in accordance with international norms. The stock and commodities exchanges have corresponding arrangements with other world exchanges. Credit is allocated on market terms.

CONVERSION AND TRANSFER POLICIES

The Australian dollar is a fully convertible currency. The government does not maintain currency controls or limit remittance, loan and lease payments. Such payments are processed through standard commercial channels without governmental interference or delay.

EXPROPRIATION AND COMPENSATION

Private property can be expropriated for public purposes in accordance with established principles of international law. Due process rights are established and respected, and prompt adequate and effective compensation is paid.

DISPUTE SETTLEMENT

1. INVESTMENT DISPUTES

Property and contractual rights are enforced through the Australian court system, which is based on English common law. There have been no investment disputes involving foreign companies in recent years. However, in 1994, the Foreign Investment Review Board (FIRB) exercised its authority to block a proposed investment involving a U.S. firm that wanted to expand its Australian health care operations.

The FIRB based its decision on concerns regarding the firm's U.S. parent and legal difficulties it experienced in the U.S. The FIRB has a history of interpreting foreign investment regulations flexibly. For example, in 1991, it approved a foreign-led takeover of Australia's second largest newspaper group, John Fairfax Group Pty., even though post-takeover foreign ownership totalled 27%. Australia is not a member of the International Center for the Settlement of Investment Disputes (ICSID).

2. COMMERCIAL DISPUTES

Australia has an established legal and court system for the conduct or supervision of litigation and arbitration, as well as alternate dispute processes. The traditional approach to commercial dispute resolution involves litigation and, more recently, arbitration. Modern methods of alternative dispute resolution, however, are becoming increasingly popular. Australia is a world leader in the development and provision of non-court dispute resolution mechanisms. It is a signatory to all the major international dispute resolution conventions and has organizations which provide international dispute resolution processes.

Dispute resolution clauses are used frequently in contracts between Australian and U.S. commercial entities. In some areas, such as construction, clauses are inserted routinely into contracts. The clauses may specify the particular process to be used (e.g., mediation, followed by arbitration), or simply state that should a dispute emerge, the parties will seek the assistance of the American Arbitration Association and/or the Australian Commercial Disputes Centre. These clauses are upheld by the courts.

POLITICAL VIOLENCE AFFECTING INVESTMENT

As in all liberal democracies, political protests (e.g. rallies, demonstrations, marches, public conflicts between competing interests) form an integral part of Australian cultural life. Australian protests cover the broad range of current issues and interests: ethnic and aboriginal concerns, pro- and anti-right wing demonstrations, environmental issues and denunciations of government policies to name a few. Such protests, while often vociferous, rarely (if ever) degenerate into violence.

PERFORMANCE REQUIREMENTS AND INCENTIVES TO SUPPORT LOCAL INDUSTRY DEVELOPMENT

1. SELLING TO THE GOVERNMENT

There are no performance requirements affecting investment per se. With the expiration of the Industrial Development Arrangements (IDA's) program in the telecommunications field on June 30, 1996, offsets will no longer be required in the civil sector. The use of offsets in defense procurement has been phased out in favor of a policy emphasizing "Australian Industrial Involvement" and "Through Life Support" concepts. Australia has not yet signed the GATT/WTO Agreement on Government Procurement, which means that it is not bound by conditions prohibiting specification of locally-made product in tenders. The Australian Government continues to review its position in relation to signature.

2. BOUNTIES

Bounties (production assistance) help domestic manufacturers maintain or increase their market share through price discounting. The Australian Government has phased out most bounties in recent years -- the only bounty remaining being for shipbuilding production. This bounty has had its expiry date extended to June 30, 1999, ostensibly to match the expiration deadlines of similar schemes in other OECD nations.

3. SPECIAL ARRANGEMENTS FOR INFORMATION TECHNOLOGY AND TELECOMMUNICATIONS COMPANIES

Since 1991, foreign information technology companies with annual sales to the GOA of US$7Ð30 million (A$10-40 million) have been asked to enter into fixed-term arrangements (FTAs) and those with sales greater than US$30 million (A$40 million) to enter into Partnerships for Development (PFDs). The FTA program was originally for overseas firms and had a minimum threshold of US$7 million (A$10 million).

The minimum threshold has been removed and Australian firms have been included since the introduction of the Endorsed Supplier Arrangement. The ESA has added a step in the procurement process whereby, before access to government IT business will be considered, firms must undertake long-term value-adding in Australia and demonstrate a commitment to "world best practice". Other endorsement criteria relate to "world best practice" matters, such as reference sites, compliance with government policies, quality, standards, services, and financial viability. This may be an obstacle to new firms seeking to enter the market, as it can prevent firms from testing the market with imports prior to undertaking a more long-term commitment.

Under FTAs, a foreign company or its subsidiary, as with local companies, commits to undertake local industrial development activities worth 15 percent of its projected amount of government sales over a four-year period. Under a PD, the headquarters of the foreign firm agrees: to invest 5 percent of its annual local turnover on research and development in Australia; to export goods and services worth 50 percent of imports (for hardware companies) or 20 percent of turnover (for software companies); and to achieve 70 percent local content across all exports within the seven-year life of the PD. In 1992, this scheme was extended to the telecommunications customer premises equipment (CPE) sector, replacing, in large measure, the requirement that suppliers of cellular mobile telephones, PABX, small business systems, and first telephones have industrial development arrangements (IDAs) in place before obtaining licenses to connect their equipment to the public switched network.

4. INFORMATION TECHNOLOGY SERVICES COMMON USE CONTRACT PANEL (ITSCUCP)

In 1995, the Australian Government established the ITSCUCP, to determine which companies will be used as sources for Commonwealth information technology requirements involving systems integration activity (excluding purchases of less than $1 million). Any information technology company may join upon demonstrating "acceptable levels" of Australian product development, investment in capital equipment, skills development and/or services support, and local sourcing. Potential members of the ITSCUCP will also be evaluated on their Australian R&D activities, export orientation, and development of relationships with Australian and New Zealand suppliers and consumers.

5. GOVERNMENT BUSINESS ENTERPRISES

Since July 1, 1993, the Australian Government has required Government Business Enterprises (GBEs are central governmentÐowned companies such as Telstra and the Civil Aviation Authority) to consider "industrial development objectives" such as local content and export potential in their procurement activities. The objective is to allow "local companies the maximum opportunity to compete for government business consistent with the commercial objectives of GBEs and the need to obtain value for money".

6. LOCAL INDUSTRY DEVELOPMENT IMPACT

After a recent review of its purchasing practices, the Australian Government announced its commitment to source at least 10 percent of its purchases from Australian small-to-medium size enterprises. The Government will continue to require tenderers to include industry development objectives in tender documents, with model guidelines to be developed in consultation with industry during 1998. The two-envelope tendering system and the requirement for industry impact statements to accompany all procurements of more than A$10 million was abolished in 1997.

7. EXPORT MARKET DEVELOPMENT SCHEME GRANTS

EMDG grants are provided to partially reimburse Australian residents who have incurred eligible expenditures while developing overseas markets for Australian products and services. Access to Export Market Development Scheme grants is determined, in part, by the degree of local content contained in the product to be exported. To qualify, goods manufactured, produced, or assembled in Australia must contain at least 50 percent local content. Goods produced outside Australia must have at least 75 percent Australian content.

RIGHT TO PRIVATE OWNERSHIP

As a general rule, foreign firms establishing themselves in Australia are accorded national treatment. They do not have to seek government permission to establish and own businesses unless their proposed activity meets tests established in law and regulation that trigger notification/review by the Foreign Investment Review Board (FIRB). These FIRB requirements are a matter of public record and are available upon application to FIRB. (See I.1. below for discussion of FIRB. See Appendix E.4. for contacts.)

Firms may, if they wish, seek "naturalization" (conversion to full Australian, as opposed to foreign, status). To be naturalized, a firm must be at least 51 percent Australian-owned; its articles of association must provide that a majority of its board be Australian citizens; and it must reach an agreement with the Government regarding the exercise of voting powers in respect of the firm's business in Australia. The only practical advantage of naturalization is relief from the requirement that the FIRB be notified of proposed investment activities.

In general, participation in privatization schemes is regulated in accordance with overall investment policy. The Qantas privatization, for example, was limited by the restrictions on foreign investment in civil aviation discussed above. Most sectors are uncontrolled and are open to foreign participation.

PROTECTION OF PROPERTY RIGHTS

Patents, trademarks, designs, copyright and integrated circuit layout rights are protected by Australian law. Australia is a member of the World Intellectual Property Organization, the Paris Convention for the Protection of Industrial Property, the Berne Convention for the Protection of Literary and Artistic Works, the Universal Copyright Convention, the Geneva Phonogram Convention, the Rome Convention for the Protection of Performers, Producers of Phonograms, and Broadcasting Organizations, and the Patent Cooperation Treaty.

IP Australia is the Federal Government agency responsible for registrations of patents, trademarks and designs. Contact details are: IP Australia, Tel: 61-2 6283 2000 or Fax: 61-2 6285 4149, attention the Director-General (Commissioner of Patents, Registrar of Trade Marks & Registrar of Designs).

1. PATENTS, TRADE SECRETS, DESIGNS

Patents are available for inventions in all fields of technology and are the principle system for protecting ownership of any device, substance, method or process which is new or inventive. They are protected by the Patents Act, 1990, which offers coverage for 20 years, subject to renewal. An application for patent in Australia provides international priority rights if applications follow in overseas jurisdictions within 12 months.

Trade secrets are protected by common law.

Design features, such as shape or pattern, can be protected from imitation by registration under the Designs Act, 1906 for up to 16 years. An important aspect of a design is that it must be applied industrially. Registration cannot be granted for a design which is purely artistic. An application for registration can only be made by the owner of the design.

2. TRADE MARKS

Trade marks may be protected for ten years and renewed indefinitely upon request by registration under the Trade Marks Act, 1995. Once used, trade marks may also, without registration, be protected by common law, however, registration with IP Australia does make enforcement easier. It is wise for any U.S. exporter intending to market a product in Australia to check with the trade marks office at IP Australia to ensure that its mark or name is not already in use.

3. COPYRIGHT

Copyrights are protected under the Copyright Act, 1968. Works do not require registration, and copyright automatically subsists in original literary, artistic, musical and dramatic works, film and sound recordings. Computer programs are considered in law to be literary works. Copyright protection is for the life of the author plus 50 years.

The Australian Copyright Act provides protection for public performances in hotels and clubs and against video piracy and unauthorized thirdÐcountry imports. No complaints about unauthorized public showings of films have been received for over five years.

4. COPYRIGHT, PATENTS, TRADEMARKS, DESIGNS AND PARALLEL IMPORTS

Parallel imports refers imports of legally manufactured products ordered by someone other than a person or firm having exclusive distribution rights in Australia. Books, sound recordings, films, computer software and other products subject to copyright cannot be imported without licence from the copyright owner.

Drugs, inventions and other products which are subject to patent cannot be imported without licence from the owner. In some cases, government approval is also required. Goods that are the subject of a registered trademark can be imported without the permission of the trademark owner or the registered local distributor. However, copyright over the labeling and packaging prevent this practice occurring.

Goods which are the subject of a registered design can be imported without the approval of the design holder, however, labeling and packaging copyright prevent this from occurring.

There are, however, two bills that have been passed by the House of Representatives and are currently being debated by the Senate which could open up Australia to parallel importation.

These are:
Copyright Amendment Bill No. 1. Removes copyright ban over parallel imports of packaging, labeling and accessories, which will allow the importation of brand goods without a licence.

Copyright Amendment Bill No. 2. Removes the copyright ban on parallel imports of sound recordings.

It is anticipated that the minor parties in the Senate will decide the fate of the abovementioned bills. At present, some parallel importation is allowed for books under strictly limited conditions (cases in which newly-published works are not made available in Australia within 30 days of publication).

LAWS, PROCEDURES AND TAXES

Australia subscribes to the 1976 declaration of the Organization for Economic Cooperation and Development (OECD) concerning international investment and multinational enterprises. The instruments cover national treatment and investment incentives and disincentives and spell out voluntary guidelines for the conduct of multinational enterprises in member countries. Australia also subscribes to two OECD codes of liberalization, one covering capital movements and the other, invisible transactions.

Both Australian law and government practice foster transparency and favor competition. Taxation policy does not impede the efficient mobilization and allocation of investment, although there are a number of differences between the U.S. and Australian tax systems that have potential implications for business. Businesses are advised to seek counsel from accounting and law firms familiar with the tax policies of both countries. In early 1990, the Australian Taxation Office and the Internal Revenue Service formalized a simultaneous audits agreement to investigate suspected non-compliance with tax laws of both countries.

The U.S. and Australia Double Taxation Treaty affects business investment between the two countries. The treaty applies to federal income tax of the U.S., excluding accumulated earnings tax, personal holding company tax and Australian income tax. Separate agreements apply to gift and estate taxes. The Controlled Foreign Corporation and Controlled Foreign Trusts legislation, effective July 1, 1991, provides for taxing income that accrues to corporations or trusts arranged after residency is established.

FOREIGN INVESTMENT REVIEW BOARD (FIRB)

Australia has an investment screening mechanism administered by the FIRB which tracks foreign investment developments through a notification system, and, if certain criteria are present, examines specific proposals. The FIRB must be notified of investment proposals in the following categories:

- acquisitions of substantial interests in existing Australian businesses with total assets over A$5 million (A$3 million for rural properties);

- plans to establish new businesses involving a total investment of over A$10 million or more;
- investments in the media, irrespective of size;
- direct investments by foreign governments or their agencies, irrespective of size;
- acquisitions of non-residential commercial real estate valued over A$5 million;
- acquisitions of residential real estate, irrespective of size (unless exempt under the regulations);
- takeovers of offshore companies whose Australian subsidiaries are valued over A$20 million or more, or account for more than 50 percent of the target company's global assets; and,
- proposals where any doubt exists as to whether they are notifiable.

Most foreign investment proposals notified to the FIRB are granted automatically without examination. Proposals above the A$50 million threshold are examined, but FIRB policy is to approve them unless they are found contrary to the national interest. The criteria governing that decision are:

- the proposal involves one of the following sectors: rural properties; agriculture; forestry; fishing; resource processing; oil and gas; mining (excluding uranium); manufacturing; non-bank financial intermediaries; insurance; stockbroking; tourism (hotels and resorts); and most other services;

and
- the proposal is an acquisition of 15 percent or more of a company or business with total assets below A$50 million; or
- the proposal is to establish a new project or business with a total investment below A$50 million, or to take over an off-shore company with Australian subsidiaries valued below A$50 million.

The above policy does not apply to uranium mining, civil aviation, the media and urban real estate, all of which have separate limitations on foreign investment. Nor does it alter the notification requirements of the Foreign Acquisitions and Takeovers Act. During FY 1996Ð97, 4,544 proposals for investment in Australia were submitted to the FIRB: 4,096 were approved (2,610 with conditions); 343 were withdrawn; and only 105 were rejected (0.3 percent by value). The U.S. has objected to the continued utilization of the screening mechanism.

BILATERAL INVESTMENT AGREEMENTS

Australia subscribes to the 1976 declaration of the Organization for Economic Cooperation and Development (OECD) concerning international investment and multinational enterprises. The instruments cover national treatment and investment incentives and disincentives and spell out voluntary guidelines for the conduct of multinational enterprises in member countries. Australia also subscribes to two OECD codes of liberalization, one covering capital movements and the other, invisible transactions. It maintains a limited reservation under the Capital Movements Code, because FIRB practice historically favored the use of Australian contractors and consultants when reviewing foreign investment proposals.

Australia is bound by the Nara Treaty not to discriminate against Japan in the investment area. This has proved a sticking point in bilateral negotiations on an investment agreement with New Zealand.

OPIC AND OTHER FOREIGN INVESTMENT INSURANCE PROGRAMS

Australia provides foreign investment insurance to its firms investing abroad through the Export Finance and Insurance Corporation (EFIC). OPIC does not extend coverage to Australia, as it is not a high risk or developing country.

LABOR

Historically, Australia's tradition of centralized contract bargaining created an industrial environment where both management and labor tended to look to government to resolve their conflicts by compulsory arbitration and to regulate their interactions. Under the complex centralized system of industrial "awards", all contracts for wages and working conditions in specific industries are based on a model contract negotiated between the relevant union(s) and a large firm or industrial association.

Other firms in related sectors either copy or base their pay on whatever award seemed to be a reasonable guideline for their type of business. Conflicts that arose in either the negotiation of contracts or in the workplace could be referred to the Australian Industrial Relations Commission, a quasi-judicial/ arbitration organization. Approximately 35 percent of the workforce was covered by the award system. Basic wages and benefits are set by "awards" determined by federal and state Industrial Relations Commissions (IRCs) through complicated sets of criteria. Until 1991, there was usually one "national wage case" annually which determined prevailing wage patterns.

More recently, however, productivity measures at an individual-enterprise level have taken root as the emerging norm. In April 1998, the Australian Industrial Relations Commission raised the national minimum wage to A$373.40 per week. This approximates A$9.83 per hour (around US$6.00).

The negotiation of contracts covering wages and working conditions is gradually shifting away from the centralized system. There are several choices in addition to basing pay and working conditions on the award system. The first is an enterprise agreement which is negotiated by individual companies with their workers as a group or with the relevant union(s). The second choice is individual contracts with individual workers.

This choice has always existed but was redefined under the 1996 Workplace Relations Act, which went into effect on January 1, 1997. These agreements are subject to far fewer government regulations than the awards are, and are similar in style to American contracts. Australian Workplace Agreements (as they are known) are required to be roughly equivalent to the basic working conditions in the award that would apply to the sector the firm belongs to.

The working conditions and regulations, as outlined in the awards (many of which also apply to enterprise agreements and Australian workplace agreements) are due to be substantially modified by the end of 1998. There would then be only 20 "allowable matters" that could be included in awards. On the one hand, this will substantially reduce the number of government regulations and red tape that employers face. At the same time, however, it will require that additional matters pertaining to working conditions and employee benefits be covered in the enterprise agreements and the Australian workplace agreements.

As a result of the awards simplification process, many firms with operations in Australia will probably require more legal services than was the case in the past. Most industry employers associations recommend that enterprise agreements and Australian workplace agreements contain specific provisions for arbitration by either the Australian Industrial Relations Commission or by other means. This will avoid potentially costly civil court damages claims from employees or groups of employees if disputes arise.

The leadership of the Australian Council of Trade Unions (ACTU) is an enthusiastic booster of workplace reform, but is adamantly opposed to a number of provisions in the Workplace Relations Act, which would substantially reduce their role in contract negotiations. The majority of the union leaders are willing to support workplace reforms that will enhance productivity and Australia-based firms' ability to compete internationally. Many see this type of change as essential to deal with Australia's persistently high unemployment rate.

Albeit much reduced in size from a decade ago, Australia's union movement still exerts considerable influence over the marketplace. Unions have organized 32 percent of the private sector workforce, but this average figure underestimates their pivotal influence in key sectors, such as mining (88 percent), transport (81 percent), construction, and manufacturing.

For foreign investors, developing a thorough understanding of labor conditions affecting specific business or manufacturing establishments is essential during the planning stages of a new venture. Enterprise agreements are especially attractive, since they allow investors more freedom to tailor their labor-relations environment to their specific operating concerns rather than to a centrally imposed template.

Australia's Liberal-National Coalition Government has made further industrial-relations reform one of its highest priorities. In fact, its first significant new piece of legislation, introduced in May 1996, was "The Workplace Relations and Other Legislation Amendment Bill". It replaces the Industrial Relations Act of 1988. Key elements of interest to possible investors include:

- a streamlined "award" system, which becomes a safety net of minimum wages and conditions;
- a new enterprise bargaining system, shifting still more responsibility for industrial relations to employer and employees at the enterprise level;
- curbs on union power, including abolition of closed shops and union demarcations. Although unions will be weakened, this provision risks creating a plethora of small and competing unions at an individual worksite, which would be a reversal of the strong trend in the opposite direction to reduce the number of competing unions;
- restrictions on strikes, including heavy fines for labor unrest during the life of an agreement (the norm in the U.S., but still a new concept in Australia), and tougher secondary-boycott provisions;
- a new unfair-dismissal system, to further limit redress and compensation claims.

Overall, the new legislation promises to make it easier for employers to reach flexible enterprise agreements with their employees, whether unionized or not.

Elsewhere, the current government has indicated that it will retain the basic system of "superannuation" (a privately run, defined-contribution retirement system) introduced by the previous Labor Government. This compulsory pension fund differs significantly from the U.S. social security system since it is privately run and firms and their employees choose which investment company or companies will administer their pension funds. Employers pay six percent (rising to nine percent by the year 2002), employees three percent, and the Federal Government three percent of the employees' base salaries into their "superannuation."

FREE TRADE ZONES (FTZ) AND FREE PORTS

The Darwin Trade Development Zone, Northern Territory, is Australia's attempt to increase exports via a geographically defined free trade zone. Incentive packages, individually tailored for each prospective company, include subsidies for many up-front property, plant, and equipment costs, as well as relocation assistance. In practice, the Darwin initiative is focused almost exclusively on its Asian neighbors to the North and West.

On December 8, 1997, the Commonwealth Government adopted "Manufacturing-in-Bond (MIB)designating the BHP Steel River Facility in Newcastle as the first Australian site selected. The big difference - and advantage - over the existing Darwin FTZ structure, is that export manufacturers no longer are required to pay up front customs, excise and sales tax outlays on imported componentry and materials. Goods only become subject to duties and taxes if removed for sale or use in Australia .

While the Newcastle site is the first MIB established in Australia, it never was the intention to limit the benfits of MIB to one location. It is anticipated that over the next two years MIB operations will be licensed in several states. (See Appendix E.4.B for contact information).

CAPITAL OUTFLOW POLICY

Private foreign investment decisions are left to the discretion of private sector firms. There are no prohibitions on overseas investment or capital repatriation.

MAJOR FOREIGN INVESTORS

Hundreds of major foreign firms in many industry sectors invest in Australia. The Australian Federal Government, and each of the State Governments, vigorously encourages investment by offering incentives to multi-national companies to set up regional headquarters for financial and other services, and manufacturing operations. At first aimed at attracting information technology companies, the campaign has widened in scope to include manufacturing and provision of financial and administrative services for the Asia-Pacific region. The Government touts the benefits of Australia's safe, stable business environment, skilled work force and lower facility, site and operating costs in comparison to other regional centers, such as Singapore, Hong Kong and Taiwan.

CORRUPTION

Australia maintains a thorough system of laws and regulations designed to counter corruption. In addition, the government procurement system generally is transparent and well regulated, thereby minimizing opportunities for corrupt dealings. Accordingly, corruption has not been a factor cited by U.S. businesses as a disincentive to investing in Australia, or to exporting goods and services here. Non-governmental organizations interested in monitoring the global development or anti-corruption measures, including Transparency International, operate freely in Australia.

Australia was an active participant in negotiations within the Organization for Economic Cooperation and Development, which led to the 1996 Ministerial Commitment to Criminalize Transnational Bribery. The government is in the process of drafting laws and regulations to give effect to the anti-bribery convention. It is expected that legislation will be enacted before the end of 1998. At the federal level, enforcement of anti-corruption laws and regulations is the responsibility of the Attorney General's Department.

PRACTICAL INFORMATION FOR CONDUCTING BUSINESS IN AUSTRALIA[30]

MARKETING PRODUCTS AND SERVICES

Market entry strategies for U.S. firms are straightforward. They include exporting of products and services through the use of agent/distributorships, license/technology transfers, franchise arrangements, joint ventures, strategic alliances, and wholly- owned subsidiaries/branches. As Australia restructures economically, there are significant opportunities to participate in major public-funded projects and to win major infrastructure and services projects made available through public sector divestment and privatization.

RETAILING TRENDS

Australian retailing has long been predominantly characterized by department stores and speciality shops with high markups. However, in recent years Australians' consumer appetites have been whetted by discount buying available through the introduction of superstores and warehouse sales outlets.

According to the results of a survey released in January 1997 that was undertaken among the country's major retailers and property investors, Australia's retail market will be almost unrecognizable within two decades -- shaped by new technologies, an ageing population, and changing consumer needs.

The survey found that the Australian retail industry is changing faster than at any other time in the country's history. The outlook is for even bigger regional centers with a strong leisure element, emerging strength in strip shop locations targeting the "time poor" consumer, an influx of new international players, the death of many traditional specialty retailers, strong growth in the bulky goods sector, and a potential rise in electronic shopping. The Internet will provide strong competition within the Australian retail industry.

To compete, retailers will be forced to become more focused on marketing and information management. They will change from being property and inventory driven to supplying information. Retailers will collect information about suppliers, merchandise, and customers and sell and network these details. The one certainty facing the retail industry in Australia is further change and a faster pace of change.

DISTRIBUTION AND SALES CHANNELS

Australia's extensive distribution and sales channels are comparable to those in other industrialized countries. Channels of distribution are through direct sales, use of distributors or agents, and also through direct investment. Financing of exports is effected through open account, commercial bills of exchange (sight and time drafts), letters of credit, and cash in advance.

Foreign exchange is readily available to the Australian importer through the local banks. There is virtually no exchange control or import licensing applicable to imports of goods and services. Both

[30] This section basd in part on the materials of the US Department of Commerce

direct and indirect foreign investment is encouraged with only minimal requirements for government review in certain sectors, e.g. residential housing and media.

USE OF AGENTS AND DISTRIBUTORS

U.S. businesses marketing their products in Australia usually establish relationships with sales agents, distributors, franchisees, and licensees.

1. Sales Agents

Sales agents or representatives solicit business for the foreign company, and serve as a conduit for purchase agreements. In most cases, a sales agent does not have the power to negotiate terms, or to finalize the sales contract. Instead, the sales representative forwards the contract to the foreign company, which either accepts or rejects it. It should be noted, however, that because the sales representative is considered to be an agent of the foreign corporation, under the general laws of agency, the foreign corporation may be bound by the acts of its agent.

Agents assume a number of duties and obligations once a representation contract with a foreign company is finalized, including adherence to the principal's instructions, good faith in the interests of the principal, and maintenance of proper accounts.

The agent retains the right to remuneration and the right to an indemnity for liabilities or for losses incurred due to improper termination. However, there is no precedent for required indemnity payments in Australian law. Parties may stipulate specific causes for termination in the agreement. Either party may terminate the agreement upon receipt of reasonable notice of termination. Although no specific time period exists which defines a "reasonable notice period", courts may take into consideration the nature and length of the contract when determining whether reasonable notice was given.

2. Distributors

A distributor acts as an independent contractor, purchasing products from the foreign corporation and distributing them to wholesale buyers or, on occasion, to retailers. Generally, the foreign corporation cannot restrain the distributor from selling competitors' products. However, because the distributor is not considered to be an agent of the foreign corporation, it is not bound by the acts of the distributor. It is common practice for Australian distributors to ask for exclusive geographic rights to market a foreign corporation's products. Because of the size of the market, these rights often cover several states or are nation-wide.

Parties are free to choose between Australian and foreign (in this case U.S.) law governing the contract when drafting an agreement. However, the choice of foreign law does not preclude application of mandatory provisions of Australian law. Without a stipulation of law, Australian courts will apply the law of the jurisdiction where the agent or distributor works (i.e., Australian federal law, and appropriate state and local law).

Therefore, notification of agent appointments should be submitted in writing to satisfy various state jurisdictional laws, especially when they last for more than one year or include terms for commissioning the agent. Either fixed or indefinite-term contracts may be employed. However, repeated renewal of fixed-term contracts will not cause the contract to achieve indefinite-term status.

FINDING A PARTNER

Commercial Service of Australia provides a range of business facilitation services to help American companies identify potential partners. All services are arranged by the U.S. company contacting its local U.S. Department of Commerce District Office in the United States.

Business Facilitation Services include:

AGENT DISTRIBUTOR SEARCH (ADS)

CS Australia will locate, screen, and assess Australian agents, distributors, and representatives for U.S. companies. After an investigation that determines there is potential interest in a product, CS Australia will send the U.S. firm contact information on companies that have reviewed the product literature and expressed interest in representing the firm in Australia. U.S. companies then contact the potential representatives directly.

GOLD KEY SERVICE (GKS)

Designed to make a U.S. company representative's visit to Australia more productive, the GKS provides a combination of many services, such as market orientation briefings, market research, agent distributor search and screening, introductions to potential partners, and assistance in developing a sound market strategy and an effective follow-up plan.

CUSTOMIZED MARKET ANALYSIS (CMA)

Formerly called the Customized Sales Survey (CSS), a CMA provides a quick and accurate assessment of how an American product will sell in Australia. Especially valuable for first-time exporters with few Australian contacts and limited overseas expertise, a CMA provides current data with which to make marketing decisions without extensive travel, investigative, and other expenses associated with overseas product research.

PARTICIPATION IN CATALOG EXHIBITIONS

CS Australia takes booth space in selected Trade Shows and runs separate catalog exhibitions in association with a variety of trade promotion events, conferences, symposia etc. U.S. firms are invited to participate either directly or by providing catalogs for display.

ACCESS AUSTRALIA

CS Australia has developed a market entry program called "Access Australia", which offers U.S. firms an effective, yet very inexpensive, way to test the Australian market. Through this program, CS Australia contacts American firms in a specific industry sector, and invites the companies to participate by completing an application form and forwarding copies of product literature. A special mailing then is sent to hundreds of local agents, distributors, wholesalers, and end-users in that particular industry. Interested respondents are sent product literature. The U.S. participants are advised of the names of the local companies that requested their catalogs so they can follow-up directly.

Participation in Trade Missions

CS Australia organizes and supports trade missions sponsored by the Department of Commerce and by State Governments.

Trade Events

CS Australia organizes U.S. booths and support for companies participating in Trade Shows and Exhibitions in Australia (see Appendix G for full Trade Event Schedule).

Trade Opportunities Program (TOP)

This program provides U.S. suppliers with credible, complete, and timely trade leads gathered by FCS Australia. The trade leads may be requests for representation, manufactured goods, services, investment, joint ventures, licensing, or foreign government procurement bids. Opportunities are publicized by the Department of Commerce through the NTDB and other avenues.

Market Research and Reporting

CS Australia reports continually on industry sector developments, major projects, program and policy developments. These reports are available through the Department of Commerce and the NTDB (see Appendix F for a list of available documents).

Commercial News USA

This monthly publication provides summary information on new U.S. products being offered to the export market. CS Australia distributes the publication free of charge to over 1,600 potential agents and distributors throughout Australia. Interested companies contact the U.S. firm directly.

FRANCHISING

Franchising is a well established way of life in Australia, with more franchising outlets per capita than in any other country in the world. The Australian franchising industry's annual turnover is estimated at US$33 billion. In 1997 franchising grew by 12.7 percent compared to between 4 and 5 percent in the United States. While growth in franchising will continue, a weakened Australian dollar combined with the current Asian economic crisis is likely to place some downward pressure on franchising's growth rates.

Nevertheless, franchising remains popular in Australia because franchise businesses enjoy more than twice the success rate of other types of small enterprises. With a total number of 26,000 franchisees and 30,500 business outlets, franchising accounts for nearly 25 percent of all retailing. While major franchises are still the large, old established US fast food conglomerates, franchising is now seen to cater for every type of Australian enterprise and has become very competitive.

Market entry opportunities exist, but there is an inherent reluctance by local companies to fund new master franchises as venture capital is not easily found. Preferences are for foreign franchisors to make the initial investment by establishing a subsidiary or branch office and to sell licenses to franchisees.

Until recently the industry operated under a voluntary Code of Practice. The breakdown of the Code in 1996 saw the establishment of the Franchise Council of Australia (FCA), the industry's new association. In 1998, the Australian Competition and Consumer Commission (ACCC) announced the launch of the Franchising Code of Conduct. The new mandatory Code is expected to improve franchisor/franchisee relations and overall confidence within the industry.

Elements of the Code will be enforceable from July 1, 1998 with the remainder effective from October 1. One of the key features of the Code is a requirement for franchisors to provide a disclosure document to potential franchisees. The disclosures include information about the directors, executives and associates of the franchisor, commission payments to brokers, trademarks, territory details, a solvency statement and two years of financial statements. This disclosure document must also be made available to existing franchisees on request.

Other features include; an obligation on the franchisor to keep franchisees informed of specific information or developments that may have an adverse effect on the franchisee or franchise system (ie. Changes in ownership or litigation), and, a mandatory dispute resolution process that also deals with changing, selling or terminating an agreement.

DIRECT MARKETING

A 1997 report by the Commercial Economic Advisory Service of Australia (CEASA) revealed that the business of direct marketing elicits almost as much advertising spending as mainstream media. In 1996 advertisers spent US$4.13 billion on direct mail, inserts, telemarketing, mail order, the Internet, and exhibitions compared with US$4.45 billion on mainstream media advertising. The sector grew by an estimated 14.5 percent and mainstream advertising 1.9 percent.

Telemarketing was the biggest form of direct marketing, with expenditure of US$1.04 billion. Catalogs came second at US$700 million followed by direct mail US$599.7 million. Marketing through the Internet was the fastest-growing form of direct marketing, up 171.7 percent. Other thriving categories included direct-response advertisements in magazines (up 37 percent), exhibitions (25 percent), telemarketing (17.6 percent), and addressed direct mail (8.8 percent). The CEASA survey showed that companies in the financial services, telecommunications, travel and hospitality sectors are still the biggest fans of direct marketing, but new converts are emerging from the retail, alcoholic beverages, motor vehicles, and packaged goods industries.

Two of the key reasons for more widespread use of direct marketing in Australia are believed to be the relative efficiencies of the industry and the ability to accurately track results. Direct mail and other forms of direct communication are becoming highly sophisticated as technology allows the development of extensive databases where particular groups can be specified targeted. Interactive marketing and the Internet are providing new opportunities for direct marketers and expanding horizons to allow global reach.

JOINT VENTURES AND LICENSING

JOINT VENTURES

Joint ventures are a common feature of Australia's commercial and legal environment. Broadly similar to U.S. practice, forms of joint venture in Australia include:

a) Unincorporated Joint Ventures may, in colloquial terms, be described as "contractual joint ventures" that do not create a separate corporate entity and which lack equity capital, i.e., no shares are allotted for the consideration of a payment of money or money in kind. Such joint ventures look much like partnerships, because partnerships are also forms of contractual association that do not create a separate corporate entity or equity capital.

b) Incorporated Joint Ventures are companies. The shareholders in the company are the joint venture participants. Unlike in an unincorporated joint venture or partnership, the shareholders have no rights in relation to the company's assets; and they can participate in the profits (distributed as dividends), but not in losses.

c) Unit Trusts are devices that enable the separation of legal and beneficial interests in assets and the income derived therefrom. In a joint venture situation, the participants wish to insure that their entitlements are fixed rather than discretionary. A unit trust is a configuration in which the entitlement of beneficiaries is expressed in units relative to the total number of fixed units.

d) Limited Partnerships are creations of statute. They remain partnerships at general law and, therefore, do not give rise to the existence of separate legal entities. A limited partnership structure requires at least one general partner to have unlimited liability and limited partners who have liability limited to the extent of their investment in the partnership. It is used rarely in Australia.

e) Hybrid Forms are forms of joint venture comprising elements of each of the preceding. They can also be created to suit the needs of the particular participants. For example, one participant in an unincorporated joint venture could be the trustee of a unit trust, while one shareholder in an incorporated joint venture could also be the trustee of a unit trust.

LICENSING

Australian industry is known for its ingenuity and practical approach to problem solving. In this context, the role of licensing is of particular importance for Australian commerce and industry.

License agreements involving Australian licensees should contain the usual terms one would find in a license in the United States, including; the type of license being grant i.e., sole, exclusive or nonÐexclusive; the territory being covered; the license fee or royalty; licensee's duties and obligations; period of grant and field use of the technology involved; maintenance of quality control; ownership rights in improvements and innovations made by licensee; warranties and indemnities; technical assistance and confidentiality; subÐlicensing and assignments; termination.

On the whole, there are few legal and administrative requirements governing the field of licensing in Australia. Exclusive licenses of patents, copyright and other statutory rights require compliance with certain minor formalities. The Trade Mark Act in Australia provides for the registration of licensees or "users" as they are called in the legislation.

In the final analysis, there is no alternative to a carefully drafted license agreement which provides certainty in defining the parties' mutual obligations. This is true in Australia as it is anywhere else in the world. However, the commonality of language and culture between Australia and the United States makes negotiations involving an Australian licensor or licensee easier.

ESTABLISHING AN OFFICE

The Australian Securities Commission (ASC) is the sole national authority responsible for the administration of companies and securities law throughout Australia. It provides a nationwide system for the registration and regulation of companies, securities and futures markets. The requirements for starting a business are uniform in each state, and the same rules apply for local and overseas companies. While companies are registered with the national body (ASC), business name registration is required in each state where business is transacted.

Because Australian business practices are similar to those in the United States, it relatively straightforward for foreign investors, either in partnership with local companies or on their own account, to establish a business in Australia. A foreign company has a range of business structures from which to choose. The most common forms of business organizations are: representative offices; branches of parent companies; subsidiaries; sole traders; partnerships; trusts; companies; and joint ventures. Overseas investors may set up an operation using any of these forms, irrespective of the business structure they have elsewhere.

Most significant businesses operating in Australia are incorporated as either private or public companies. Under the Corporations Law, the entity is registered automatically as an Australian company, enabling it to conduct business throughout Australia without further registration in individual states or territories. Local companies may be fully controlled by foreign owners. All registered companies must conform to Australian company law administered by the ASC, covering: accounting; financial statements; annual returns; auditing and general meeting requirements; and the necessity to maintain a registered office open to the public.

A private company is the most typical structure for an overseas investor if it is to be a wholly-owned subsidiary of a foreign company and if public offering of shares is not intended. The regulations that apply to a private company are simpler and less costly than those that apply to a public company. A private company may be converted into a public company at any time. Branch offices of overseas companies are established in Australia by registering the overseas corporation as a foreign company under Australia's Corporation Law. A branch office does not require directors to be Australian residents, but must have a registered office address and a statutory agent responsible for requirements of the Corporations Law. The branch will be assigned an Australian Registered Body Number (ARBN) which must be shown with the corporation's name on public documents.

While the procedure to establish an office is fairly straightforward, as in the U.S., it often is done best with expert legal and financial advice readily available from Australian and multinational service providers. Nominal costs for company incorporation include filing fees payable to the ASC, legal costs for preparing the charter and bylaws, and registration. Application forms are available from ASC Business Centers in any state and can be lodged for any city.

SELLING FACTORS AND TECHNIQUES

While Americans find it easy to do business in Australia because of the similarities in cultural and business practices, to understand the market better, there are some precautions to be observed, and some key selling factors to be considered. Australians are very quality conscious. The principles that apply to all sales methods are: product quality, company integrity, and good ongoing service. With a history of geographic isolation, and reliance on imported manufactured goods, Australians are very sensitive to product reliability and assurances of back-up product service, where necessary.

Market Research

Before entering the market, prospective exporters to Australia should evaluate their proposed selling technique thoroughly to ensure that it is responsive to market demand for their product, technology or service in Australia. An effective way to evaluate the situation is to do some basic market research and then to follow through with a personal visit. There is no substitute for a first-hand look.

COMMON SALES ARRANGEMENTS

The use of agents and distributors is the most common way for U.S. companies to sell products in Australia, as discussed in more detail in Section B. above. Because of market size, it is common practice for Australian distributors to ask for exclusive geographic and/or product rights.

Franchising, licensing, joint ventures, and direct marketing, as discussed in Sections E-G above, are all good alternative market entry techniques. These methods entail more investment and commitment than simply appointing an agent or distributor, but they may be more appropriate in the long run.

ADVERTISING AND TRADE PROMOTION

U.S. companies can promote their products in the major newspapers of each Australian state and/or national and state trade and industry magazines. The Commercial Service in Australia publicizes Trade Missions and Seminars by advertising in the financial sections of the major newspapers, in industry magazines, and in newsletters of associations. It also compiles industry-specific mailing lists, sourced from a variety of business directories, both print and electronic, to send material by post or faxstream, using automated mailing list products and search techniques.

PRODUCT PRICING

Australia is a free enterprise economy, and basic market factors of supply and demand apply in product pricing. In order to complete successfully in this small, but highly competitive market, U.S. exporters to Australia must be prepared to offer flexible prices, with, perhaps, lower than usual profit margins, and for smaller minimum quantities. Some factors to consider are:

1. SELLING COSTS AND PRICE COMPETITIVENESS

It is important for U.S. exporters to Australia to competitively price their products. They will be selling in an active, highly competitive and vibrant market with a geographical area like that of the USA and a population slightly more than that of greater Los Angeles. Products from all over the world are represented in this extremely sensitive market where sellers and end-users alike are all searching for something new.

To structure prices competitively, suppliers must consider all the cost elements imported products have to bear. The key factors are freight rates; handling charges; import tariffs; marketing costs, such as for advertising and trade promotion; sales tax; and agent or distributor commissions.

- Sea freight rates from the U.S. to Australia are high when compared with those from within Asia, and even from Europe.
- Imports from competing European nations and many Asian nations including Japan, have the same tariff rates as those from the United States. Tariff rates on imports from nations designated by Australian Customs as Developing Countries are five percent less than the general tariff rate.

- Sales tax is applied equally to most imported and locally made products at the wholesale level at the rate of 11%, 22% or 32% depending on the product. It can make a difference to the end price of imported products, where sales tax is applied by Australian Customs at a nominal, as opposed to actual, wholesale value. If the nominal wholesale value is more than the mark-up generally applied by local manufacturers, imported products may be out-priced.

2. VOLUME BUYING/SELLING AND DISCOUNT PRICING

Australian wholesalers and retailers traditionally have sought the highest markup the market would absorb, rather than thinking of volume buying or selling. This pattern is changing as open markets and the influx of franchisers and other high-volume businesses have alerted the increasingly cost-conscious consumer to competitive discount sales and services. Suppliers need to be able to deliver quality products and/or services at attractive prices. To compete successfully, exporters should consider granting maximum wholesale discounts, keeping in mind that a significantly-sized order to an Australian buyer may still seem like a small order to the U.S. exporter.

Some Australian importers prefer to deal directly with manufacturers. They have the perception that it is cheaper to deal with the overseas manufacturer rather than sourcing from overseas distribution houses. This cultural perception is gradually changing but could result in a U.S. mass merchandiser being called on by a potential importer to justify its pricing system.

3. INDUSTRIAL PRICING

Factors of price, quality, reliability and support in the way of service, are prime considerations when selling industrial products or capital equipment. While price is certainly a major factor, a purchaser may decide to pay more for a piece of equipment known to be of better quality and more reliable than a competing product. However, U.S. exporters must be prepared to negotiate on price or other aspects of the purchase.

In general, Australians are conservative when purchasing capital equipment to upgrade their manufacturing processes. They take time to make purchasing decisions, weighing them carefully against their perceived pay off to increase bottom line profits. If the bottom line does not appear to offer much gain, they may simply defer the purchase.

4. PRICE CONTROLS

There is little formal price control. The national regulator, the Australian Competition and Consumer Commission (ACCC), has the power under the Prices Surveillance Act 1983 to investigate, vet or monitor the prices charged by businesses. These statutory pricing powers, which are designed to make particular businesses or industries publicly accountable for the prices they set, can only be employed where the Federal Government has authorized their use. The ACCC generally uses its pricing powers to examine prices charged by companies and government enterprises that hold substantial power in a market. The Commission's use of its enquiry and monitoring powers culminate in a public report and, where necessary, recommendations to the Government.

Companies "declared" by the Government are required to notify the ACCC of proposed price rises. The Commission usually has 21 days in which to endorse, object or suggest a different price to that proposed. Companies tend to follow the recommendations of the ACCC. The list of declared companies has been reduced significantly in recent years because of increased competition. Oil, beer and cigarettes are the areas where it still applies in the private sector. Airport and postal services are the areas affected in the public sector.

State governments have the power to control prices, but in recent decades have rarely done so.

SALES SERVICE AND CUSTOMER SUPPORT

Generally, doing business in Australia is simple for U.S. exporters when compared with other foreign markets. Culture, language, and business practices are remarkably common. However, subtle cultural differences do exist that can either invigorate or undermine a business relationship. In their dealings, both Americans and Australians are wise to take the time and effort to confirm that their perceptions about roles and expectations are consistent with those of their counterparts.

Depending on the product or service to be exported, Australian agents/distributors expect support from their U.S. suppliers. Examples of this support include product warranty for a specified time, training, advertising, and promotion.

Timely delivery of goods, including spare parts, is expected and is rarely a problem, as major U.S. freight forwarders have offices in Australia. Air freight is used commonly for smaller items. Shipping schedules are reliable. Where necessary, U.S. firms should ensure that their representatives can service the imported equipment or that there are service arrangements in place.

SELLING TO THE GOVERNMENT AND LOCAL INDUSTRY DEVELOPMENT ENCOURAGEMENT

Australia has not yet signed the GATT/WTO Agreement on Government Procurement, which means that it is not bound by conditions prohibiting specification of locally-made product in tenders. The Australian Federal Government has made recent overtures to individual States but to date consensus on signature has not been reached.

Although Australia's government procurement process generally is considered to be well documented and fair, with few restrictions on foreign bidders, there exist a number of qualitative decision factors relating to local industrial development. It is becoming increasingly important for U.S. companies considering bidding for major government business to understand, and to take this into account in their bid structuring. This applies particularly to their consideration of whether to team with Australian industry partners, or to go it alone.

Australia does not impose an overt system of offsets, as it did in the period from the mid-sixties to the mid-nineties. However, it is a feature of the local landscape that some form of commitment to counter-expenditure will be necessary for an overseas company to be successful in winning a large government tender. Government business is increasingly won or lost, not on the price/performance/service package, but on the amount of local industry participation, and even research and development activities undertaken in Australia as a result of the business.

Federal and State governments actively encourage local industry participation in government procurement through purchasing policies and clauses contained in tender documents. Bidders and purchasing agencies are often required to submit separate industry impact statements. In some cases where local participation is a requirement, such as in defense contracts, a two-envelope bid is required, one specifying minimum local involvement (failure to meet minimum objectives renders the bid non-compliant), the other specifying maximum local industry participation. Most governments stop short of directing their agencies to give preference to local suppliers. The Sydney Olympics organizers, however, do give preference to Australian and New

Zealand companies for 2000 Games requirements, not in monetary terms, but in choice of supplier.

Foreign information technology companies with annual sales to the Australian Government in excess of AUD40 million are encouraged to participate in the Partnership for Development scheme (which replaced civil offsets), and those with sales of less than this figure, in fixed-term arrangements. In recent times these schemes have been expanded to include domestic companies. It is not legislated that companies participate, but there is strong pressure to sign up in order to continue business with the Australian government. The schemes promote research and development, training, technology transfer, capital investment and jobs.

PROTECTING YOUR PRODUCT FROM INTELLECTUAL PROPERTY RIGHTS (IPR) INFRINGEMENT

Copyrights, patents, trademarks, industrial designs and integrated circuits are protected under Australian law. Australia is a member of the major global intellectual property protection organizations and conventions. American patent holders planning extensive sales or manufacturing in Australia should not assume that a U.S. patent provides comparable protection in Australia and should seek legal advice as to the advisability of registering their patents under Australian law. For a full discussion of Intellectual Property Rights see Chapter VII, Investment Climate, H.

Copyrights are protected under the Copyright Act of 1968 for the life of the author plus 50 years and in most cases apply to books, sound recordings, films and computer software. The parallel importation of overseas sound recordings and computer software is illegal. It is regarded as an infringement of copyright, under Sections 37 and 38 of the Act. However, the Senate is presently debating amendments to Australian copyright law which could open up the Australian market to numerous non approved importers; Copyright Amendment Bill No. 1 would remove copyright bans over parallel imports of packaging, labeling and accessories allowing the importation of branded goods without a licence; Copyright Amendment Bill No. 2 would remove copyright bans on parallel imports of sound recordings. The fate of both these bills rests in the hands of the minor parties in the Senate. Limited parallel importation is permitted for books in cases where the original editions are not made available in Australia in a timely fashion.

Patents are available for inventions in all fields of technology under the Patent Act of 1990. Trade secrets are protected by registration under the Designs Act for one year, with extensions. Trade names and marks may be protected for seven years and renewed at will by registration under the Trademark Act of 1955. Once used, trade names and marks may also, without registration, be protected by common law.

The Australian Patent, Trademarks and Designs Office of IP Australia handles inquiries regarding laws, regulations and procedures applicable to patents, trademarks, other industrial property rights protection, and copyrights.

NEED FOR A LOCAL ATTORNEY

As in the United States, in Australia it is common practice - and makes good business sense - to retain the services of a reputable attorney familiar with local business conditions, local law, and regulations. Legal expertise is needed to execute legal documentation, interpret laws and regulations, and ameliorate disputes. Most businesses also use the services of a professional accounting firm.

Many well-known local and international law and accounting firms practice in Australia, some with offices throughout Asia and the United States. The Commercial Service in Australia and the American Chamber of Commerce maintain lists of law and accounting firms, as do legal and accounting associations.

LEADING SECTORS FOR U.S. EXPORTS AND INVESTMENT

BEST EXPORT PROSPECT SECTORS

1. INFORMATION TECHNOLOGY SERVICES/E-COMMERCE (CSV)
2. COMPUTERS AND PERIPHERALS (CPT)
3. COMPUTER SOFTWARE (CSF)
4. MEDICAL EQUIPMENT (MED)
5. TELECOMMUNICATIONS PARTS AND EQUIPMENT (TEL)
6. TRAVEL AND TOURISM (TRA)
7. AIRCRAFT AND PARTS (AIR)
8. TELECOMMUNICATIONS SERVICES (TES)
9. INDUSTRIAL AND SPECIALTY CHEMICALS (ICH)
10. ENVIRONMENTAL TECHNOLOGIES (POL)
11. AUTOMOTIVE PARTS & ACCESSORIES (APS)
12. LABORATORY & SCIENTIFIC EQUIPMENT (LAB)
13. BIOTECHNOLOGY (BTC)
14. CONSTRUCTION MACHINERY (CON)

A. EXPORTS

All statistics are calculated using the following conversion rates:

CY 1998 A$1 = US$0.63
FY 1998 A$1 = US$0.62
CY 1999 A$1 = US$0.64
FY 99-00 A$1 = US$0.64
CY 2000 A$1 = US$0 59
CY 2004 A$1 = US$0.53

INFORMATION TECHNOLOGY SERVICES/E-COMMERCE (CSV)

Rank of sector: 1
Name of sector: INFORMATION TECHNOLOGY SERVICES
ITA Industry Code: CSV

The Australian IT services industry accounts for approximately 30 percent of the total IT market and last year 2000 generated US$5 billion in revenue. The services sector recorded 32 percent growth from 1995-1996 to 1998-1999. Industry analyst Gartner Group estimates that the sector will double within the next four years and will account for more of the IT industry than hardware and software revenue combined. Key drivers of the IT services sector are the increased adoption of outsourcing programs, the increase in numbers of Application Service Providers (ASPs), Customer Relationship Management services (CRM), E-commerce applications, and managed or hosted Internet Services.

Over the last few years, outsourcing has been one of the single largest contributors to the local services sector, led by the Federal Government's drive to outsource the majority of its agencies' and departments' provision of IT requirements. According to research group IDC, the local outsourcing sector grew by 17 percent to US$1.45 billion last year. The three largest companies in the local outsourcing market are IBM Global Services Australia (IBMGSA), EDS and CSC, which together account for 65 percent of the total market. In 1999, IBMGSA generated revenue of US$528 million, EDS US$373 million, and CSC US$151 million.

There are few Australian-owned companies that compete in this space, given the size and complexity of Federal Government tenders. In this market segment, some U.S. companies have entered the market by acquiring one of the larger local integration companies (for example, GEIT's acquisition of Ferntree and the recent buyout of BHPIT by CSC). While the majority of the Federal Government contracts have been awarded, many integration providers will be focusing on providing solutions to local small-to-medium sized enterprises (SMEs).

The CRM market is very young in Australia; in 1998 the sector was valued at US$20 million and in 1999 US$38 million. Observers are predicting that there will be approximately 44 percent compound growth over the next five years, given that most companies have yet to implement a CRM solution. Recent research has found that 65 percent of local companies considered CRM to be their first or second development priority; up to 27 percent were evaluating or in the early stages of planning and implementing a system; and 48 percent had no form of CRM in place at all.

Another service sub-sector in its infancy is the ASP market, which is predicted to show robust growth into the foreseeable future. Many local "box selling" companies, faced with dwindling margins in the sales area, have been forced to incorporate value-added services into their range of solutions. Many of these companies are moving to the ASP model and are providing customers with a range of client-based applications on-demand, effectively blurring the area between application providers and ISPs. Many of the approximately 500-strong local ISPs are also moving into the ASP arena, offering a range of services that a couple of years ago would have been the domain of IT consulting companies. We are also noticing an increase in the number of companies offering managed or hosted Internet services. Many local companies are looking to third party hosting providers to provide expert security, site redundancy, and managed services for their Internet site assets. This market segment is predicted to grow strongly over the next year.

The gap between reality and hype surrounding the local uptake of B2B and B2C applications is still large. Much has been said about the projected growth of this market segment, but the reality is that this growth has failed to materialize thus far. The dot com collapse of last year has meant that traditional bricks and mortar companies are not as obliged to race into the adoption of Internet commerce applications as they would have (if the dot com business paradigm had proven to be sustainable and successful).

Presently, travel bookings make the biggest contribution to local consumer online sales (US$43.5 million), although consumers are also purchasing books, CD's, toys, and other items, and using the internet to transact financial services as well.

DATA TABLE (Millions US$)

YEAR	1999	2000	2006
A. TOTAL MARKET SIZE	3,000	4,000	5,000
B. TOTAL LOCAL PRODUCTION	1,700	2,300	2,500
C. TOTAL EXPORTS	200	300	350

D. TOTAL IMPORTS	1,500	2,000	2,000
E. IMPORTS FROM THE U.S.	1,000	1,500	1,700

COMPUTERS & PERIPHERALS (CPT)

Rank of Sector: 2
Name of Sector: COMPUTERS & PERIPHERALS
ITA Industry Code: CPT

The Australian hardware market was patchy over the last year. Certain sub-sectors of the industry showed reasonable growth and others struggled. For example, lower-end server sales were strong, but high-end sales (US$600,000 and above) were flat over the same period. Last year, the government abolished the local sales tax and introduced a general impost of 10 percent on most goods and services. The reverberations and economic disruption caused by the introduction of the GST are still being felt in the local economy and, as such, IT sales across the board have suffered.

PC sales have been robust over the last year, with sales growing by 15 percent. The five major vendors are Compaq (16 percent of total local desktop, notebook and server markets), IBM (11 percent), HP (10.6 percent), Dell and Toshiba. In the local market, about 2 million PCs are shipped annually. Of these, 500,000 are destined for the consumer desktop sector. Local brand and clone manufacturers have an estimated fifty percent share of the local desktop market. The laptop/notebook market grew 25.2 percent over the past year.

With prices dropping significantly on hand-held devices, such as the Palm Pilot, their uptake in the local economy has been assured. Sales on other hand-held devices, such as PocketMail, have been far more disappointing. Wireless Application Devices (WAP) have also been heavily promoted in the local market. With 40 percent of the local population owning a cellular phone, the market should have proven a strong revenue earner for service providers. Unfortunately, the carriers have not been able to find compelling services to offer on customer cell phones, and uptake of WAP services has been slow.

Australia ranks just behind Sweden, Canada and the U.S. in terms of Internet access, with 36 percent of the local population now accessing the Internet. Hardware sales related to Internet access will continue to grow very strongly over the next couple of years.

In Australia, a large number of service providers are moving to provide Application Services (ASPs). It is expected that sales to ASPs will drive the server market as well. IBM, Hewlett-Packard, Compaq and Sun Microsystems account for 80 percent of total local sales. IBM lays claim to 30 percent of the local server market. At present, local white box server assemblers account for only 10 percent of the Australian market.

Good opportunities exist for U.S. vendors of Storage Area Networks (SANs) in the local market, especially in the corporate space. With corporate storage requirements growing at between 60 and 80 percent annually, U.S. vendors should be well-placed to tap into this extra demand for robust, reliable solutions.

The networking market has been growing in excess of 20 percent per annum and shows no signs of slowing in the near future. Strong demand will continue for routers and switches.

There is always strong interest from Australian resellers and distributors for new sources of PC memory, video and sound cards, and storage devices. In this segment, price becomes a critical factor for U.S. companies to compete successfully against cheaper Asian imports.

DATA TABLE (Millions US$)

YEAR	1999	2000	2006
A. TOTAL MARKET SIZE	5,605	5,970	6,000
B. TOTAL LOCAL PRODUCTION	1,700	1,980	2,000
C. TOTAL EXPORTS	1,220	1,350	1,350
D. TOTAL IMPORTS	5,125	5,350	5,500
E. IMPORTS FROM THE U.S.	2,700	2,950	3,000

COMPUTER SOFTWARE (CSF)

Rank of Sector: 3
Name of Sector: COMPUTER SOFTWARE
ITA Industry Code: CSF

The Australian software market has grown at approximately 15 percent over the last year and is valued at US$3 billion.

The Customer Relationship Management (CRM) software and Knowledge Management (KM) software markets are growing in excess of 40 percent annually and excellent opportunities exist for U.S. vendors of these solutions. Many Australian integrators and solutions providers have identified that these two sectors will also show rapid growth in the medium term. As such, they are developing business models incorporating KM and CRM solutions with their existing suite of solutions and are actively looking to form partnerships with U.S. vendors. This window of opportunity for U.S. firms could close by the end of 2004.

Networking solutions are always in high demand in the local market, including solutions designed to monitor, document and analyze networks. The network and website security markets are beginning to develop as many Australian companies are realizing the importance of keeping their Web assets secure. It is anticipated that the market for security applications will grow strongly over the next two years and excellent opportunities exist for U.S. developers of these programs.

The Australian call center market has been growing rapidly over the last few years. U.S. software vendors will find their network documentation, management and monitoring software in large demand from local integrators and consultants. The document management and imaging markets have matured over the last two years. Opportunities exist in the local market for new vendors, although some of the incumbents are well- entrenched, so securing market share could be a long and costly exercise.

Observers are predicting that the application server middleware market will show strong growth in the local market. With Y2K fixes now well off the books of large corporations and mid-sized companies, those firms that have not fully implemented a web strategy will be well into their implementation phase. Given that middleware is the ideal method of getting legacy data onto the web, and that the number of companies developing web strategies is increasing rapidly, U.S. vendors should be well-placed to serve the local market.

The collapse of the local dot com sector over the last year has left many "bricks and mortar" companies cautious with regard to implementing B2B and B2C online E-commerce strategies. Many companies have re-evaluated their business models in terms of Internet strategies, and as such, are adopting a wait and see approach to what systems (if any) they will purchase. U.S. vendors of these systems will face a difficult job of obtaining market share in this market segment.

In the corporate web authoring space, good quality graphics packages are still heavily in demand. Industry-standard tools include most Macromedia products (especially Dreamweaver, with its quality HTML generator), Adobe Photoshop (the standard in the publishing and content industries), and Jasc Paintshop Pro (an affordable graphics graphics package, which has proven a favorite in the retail space as well). There are a number of resellers and distributors who specialize in the multimedia space and all of them are looking for new products to add to their business lines.

At the retail level, Internet-centric software applications are in high demand. These include non-commercial web authoring packages (of which Front Page is a clear leader), graphics packages, diagnostics tools and reference titles. Pricing is a key factor to gaining market share in this segment.

DATA TABLE (Millions US$)

YEAR	1999	2000	2006
A. TOTAL MARKET SIZE	2,754	2,975	3,005
B. TOTAL LOCAL PRODUCTION	749	780	785
C. TOTAL EXPORTS	270	279	280
D. TOTAL IMPORTS	2,700	2,850	2,850
E. IMPORTS FROM THE U.S.	1,755	1,900	2,000

MEDICAL EQUIPMENT

Rank of sector: 4
Name of sector: MEDICAL EQUIPMENT
ITA Industry Code: MED

Medical equipment is one of Australia's largest markets for exporters of U.S. products. The market is valued at approximately A$1.8 billion, representing about one percent of the global market. It is a mature market, characterized by modest sales growth and strong competition. A large number of small companies and a small number of multinational firms serve the market. The U.S. is the world's largest producer of medical equipment, and thus, most of the major U.S. medical companies are represented in Australia, either through local representatives or subsidiary companies.

Although a relatively small market, Australia's high per capita income means that there is demand for the full range of sophisticated medical equipment. In addition, Australia enjoys a high standard of medical practice. This, together with the expectation of state-of-the-art medical treatment by an educated population, ensures a continuing need for high quality and innovative medical equipment and products. Approximately 80% of local requirements are met by imports. Of this, U.S. imports account for approximately 50%. Other major market suppliers are Germany, Japan and the EU.

The Government is the primary purchaser of medical equipment in Australia. Industry estimates that public hospitals account for 85% of sales of medical equipment, while State and Territory tenders account for 65% of medical consumables. The Government is also a major buyer of dental equipment, which is around 15-20% of the total market. Thus, government policy and activity in the provision of public health services is a major factor in the demand for medical equipment. However, the provision of health services by the private sector is increasing. Further increases are likely due to the rise in the number of Australians with private health insurance, the corporatization of services such as pathology, radiology and general practice, and the considerable role of the private sector in the care of Australia's aging population.

Locally-manufactured medical equipment accounts for a modest share of the Australian market. However, over the past twenty years, the number of establishments manufacturing medical and surgical equipment has grown at an average rate of 3.5%. Turnover has also averaged 3.0% growth during this time. Most local manufacturers operate in niche markets and are strongly export-oriented. The principal markets for exports of Australian medical equipment are Asia, the U.S., and New Zealand. The value of exported medical equipment has varied significantly during the 1990s, due to the relocation offshore of the manufacturing facilities of several major multinationals.

The medical equipment market in Australia is regulated by the Therapeutic Goods Administration (TGA). A new regulatory framework, based on global harmonization, is scheduled to come into force at the end of 2004. Both the current and the new systems classify devices according to the degree of risk associated with their application. Thus, medical equipment, such as electromedical products, sterile devices, and implantables from all sources are likely to require the most rigorous assessment by the TGA before they can enter the Australian market. As this approval can only be obtained by an Australian sponsor, U.S. exporters need to appoint an Australian representative before their products can be approved by the TGA.

U.S. medical equipment is traditionally well-received in Australia, due to its perceived high quality. Opportunities exist for state-of-the-art and innovative medical equipment and products which lead to a significant improvement in clinical outcomes. In particular, products which serve Australia's aging population, such as treatments of diseases of the aged, like arthritis, or equipment which assists aged people to live independently, are likely to experience growth. Also in demand are information technology applications which facilitate information sharing and service delivery over distances, along with those relating to practice and records management and supply chain management.

DATA TABLE (Millions US$)

YEAR	**1999**	**2000**	**2006**
A. TOTAL MARKET SIZE	1,024	960	936
B. TOTAL LOCAL PRODUCTION	451	401	391
C. TOTAL EXPORTS (INC. RE-EXPORTS)	185	290	292
D. TOTAL IMPORTS	758	849	837
E. IMPORTS FROM THE U.S.	379	425	418

TELECOMMUNICATIONS PARTS & EQUIPMENT (TEL)

Rank of Sector: 5
Name of sector: TELECOMMUNICATIONS PARTS & EQUIPMENT
ITA Industry Code: TEL

In this exciting and rapidly advancing sector, U.S. exports of telecommunications equipment to Australia represent about 20 percent of the total import market and have the potential to continue to grow. Growth in the telecommunications industry is estimated at 9% for 2004.

Australia's telecommunications industry is well-developed and mature. Telephone lines are connected to 96 percent of all Australian households, and total telecommunications revenue for 2004 is estimated at US$21.9 billion. Australia is implementing a range of broadband infrastructure, and has seen significant expansion in the telecommunications market following deregulation in July 1997. 2000 saw the end of Telstra's monopoly for carrying local calls, with the unbundling of the local loop. Deregulation has resulted in more than 70 licensed carriers (from an initial two), offering a range of telecommunications services, including long-distance and local telephony, broadband services, and wireless services.

Telecommunications products are segmented into customer premises equipment (CPE), such as telephone handsets, and network equipment and infrastructure. Customer premises equipment is defined as products attached to the network at the customer end, and includes not only telephones, small business systems and PABXs, but any piece of equipment attached to the network. U.S.-made CPE equipment will not be permitted in Australia without modification to comply with regulations set down by the Australian Communications Authority (ACA).

Other key niche segments include the mobile market and, more importantly, Internet networks. These two segments have opened up major areas of equipment provision previously not required. XDSL technologies were launched to the public in August 2000, and a range of other services, including satellite and cable are also being offered to provide broadband access to the Internet.

Although U.S.-made analog phones sold well in the past, the closure of the Australian analog AMP network have in early 2000 and the spread of the digital GSM network has meant that U.S.-made products lost market share to European-made GSM products. However, the introduction of the CDMA mobile networks (which has replaced the analog system in rural areas), as well as Hutchison Telecommunication's Orange One, are important for suppliers like Motorola, which is strong in the handset provision segment. Motorola recently won the contract to supply equipment for Hutchison Telecommunications' new 3G network.

All carriers, including Telstra, continue to develop and upgrade existing networks, and it is estimated that it costs US$2.5 billion each year to maintain the existing networks. These carriers usually undertake network infrastructure purchases on an "invitation only" basis to selective international telecommunications suppliers, which must also be prepared to include some aspect of local industry development. Nonetheless, U.S. exporters of network infrastructure products should certainly consider presenting their products to the carriers.

U.S. products, including advanced network equipment like ATM switches, call processing and managing equipment, modems, and routers, are competitive in Australia. Growth areas include wireless technologies, optical technologies and communications and applications software.

A number of U.S. companies, including Lucent, Cisco, Sun Microsystems, and Canadian company Nortel, have contracts to supply network equipment. Motorola is also a major player, with products coming from the U.S. and Europe. Major network equipment competitors include

Siemens, NEC, Ericsson, and Alcatel. There are also many high-quality local suppliers, most of which are subsidiaries of international companies, including Ericsson and Alcatel.

DATA TABLE (Millions US$)

YEAR	1999	2000	2006
A. TOTAL MARKET SIZE (wholesale)	3,305	3,964	4,360
B. TOTAL LOCAL PRODUCTION	1,846	2,153	2,368
C. TOTAL EXPORTS	727	446	490
D. TOTAL IMPORTS	2,186	2,257	2,482
E. IMPORTS FROM THE U.S.	460	499	549

TRAVEL AND TOURISM (TRA)

Rank of sector: 6
Name of sector: TRAVEL AND TOURISM
ITA Industry Code: TRA

Australia is a major source of export earnings for U.S. travel and tourism services. In 1999, travel receipts from Australian travelers totaled US$1.5 billion. As a market for U.S. tourism, Australia is a major source of export earnings. Since 1986, Australia has ranked as one of the top fifteen most important markets for the U.S. In 2000, Australia claimed the number 10 spot. The 540,000 visitors in 2000 from Australia was an increase of 12 percent from 1999.

The U.S. ranks as the leading long-haul destination, ahead of the UK and Europe, and is the second most popular destination behind New Zealand. Visitors from Australia to the U.S. are projected to increase steadily, by approximately 3.6 percent per annum for the next three years. It is forecast that 546,000 Australians will visit the U.S. in 2004.

Australians have a great propensity for travel and receive four weeks of annual vacation per year. Australian travelers to the U.S. are characterized by long stays and high spending, and tend to travel during the off-season months of March, May, June, September, October and December. The long distances for Australians traveling to the U.S. is reflected in their relatively long periods of stay. The average length of stay for Australians in the U.S. is 23.7 nights, which is much higher than the average for all overseas visitors 14 nights.

The U.S. can offer the Australian traveler what they seek in a vacation destination, and with no language barriers, stunning scenery, good shopping, and a variety of entertainment facilities, the steady growth of Australian travelers to the U.S. should continue in the long term. Most Australians visiting the U.S. are independent travelers and only 19 percent purchase pre-paid packages or tours. The majority of Australian visitors make use of some mode of transport to travel within the U.S., such as domestic airlines, car rentals, and bus or train services. The most popular types of accommodation are two-three star, medium-priced hotels.

The most popular activities for Australian travelers visiting the U.S. include shopping; dining in restaurants; sightseeing in cities; touring the countryside; visiting historic places, small towns, amusement/theme parks, and National Parks; visiting cultural heritage sights; and taking guided tours.

The most popular destinations for Australian travelers do not vary greatly from year to year. In 1999, Australians primarily visited California (60 percent), New York (23 percent), Hawaii (18 percent), Nevada (18 percent), Florida (13 percent) and Colorado (7 percent). The top cities visited were Los Angeles (38 percent), San Francisco (24 percent), New York City (22 percent), Las Vegas (16 percent), Oahu/Honolulu (15 percent), Anaheim (12 percent), Washington, DC (8 percent), and San Diego (7 percent).

On average, Australians visit two states and one to three cities. The destinations with the most potential for an increase in Australian visitors are West (including California), Mid-Atlantic (including New York State), and South (including Florida and Louisiana). Good development opportunities exist in specialist holidays, such as self-drive car rentals and RV holidays, skiing, and adventure travel.

Skiing is a popular holiday activity, with an estimated 85-95 percent of long-haul ski traffic from Australia heading for North America. This represents a change from 20 years ago, when Europe was the most popular long-haul skiing destination. Australians are not only going to Colorado, the traditional leader, but are also venturing to Wyoming, Idaho, Utah and Montana. Eastern ski resorts are increasingly combined with visits to New York City and Boston.

Winter is an opportune time to attract additional Australian travelers to the U.S., as it corresponds to the Australian Summer (December-January), when school vacations are longer. Australians can take advantage of off-season prices in the U.S. and lower domestic airfares. Notably, the particularly long average length of stay 24 days does not significantly vary throughout the year.

Australian tour operators and travel agents are key players in the industry and very influential in the consumer's decision-making process. Most Australians visiting the U.S. source information from local travel agents. Although the use of the Internet from home by Australians has doubled every year since 1996, a boom in home shopping, has not matched the boom in general home usage. A recent survey of Internet users revealed that the products which consumers have shown a willingness to purchase over the Internet include travel and tourism services. Australia lags behind American Internet shoppers, although tourism analysts predict that increasingly more Australians will bypass travel agents and, in the long term, Internet bookings have the potential to become an truly important part of the industry.

DATA TABLE (Millions US$)

YEAR	1999	2000	2006
A. TOTAL MARKET SIZE	4,810	5,231	5,813
B. U.S. RECEIPTS FROM AUSTRALIAN TRAVELERS	1,623	2,255	2,505

AIRCRAFT AND PARTS

Rank of sector: 7
Name of sector: AIRCRAFT AND PARTS
ITA Industry Code: AIR

The aviation industry in Australia is comprised of three main sub-sectors: commercial aviation, defense aerospace and general aviation.

Commercial aviation is comprised of aircraft used for international and domestic trunk services and regional fleets, for which the local industry provides repair and modification up to 747-size aircraft. The commuter routes between the population centers on the East Coast, notably between the cities of Sydney and Melbourne, comprise one of the busiest air traffic lanes in the world. The two major licensed airline operators, Qantas and Ansett, dominate domestic commercial aviation. Despite deregulation of the airline industry twelve years ago, attempts by others to break into the market have met with failure or limited success. According to the Bureau of Transport Economics, during the past nine years, forty airlines entered the regional aviation industry, and a similar number exited. Most of these were small. On a larger scale, of the latest to make an entry into the trunk routes, Impulse Airlines and Virgin Blue, only Virgin remains. While the Government encourages competition in the industry, the hurdles for new entrants are formidable.

The Australian Department of Defense plays a vital role in sustaining the Australian aerospace industry. The Department spends around US$700 million annually on the acquisition of new aircraft, modification of existing fleets, and maintenance and spare parts. The United States enjoys an important strategic defense relationship with Australia, and there is day-to-day cooperation in maintenance, provision of spare parts, and development of Australia's military air assets.

General aviation (GA) and charter is supported nationwide by about 120 small companies based at or near the major airports. These small enterprises supply parts and service, overhaul and maintenance, and half of these establishments account for the majority of dollar turnover. Nearly all are located in New South Wales and Victoria, where the larger airline companies have major facilities and/or large maintenance bases. The GA sector is made up of all non-scheduled flying activity by registered aircraft, other than that performed by major international and domestic airlines. Major categories of GA are private, business, training, aerial agriculture and charter. It also includes ultralight operations, gliders, hang gliders and autogyros. Charter and flight training comprise the largest share of the market, and aerial agriculture is the fastest growing sector.

The health of the domestic aviation industry is highly dependent on the efficient operation of regional aviation services. In the most recent decade, regional passenger traffic has been growing at an annual rate of around 13%.

Australia boasts one of the highest per capita uses of light aircraft in the world, with over 11,000 aircraft utilizing over 277 licensed airports (many of which can be categorized as airfields). However, eighty percent of Australian airspace (in itself, ten percent of the world's airspace) does not have radar coverage. Airservices Australia, the entity responsible for the management of air traffic control in the Australian flight information region, would like to see this situation improved, for example, through increased use of the global positioning system.

There are about forty regional commuter operators throughout Australia, providing regular public air transport services and serving 9-10% of the market. There are approximately 650 charter service operations holding a charter license; 280 establishments offering flying training and forty-five offering helicopter flying training. Other features of the general aviation segment include aerial work such as surveying, spotting and photography, police and customs functions, and aerial medical services; private piloting; large corporations, which own their own aircraft; and agricultural services, of which there are around sixty leading operations.

Total imports of aircraft goods currently run at about US$1.2 billion, representing around 4.5% of Australia's total manufactured imports. Completed aircraft comprise about 66% of the imported value, and parts and components 24%. Other aircraft-related commodities make up the remainder (10%).

DATA TABLE (Millions US$)

YEAR	1999	2000	2006
A. TOTAL MARKET SIZE	1,685	1,495	1,785
B. TOTAL LOCAL PRODUCTION	635	630	720
C. TOTAL EXPORTS	170	174	205
D. TOTAL IMPORTS	1,495	1,305	1,525
E. IMPORTS FROM THE U.S.	1,195	975	1,245
F. RE-EXPORTS	275	265	255

TELECOMMUNICATIONS SERVICES (TES)

Rank of sector: 8
Name of sector: TELECOMMUNICATIONS SERVICES
ITA Industry Code: TES

Telecommunications services in Australia are booming, with revenue of about US$17.6 billion in 2004 and an expected growth of between 10-15 percent annually. U.S. products are extremely well received, and U.S. exports of telecommunications services should continue growing by 10-15 percent annually.

The market was opened to full competition in 1997, and the last few years has seen the introduction of a plethora of carriers offering various telecommunications services new to Australian consumers. As of June 2000, there were over 70 licensed carriers. A sizeable number of these carriers include U.S. companies that have identified opportunities in Australia. This list includes Primus, PowerTel, UEComm (a subsidiary of United Energy), and MCI Worldcom (UUNET). Sprint has ALSO recently signaled its intention to re-enter the market. Of course, not all carriers offer full service to residential and business consumers - many of the 70-plus carriers provide specialized services or operate in a specific region.

Market competition has increased significantly with access to the local call market. With the unbundling of the local loop, the opportunity to offer a range of services has presented itself. In addition, carriers and resellers are exploring ways of offering new services to consumers through developing and convergent technologies.

The growth of data communications over voice has primarily been a result of the strength of the Internet, of which Australia is a major user. Internet growth in Australia has created an explosion of providers for this service, with around 700 ISPs active in the Australian market. Many telecommunications carriers have, in one form or another, seen the business opportunities in this area and set uptheir own ISPs. In addition, the growth in electronic commerce is ensuring the continuing arrival of facilitators for this service.

Strong demand for mobile communications has meant there are numerous providers who offer services. Australia now has five mobile networks: Telstra, Optus, Vodafone, Orange, and that of recently failed One.Tel. There is also considerable competition also in the reselling of mobile networks. One recent entrant to the mobile phone market in Australia was Virgin Mobile, which began operations in 2000. Virgin Mobile resells capacity on the existing networks, but offers customers no contracts: consumers purchase a handset, then either pre-pay or pay per call.

The market is rapidly growing, diversifying and adapting to swift technological change. It incorporates broadband services as well as data-based and regular telephony services. Wireless Access Protocol (WAP), bringing Internet services to the cellular phone, is growing as well, and consumers can now access a range of content. Australians have proved themselves to be quick in the uptake of new technologies, and WAP services are likely to enjoy considerable popularity in coming years.

Promising market entry opportunities are available in providing Internet access, electronic commerce, wireless communications, facilities management (billing services, call centers, etc.), electronic funds transfer at point-of-sale (EFTPOS), electronic data interchange, and the simple resale of capacity.

DATA TABLE (Millions US$)

YEAR	1999	2000	2006
A. TOTAL MARKET SIZE (wholesale)	13,190	16,000	17,600
B. TOTAL LOCAL PRODUCTION	10,223	14,679	16,146
C. TOTAL EXPORTS	1,300	1,700	2,000
D. TOTAL IMPORTS	2,967	1,321	1,453
E. IMPORTS FROM THE U.S.	1,600	945	1,039

INDUSTRIAL AND SPECIALTY CHEMICALS (ICH)

Rank of sector: 9
Name of sector: INDUSTRIAL CHEMICALS
ITA Industry Code: ICH

The Australian industrial inorganic chemical industry has a turnover of approximately US$1 billion annually. In 1998-1999, it represented approximately 8 percent of the total local chemical industry, which is valued at US$14 billion. Key product segments are chlorine, titanium oxide, sodium cyanide, ammonia (industrial), caustic soda, sulphuric acid, and soda ash. Major local players include Tiwest, Penrice Soda Products (U.S.-owned), Ticor, Incitec, Orica, Wesfarmers, and Millennium Inorganic Chemicals Ltd.

Despite its overall loss of market share, the U.S. is in an ideal position to expand total exports of inorganic industrial chemicals to Australia. The U.S. continues to have access to quality feedstock and U.S. chemical manufacturers have a reputation for supplying consistently good high-quality product. Furthermore, government and industry bodies are trying to encourage a more international focus to incorporate new technologies. As exports rise, the demand for chemicals (particularly industrial inorganic chemicals) will also rise.

The industry is in a mature phase, but it is likely to enter a growth phase in the near future. This phase is characterized by growth in the production of key industry products and demand from user industries. Australia is a world leader in the production of mineral sands containing titanium minerals (rutile and ilmenite, the main raw materials for titanium dioxide pigment). In fact, Australia possesses 30% of the world's ilmenite resources and 20% of its rutile resources. Generally, imports of chemicals exceed exports, although exports have increased over the last decade. The expansion of titanium dioxide production has contributed to much of the growth, mainly in the paint manufacturing area. However, the mining industry is probably the largest customer for a wide range (and large quantities) of industrial inorganic chemicals.

The U.S. has traditionally been the major supplier of chemical products to the Australian chemical industry. A high percentage of inorganic chemical imports are sourced from the U.S., followed by the U.K., China, Japan and Germany. A weakening Australian dollar is not likely to affect this segment of the chemical industry, which has remained static. Many of these chemicals are essential additives for the manufacturing sector and new technology is constantly being sourced from overseas countries to be used in a variety of industries. New chemicals are being registered on a constant basis with the National Industrial Chemicals Notification and Assessment Scheme (NICNAS).

DATA TABLE (Millions US$)

YEAR	1999	2000	2006
A. TOTAL MARKET SIZE	1,744	1,800	1,813
B. TOTAL LOCAL PRODUCTION	199	201	214
C. TOTAL EXPORTS	936	906	819
D. TOTAL IMPORTS	737	764	780
E. IMPORTS FROM THE U.S.	216	236	257

ENVIRONMENTAL PRODUCTS AND SERVICES (POL)

Rank of sector: 10
Name of sector: POLLUTION CONTROL EQUIPMENT
ITA Industry Code: POL

Total environmental spending in Australia is in the order of US$5.1 billion, or about 1.5 percent of the total world market. Total spending is split between goods and services, estimated at 35 and 65 percent, respectively, and is forecast to continue to grow at a rate of three percent up until 2002. The industry is made up of between 2,500 and 3,000 mostly small firms that employ a total of 100,000 people. Imports currently satisfy 70 percent of total demand for goods, but only 20 percent of the demand for services.

There is a perception in Australia that four countries lead the industry: Japan in air pollution control; France in water; and the U.S. and Germany in pollution abatement equipment and waste management technologies. Other international key players are considered to be the U.K, Canada and the Netherlands. The U.S. has an estimated overall import market share of 15 percent.

The two driving forces behind the demand for environmental goods and services are increasing community awareness and government regulations. Population pressure in part explains the demand for water and wastewater treatment, the largest sector of the environmental industry. Developments since 1998, such as the change in Australia's Corporations Law and the establishment of a database to record pollution emissions, should assist with policy and program formulation at all levels of government. A number of state-based environmental agencies have also revised and updated various environmental laws, such as those governing the management and treatment of scheduled/hazardous wastes and contaminated sites.

A relatively small population and industrial base are the major constraints on the industry. As a result, there is a shortage of venture capital to fund R&D, pilot projects, and the commercial development of new technology. These very constraints, however, explain in part why Australian firms are particularly interested in reviewing new technology and are open to discussing various forms of strategic alliances.

The strongest opportunities are in the water and wastewater treatment sector, followed by reclamation and remediation. Wastewater treatment plants have, in the past, primarily been managed by state government-owned utilities. However, the corporatization of many utilities has resulted in increased opportunities for private sector participation in the delivery of water and wastewater services. Some water authorities have outsourced the management and maintenance of existing water treatment plants, while new plants are also being created under "build-own-operate-transfer" contracts by private sector interests. Many of these projects have in recent years been awarded to French and U.K. companies, in consortia with local firms. U.S.-led consortia have been largely absent from these projects.

Opportunities are also being created by local government or council activity. In 1992, the government set a national goal of reducing waste going to landfills to 50 percent of 1990 per capita levels, by 2000. This pressure on councils, together with rising costs associated with monitoring and managing landfill sites, is creating a market for technology with applications in waste minimization, re-use, recovery, and recycling. Recycling remains the most fragile sub-sector of the industry, given near monopoly buyers and low commodity prices. Local councils are even starting to collect materials that they are unable to sell.

Despite this, regulatory pressure continues to force councils to look at more cost-effective recycling systems and services. As a result, some councils are now also exploring solid waste-to-energy recycling systems. An estimated 50 percent of greenhouse gases are created by council activity and it is claimed that Australia has managed to get more local governments involved in programs than any other country.

In addition, a "green" power market in Australia is also emerging. Electricity retailers are expected to source an extra two percent of their supply from renewable energy or specified waste energy sources by 2010. There is currently no direct regulatory pressure for industry to embrace sustainable energy technology. However, there does appear to be some moral responsibility being assumed by companies generally. This is exemplified through the Greenhouse Challenge, a cooperative effort of Australian industry and the Commonwealth Government to reduce greenhouse emissions. Through this program, Australian companies are encouraged to reduce their emissions through self-regulation.

Site remediation is considered the most competitive area within the Australian environmental management industry. Contracting companies are required to provide integrated solutions in site assessment and remediation, and consultancies for decontamination projects in industrial metals, chemical contamination and agricultural chemical contamination. Environmental liabilities associated with business and property transactions are increasingly making on-site treatment and soil remediation more economically viable than the alternative of disposing contaminants to landfill.

Environmental opportunities are ready to be found. Australia needs strategic alliances to help commercialize some of its own emerging environmental technologies, as well as adopt advanced technological developments through strong partnership relations.

DATA TABLE (Millions US$)

YEAR	1999	2000	2006
A. TOTAL MARKET SIZE	5,412	5,574	5,142
B. TOTAL LOCAL PRODUCTION	3,505	3,610	3,330
C. TOTAL EXPORTS	123	126	116
D. TOTAL IMPORTS	2,030	2,090	1,928
E. IMPORTS FROM THE U.S.	325	334	304

AUTOMOTIVE PARTS AND ACCESSORIES (APS)

Rank of Sector: 11
Name of Sector: AUTOMOTIVE PARTS AND ACCESSORIES
ITA Industry Code: APS

An estimated 11.93 million motor vehicles are currently registered in Australia, for a population of 19 million people. The average age of passenger vehicles is about 10.3 years, twice the average age of equivalent motor vehicles in Japan. The aging of the vehicle fleet translates to solid opportunities for parts and accessories firms.

While future growth is forecast for the import of U.S. automotive parts and accessories, with the U.S. holding a major share of the market, the strong U.S. dollar over the past two years has meant considerable competition for U.S. parts by cheaper, mostly Asian suppliers. Currently, the U.S. supplies nearly 20 percent of total imports. The other significant suppliers of automotive parts and accessories (in descending order) are Japan, Germany, Sweden and Italy. The automotive parts and accessories market in 2004 is valued at US$5.07 billion, around 50 percent of which is accounted for by imports.

The U.S. is Australia's second largest supplier of automotive parts and components, after Japan. Imports from the U.S. totaled US$495 million in 2004, which is a significant achievement, given the small quantity of U.S. vehicles that enter the Australian market.
The sector can be divided into original equipment (OE), which is supplied to local manufacturers, and replacement parts and accessories. Four automotive manufacturing companies operate in Australia: Ford, General Motors, Toyota and Mitsubishi, with a total production capacity of over 400,000 vehicles annually.

The Australian automotive market provides excellent opportunities for U.S. suppliers of the following: compression-ignition internal combustion piston engines, carburetors, piston rings, fuel injection products, transmission and ignition products, lubricants and fuel pumps, cruise controls, accessories and car care products, body repair kits and products, and automotive tools. Accessories which are of a high quality and competitively priced are also in demand.

Statistics for the Australian market are shown in the table below. Due to conversion to U.S. dollar amounts, the real value of the sector is slightly distorted (due to the relative decline of the Australian dollar against the U.S. dollar). Exports of components have also grown strongly, due to the competitive Australian dollar.

DATA TABLE (Millions US$)

YEAR	1999	2000	2006
A. TOTAL MARKET SIZE (wholesale)	4,416	4,438	5,077
B. TOTAL LOCAL PRODUCTION	2,529	2,548	3,100
C. TOTAL EXPORTS	623	612	792
D. TOTAL IMPORTS	2,510	2,502	2,769
E. IMPORTS FROM THE U.S.	497	492	495

LABORATORY AND SCIENTIFIC EQUIPMENT

Rank of sector: 12
Name of sector: LABORATORY AND SCIENTIFIC EQUIPMENT
ITA Industry Code: LAB

The structure of the Australian laboratory and scientific equipment industry broadly reflects that of the U.S. It features a large number of small companies and a small number of multinationals.

Australia is a small and mature market, with about 90 percent of local consumption being supplied by imports. The main suppliers are Western Europe, the U.S. and Japan. U.S. products hold approximately 38 percent of the market. U.S. products are well-regarded in the Australian market in terms of technical suitability and quality. There is no significant price advantage or disadvantage attached to U.S. products when compared with third-country suppliers.

Some consolidation has occurred in the scientific supplies industry over the past year, with the largest distributor in the sector, New Zealand-based Selby-Biolab, buying competitor, Lab Supply. Other recent takeovers include that by Radiometer Pacific, which purchased Proscience; and Technical and Scientific, which purchased the Analytical Equipment Company (AEC).

Australia has a strong, internationally-recognized scientific research sector. Public sector institutions, including universities, perform the majority of research activities. However, the sector faces several challenges, not least of which are increasing investment in research and development and commercializing scientific discoveries. The Australian Government has recognized that, in order for Australia to remain competitive in the global economy, it must nurture and support scientific research. In January 2004, the Government announced a new "Innovation Policy", which included funding, education and commercialization-related initiatives for the science sector. In addition, there is a high degree of interest on the part of Australian state governments and commercial entities in Australia's biotechnology sector, which generated A$1 billion (US$520 million) in revenue in 2000. A positive development for the sector was the announcement by the Victorian State Government (in June 2004) of the decision to build a synchrotron (an electron accelerator, which acts as an immensely powerful microscope), likely to attract research and development activities to the state. These developments bode well for the demand of scientific and laboratory equipment.

Laboratory and scientific equipment must conform to Australian electrical standards, must comply with Australian Electromagnetic Compatibility (EMC) requirements, where appropriate, and must be appropriately labeled. Best prospects are products which serve Australia's research strengths in agricultural sciences, earth sciences, biological sciences and health and medical sciences.

DATA TABLE (Millions U.S.$)

YEAR	1999	2000	2006
A. TOTAL MARKET SIZE	693	728	764
B. LOCAL PRODUCTION	321	337	354
C. EXPORTS (INCL. RE-EXPORTS)	198	208	218
D. TOTAL IMPORTS	567	559	628
E. IMPORTS FROM THE U.S.	223	240	248

BIOTECHNOLOGY (BTC)

Rank of sector: 13
Name of sector: Biotechnology
ITA Industry Code: BTC

Australia is a significant player in the global biotechnology industry and has had a long, consistent tradition of excellent research and development (R&D), particularly in medicine and agriculture. The country's R&D assets are based on a high-quality science education system and expertise across a range of fields. As a result, Australia attracts a large number of major international pharmaceutical and agribusiness companies that undertake research in Australia, or enter into alliance with Australian companies and research providers.

The biotechnology sector is experiencing rapid growth, with industry turnover estimated at US$500 million per year. Since 1999, the number of biotechnology companies in Australia has increased by 70 percent. This is due to a number of key strengths, including the low cost of running R&D facilities compared with other countries and greater domestic investment, partly fuelled by Federal and State incentives. The total number of core biotechnology companies operating in Australia is estimated to be 190, with a further 460 biotechnology-related companies. When normalized to available labor force, Australia has similar numbers of listed biotechnology companies when compared with the U.S. and far more than in the European Union.

Australia is a leader in life science research and the country's technology productivity is very high, with a per capita patent filing rate similar to that of the U.S. The Australian Government has identified biotechnology as one of the key industries of the future and plays a large role in funding biotechnology research, providing US$150 million a year through a variety of sources. In addition, the State Government of Victoria recently announced that it will be establishing Australia's first national synchrotron facility, representing a major investment in Australia's science infrastructure.

Australia is well-placed to seize biotechnology opportunities, because of its internationally recognized reputation in the sciences that underpin biotechnology, access to high growth markets of Southeast Asia, a favorable regulatory climate and positive public attitudes to biotechnology. With over 650 (core and related) biotechnology companies and research centers, Australian companies have sufficient capability of manufacturing in biotechnology to match leading companies of the world.

Australian biotechnology companies have the facilities, experience and personnel to develop a product from the concept stage, through process development, production, clinical trials, and on to international regulatory approval. Australia's scientific excellence is founded upon its expertise in a range of disciplines, including genetics, molecular biology, immunology, and plant and agricultural biotechnology. The sectors with the greatest number of products under development are human health and agriculture. Fifty percent of Australian biotechnology companies are focusing on human health, 14 percent in agriculture, and 13 percent in genomics.

Australia is striving to become the center of biotechnology in the Asia-Pacific region and has a strong intellectual property policy that meets international best practices, along with an extensive available pool of highly-skilled specialist and biotechnology technicians. While the biotechnology industry in Australia continues to grow, it remains small in global terms. The Australian biotechnology industry operates in a science-rich but investment- poor environment. As a result, alliances with larger multinationals continue to be a major route to international markets for Australian biotechnology companies.

Best prospects for U.S. companies include forming strategic partnerships, research collaborations, and licensing arrangements with Australian companies. Australian research institutions tend to license intellectual property overseas as part of the formation of alliances with pharmaceutical firms. In addition, Australian companies are forging commercial alliances with companies in Asia for marketing, distribution and manufacturing, providing market access into the Asian region.

U.S. companies will find clear business cost advantage in conducting research and product development in Australia, as highly-skilled labor costs a fraction of that in the U.S. or Europe. Salaries, the major component of R&D expense, are lower than in U.S. academic and commercial organizations.

Australia is also an attractive location for conducting all stages of clinical trials. According to industry reports, the cost of conducting clinical trials in Australia is approximately one-third less than in the U.S. The practice and standard of medicine is equivalent to the U.S. and the EU. Trial protocols are immediately transferable and results are reliable. The Australian medical R&D community is highly regarded in the fields of respiratory medicine, HIV/AIDS, oncology, and immunology. Furthermore, as Australia is located in the Southern Hemisphere, trials on seasonal-related illnesses, such as allergy/asthma or influenza conditions, can be conducted in alternate seasons, thereby accelerating therapy development times.

CONSTRUCTION MACHINERY (ENGINEERING AND NON-RESIDENTIAL)

(CON)
Rank of Sector: 14
Name of Sector: CONSTRUCTION MACHINERY (ENGINEERING AND NON-RESIDENTIAL)
ITA Industry Code: CON

The market for construction equipment depends upon the state of the construction industry and the outlook is for a decline in both the engineering and non-residential sectors over the next two years.

A recent survey by a major Australian project developer and economic forecaster estimated the value of engineering construction work for year ended June 30, 2004 at US$5.7 billion (down 11 percent from 1999-00), with US$5.8 billion forecast for 2004-02.

According to leading industry forecaster BIS Shrapnel, the extraordinary near-decade long boom in engineering construction (roads, railways, pipelines and infrastructure for electricity, telecommunications, mining, and heavy industry) has come to a temporary halt. The reason for the decline is that the biggest and most attractive projects for private investment have largely been done. Most state and territory infrastructure construction programs launched in the late

1990s have been completed and new government projects have not been brought forward fast enough to replace them. However, construction activity is expected to soar once again in June 2004-June 2005 and exceed US$10.8 billion, before peaking in 2006 at a level well above the previous peak of the late 1990s.

BIS-Shrapnel warns that the current decline should not cause alarm, as in reality the decline represents only a small proportion of the increases experienced during the last eight years. Several sub-sectors will, in fact, remain strong and perhaps even strengthen, among them mining and heavy industry construction. The rail, pipeline, and harbor sectors will perform strongly, as will water storage and supply.

After six years of solid growth, non-residential building starts are estimated to have fallen 15 percent to US$6.6 billion for the year ended June 30, 2004, with a drop of eight percent to US$6.1 billion forecast for 2004-02. The decline is blamed on a weakening economy impacting on non-residential building as well as the conclusion of Olympics-related investment.

Imports dominate the construction machinery market, accounting for about 90 percent of the total market. Leading overseas suppliers are from the U.S., Japan, the United Kingdom and Germany. Major U.S. companies in the market are Caterpillar, John Deere, Case, and Ingersoll-Rand.

No trade restrictions or other non-tariff barriers exist for imported construction equipment; however, a permit issued by the Australian Quarantine and Inspection Service (AQIS) must cover machinery used prior to importation. AQIS has strict regulations that are rigidly enforced on all consignments, including a cleanliness certificate to verify that the machinery has been fully cleaned.

Best sales prospects are considered to be wheel loaders, articulated four-wheel drive front-end loaders, hydraulic excavators, and backhoe loaders. The used equipment market for very heavy machinery, such as excavators, bulldozers, and loaders, also has good growth prospects, particularly for replacement parts.

DATA TABLE (Millions US$)

YEAR	1999	2000	2006
A. TOTAL MARKET SIZE (*)	896.2	755.1	654.5
B. TOTAL LOCAL PRODUCTION (*)	23.1	22.4	19.6
C. TOTAL EXPORTS (*)	59.2	59.2	51.4
D. TOTAL IMPORTS	932.3	791.9	686.3
E. IMPORTS FROM THE U.S.	240.0	287.7	259.7

SIGNIFICANT INVESTMENT OPPORTUNITIES

PRIVATIZATION

Since privatization began in Australia around the mid-1980s, billions of dollars worth of formerly public-owned assets have been transferred to private sector ownership and management. During this period, as a result of privatization, outsourcing and a change in technological adaptation, federal public sector employment declined by almost 50%, while the state sector declined by about one-third and local government by less than a quarter. Overall activity has slowed considerably, although there are still some large sales scheduled to take place.

Asset Sales Currently in Process:

- Australian Submarine Corporation: business and legal advisers have been appointed to provide commercial and legal advice in this process. The Australian Federal Government intends to divest all of its interest in ASC once suitable arrangements have been put in place. No decision has been made about the ultimate ownership structure for ASC or the timing of any prospective sale.

- National Rail Corporation: The shareholders, comprising the Australian Federal Government, the New South Wales and Victorian governments, have now agreed upon sale management arrangements for a joint sale of their interests in the corporation.

- Essendon Airport Limited: expected to be completed mid-2004. Essendon Airport will continue to operate as a General Aviation Airport, with the existing administrative operational guidelines being formalized in regulations to ensure noise considerations are adequately addressed.

- Sydney (Kingsford Smith) Airport: the sale process has begun and there are three bidding consortia. The Sydney Airports Corporation Limited will be privatized as two separate companies; one will operate Sydney (Kingsford Smith) Airport and the other will operate Sydney's smaller Bankstown, Camden and Hoxton Park Airports. Sydney (Kingsford Smith) Airport will be sold by way of a 100% trade sale, to be completed in the second half of 2004; the other airports will be sold by way of a 100% trade sale in the second half of 2002. The new owner of Sydney (Kingsford Smith) Airport will be given first right of refusal by the Commonwealth to build and operate any second major airport within 60 miles of downtown Sydney. Sydney's requirements for a second airport will be reviewed in 2005.

Sales managed by Australia's Office of Asset Sales include:

Apr 1988 Commonwealth Accommodation and Catering Services
Nov 1988 Defense Service House Corporation Loan Portfolio
May 1991 Australian Defense Force Home Loan Franchise
Jun 1991 Commonwealth Housing Loan Assistance Program
Jun 1992 Australian Airlines
Dec 1992 Qantas (25%)
Nov 1993 Commonwealth Bank Secondary Public Share Offer
Nov 1993 Snowy Mountains Engineering Corporation
Jun 1994 Commonwealth Serum Laboratories
Jun 1994 Moomba-Sydney Pipeline System
Jun 1994 Commonwealth Uranium Stockpile
Jun 1995 Aerospace Technologies of Australia
Jul 1995 Qantas Public Share Offer
Jul 1996 Commonwealth Bank Secondary Public Share Offer
Jan 1997 Avalon Airport Limited
May 1997 Melbourne Airport
May 1997 Brisbane Airport
May 1997 Perth Airport
Jul 1997 Commonwealth Vehicle Fleet Management
Aug 1997 Australian National Railways Corporation
Sep 1997 Australian Industry Development Corporation
Oct/Nov 97 Department of Administrative Services Business Units
Nov 1997 Telstra Corporation Public Share Offer

Feb 1998 Former Macleod Repatriation Hospital Site
Apr 1998 Australian Multimedia Enterprise
Apr 1998 Phase 2 Airports
Jun 1998 Auscript
Mar 1999 National Transmission Network
Nov 1999 ADI Limited
Nov 1999 Telstra Corporation Second Public Share Offer
Jan 2000 Removals Australia

In 1997, the Australian Federal Government decided that IT infrastructure services across all budget-funded agencies were to be outsourced, subject to the outcome of competitive processes to be undertaken within a government framework. This initiative is known as the "Whole of Government IT Infrastructure Initiative", and is led and managed by the IT Outsourcing Team within the Office of Asset Sales and IT Outsourcing. The scale of the Initiative is very large and involves the transfer to the private sector of around US$2.2 billion worth of work, across some 100 Australian Federal Government agencies.

MAJOR INFRASTRUCTURE DEVELOPMENT PROJECTS BY SECTOR

AIR TRANSPORT

Air transport is used extensively within Australia, which, including its territories, has around 280 licensed airports. The major international gateways, of which there are nine, include Sydney, Melbourne, Brisbane, Perth and Cairns. The majority of all airports are owned and operated by local and state governments, private companies and the Department of Defense. International passenger and cargo flights are frequent and reliable.

Air is used extensively for lighter cargo, small high-value items, and for urgent needs. Domestic airlines carry about 200,000 tons of cargo per annum. An extensive network of air cargo operators, including major international companies, offers a full range of cargo services, processing of documentation relating to the importation and clearance of goods, and follow-on-delivery to regional centers. Australia is serviced by most of the world's major air carriers, feeding into a well-established domestic network covering the trunk commuter routes. An active regional airline service links regional centers with capital cities. Almost all Australia's airports have been privatized and now operate on a commercial, profit-oriented basis, competing for passenger and freight revenue. Australia's major airport, Sydney's Kingsford Smith, is in the process of being sold by the Federal Government which, should be completed by the end of 2004. The aviation industry is unregulated, and is dominated by long-time carriers Qantas and Ansett. Virgin Blue is operating on a limited service basis and is exerting a moderating influence on fares for air transport users.

Australia is a member of the International Civil Aviation Organization and is represented on the Air Navigation Commission. It has full treaty air service agreements with forty countries. Within Australia, Airservices Australia manages air traffic control over Australia's eleven percent of the earth's surface, and the Civil Aviation Safety Authority is responsible for ensuring aviation safety.

RAIL TRANSPORT

The Federal Government's aim is to create a more competitive rail industry through private sector involvement in areas ranging from operations and infrastructure to maintenance and engineering. The reforms -- including corporatization, increasing competition, contracting out of maintenance services, new private-sponsored rail projects, and full privatization -- have created intense interest from both local and overseas freight/transport operators and investors.

In 1997, the Federal Government sold Australian National Railways (AN), which operated the short haul freight railways in Tasmania and South Australia and was responsible for interstate passenger services, the Indian Pacific, the Ghan, and the Overland. AN was split into three divisions and sold to foreign consortia for US$96 million. Two of the three divisions went to U.S.-based consortia.

In January 1999, the Victorian Government sold its freight business, V/Line Freight, to a consortium comprising U.S. and local interests. The Victorian Government has also franchised its passenger train and tram operations. In October 2000, the Western Australian Government sold its freight business for US$330 million, the highest price paid so far for a public rail asset.

Strong interest from local and overseas consortia is also expected for the proposed sale of the National Rail Corporation (NR), a $300 million interstate freight rail operator, owned by the Federal, New South Wales and Victorian Governments. NR operates 300 trains, has over 250 customers, and handles about 20 percent of all land-based, inter-capital freight.

Major projects include:

Rail line linking Melbourne to Darwin via NSW and Queensland US$5 billion
Rail line linking Darwin to Alice Springs US$1.2 billion
Rail lines connecting the Central Coast with Sydney US$920 million
Rail lines connecting Parramatta to Chatswood US$882 million

SEA TRANSPORT

The growth in cruise shipping has stimulated the development of port infrastructure in Australia to meet the needs of cruise operators, now forming an integral part of overall port infrastructure development. The Australian Government introduced a ship building innovation program on July 1, 1999, to develop a sustainable shipbuilding industry. Under the program, shipbuilders are entitled to the payment of a benefit rate of fifty percent of eligible research and development expenditures, up to two percent of the eligible production costs of bountiable vessels. This shipbuilding bounty is due to continue until at least 2003, providing the local shipbuilding industry with transitional support while international measures are being developed to phase out these industry subsidies.

TELECOMMUNICATIONS

The second stage in the privatization of Telstra (Australia's former carrier monopoly) was completed in 1999, with private ownership now amounting to 49%. The Australian Government remains the majority owner, with 51%. While the current Federal Coalition Government would like to fully privatize the carrier, this is unlikely to happen, as there is considerable opposition from both the Australian Democrats and the Australian Labor Party.

The constant growth in telecommunications segments has provided a whole new scenario in terms of investment in the telecommunications sector. This has included investment in large projects like the "Southern Cross Underwater Cable Project" and the development of networks by some of the newer carriers, but also the very strong segment growth in Internet access and the mobile phone/communications boom.

Telstra still remains the dominant investment provider and with 99% of Australia's 10 million-plus telephone lines, it is no surprise. The technology drivers remain mass Internet access, broadband rollout, and mobile communications, along with the phenomenal growth in data traffic. While it is not usual for Australia's major telecommunications carriers to go to open tender for the supply of products, they sometimes prefer to invite selected suppliers to tender for major works. Telstra has 'preferred suppliers' from which it sources network equipment for its upgrading and development program. Optus Communications has Strategic Supplier Partnerships with companies, including Digital Equipment Corp., Nortel Australia, Nokia Telecommunications, Fujitsu Australia, and Leighton Contractors, for the supply of network infrastructure.

The increase in the number of carriers in Australia to more than 70 has meant that there is significant activity. Newer carriers are developing their own networks, such as Hutchison Telecommunications' wireless "Orange One" network and their proposed 3G network. This new network will comprise infrastructure provided by Ericsson, Motorola and Cisco, and will cost more than US$400 million. Other carriers, such as Davnet, are combining a range of technologies (microwave, laser) to provide specific services (wiring-up office buildings, in the case of Davnet). New services are constantly being launched: Cable and Wireless Optus has just announced a two-way broadband satellite service for the business market, using technology from Israeli company Gilat.

Telstra has also been forced to unbundle its local loop, which should provide further opportunities for the newer carriers. However, given the slow progress of xDSL technologies being offered to the public, access may be slow.

WATER AND SEWERAGE

The sewage systems in most of Australia's major cities are old and, in many cases, overloaded. Upgrades will have to address sewer capacity and condition equally with treatment. About 70 percent of expenditures relate to water collection/distribution and sewage collection/disposal. The remaining 30 percent is concerned with product quality or treatment, with about 10 percent of this related specifically to process equipment. While the public sector accounts for most of the demand, private enterprises are becoming increasingly environmentally aware. Their environmental practices are under the microscope, and many are using "green" issues to position products.

Australian state governments are increasingly turning to restructuring and reforming public utilities. This is resulting in the corporatization of government-owned enterprises, as well as contractual arrangements with private enterprises. Impetus for these changes comes from the Hilmer Report (into competition) and COAG (the Council of Australian Governments).

Significant expenditure by water authorities will continue in the traditional purchase areas of pipelines, storage, clean-up projects, pump stations and treatment plants. For example, Sydney Water, a state government water agency, is in the process of delivering a multi-billion dollar program of capital works. The agency has developed Waterplan 21, a long-term strategic plan for sustainable water and wastewater management. Information on some of the projects developed under the plan can be viewed on the agency's website at www.sydneywater.com.au.

CONSTRUCTION

The predicted decline in Australia's engineering construction industry over the next two years is expected to be moderated by strong performances in several sectors, including mining, water storage and supply, heavy industry, and pipelines.

Some other major development and road construction projects already started or committed include:

Project	Value	Estimated Completion Date
Melbourne Docklands, Victoria	US$2.4 billion	2010
Urban Redevelopment of South Sydney	US$1 billion	2005
Linking Victoria Transport Program	US$795 million	2003
Pacific Highway Upgrade, New South Wales	US$636 million	2006
Rebuilding New South Wales Country Roads	US$530 million	2010
Rapid Bus Transitways, Sydney	US$424 million	2010
Darling Harbour Wharves 9-10, Sydney	US$397.5 million	2005
Honeysuckle Redevelopment Project, Newcastle, New South Wales	US$371 million	2014
Newcastle High Speed Rail	US$344.5 million	2003
South West Metropolitan Rail, Perth	US$265 million	2003
VicRoads, Victoria	US$243.2 million	2003

ENERGY

Australia needs to develop US$15 billion worth of electricity supply infrastructure this decade. This means that this Government has a window of 12-18 months to evaluate and pursue changes in the energy sector to avoid the "shadow" of the California crisis in the power sector. A complete overhaul of the market and accelerated national reform will have to be implemented.

The Australian market will now offer major growth opportunities for the international power industry to produce further gains in productivity and efficiency. There will be a major shift towards deregulation of the whole of the Australian electricity and gas sectors and more private ownership of major infrastructure for the industry. Australia is an extremely attractive destination for foreign investment -- the country is politically stable and has vast reserves of a variety of fuels for the generation of electricity. Yet, regulatory risks do exist on both federal and state levels.

Significant investment and infrastructure opportunities exist for U.S. firms to participate in the following proposed projects in Australia. In addition, American companies will be able to provide services and technologies for many proposed renewable energy projects. The Commonwealth Government is awarding grants to build new wind farms, solar farms, and co-generation projects throughout Australia.

STATE	US$ value
NEW SOUTH WALES	
Privatization of the NSW electricity generators, distributors and the transmission assets still a possibility.	$17 billion

NORTHERN TERRITORY	
Shell/Woodside in the development phase for a LNG plant using gas from the Greater Sunrise and Evans Shoal gas fields in the Timor Sea, off the coast of Darwin. Sea-bed sampling has commenced.	$ 5 billion
Phillips Petroleum and Epic Energy have entered into an alliance to conduct the market development for the commercialization of the Bayu-Undan oil field. This includes building an onshore pipeline from Darwin and firming up potential gas customers and markets. Several billion dollar major contracts have already been awarded for supply and installation of the production facility.	$ 1 billion
Woodside Energy is in the development phase of the Laminaria/Corallina oil fields in the Timor Sea.	$750 million
QUEENSLAND	
3,200 km gas pipeline from oil and gas fields in Kutubu, Papua Guinea, to Townsville, with an extension to Gladstone.	$3.5 billion
Transmission link between Queensland and New South Wales now named QNI).	$284 million
Following are proposed power plants for Queensland to meet future power demand, with the parties involved and projected values. However, many are dependent on the PNG gas pipeline being completed.	
▪ 840 MW advanced-cycle boilers at Callide power plant near Gladstone. Plant is under construction and due to be completed December 2004. CS Energy/Shell Coal.	$650 million
▪ 120 MW combined-cycle natural gas turbine plant at Gladstone, open to tender for construction. NRG/Comalco.	$130 million
▪ Mine-mouth, coal-fired boilers for Milmerran generator. Construction has commenced and equipment will be required. Itergen/Normandy/Mitsui.	$850 million
▪ Open-cycle gas turbine - natural gas, Energy Resource Management, Wambo.	$150 million
▪ Coal-fired generator for Kogan Creek - license has been granted; however, the project is on hold due to the construction of the other coal-fired plant at Milmerran and environmental issues. Southern Energy.	$850 million
SOUTH AUSTRALIA	
Texas Utilities has commenced a feasibility study to transport gas from Victoria to South Australia. Tenders for an operator are under consideration.	N/A
Exploration for more gas in the Cooper/Eromonga Basin by Santos Ltd.	$ 75 million
TASMANIA	

Tender was awarded to National Grid (U.K.) to build and operate Basslink - an undersea cable, which will connect Tasmania to Victoria's electricity system by the year 2002. The project has been granted Major Project Facilitation Status by the Government.	$300 million
VICTORIA	
Loy Yang -A 200 MW coal-fired electricity generator, owned by U.S. firm CMS Energy, is to be resold.	$3.4 billion
Duke Energy plans to transport gas from the Bass Strait gas fields in Victoria to Bell Bay in Tasmania via a 333 km sub-sea pipeline and convert the existing power plant at Bell Bay to gas.	$300 million
Two new gas-fired power plants to be built in Victoria. AGL plans to build a 150 MW gas-fired power plant near to Melbourne.	$300 million
Edison Mission Energy (operator of the Loy Yang-B power plant in the Latrobe Valley) will build a 300 MW gas-fired station near their existing plant.	N/A
WESTERN AUSTRALIA	
Chevron and partners (Mobil, Texaco and Shell) to develop the Gorgon/Chyrsaor gas fields for LNG exports.	$ 6 billion
1 new LNG production/processing train for the North West Shelf project will be built to expand the LNG export market into Asia and the U.S.	$1.5 billion

U.S. FOREIGN DIRECT INVESTMENT

The Government of the United States acknowledges the contribution that outward foreign direct investment makes to the U.S. economy. United States foreign direct investment is viewed as a complement and necessary component of trade. For example, roughly 60 percent of U.S. exports are sold by American firms that have operations abroad. Recognizing the benefits that U.S. outward investment brings to the U.S. economy, the Government of the United States undertakes initiatives, such as Overseas Private Investment Corporation (OPIC) programs, investment treaty negotiations, and business facilitation programs that support U.S. investors.

TRADE REGULATIONS & STANDARDS

TRADE BARRIERS

1. TARIFFS

Australia's long-standing policy of using tariffs to protect its local industry began changing in the early 1970s and was accelerated in 1988 by the Federal Government's program of economic reform directed toward moving the country toward a globally competitive economy.

Initially general in scope, the program now is focused on microeconomic changes to help business become more competitive. The strategy has three principal premises: tariffs and other forms of protection must be reduced; industry must drop its preoccupation with protection and turn its attention to becoming more competitive; and, improvements must come from both labor and management.

On a trade-weighted basis, Australian duties on manufactured goods currently average 3 percent, with 94 percent of its industrial tariff lines GATT-bound. All tariffs were reduced to 5 percent or below in 1996, except for textiles, clothing, and footwear (TCF), and certain automotive products. By 2000, apparel and certain finished textile tariffs will be reduced to 25 percent; footwear, sheeting and certain other fabrics to 15 percent. Nonetheless, tariff rates do affect competitive pricing of imported goods.

The tariff rate on passenger motor vehicles and their original equipment components, currently 20 percent, will be reduced in stages to 15 percent by 2000. Tariffs on light commercial and four-wheel drive vehicles and components were reduced to 5 percent in 1996. Replacement components for passenger vehicles will remain at 15 percent from 1996 until 2000, with special provisions for automobile manufacturers.

Automotive tariffs will be frozen from 2000 to 2004, when they will undergo further review. Under the terms of the government's export facilitation scheme, automobile manufacturers may also offset tariffs payable on the importation of specified automotive products by exporting Australian-made automotive products.

In May 1996, the Australian Government reduced the value of tariff relief available to importers of goods through changes to the Tariff Concession Scheme (TCS). The TCS applies to goods imported into Australia for which there is no no substitutable good produced domestically. The TCS waives any duties payable on imported business inputs and consumer goods, but requires that minimum 3 percent concessional duty be paid.

2. NON-TARIFF BARRIERS

Although Australia became a signatory to the GATT Standards Code on March 1, 1992 (and has now acceded to the World Trade Organization (WTO) Agreement on Technical Barriers to Trade), it maintains some restrictive standards requirements and design rules that have an impact on the free flow of goods. However, Australian standards are being rewritten in a number of areas to bring them into conformity with Australia's new international obligations under various trade agreements.

3. IMPORT TAXES AND SALES TAXES

There are no import taxes in Australia. The Australian government does, however, impose a tax on the sale of both domestically-manufactured and imported goods. Generally speaking, for domestic consumption, the tax is imposed on the last wholesale sale. The wholesaler or manufacturer, upon whom the tax is imposed, can, in turn, pass the tax on to the retailer who, in turn, passes it to the consumer.

There is no additional sales tax imposed at the retail level. Manufacturers and wholesale merchants are required to register for sales tax. Importers of goods who are not manufacturers or wholesalers are not required to register but are liable for sales tax on the entry of goods into Australia. The general rate of this tax is 22 percent of the sale value (broadly equal to the fair wholesale value) of the goods.

There are a large number of exempt goods set out in a schedule to the Sales Tax (Exemptions and Classifications) Act. There are also categories of goods subject to tax at 12 percent (household goods) and 32 percent (luxury goods). Exporters should clarify with their agent, distributor, or representative the tax level to be imposed on their goods and take this into consideration in calculating product pricing. Australia's anti-dumping legislation defines dumping as occurring when the FOB price at which goods are exported to Australia (the "export price") falls below the price at which the same goods are sold domestically in the country of export. When dumping is found to occur, dumping duties are imposed on the importer.

Further information on tariffs and anti-dumping regulation can be obtained from the Australian Customs Service, the Embassy of Australia, or the Anti-Dumping Authority (see Appendix E.4).

B. CUSTOMS VALUATION

The Australian customs valuation system is based on self-assessment, i.e., the importer is responsible for valuing imports correctly. While Australian legislation conforms generally with the terms of the GATT Code on customs valuation, there are important differences. Imported goods are valued under one of nine different methods of valuation in a sequence established in the legislation. The first and most common is the transaction value method. There are alternative methods, e.g., where goods are exported to Australia on consignment.

The United States believes that the Australian Customs Act of 1901, as amended July 1, 1989, is inconsistent with the GATT Agreement on customs valuation because its treatment of royalties and buying commissions, could lead to certain impermissible additions being made to the dutiable value of merchandise.

The amendment also increases the amount of inland freight that can be included in the dutiable value of the goods. While not inconsistent with the GATT Agreement on customs valuation, the amended Australian law may impair or nullify tariff concessions on products that are exported on an ex-factory basis. Customs and quota information is available from the Australian Customs Service (Appendix E.4)

C. IMPORT LICENSES

Australia has phased out its import licensing requirements. The only commodities subject to import quotas are certain types of cheese and curd. These quotas were established in the mid-1980s in response to dumping by European producers and have a sunset clause of 2000.

D. EXPORT CONTROLS

Australia exports over one million individual consignments each year, 40 percent of which are subject to some kind of restriction. Controls are applied through permits issued by the Department of Defence and licenses issued by various Government agencies. Australia's controls on exports are documented in the publications "Australian Controls of the Export of Technology with Civil and Military Applications" and "Australian Control of Defence and Related Goods - a Guide for Exporters", available through the Acquisition and Logistics Branch of the Department of Defence (see Appendix E.4. for contact information).

Export Clearance Numbers are issued by the Customs Service based on export data lodged by shippers. Consignments are checked by computer against required permits and licenses (97 percent of export consignments are entered electronically). Cargo may not leave Australian points of departure unless allocated an Export Clearance Number.

Australia was a member of COCOM until its conclusion and is a signatory to the Missile Technology Control Regime. Permits are issued for the export of military and dual-use goods and technology as formerly defined by COCOM, and in keeping with Australia's international agreements. Revised guidelines were issued in March, 1994.

IMPORT/EXPORT DOCUMENTATION

1. IMPORTS

Importers are responsible for obtaining Customs clearance for consignments of goods above set value limits. The minimum documentation required includes an air-way bill or bill of lading, invoices and any other papers relating to the shipment.

2. EXPORTS

Goods may not be exported until all necessary export permits, including an Export Clearance number, are obtained from the relevant permit issuing agency (See Section D. above).

F. TEMPORARY ENTRY

Goods may be imported into Australia duty free for a temporary period if they are for display purposes in a trade show certified by the Australian Customs Service. The ATA Carnet is a special international customs document accepted in 46 countries used for temporary imports/exports, particularly professional equipment and commercial samples. The Carnet, issued in lieu of the usual customs documents, eliminates value-added taxes, duties and temporary import bonds.

G. LABELING, MARKING REQUIREMENTS

U.S. suppliers need to be aware of Australian legislation regulating the packaging, labelling, ingredients, marketing, and sale of specific products, and of general weights and measures. Legal import and sale of products packaged and labelled overseas may not be possible without modification. U.S. exporters should ask their Australian importer to ensure that products comply with Australian Federal and State Government labeling regulations.

H. PROHIBITED IMPORTS

Australia has stringent prohibitions and/or quarantines imposed against a number of products, particularly those considered to be of potential public danger and agricultural products that are considered to have the potential to introduce contamination or disease. Restricted items include drugs, steroids, weapons/ firearms, heritage items and cordless telephones and CB radios (unless they have been approved by the Department of Communications and the Arts), food, plants and animals and protected wildlife. It is important to note that while some items may be imported, their use may be prohibited under individual State laws. (Contact information for Australian Customs is found in the Supplement). 1.

PHYTOSANITARY RESTRICTIONS AFFECTING IMPORTS OF FRESH FRUIT AND VEGETABLES

Australia has stringent phytosanitary restrictions affecting imports of fresh fruit and vegetables and other requirements affecting imports of meat and poultry products. The subject of a WTO complaint, phytosanitary barriers to the importation of fresh and frozen salmon are under review. A ban on importation of cooked chicken is still under review.

Appendix C., Part II contains information on a partial listing of fruits and vegetables and their import status relative to Australian phytosanitary import regulations. This list is constantly changing and U.S. exporters should check with Australian Quarantine officials to make sure that their product is, or is not, allowed entry to Australia.

All produce should have an Australian import permit and a U.S. phytosanitary certificate. The import permit can be requested from the Australian Department of Primary Industries and Energy in Canberra, or from appropriate State Departments of Agriculture located in the State capitals. The permit may specify additional import requirements to those noted below. (See Appendix E. 4. and 10 for contact information.)

When applying for import permits, as much detail as possible should be provided as to where the product is grown and how it is processed, so that the appropriate advice on treatments, etc. can be given without having to request additional information from the U.S. exporter. Products falling under the Fruit Fly Rule must be accompanied by a phytosanitary certificate endorsed to indicate that no species of fruit fly which attacks this product has been trapped within 80 km (50 miles) of the area of production within the last 12 months.

All meat and poultry products must be accompanied by an Australian Import Permit and appropriate USDA Animal Health Certificates and must originate from a plant approved for export to Australia. Appendix C., Part II contains further information on requirements.

Livestock imports, with the exception of horses, are limited under quarantine regulations. Breeder, feeder and slaughter steers may be imported on quarantine grounds, but all must undergo the same tests as breeders. With the exception of anticipated changes in the case of cooked chicken, U.S. poultry cannot be imported due to phytosanitary restrictions. Restrictive plant health regulations prohibit or limit the entry of many fruits.

STANDARDS (E.G. ISO 9000 USAGE)

Australia is a signatory to the GATT Standards Code. Use of quality standards such as the IS0 9000 series is increasing. Standards Australia, the national standards body, has a Quality Assessment section attached to it and can provide a list of those companies adhering to the IS0 9000 series

Australia still has in place some standards that can restrict product entry. In particular, the Australian standards for telecommunications Customer Premises Equipment (CPE), such as telephones, usually require a product's modification prior to market entry. Safety related automotive parts and accessories on a vehicle or for environmental (EPA) compliance, must adhere to Australian Design Rules and Australian automotive standards. Certain medical equipment also must be approved prior to use; and, after December 1997, the supply of OE (Original Equipment) automotive parts must adhere to Quality System QS9000, the system adopted in the U.S. by Ford, General Motors and Chrysler.

Australian electrical voltage is 220-240 Volts, 50 cycle, meaning electrical equipment and machines running on electrical cycles must be modified or made for use at this higher (than the U.S. and Europe) voltage level. Alternatively, for electrical equipment, transformers can be purchased; but this is not common.

Imported consumer products, mainly foodstuffs, should comply with state packaging regulations. States agree that any product, including imports, meeting the legal requirements of one state, may be sold in all other states and territories. State agricultural quarantines prohibit interstate trade of some items.

Standards Australia and the American National Standards Institute (ANSI) in New York have full information on Australian Standards.

FREE TRADE ZONES/WAREHOUSES

The Darwin Trade Development Zone (TDZ) in Australia is located in Darwin, Northern Territory. The Darwin TDZ is concentrating on developing Australia's trading relationships with its Asian neighbors to the north and west. Since 1986, the TDZ has fostered close working relationships with other Industrial Estates and Export Processing Zones within Asia, particularly the Eastern States of Indonesia. Industries established include manufacturers of: knitted textiles; cardboard and packaging; color repro-graphics; computer software development; brewery supplying beer to Asia; fish emulsion and plant food; plastics extrusion injection blow molding; and engineering-based manufactures. The Zone also has access to the services of international financial consultants and customs agents, and other industries are scheduled to be established.

On December 8, 1997, the Commonwealth Government adopted "Manufacturing-in-Bond (MIB)designating the BHP Steel River Facility in Newcastle as the first Australian site selected. The big difference - and advantage - over the existing Darwin FTZ structure, is that export manufacturers no longer are required to pay up front customs, excise and sales tax outlays on imported componentry and materials. Goods only become subject to duties and taxes if removed for sale or use in Australia. While the Newcastle site is the first MIB established in Australia, it never was the intention to limit the benfits of MIB to one location. It is anticipated that over the next two years MIB operations will be licensed in several states. (See Appendix E.4.B for contact information).

SPECIAL IMPORT PROVISIONS

There are no special import provisions in Australia.

MEMBERSHIP IN FREE TRADE ARRANGEMENTS

Australia is a key member of the evolving Asia Pacific Economic Cooperation (APEC) forum.

The Australia New Zealand Closer Economic Relations Trade Agreement (ANZCERTA - usually abbreviated as CER) entered into force in January, 1983. Bilateral trade in all products originating in the two countries is free of tariffs, quantitative restrictions, anti-dumping measures, and production subsidies and like measures. A 1988 protocol on trade in services provides for market liberalization, national and MFN treatment and free choice of commercial presence. The merger between Air New Zealand and Ansett and recent positive negotiations between the Australian and New Zealand governments looks set to create a unified aviation market in the near future.

TRADE AND PROJECT FINANCING

BANKING SYSTEM

Up until recently, the Reserve Bank of Australia (RBA) carried out the prudential regulation of Australia's banks, not unlike the Federal Reserve does in the U.S. Changes brought about by the Wallis Inquiry into the Australian financial system see the RBA's key roles as monetary policy, systemic stability and payments system regulation. While the banking system in Australia is reliable and transparent, there are structural and operational differences between it and the American system. Historically, Australian banks have not operated under the restrictions that have limited U.S. bank operations since 1933. In Australia, the distinction between retail banks and investment banks is blurred.

The Australian banking system is undergoing progressive deregulation and privatization. Beginning with deregulation of the financial markets in the 1980s, foreign banks have been allowed to enter the market. Retail banks, in general, now provide a wider range of financial services, including life and general insurance, stock brokering and security underwriting to their retail customers, in addition to making corporate and consumer loans. This places them in competition with brokerage houses and merchant banks.

In early 1992, the government further liberalized the banking system by abolishing limitations on the number of foreign bank licenses. This permits non-Australian banks to operate as branches to serve the wholesale market. However, retail banking activities may be conducted only through a locally-incorporated subsidiary.

Governments, both state and federal, have, as part of an economy-wide trend of deregulation and privatization, divested themselves of their banking interests over the past few years. There are now no government-owned banks in Australia. The State Bank of New South Wales was sold in December, 1994. The South Australian Government accepted an offer for the State Bank of South Australia in 1995 from the Advance Bank, and the Western Australian Government floated BankWest in January, 1996. The Federal Government completed its privatization of the Commonwealth Bank in 1996.

Australia has 46 authorized banking groups, 32 of which are foreign-owned. Of the latter, 16 are incorporated locally and 16 are branch operations. There are 7 American licensed banks: Bank of America (both as a locally-incorporated subsidiary and a branch operation); Bankers Trust; The Chase Manhattan Bank; Citibank; First National Bank of Chicago; Morgan Guaranty Trust Company of New York; and State Street Bank and Trust Company Another 20 U.S. banks have local representative offices. The major Australian commercial banks are Westpac Banking Corporation, ANZ Bank, National Australia Bank, and the Commonwealth Bank of Australia. (See Appendix E.6.) There is momentum in the banking sector to use Australia as a regional financial services center.

The recently tabeled Wallis inquiry, the first analysis of the Australian financial system since the Cambell Committee in 1981 has seen the government endorce a number of Wallis recommendations, the most notable being;

- changes to the prudential regulation regime. The main feature being the establishment of the Australian Prudential Regulation Authority (APRA) which has the role of regulating the banks, life offices, general insurers, superannuation, building societies, credit unions and friendly societies. It is expected that APRA will be operational by July 1, 1998.

- creating the Payments System Board within the Reserve Bank to supervise the opening of the payments system to non-banks, including companies outside the finance sector.
- removing prohibitions on life offices taking over banks, while stipulating that the "four pillars" (National Australia Bank, ANZ, Commonwealth Bank and Westpac) could not merge. The Treasurer, however, has openly stated that the government would not be adverse to one foreign takeover of one of the abovementioned banks.
- the Australian Competition & Consumer Commission to carry out prices surveillance, monitor for restrictive trade practices and provide non financial consumer protection.

FOREIGN EXCHANGE CONTROLS AFFECTING TRADING

Australia does not restrict the flow of currency into or out of the country. There are, however, cash reporting obligations under the Cash Transaction Reports Act (CTRA). International currency transfers of A$5,000 or more, or A$50,000 in any form in one year, must be reported to the Cash Transaction Reports Agency. The purpose is to control tax evasion and money laundering and does not inhibit currency transfers associated with international trade.

The Australian dollar has been allowed to float since 1983. The currency is freely convertible, and exchange rates are determined by international demand and supply. Official policy is not to defend any particular exchange rate level. Intervention by the Reserve Bank is minimal and is exercised to accommodate government economic policy adjustments. Transactions in foreign exchange are made through authorized foreign exchange dealers, including trading banks and most merchant banks. There are no specific restrictions regarding the remittance of profits, dividends, or capital.

GENERAL FINANCING AVAILABILITY

The major finance companies, which control about three-quarters of the total assets of the industry, are owned wholly or predominantly by the major trading banks. Commercial banks are the major source of medium-term loans. A wide range of merchant banks operate in Australia, many of which are associated with some of the world's largest financial institutions. They also provide short-to-medium term funding. Venture capital finance usually is available from management and investment companies, which are funded by tax-deductible capital subscriptions. Other alternatives include obtaining funds from finance companies (including leasing arrangements), building societies, credit co-operatives or unions, insurance companies, pension and superannuation funds and cash management trusts.

The larger finance companies obtain their funds mainly by public issues of debentures and unsecured notes with terms of up to five years. Long-term financing, generally, is supplied by syndicated Australian and overseas bank lending. A specialized market exists for direct borrowing and lending on an unsecured basis between large, well-established companies. Factoring of book debts also can be arranged with finance companies but is not widespread.

Unlike their U.S. counterparts, Australian banks are free to participate in virtually all forms of financial services, including overdrafts (a traditional form of borrowing), fixed-term loans, commercial bills of exchange, letters of credit, domestic and international debt and equity issues, underwriting, leasing and Euro currency borrowing. Increasingly, financial services to business also are provided through a wide range of non-bank institutions.

HOW TO FINANCE EXPORTS AND METHODS OF PAYMENT

As in other industrialized countries with mature financial systems, Australia has a range of export finance methods available. The method chosen should depend upon the individual circumstances of a transaction.

1. **Cash in Advance:** The exporter demands cash in advance before exporting. This is the least popular method used. It is acceptable if the client does not have access to other forms of financing
2. **Letter of Credit:** Payment is guaranteed by the issuing bank. A confirmed letter of credit guarantees payment by a foreign bank as well. This is a very secure form of payment and is used frequently for unknown clients, or those perceived to be risky accounts.
3. **Commercial Bills of Exchange** (sight and time drafts; cash against documents): These bills of exchange are processed through the exporter's and importer's banks. The banks do not guarantee payment, but they will not release shipping documents until the terms of the bill of exchange are met. This is the most widely used form of trade finance, but the risk is higher, as the importer may refuse to pay. The exporter should obtain credit references, or have had a long standing relationship with the importer, before offering this form of financing. Importers prefer this method because it does not affect their cash flow or tie up their commercial credit lines.
4. **Open Account:** The exporter ships the goods and sends a bill for payment. These accounts are used widely, particularly with shipments to U.S. subsidiary operations in Australia. Because this is the least secure form of financing, it is also used for the very best and long-established accounts.

Eighty percent of Australian imports from the U.S. carry payment terms of 30 to 180 days from the date of the shipping documents. Importers normally will request terms, the cost of which should be built into the export price. Importers prefer extended terms to allow them to receive, inventory and sell the goods before paying. They may also wish to use exporters' credit.

TYPES OF AVAILABLE EXPORT FINANCING AND INSURANCE

Several U.S. government agencies, as well as state and local bodies, offer programs to assist exporters with their financing needs. Some are guarantee programs that require the participation of an approved lender; others provide loans or grants to the exporter, or to a foreign government. Many financing and guarantee programs apply only to high-risk or developing countries. Therefore, business dealings with Australia do not qualify for coverage. However, some programs do extend to Australia. Exporters should seek counseling on availability.

The Export-Import Bank of the United States (Eximbank) is the federal government's trade finance agency, offering numerous programs to finance and facilitate U.S. exports by making loans and providing guarantees and insurance for loans from commercial sources. Although Australia does participate in Eximbank programs for some major projects, such as commercial aircraft sales, there is relatively little EXIM activity in Australia.

Other organizations fill various market niches. The Private Export Funding Corporation (PEFCO) is owned by a group of large banks, and makes EXIM-guaranteed loans to foreign purchasers of U.S. goods. The Department of Agriculture offers a variety of programs to foster agricultural exports. The Small Business Administration addresses the needs of small exporters.

Because Australia is an industrialized country, and a donor nation to the multilateral development banks (MDBs), lending institutions such as the World Bank and the Asian Development Bank do not operate here. Like other prosperous countries, Australia has a large pool of private funding available for debt financing of projects. World Bank and Asian Development Bank support for development projects in the developing countries of Asia provides opportunities for American/Australian consortia to compete for MBD-funded contracts in these countries. Australian companies often have established relationships in the region and are in a strong position when teamed with U.S. companies to offer very competitive bids and performance qualifications. (See Appendix E.7 for MBD contact information.)

PROJECT FINANCING AVAILABLE

A number of national and international financial management companies practice in Australia. They provide the complex financial structuring services required to fund projects, using the most competitive financial package available for a particular project. Long-term debt can be financed from a variety of sources and methods. These include:

-- Banks
-- Financial institutions
-- Retail investors
-- Government loans
-- Export credit agencies
-- Credit enhancement agencies -- Bonds
-- Formation of national and international banking consortia
-- BOOT (build, own, operate and transfer)
-- Direct investment by local and international companies
-- Formation of loan syndications
-- Formation of joint ventures

Project financing includes both finance made available by non-participants (i.e., loan funds by financial institutions), and finance provided by participants (i.e., shares in a stock company), as well as a host of hybrid arrangements. U.S. companies participate actively in all types of project financing in Australia.

Traditionally, banks have provided project finance term debt and currently are the only source of project credit. While other sources might fund project loans, funding is undertaken only on the basis of bank credit enhancement through a bank guarantee or letter of credit. However, the development of new and innovative funding mechanisms is a key element in financing projects and infrastructure development as public projects at the federal, state and local levels are made available for privatization.

BANKS WITH CORRESPONDENT U.S. BANKING ARRANGEMENTS

All major banks in Australia have correspondent relationships with U.S. banks

BUSINESS TRAVEL TO AUSTRALIA

U.S. STATE DEPARTMENT SUGGESTION

Country Description: Australia is a highly developed, stable democracy with a federal-state system. Tourist facilities are widely available.

Entry Requirements: Information about entry requirements may be obtained from the Embassy of Australia at 1601 Massachusetts Avenue, N.W., Washington, D.C. 20036, telephone (202) 797-3000, or via the Australian Embassy home page on the Internet at http://www.austemb.org, or from the Australian Consulate General in Los Angeles, telephone (310) 229-4840.

Medical Facilities: Good medical care is available. Doctors and hospitals often expect immediate cash payment for health services. The Medicare/Medicaid program does not provide payment of medical services outside the United States. U.S. medical insurance is not always valid outside the United States. Travelers have found that, in some cases, supplemental medical insurance with specific overseas coverage, including provision for medical evacuation, has proven to be useful. Useful information on medical emergencies abroad is provided in the Department of State, Bureau of Consular Affairs' brochure, *Medical Information for Americans Traveling Abroad* available via our home page and autofax service. Information on vaccinations and other health precautions may be obtained from the Centers for Disease Control and Prevention's international traveler's hotline at 1-877-FYI-TRIP (1-877-394-8747), via the CDC autofax service at 1-888-CDC-FAXX (1-888-232-3299), or by visiting the CDC Internet homepage at http://www.cdc.gov.

Information on Crime: Australia's crime rate is low. However, foreign visitors from the U.S. or elsewhere are targets for pick-pockets, purse snatchers and petty thieves. Automobile burglaries and theft of personal belongings also occur. The loss or theft abroad of a U.S. passport should be reported immediately to the local police, and the nearest U.S. embassy or consulate. Useful information on guarding valuables and protecting personal security while traveling abroad is provided in the Department of State pamphlet *A Safe Trip Abroad*, which is available from the Superintendent of Documents, U.S. Government Printing Office, Washington D.C., 20402 or via the Internet at http://www.access.gpo.gov/su_docs.

Customs Regulations: Customs officials encourage the use of an ATA (Admission Temporarie/Temporary Admission) Carnet for the temporary admission of professional equipment, commercial samples, and/or goods for exhibitions and fair purposes. ATA Carnet Headquarters, located at the U.S. Council for International Business, 1212 Avenue of the Americas, New York, NY 10036, issues and guarantees the ATA Carnet in the United States. For additional information, please call (212) 354-4480, or send e-mail to atacarnet@uscib.org or via their website at http://www.uscib.org.

Criminal Penalties: While in a foreign country, a U.S. citizen is subject to that country's laws and regulations, which sometimes differ significantly from those in the United States and may not afford the protections available to the individual under U.S. law. Penalties for breaking the law can be more severe than for similar offenses in the United States. Persons violating the law, even unknowingly, may be expelled, arrested or imprisoned. Criminal penalties for possession, use, or trafficking of illegal drugs are strict, and convicted offenders can expect severe jail sentences and fines.

Road Safety: Visitors are reminded that all traffic operates on the left side of the road, and that all vehicles use right-hand drive. Visitors should use caution when crossing streets and when driving. When crossing roads, pedestrians are reminded to look carefully in all directions. Seat belts are mandatory. Speed limits and laws regarding driving while intoxicated are rigorously enforced. Roads and streets are frequently more narrow and less graded than U.S. highways. Outside the major metropolitan areas, most highways are two-lane roads with significant distances between destinations.

Drivers are urged to exercise caution while passing or merging with adjacent traffic. When driving in rural areas, particularly in the Northern Territory where there are no speed limits, drivers should be cautious of free-roaming animals and "road-trains" (several semi-truck trailers hooked together). It is dangerous to pass road-trains, and it is advisable to pull over and allow on-coming road-trains to pass to avoid being sideswiped. A number of fatalities have occurred in the Northern Territory when vehicles, driven at high rates of speed, have skidded and overturned after hitting the loose gravel shoulder of the road. U.S. drivers, especially those inexperienced with 4-wheel drive vehicles, should exercise common sense judgment when driving in outback Australia.

Aviation Oversight: The U.S. Federal Aviation Administration (FAA) has assessed the Government of Australia's civil aviation authority as Category 1 -- in compliance with international aviation safety standards for oversight of Australia's air carrier operations. For further information, travelers may contact the Department of Transportation within the U.S. at tel. 1-800-322-7873, or visit the FAA Internet home page at http://www.faa.gov/avr/iasa/index.htm. The U.S. Department of Defense (DOD) separately assesses some foreign air carriers for suitability as official providers of air services. For information regarding the DOD policy on specific carriers, travelers may contact DOD at 618-256-4801.

2000 Summer Olympic and Paralympic Games in Sydney, Australia: The 2000 Summer Olympic Games will be held in Sydney from September 15 to October 1, 2000. The 2000 Summer Paralympic Games will be held in Sydney from October 18-29, 2000. Please monitor the home pages of the Department of State and the U.S. Embassy and U.S. Consulates in Australia for information about consular services available during the Games. For more general information on both events, please see the Internet home pages for the Sydney Olympic Organizing Committee at http://www.sydney.olympic.org, the International Olympic Committee at http://www.olympic.org/future/sydney, and the U.S. Olympic Committee at http://www.olympic-usa.org.

Registration/U.S. Embassy and Consulate Locations: U.S. citizens living in or visiting Australia are encouraged to register at the U.S. Embassy or at the nearest U.S. consulate and to obtain updated information on travel and security within the country. The U.S. Embassy in Canberra is located on Moonah Place, Yarralumla, A.C.T. 2600, telephone (61)(2) 6214-5600, fax (61)(2) 6273-3191, home page http://www.usis-australia.gov/embassy.

The U.S. Consulate General in Sydney is located on Level 59, MLC Centre, 19-29 Martin Place, Sydney NSW 2000, telephone (61)(2) 9373-9200, fax (61)(2) 9373-9184, home page http://www.usconsydney.org.

The U.S. Consulate General in Melbourne is located at 553 St. Kilda Road, P.O. Box 6722, Melbourne Vic 3004, telephone (61)(3) 9526-5900, fax (61)(3) 9525-0769, home page http://www.usis-australia.gov/melbourne.

The U.S. Consulate General in Perth is located on Level 13, 16 St. Georges Terrace, Perth WA 6000, telephone (61)(8) 9231-9400, fax (61)(8) 9231-9444, home page http://www.usis-australia.gov/perth.

American business travelers to Australia should not encounter any particular difficulties. Visitors should make preparations as they would when traveling in the U.S., using normal reservation services for travel and accommodation, plus taking into account the requirement to have either an electronic travel authority or a valid Australian visa.

Despite the old image of being a far distant shore, travel time from the U.S. to Australia is comparable to that of other Asian destinations, a 14 hour non-stop flight from the West Coast, with a choice of flights on several reliable international airlines including United Airlines, QANTAS and Air New Zealand. Most departures from the U.S. leave in the evening and arrive in Australia early in the morning (with a day lost at the international date line). Travel to or from the rest of Asia, Europe, South America and South Africa also is convenient. Around 30 international airlines fly into Australia every week from 37 countries around the globe.

Frequent interstate flights connect the five major Australian cities. Savings are available on internal air fares when purchased in conjunction with international tickets. Australia has a very extensive, efficient domestic transportation system including air, rail, coach, sea, chauffeured and rental cars, and urban public transport between cities and country areas, and within the urban areas.

Australia's many attractions as a tourist and holiday destination finally are becoming well known, and the country is experiencing a tourism boom that surpasses that of any other western country. In the past ten years, tourism has become one of Australia's largest export earners, with the number of international visitors increasing from 1.4 million in 1986 to 3.7 million in 1995 and 4.3 million in 1997. The Australian Tourist Commission, Australia's national tourist office, has an office in Los Angeles (see Appendix E, Section 4A). The commisison can assist with travel advice and information on where to go and what to see.

Australia is a desired international destination for conventions and corporate meetings and corporate incentive travel. Its convention centers and trade show facilities in capital cities and resort areas offer state-of-the-art technology, some accommodating as many as 10,000 delegates. Many executives and conference delegates extend their stays in Australia with a holiday.

BUSINESS CUSTOMS

Doing business in Australia is comfortable for American companies because the language, the cultural environment, business practices and customer expectations are very similar. Business etiquette is familiar to Americans, with attention paid to advance planning, promptness, punctuality, and follow through.

Australians are personally gracious, yet informal and direct in their business dealings. Very soon after meeting, Australians do business on a first name basis. Business cards are exchanged for information purposes, but without any special ceremony. Token gift exchange is not common. Luncheon meetings are common, but Australians do not usually schedule business functions during the evening or on week-ends, which are dedicated to family and friends. Normal business attire is worn in the cities, with country areas being more informal.

TRAVEL ADVISORY AND VISAS

1. TIME ZONES

Australia's three time zones, Eastern, Central and Western, are parallel to those in Asia. Eastern Time, (Sydney, Melbourne, Canberra, Brisbane, Cairns), is one hour ahead of Tokyo. The reversal of the seasons (and hence of daylight saving time in the Northern and Southern Hemispheres) complicates the time zone calculation. Not all Australian states have daylight saving. Between the months of April-October, when it is 8:00 am in New York and 11:00 am in Los Angeles, it is 10:00 pm in Sydney and 8:00 pm in Perth. From November-March, at 8:00 am in New York it is 12:00 pm in Sydney and 9:00 pm in Perth.

2. INTERNATIONAL AIR TRAVEL TIMES

Los Angeles to Sydney 14 hrs 20 mins
New York to Sydney (via Los Angeles) 21 hrs 30 mins (via Japan) 25 hrs 20 mins
Honolulu to Sydney 9 hrs 55 mins
Tokyo to Sydney 9 hrs 20 mins
Hong Kong to Sydney 9 hrs 00 mins
Singapore to Sydney 7 hrs 50 mins

3. AIR TRAVEL TIMES WITHIN AUSTRALIA

Sydney to Melbourne 1 hr 10 mins
Sydney to Brisbane 1 hr 25 mins
Sydney to Perth 4 hrs 10 mins
Sydney to Canberra 35 mins
Melbourne to Brisbane 2 hrs
Melbourne to Perth 4 hrs
Brisbane to Perth 6 hrs 20 mins

4. VISAS

A valid U.S. passport and either a visa or an electronic travel authority are required for Americans traveling to Australia for business and/or tourism. The electronic travel authority is obtained from approved U.S. travel agents and airlines when purchasing the airline ticket. The Australian Embassy has lists of approved travel agents. U.S. citizens traveling to Australia should note that the electronic travel authority can only be obtained in the U.S. Requirements for work and resident visas are more stringent. The nearest Australian visa office should be contacted well in advance Visas are issued by Australian Embassies and Consulates. (The addresses of Australian Government offices in the U.S. are listed in Appendix E.4A.)

HOLIDAYS

Australians tend to take their long annual holiday in December and January, combining Christmas/New Year celebrations with the long summer school holidays. Consequently, business slows down and it is usually difficult to make appointments. Business travelers should be sure that their contacts will be available during this period before scheduling trips.

Listed below are the national public holidays observed in Australia. Some dates may vary from state to state, and individual states have their own additional public holidays. For example, all states have a public holiday for the Queen's Birthday, but the date varies.

- **New Year's Day January 1**
- **Australia Day January 26**
- **Good Friday April 3**
- **Easter Monday April 5**
- **Anzac Day April 25**
- **Christmas Day December 25**
- **Boxing Day December 26**

BUSINESS INFRASTRUCTURE

1. BUSINESS HOURS AND BANKING

Office business hours generally are 9:00 am- 5:00 pm, Monday through Friday. Retail shops increasingly keep longer business hours, and all city centers have evening shopping at least one day per week along with Saturday and, in some areas, Sunday also. However, Australia has not yet gone to the 7 day/24 hour shopping mode characteristic of most of the U.S. Banks are open to the public from 9:00 a.m. to 4:00 p.m. Monday through Friday, with 7 day/24 hour ATM service. Restaurants and convenience stores are open long hours.

2. CURRENCY

Australia's unit of currency, the Australian dollar (A$), is freely traded. The conversion rate is variable. In 1996 the average rate was A$1 to US$0.78; in 1997 it was A$1 to US$0.74 and for the first four months of 1998 it was A$1 to US$66. Travelers checks are accepted widely. Currency can be exchanged easily at international airports and most major banks, and ATM machines are everywhere. There are no major restrictions on importing or exporting currency or travelers checks to/from Australia, although a customs declaration is filed when taking out large amounts of cash.

3. CREDIT CARDS/ATMS

Most international credit cards are accepted in Australia and, as in the U.S., can be used for purchases of goods and services and to confirm hotel and other travel arrangements. ATM machines have most international cash access systems available so that travelers can draw cash directly from their U.S. accounts.

4. TELEPHONES AND FACSIMILES

Australia's telecommunications infrastructure is excellent, national and international prices continue to decline as competition increases. Services to businesses include ISDN, Frame Relay, E-mail, voice messaging, Internet access, electronic mail boxes, and faxstream. A number of companies provide call-back services by leasing excess capacity lines from the telecommunications operators, then offering national or international calls. The use of phone cards is common, and most major international phone cards can be used. Phone cards are available locally from numerous retail outlets.

For international travelers wanting to use a mobile phone, it is easier to rent one in Australia. Business visitors from the U.S. can use Analog AMPS mobile phones in Australia, but they must obtain a compliance certificate from the local manufacturer, plus an Electronic Serial Number (ESN). Compliance certificates cost between A$100 and A$400. Local manufacturers say that phones may be used without a compliance certificate for a short period of time by going to phone shops who could connect short term users to the network directly. But phone shops, in turn, advise they will only connect a mobile phone if it has a compliance certificate and ESN, and then only if the account will be paid by an Australian resident. In other words, if you need a mobile phone while in Australia, you should rent one here. Facsimile services are widely available for public use in Post Offices, hotels, and some copying shops.

5. POSTAL AND COURIER SERVICES

Australia Post supplies modern and efficient postal services within Australia and overseas. Express delivery and insured service is available. Domestic and international faxes can be sent from Post offices. Several international courier services operate from major cities offering express world-wide delivery of documents and packages.

6. HOTELS AND BUSINESS SERVICES

The business traveler to Australia can choose from a full range of hotels, from budget to international standard. Bookings for major chains can be made before leaving the U.S. Accommodations range from rooms to elaborate suites. Serviced apartment hotels with kitchens and living rooms are available. Most large hotels offer a full range of business and communications services including fax, word processing and copying. Temporary worker-serviced office suites are available for short-term rental.

7. RENTAL CARS AND LOCAL TRANSPORTATION

As in Britain and most of Asia, Australians drive on the left side of the road. Major U.S. and Australian car rental agencies operate throughout the country. Reservations can be made through airports, hotels, travel agents or directly, using a credit card and a U.S. or international driver's license. Throughout the urban areas, public transportation is well developed and safe. Urban crime is not a common fear. Comfortable and convenient bus, rail, and air services are available between cities and country towns.

8. ELECTRICAL POWER

Voltage in Australia is 220-240V, 50 cycles. Three-prong conversion plugs are available widely in retail stores. Voltage transformers to convert American 110V appliances are available, but not found so easily. Dual-voltage devices are more practical.

9. TAXES AND CUSTOMS DUTIES

There is no retail sales tax in Australia. Instead, wholesale taxes are levied at either manufacturer or wholesaler level by the Commonwealth Government and passed along to the consumer as part of the retail price. Passengers with airline tickets can buy items at duty-free shops in major cities and airports, although sometimes the prices are better in regular shops. It pays to compare. Customs information is available from the Australian Customs Service.

10. HEALTH

Australia is a healthy place, with no notable problems. Public water is safe everywhere. There are active campaigns to get people to protect themselves from the sun, skin cancer, and AIDS, and visitors should pay them heed. Medical and dental services, and all types of health facilities are comparable with those in the U.S. Visitors needing medical attention can receive it easily, but may be required to pay for services immediately by cash or credit card. Therefore, visitors should have their own health insurance arrangements in the U.S. from which to seek reimbursement.

11. FOOD AND DRINK

Australia's reputation as a world gourmet destination is growing, as understanding spreads of Australia's abundance of fresh, pure, and prime quality fruits, vegetables, meats, seafood, dairy products, specialty cheeses and fine wines. Australia's cultural diversity provides a broad choice of cuisines, and modern Australian chefs are reaching new heights of creativity. The coastal cities are renowned for fresh seafood, and the traditional Australian barbecue is a way of life. Australia is winning international wine awards; and its wine industry export earnings are growing exponentially. Of course, the Aussies' traditional dedication to their beer is legendary.

12. CULTURAL OPPORTUNITIES

Australia's vibrant, multi-cultural society offers cultural events to suit every preference. In major cities opera, ballet, and theater companies have full seasons. There is a myriad of art exhibitions, classical, rock, and country and western music festivals and concerts. Books and movies are current. Country areas hold folk, historic and food and wine festivals. Ethnic groups stage their own celebrations. Sport of all types is a national obsession - whether as a participant, or stadium fan, or television viewer. After sampling some of these attractions, most business visitors decide they want to spend their next holiday in Australia.

Copies of the State Department's publication, "Key Officers of Foreign Service Posts - Guide for Business Representatives" are available for sale by the Superintendent of Documents, U.S. Government Printing Office, Washington, D.C. 20402; Tel: 202 512 1800; Fax: 202 512 2250. Business travelers to Australia seeking appointments with U.S. Embassy/Consulate officials in Australia should contact the Commercial Service, Sydney in advance (telephone: 61 2 9373 9205; fax: 61 2 9221 0573; email: osydney@cs.doc.gov).

TRAVEL TIPS

- Protect against sunburn at all times, but especially in summer. Use a wide brimmed hat, 15+ sunscreen, sunglasses, protective clothes and shoes. Australian sunlight has very high UV levels and skin damage occurs rapidly, especially during the middle of the day.

- Check approaching storm fronts for signs of a greenish tinge. This often indicates a hail storm that may cause damage to persons and property.

- Always observe correct beach safety. Swim only at patrolled beaches. Only swim between flagged areas. If in doubt, ask. Always check for warning signs.

- If you intend to swim in shallow coastal waters north of Gladstone, make it your business to be informed about box jellyfish (marine stingers). Generally found in shallow water near creek or river mouths, more likely after local rain, usually absent in rough water. Not usually found over deep water or coral. Stinger season is usually from December to March in the Gladstone (south) area and longer, from October to June, in the Cairns (north) area. Most popular beaches in the stinger areas are netted to provide swimmer protection.

- Always wear thick soled shoes when walking in shallow tropical waters or reef walking as protection against the highly camoflaged stonefish. It has dorsal spikes which will rupture the skin of the foot and inject poison causing extreme swelling and agony. Deaths have been recorded as a result of stonefish poisoning.

- There are other poisonous creatures on the reef such as some of the cone shell species and coral snakes, both of which are capable of causing death. If you intend spending time on the Barrier Reef without expert guidance, ensure you have a sound knowledge of what can hurt you before you start.

- Australian traffic drives on the left hand side of the road.

- If you are in doubt about your driving license being accepted in Australia, rather obtain an International Licence from your local automobile association prior to your departure.

- Road speed limits differ between states but are generally 100-110kph on the highways and 50-60kph in built-up areas. Interstate highways are not of the same standard as USA and European highway systems but nor do they carry the same traffic volumes.

- Don't hitch-hike, it is illegal.

- Never leave small children or animals locked in vehicles in very hot weather. Dehydration occurs very quickly. This practice is illegal.

- The most serious danger on the road is fatigue. Look for driver refreshment stations and pull off and rest after driving for several hours.

- Be careful when driving on country roads at night in cold weather. Cattle and native animals such as kangaroos lie on the bitumen road surface which holds the warmth of the sun. Car lights blind and mesmerize the animals and they may just as easily run into your vehicle as run away from it.

- When traveling on remote outback roads/tracks, always advise someone at the destination of your expected arrival time and number of people in your party. If you fail to arrive within a reasonable time, help procedures can be started. Do **NOT** leave your vehicle as a missing vehicle is much easier to find that a missing person.

- When traveling on unsurfaced or poor quality roads, always conduct a vehicle check before starting off on the next sector.

- Extra care is needed when sharing the road with roadtrains (tractor trailers). These are prime movers with multiple trailers of cattle attached and are about 50 meters (170 feet) long. Always give them plenty of room as the buffeting from displaced air as you pass in opposite directions can be quite severe. Allow at least 1 kilometer (3000 feet) of clear road before overtaking a road train.

- Do not attempt to cross flooded rivers and causeways unless you are sure of the water depth and road surface damage. Most flash floods recede within 24 hours.

- Dust from passing vehicles on outback roads can obscure your vision. Don't take risks, slow down or stop until it settles.

- Avoid flying early morning and late afternoon on the eastern seaboard routes. These flights are usually heavily booked by business people traveling between the capital cities.

- Need extra leg room? Ask to be seated in a row that serves the exit doors as these rows seem to have more room.

- When checking in and getting seat allocation, ask if your seat is in the first row immediately adjacent one of the large central video screens. You may wish to ask for a different location, especially if on a long international flight.

- A departure tax of A$27 per adult is payable when leaving Australia.

- Need an interpreter? The telecommunications provider Telstra offers a 24 hour translation and interpreter service for an extensive range of languages. Dial 13 14 50. The local white pages telephone book will provide more information.

- Australian nationals and New Zealand visitors are covered by Medicare, the national health insurance scheme. It does not apply to visitors from any other country.

- Visitors should always obtain medical cover insurance prior to departure from their home country.

- Visitors will only require specific vaccinations if they have traveled through an area infected with yellow fever. Visitors passing through other countries when entering or leaving Australia should check the vaccination requirements of those countries.

- All cities and most towns offer 24 hour medical facilities by way of private practice clinics or government run hospital facilities. They will be listed in the telephone book of the area you are visiting.

- Drug stores are located in all towns and cities throughout Australia. The Australian chemist does not operate the "soda fountain" type of drug store found in the USA.

- In an emergency dial 000 (not 999). This will link you to the ambulance, fire and police services.
- Phone cards are a popular way of accessing the public phone system. Cards are available from selected newsagents and stores. Selected public phones also accept credit cards. Public phone call assistance is available by dialing 013.

- Australians working in the tourist, hospitality and transport industries are paid a minimum salary. Tipping is not standard practice but is generally considered an appropriate gesture of appreciation when the level of service has exceeded expectations.

  A tip of around 10% would be considered appropriate.

- To enter Australia you will need a current passport valid for the duration of your stay and a valid tourist visa issued in the your own country and entered into the passport before the travel date. New Zealand visitors are exempt from these requirements and are granted an entry permit on arrival.

  Visa applications are made to the Australian Embassy, Consulate or High Commission, as applicable, in your home country. Make sure you apply for the correct visa type. For example, if you plan to work, you will need to apply for a work permit which is generally limited to single under 25's and which only allows for casual work to be performed for up to 3 months.

  Tourist visas are generally valid for a stay of 3 or 6 months. At the time of making your visa application you will have to sign an undertaking that you have an outward bound ticket and sufficient funds for the duration of your stay.

- No duty is payable on personal effects. Adults may carry up to 250 cigarettes and 1 liter of alcoholic liquor in their personal effects provided it is carried with them.

  Duty and sales tax is applied to dutiable goods exceeding A$400. Strict regulations apply to narcotics and controlled substances.

- When entering Australia you will have to surrender all fresh food, animal and plant products and any unprocessed foodstuffs. You will be required to sign a declaration to this effect. This is a quarantine requirement to prevent the entry of foreign organisms that may have a harmful effect on Australia's native vegetation, wildlife and farming products.

- Strict regulations apply to the import and export of protected wildlife and items made from protected species. Any such items will be seized by customs officials upon arrival.

- Major shopping centers do not open on Sundays. Tourism oriented outlets do have a 7 day trade as do convenience stores supplying basic needs.

- Banks are only open Mondays through Fridays and generally only between the hours of 9.00 to 4.00. Most towns have automatic teller machines to cater for after-hours transactions.

- Australian currency consists of 5c 10c 20c 50c $1 $2 as coins. Notes are $5 $10 $20 $50 and $100.

- Australian electricity supply is 220-240 volts. Most electronics stores stock adaptors for 110v appliances as well as adaptors for 220-240v appliances with different plug types.

MONEY & COSTS

Currency: Australian dollar

Relative costs:

- Budget room: US$6-12
- Moderate hotel: US$20-60
- Top-end hotel: US$70 and up

- Budget meal: US$3-5
- Moderate restaurant meal: US$7-15
- Top-end restaurant meal: US$17 and up

If you're coming from Europe or the USA, Australia is going to look pretty cheap. Food, in particular, is great value. Accommodation is also reasonably priced, and if you're staying in hostels or on-site caravans or camping, and mostly making your own meals you could conceivably get by on about US$18 a day. Travel will be your biggest expense - distances are long and fuel's pricey - so if you're moving around a bit, eating out once or twice a day and staying in low-end hotels, budget around US$50 a day. If you're only coming for a couple of weeks and plan to take a few internal flights, you'll be looking at more like US$100 a day.

You'll have no problems changing foreign currencies or cash at almost any bank or exchange agent. Travelers checks generally get a better rate than cash. Credit cards are widely accepted (and pretty much compulsory if you're going to rent a car), and ATMs all over the country accept credit and Cirrus cards.

Tipping is getting a foothold in Australia, particularly in cafes and restaurants in the bigger cities - 10 or 15% is the usual. However, you won't be looked down upon if you don't tip. Taxi drivers are always grateful if you leave the change.

SUPPLEMENTS

THE AUSTRALIAN GOVERNMENT'S 2010-11 SCIENCE, RESEARCH AND INNOVATION BUDGET TABLES

(1)The Science, Research and Innovation Budget Tables provide an overview of whole-of-government support for science, research and innovation by the Australian Government over a 10 year period.

(2) The current tables generally retain the format used in earlier years, thus providing continuity and comparability with earlier budget tables. Since the 2004-05 publication, the groupings in Table 1 have been reclassified according to sectors of the economy. This is consistent with the nomenclatural conventions recommended in the Frascati Manual (2002, OECD).

(3)The tables also conform as closely as possible with the standards for reporting government budget appropriations and outlays on research and development as recommended in the 2002 edition of the Frascati Manual published by the OECD. Accordingly, extramural expenditures report only current costs and capital expenditures. It is important to note that the expenditure categories reflect the funder's perspective, which are then aggregated according to the sectors of performance.

(4)The support for science, research and innovation programs, administered on behalf of the Australian Government, may be provided either through annual appropriations (see Table 3) or through special appropriations (see Table 4). All expenditures reported in these tables have been recorded in accordance with the principles of accrual accounting.

(5)Table 1 summarises the total Australian Government support by sector of performance. Tables 2, 3 and 4 provide a detailed disaggregation of the total expenditure identified in Table 1 by program, which can be identified by the posting references. Table 5 identifies the allocation of science, research and innovation support by socio-economic objectives. To assist with the use of the tables, definitions are provided below for key terms that are used in these tables.

(6)The financial data have been supplied by the departments and agencies responsible for administering the programs listed in the tables. Previous estimates are adjusted by Departments and Agencies as data becomes available on actual expenditure and R&D content of programs.

(7)The most significant change from the estimates to actuals for 2009-10 (see Table 1) was a rephasing of funding relating to the Clean Energy Initiatives to 2013-14.

DEFINITIONS

Budget and Special Appropriations. Budget appropriations refer to funding appropriated annually, in particular, under *Appropriation Act No.1* and *No.2* of a given financial year (additional funding is appropriated under *Appropriation Acts No.3* and *No.4*). Special appropriations refer to funding appropriated through provisions in other legislation such as the *Higher Education Support Act (2003)* , the *Income Tax Assessment Act (1936),* the *Industry Research and Development Act (1986) and the Nation-building Funds Act (2008).*

Intramural Expenditure. Intramural expenditures are all expenditures for R&D performed within a statistical unit or sector of the economy during a specific period, whatever the source of funds (Frascati Manual, 2002, OECD).

Extramural Expenditure. Extramural expenditures are sums that a unit, organisation or sector reports having paid or committed to pay to another unit, organisation or sector for the performance of R&D during a specific period. This includes acquisition or R&D performed by other units and grants given to others for performing R&D (Frascati Manual, 2002, OECD).

TABLE 1. SUMMARY OF MAJOR AUSTRALIAN GOVERNMENT SUPPORT FOR SCIENCE, RESEARCH AND INNOVATION THROUGH THE BUDGET AND OTHER APPROPRIATIONS - ACTUAL COST IN YEAR INCURRED a, f

	Ref. no. a	2001-02	2002-03	2003-04	2004-05	2005-06	2006-07	2007-08	2008-09	Estimated Actual 2009-10	Budget Estimate 2010-11
		$m	$m	$m	$m	$m	$m	$m	$m	$m	$m
INTRAMURAL EXPENDITURE ON SCIENCE, RESEARCH AND INNOVATION b											
Major Australian Government Research Agencies											
· Defence Science & Technology Organisation	1	275.0	283.4	293.9	314.4	349.1	406.0	401.0	427.3	433.0	438.6
· CSIRO	2	509.6	532.1	568.6	577.1	593.9	610.1	663.1	675.8	726.8	780.8
· Other R&D Agencies	3	429.4	447.8	571.3	486.8	469.6	486.8	562.4	552.3	578.5	568.6
SUB-TOTAL		1,214.0	1,263.3	1,433.9	1,378.3	1,412.6	1,502.9	1,626.6	1,655.3	1,738.3	1,788.0
EXTRAMURAL EXPENDITURE ON SCIENCE, RESEARCH AND INNOVATION b											
Business Enterprise Sector											
· Industry R&D Tax Concession c	4	370.0	587.0	665.0	729.0	867.0	1,045.0	1,208.0	1,369.0	1,563.7	1,606.1
· Other R&D Support	5	237.9	158.6	230.8	200.2	222.6	244.2	270.2	215.8	94.4	80.1
· Other Innovation Support	6	291.7	264.7	266.9	223.7	242.4	255.1	272.4	292.0	605.7	423.7
SUB-TOTAL		899.6	1,010.2	1,162.7	1,152.9	1,332.0	1,544.3	1,750.6	1,876.8	2,263.8	2,109.9
Higher Education Sector											
· Australian Research Council	7	265.8	298.3	399.6	480.9	544.4	570.3	571.8	585.9	664.2	717.2
· Performance Based Block Funding	8	1,073.2	1,133.4	1,215.2	1,223.7	1,271.2	1,282.4	1,270.4	1,282.1	1,146.9	1,007.9
· Other R&D Support	9	538.3	541.1	551.7	111.8	243.7	120.2	124.8	135.0	559.1	825.0
SUB-TOTAL		1,877.3	1,972.8	2,166.5	1,816.3	2,059.3	1,972.9	1,967.0	2,003.0	2,370.2	2,550.1

Multisector d											
· NHMRC and Other Health	10	243.8	291.3	365.6	371.4	653.3	959.1	620.1	836.9	880.5	1,067.3
· Cooperative Research Centres	11	145.3	148.6	201.8	194.5	208.1	189.3	211.9	182.3	178.9	172.6
· Rural	12	197.5	204.3	210.7	210.9	218.5	222.3	222.9	226.4	231.0	222.9
· Energy and the Environment	13	33.6	33.1	62.3	40.7	46.0	75.6	130.3	215.2	382.4	571.2
· Other Science Support	14	13.3	39.2	50.3	57.6	72.3	150.9	152.8	169.2	364.7	441.4
SUB-TOTAL		633.5	716.6	890.7	875.1	1,198.1	1,597.3	1,338.1	1,629.9	2,037.5	2,475.4
TOTAL AUSTRALIAN GOVERNMENT SUPPORT		4,624.4	4,962.8	5,653.7	5,222.7	6,002.1	6,617.4	6,682.2	7,165.1	8,409.8	8,923.4
% Total Australian Government Expenditure e		2.40%	2.47%	2.63%	2.28%	2.48%	2.55%	2.39%	2.21%	2.47%	2.59%

Notes:

a. The financial data presented in this table are an aggregate of the expenditure data sourced from Tables 2, 3 & 4. Reference numbers in Column 2 identify their respective disaggregated source data in Tables 2, 3 and 4.

b. A definition of the expenditure categories is provided on Page 1.
c. The amounts indicated for the R&D tax concession are estimates only.
d. 'Multisector' includes programs that may be accessed by several sectors, including Australian Government agencies.
e. The ratio is calculated based on the expenditure (and forward estimate) published in Appendix D: Historical Australian Government Data, Mid-year Economic and Fiscal Outlook 2009-10.
f. A breakdown of the total expenditure by portfolio is summarised in the table below. Tax measures are included in the relevant policy portfolio rather than Treasury.

PORTFOLIO SUMMARY

		2001-02	2002-03	2003-04	2004-05	2005-06	2006-07	2007-08	2008-09	Estimated Actual 2009-10	Budget Estimate 2010-11
PORTFOLIO		$m	$m	$m	$m	$m	$m	$m	$m	$m	$m
AGRICULTURE, FISHERIES AND FORESTRY		207.1	217.2	232.0	235.8	247.5	248.4	245.7	245.4	254.8	246.9
BROADBAND, COMMUNICATIONS AND THE DIGITAL ECONOMY		0.0	10.3	11.3	17.2	23.5	24.0	26.8	27.3	25.4	25.9
CLIMATE CHANGE AND ENERGY EFFICIENCY		4.8	3.2	3.6	6.9	6.7	9.4	12.0	18.5	15.0	15.0
DEFENCE		275.0	283.4	293.9	314.4	349.1	406.0	403.3	438.1	446.2	454.3
EDUCATION, EMPLOYMENT AND WORKPLACE RELATIONS		589.0	585.0	585.0	154.9	165.2	166.6	167.7	170.1	171.1	174.2
ENVIRONMENT, WATER, HERITAGE AND THE ARTS		144.8	140.2	166.7	143.5	152.1	188.5	186.6	192.3	188.4	174.4
FOREIGN AFFAIRS AND TRADE		39.7	41.3	41.2	42.8	46.4	51.3	56.8	56.1	72.8	78.3
HEALTH AND AGEING		244.6	292.1	366.5	372.0	653.8	959.7	621.3	838.2	881.3	1,068.2
INFRASTRUCTURE, TRANSPORT, REGIONAL		1.8	1.8	1.9	1.9	2.2	7.1	9.1	7.0	3.4	3.3

DEVELOPMENT AND LOCAL GOVERNMENT											
INNOVATION, INDUSTRY, SCIENCE AND RESEARCH		3,036.3	3,299.6	3,854.8	3,829.6	4,239.9	4,422.7	4,736.9	4,895.0	5,898.8	6,153.8
PRIME MINISTER AND CABINET		0.0	0.0	0.0	1.0	2.0	2.1	5.0	4.6	4.5	4.1
RESOURCES, ENERGY AND TOURISM		81.3	88.8	96.9	102.6	113.6	131.5	210.9	272.5	448.2	525.0
TOTAL		4,624.4	4,962.8	5,653.7	5,222.7	6,002.1	6,617.4	6,682.2	7,165.1	8,409.8	8,923.4

TABLE 2. MAJOR AUSTRALIAN GOVERNMENT RESEARCH AGENCIES - BUDGET EXPENDITURES a

	Ref. no. a	2001-02	2002-03	2003-04	2004-05	2005-06	2006-07	2007-08	2008-09	Estimated Actual 2009-10	Budget Estimate 2010-11
PORTFOLIO / AGENCY		$m	$m	$m	$m	$m	$m	$m	$m	$m	$m
AGRICULTURE, FISHERIES AND FORESTRY											
Australian Animal Health Laboratory	3	5.8	6.1	6.2	6.8	6.9	7.0	5.7	7.1	7.2	7.3
DEFENCE											
Defence Science and Technology Organisation	1	275.0	283.4	293.9	314.4	349.1	406.0	401.0	427.3	433.0	438.6
FOREIGN AFFAIRS AND TRADE											
Australian Centre for International Agricultural Research	3	39.7	41.3	41.2	42.8	46.4	51.3	56.8	56.1	72.8	78.3
INNOVATION, INDUSTRY, SCIENCE AND RESEARCH											
CSIRO	2	509.6	532.1	568.6	577.1	593.9	610.1	663.1	675.8	714.8	730.8
Australian Nuclear Science & Technology Organisation b	3	158.7	173.2	290.4	196.4	158.5	141.6	185.7	174.7	175.2	189.7
Australian Institute of Marine Science	3	22.4	24.3	22.1	22.5	23.1	24.5	26.6	27.6	30.4	30.9
Anglo-Australian Telescope Board c	3	3.8	3.9	4.0	4.1	4.6	4.7	4.8	4.9	5.0	0.0
Australian Institute of Aboriginal and Torres Strait Islander Studies	3	3.8	3.8	3.9	4.0	3.9	4.0	3.6	3.8	3.8	4.4
ENVIRONMENT, WATER, HERITAGE AND THE ARTS											
Antarctic Division	3	92.0	84.6	85.5	86.5	94.6	99.6	105.5	104.6	116.9	103.8
Bureau of Meteorology Research Centre	3	9.4	9.7	10.1	11.0	11.7	12.8	12.6	19.9	22.6	24.3
Great Barrier Reef Marine Park Authority	3	4.1	4.1	3.9	4.0	4.9	4.8	4.8	3.4	3.0	2.8
Supervising Scientist Division d	3	8.4	8.0	7.1	7.8	7.5	11.1	11.2	11.0	11.0	11.0
RESOURCES, ENERGY AND TOURISM											
Geoscience Australia	3	81.3	88.8	96.9	100.	107.	125.	145.	139.	130.6	116.2

					9	4	4	0	0		
TOTAL		1,21 4.0	1,26 3.3	1,43 3.9	1,37 8.3	1,41 2.6	1,50 2.9	1,62 6.6	1,65 5.3	1,726. 3	1,738. 0

Notes:

a. The financial data have been supplied and confirmed by the Departments and Agencies responsible for administering the programs listed in the table. Reference numbers in Column 2 reconcile agency expenditures with their respective sector aggregates in Table 1.

b. The reduction in budget expenditures for 2004-05 when compared to 2003-04 is a timing issue relating to two special purpose projects: disposition of spent fuel and replacement research reactor. The fluctuations in the years 2007-08 onwards are timing issues relating to several large equity projects and two special purpose expense areas: disposition of spent fuel and ANSTO's decommissioning program.

c. The Anglo-Australian Telescope Board will be dissolved with effect 1 July 2010 and replaced by the Australian Astronomical Observatory within the Department of Innovation, Industry, Science and Research. Thus funding for 2010-11 appears in Table 3 under the DIISR portfolio.

d. Formerly referred to as the Environmental Research Institute of the Supervising Scientist. From 2006-07, total Divisional expenses have been assessed as supporting research and innovation.

source data: to be outside print area

Higher Education Sector		2550.10	28.6%
Australian Government Research Agencies		1787.99	20.0%
Business Enterprise Sector		2109.91	23.6%
Multisector		2475.40	27.7%
		8923.42	100.0%
		8923.42	

TABLE 3. MAJOR R&D GRANTING PROGRAMS AND OTHER SUPPORT FOR SCIENCE, RESEARCH AND INNOVATION THROUGH THE BUDGET a,b

	Ref. no. a	2001 -02	2002 -03	2003 -04	2004 -05	2005 -06	2006 -07	2007 -08	2008 -09	Estimated Actual 2009-10	Budget Estimate 2010-11
PORTFOLIO / PROGRAM		$m	$m	$m	$m	$m	$m	$m	$m	$m	$m
AGRICULTURE, FISHERIES AND FORESTRY c											
Centres of Excellence - Biosecurity Risk Analysis and Research	14	0.0	0.0	0.0	0.4	1.7	1.7	1.7	1.7	1.7	1.7
Centres of Excellence - National Food Industry Strategy	6	0.0	0.9	3.0	3.4	2.4	2.3	0.0	0.0	0.0	0.0
Climate Change Research Program	13	0.0	0.0	0.0	0.0	0.0	0.0	0.0	10.0	15.0	15.0
Fishing Industry Research	12	15.8	25.5	27.9	31.7	32.8	28.0	14.9	21.4	16.4	16.4
Food Innovation Grants - National Food Industry Strategy	6	0.0	1.9	8.9	10.8	15.4	13.1	13.1	0.0	0.0	0.0
Grains	12	40.8	39.2	39.2	35.1	35.1	35.8	37.5	42.2	50.4	47.1
Horticulture Research	12	29.5	30.2	30.0	30.0	32.9	34.0	36.2	32.4	38.5	38.5
Land & Water Research	12	11.6	11.9	12.2	12.5	12.5	12.8	13.0	13.0	6.7	0.0
Meat Research	12	23.5	26.3	28.5	35.6	36.3	37.6	45.0	42.8	40.3	41.8
National Weeds and Productivity Research Program	12	0.0	0.0	0.0	0.0	0.0	0.0	0.0	3.1	4.2	4.0
New Industries Development Program	6	3.8	4.0	3.2	3.5	2.6	2.0	2.3	0.2	0.0	0.0
Other Rural Research	12	36.6	40.1	41.9	37.7	37.8	47.6	50.8	45.9	46.8	46.8
Regional Food	12	0.0	0.0	0.0	0.0	0.0	0.0	0.0	0.0	6.9	7.0

Producers/Seafood Industry Innovation and Productivity Program											
Rural Industries R&D Corporation	12	17.2	14.9	14.8	14.6	14.9	14.9	13.4	13.3	10.4	10.5
Wool Research	12	22.5	16.2	16.2	13.7	16.2	11.6	12.1	12.2	10.4	10.8
BROADBAND, COMMUNICATIONS AND THE DIGITAL ECONOMY											
ICT Centre of Excellence	5	0.0	10.3	11.3	17.2	23.5	24.0	26.8	27.3	25.4	25.9
CLIMATE CHANGE AND ENERGY EFFICIENCY											
Australian Climate Change Science Program	13	0.0	0.0	0.0	6.7	6.6	8.3	8.3	8.8	7.8	7.8
Bilateral Climate Change Partnerships Program d	13	0.0	0.0	0.0	0.2	0.1	1.1	1.2	6.5	0.0	0.0
National Carbon Accounting System	13	4.8	3.2	3.6	0.0	0.0	0.0	2.5	3.2	3.2	3.2
National Carbon Accounting Toolbox	13	0.0	0.0	0.0	0.0	0.0	0.0	0.0	0.0	4.0	4.0
DEFENCE											
DMO - Capability Technology Demonstrator - Extension Program	14	0.0	0.0	0.0	0.0	0.0	0.0	2.2	10.9	10.4	11.2
DMO - Defence Industry Innovation Centre	14	0.0	0.0	0.0	0.0	0.0	0.0	0.0	0.0	2.8	4.5
EDUCATION, EMPLOYMENT AND WORKPLACE RELATIONS											
Bond University - Grant for Clinical Education and Research Centre Building	9	0.0	0.0	0.0	0.0	0.0	0.0	0.0	2.5	0.0	0.0
Bond University - Grant for Health Science and Medicine Building	9	0.0	0.0	0.0	0.0	4.5	0.0	0.0	0.0	0.0	0.0
ENVIRONMENT, WATER, HERITAGE AND THE ARTS											
Australian Biological Resources Study	13	4.5	3.7	3.1	3.0	3.0	1.9	2.0	2.0	2.0	2.0
Australia Council - Synapse Program	14	0.0	0.0	0.1	0.0	0.3	0.1	0.1	0.2	0.2	0.1
Commonwealth Environment Research Facilities	13	0.0	0.0	0.0	0.0	2.9	15.5	23.0	25.4	24.4	23.3
Emissions Measurement and Analysis d	13	0.0	0.0	0.0	7.7	6.8	6.3	6.1	6.6	0.0	0.0
Greenhouse Gas Abatement Program	13	9.0	11.2	38.9	15.4	13.3	17.7	7.9	1.5	0.0	0.0
Greenhouse Research (NGRP)	13	3.9	3.9	4.1	0.0	0.0	0.0	0.0	0.0	0.0	0.0
Low Emissions Technology and Abatement	13	0.0	0.0	0.0	0.9	2.0	6.7	3.1	1.7	0.0	0.0
Marine and Biodiversity Research	13	0.0	0.0	0.0	1.8	2.1	9.6	8.5	13.9	6.4	4.2
Reef Water Quality	13	0.0	0.0	0.0	0.0	0.0	0.0	0.0	2.0	2.0	3.0
Renewable Energy Commercialisation Program	13	8.9	9.2	9.2	2.9	1.7	1.5	0.0	0.0	0.0	0.0
Renewable Energy Equity Fund	13	2.5	1.9	3.4	0.4	1.3	0.8	1.8	0.0	0.0	0.0
HEALTH AND AGEING											

Adult Stem Cell Research Centre	10	0.0	0.0	0.0	0.0	0.0	5.0	5.0	5.0	5.0	0.0
Anti-Doping Research Program (ADRP)	14	0.8	0.8	0.9	0.6	0.5	0.6	1.2	1.3	0.8	0.9
Attacking Lung Cancer	10	0.0	0.0	0.0	0.0	0.0	0.0	0.0	0.0	0.9	2.4
Cancer Data	10	0.0	0.0	0.0	0.0	0.0	0.0	0.0	0.0	0.5	0.5
Cancer Research	10	0.0	0.0	0.0	0.0	3.0	5.1	5.7	5.9	4.4	4.4
Cooperative Research Centre for Aboriginal and Torres Strait Islander Health	10	0.0	0.0	0.2	0.2	0.2	0.2	0.2	0.2	0.2	0.2
Health Sciences - Australian Longitudinal Study on Women's Health e	10	0.8	0.9	1.7	1.1	1.4	1.4	1.4	1.4	1.3	1.4
Investing in Hearing Research	10	0.0	0.0	0.0	0.0	0.0	0.0	0.5	1.2	1.4	4.5
Medical Research Infrastructure Projects	10	0.0	0.0	31.2	0.0	215.0	435.8	0.0	64.8	100.7	223.8
National Cancer Plan - Boost Cancer Research	10	0.0	0.0	0.0	0.0	0.0	0.0	0.0	5.0	5.0	5.0
National Illicit Drug Strategy Research	10	0.0	0.0	0.0	0.2	0.2	0.7	0.5	0.3	0.5	0.5
National Public Health Communicable Disease Control - Research Centres	10	0.0	0.0	0.0	0.0	8.2	8.2	8.5	8.9	9.0	9.2
NHMRC Research Grants f	10	243.0	290.4	332.4	369.4	403.5	474.0	566.1	707.3	723.3	791.7
Onemda VicHealth Koori Health Unit - University of Melbourne	10	0.0	0.0	0.0	0.2	0.2	0.2	0.2	0.3	0.3	0.3
Pandemic Vaccine Accelerated Development	10	0.0	0.0	0.0	0.0	2.0	2.5	2.5	0.0	0.0	0.0
Primary Care Policy, Innovation and Research	10	0.0	0.0	0.0	0.0	14.6	14.2	16.4	14.6	16.3	14.5
Priority Medical Research	10	0.0	0.0	0.0	0.0	0.0	5.0	5.0	5.0	0.9	0.9
Radiation in Health Care - Safe and Better Use	10	0.0	0.0	0.0	0.0	0.0	0.0	2.1	4.3	2.0	2.0
Support for Diabetes Research	10	0.0	0.0	0.0	0.2	4.9	6.8	6.0	9.8	6.7	3.0
Two Dedicated Prostate Cancer Research Centres	10	0.0	0.0	0.0	0.0	0.0	0.0	0.0	3.0	2.0	3.0
INFRASTRUCTURE, TRANSPORT, REGIONAL DEVELOPMENT AND LOCAL GOVERNMENT											
Air Cargo X-ray Trials	14	0.0	0.0	0.0	0.0	0.0	4.9	3.8	0.0	0.0	0.0
Liquids, Aerosols and Gels Screening Technology Trials	14	0.0	0.0	0.0	0.0	0.0	0.0	0.9	3.5	0.0	0.0
Low Volume Roads Research	14	0.0	0.0	0.0	0.0	0.0	0.0	1.6	0.6	0.3	0.1
Payments to Austroads/ARRB Transport Research Ltd.	14	1.8	1.8	1.9	1.9	2.2	2.2	2.8	2.9	3.1	3.2
INNOVATION, INDUSTRY, SCIENCE AND RESEARCH											
Anglo-Australian Observatory	14	0.0	0.0	0.0	0.0	0.0	0.0	0.0	0.0	4.0	1.5
Australian National University Research Infrastructure Projects	9	0.0	0.0	0.0	0.0	125.0	0.0	0.0	0.0	0.0	0.0
Australian Square Kilometre Array (SKA) Pathfinder Telescope g	14	0.0	0.0	0.0	0.0	0.0	0.0	1.5	1.1	1.3	1.1
Australian Space Research	14	0.0	0.0	0.0	0.0	0.0	0.0	0.0	0.0	5.8	12.2

PORTFOLIO / PROGRAM	Ref. no.a	2001-02	2002-03	2003-04	2004-05	2005-06	2006-07	2007-08	2008-09	Estimated Actual 2009-10	Budget Estimate 2010-11
Program and Space Policy Unit											
Australian Synchrotron Contribution	14	0.0	0.0	0.0	0.0	0.0	50.0	0.0	0.0	0.0	0.0
Automotive Competitiveness and Investment Scheme	6	142.6	134.8	128.7	130.4	145.7	168.9	178.4	202.4	233.8	137.0
Automotive Transformation Scheme	6	0.0	0.0	0.0	0.0	0.0	0.0	0.0	0.0	0.0	52.0
Biotechnology Innovation Fund h	6	4.0	11.9	13.4	0.0	0.0	0.0	0.0	0.0	0.0	0.0
Building Information Technology Strengths – Advanced Networks Program	6	21.9	8.8	6.6	8.0	7.0	5.0	0.0	0.0	0.0	0.0
Building Information Technology Strengths – Incubators	6	22.7	16.1	11.6	12.6	10.6	5.0	3.5	0.0	0.0	0.0
Building Information Technology Strengths – Intelligent Island (Tas.)	6	20.0	0.0	0.0	0.0	0.0	0.0	0.0	0.0	0.0	0.0
Clean Business Australia - Climate Ready Program	6	0.0	0.0	0.0	0.0	0.0	0.0	0.0	15.9	37.6	18.5
Commercial Ready Program h, i	5	0.0	0.0	0.0	152.1	163.4	172.1	186.0	132.3	41.3	11.7
Commercialising Emerging Technologies (COMET) i	6	12.2	11.4	8.7	7.9	8.4	9.7	14.0	13.5	11.2	7.6
Commercialisation Australia i	6	0.0	0.0	0.0	0.0	0.0	0.0	0.0	0.0	15.0	31.9
Commonwealth Strategic Relationship with ANU											
· Australian National Institute for Public Policy	9	0.0	0.0	0.0	0.0	0.0	0.0	0.0	0.0	0.0	3.1
· Australian Centre on China in the World	9	0.0	0.0	0.0	0.0	0.0	0.0	0.0	0.0	0.0	25.2
· National Security College	9	0.0	0.0	0.0	0.0	0.0	0.0	0.0	0.0	0.0	2.7
· Sir Roland Wilson Foundation	9	0.0	0.0	0.0	0.0	0.0	0.0	0.0	0.0	0.0	7.0
Collaborative Research Networks	9	0.0	0.0	0.0	0.0	0.0	0.0	0.0	0.0	0.0	9.7
Cooperative Research Centres (CRC)	11	145.3	148.6	201.8	194.5	208.1	189.3	211.9	182.3	178.9	172.6
		$m	$m	$m	$m	$m	$m	$m	$m	$m	$m
EMBL Partner Laboratory	14	0.0	0.0	0.0	0.0	0.0	0.0	0.0	0.0	2.0	2.0
Enterprise Connect Innovation Centres	6	0.0	0.0	0.0	0.0	0.0	0.0	5.3	6.9	1.0	0.9
Excellence in Research for Australia (ERA)	7	0.0	0.0	0.0	0.0	0.0	0.0	0.0	0.0	9.1	1.4
Green Car Innovation Fund	6	0.0	0.0	0.0	0.0	0.0	0.0	0.0	0.0	132.7	103.5
Industry Co-operative Innovation Program	6	0.0	0.0	0.0	0.0	1.9	3.7	4.5	5.2	4.2	1.5
Industry Innovation Program (Includes R&D Start Grants) h	5	207.0	115.5	132.8	0.0	0.0	0.0	0.0	0.0	0.0	0.0
Information Technology Online (ITOL)	6	0.8	2.3	2.2	1.9	2.2	1.3	0.0	0.0	0.0	0.0
Innovation Access Program –	5	0.0	5.0	11.0	2.1	0.0	0.0	0.0	0.0	0.0	0.0

Industry (IAccP) h											
Innovation Investment Fund including Innovation Investment Follow-on Fund i	6	27.3	24.7	17.6	19.6	14.7	12.3	12.1	8.1	121.8	23.4
Intermediary Access Program (Pilot)	6	0.0	0.0	0.0	0.0	0.0	1.0	3.0	0.0	0.0	0.0
International Education and Training (Australia-India Strategic Research Fund)	6	0.0	0.0	0.0	0.0	0.0	0.0	2.1	6.9	5.6	9.5
International Science Linkages j	14	4.1	7.6	7.6	9.3	10.2	11.1	11.4	11.7	10.1	12.3
James Cook University - Cairns Institute Tropical Innovation Hub	9	0.0	0.0	0.0	0.0	0.0	0.0	0.0	0.0	0.0	15.0
Major National Research Facilities k	14	4.5	25.0	38.5	42.3	42.2	0.0	0.0	0.0	0.0	0.0
Motor Vehicle Producer R&D Scheme	5	0.0	0.0	0.0	0.0	6.7	12.0	15.0	15.9	12.7	28.0
National Collaborative Research Infrastructure Strategy l	14	0.0	0.0	0.0	0.0	13.1	78.2	120.6	102.8	105.3	107.1
National Enabling Technologies Strategy	6	0.0	0.0	0.0	0.0	0.0	0.0	0.0	0.0	0.9	0.9
National Measurement Institute	5	0.0	0.0	0.0	8.0	8.0	8.0	8.5	8.5	9.0	9.0
National Stem Cell Centre	5	0.8	3.6	4.6	5.8	7.1	6.5	6.0	5.5	5.0	4.5
Pharmaceutical Industry Investment Program	5	14.0	16.4	59.3	0.4	0.0	0.0	0.0	0.0	0.0	0.0
Pharmaceutical Partnerships Program	5	0.0	0.0	0.0	4.2	12.4	21.6	26.9	25.3	0.0	0.0
Pre-Seed Fund i	6	0.0	4.2	6.4	6.7	12.5	8.8	11.1	6.9	13.1	3.0
R&D Start Loans program	5	16.1	7.8	11.8	10.4	1.5	0.0	0.0	0.0	0.0	0.0
Shipbuilding Innovation Scheme	6	6.4	8.7	7.0	2.9	0.0	0.0	0.0	0.0	0.0	0.0
Small-Scale Mammalian Cell Production Facility	5	0.0	0.0	0.0	0.0	0.0	0.0	1.0	1.0	1.0	1.0
Société Internationale de Télécommunications Aéronautiques	6	2.3	1.7	0.3	0.0	0.0	0.0	0.0	0.0	0.0	0.0
Software-Engineering Australia	6	3.3	2.0	1.1	0.0	0.0	0.0	0.0	0.0	0.0	0.0
Technology Diffusion Program	6	14.2	12.9	4.2	0.0	0.0	0.0	0.0	0.0	0.0	0.0
Test-It	6	0.7	0.4	0.0	0.0	0.0	0.0	0.0	0.0	0.0	0.0
PRIME MINISTER AND CABINET											
Research Support for Counter Terrorism	14	0.0	0.0	0.0	1.0	2.0	2.1	4.0	4.4	4.0	3.3
US Department of Homeland Security Collaborative Research	14	0.0	0.0	0.0	0.0	0.0	0.0	0.1	0.0	0.2	0.4
US Technical Support Working Group (TSWG) Collaborative Research	14	0.0	0.0	0.0	0.0	0.0	0.0	0.9	0.3	0.3	0.4
RESOURCES, ENERGY AND TOURISM											
Advanced Electricity Storage Technologies	13	0.0	0.0	0.0	0.0	0.2	0.8	6.1	7.8	0.0	0.0
Clean Energy Initiative m											
· Australian Centre for Renewable Energy	13	0.0	0.0	0.0	0.0	0.0	0.0	0.0	0.0	42.1	104.4
· Australian Solar Institute	13	0.0	0.0	0.0	0.0	0.0	0.0	0.0	0.0	49.8	25.0
· National Low Emission Coal Initiative	13	0.0	0.0	0.0	0.0	0.0	0.0	0.0	0.0	87.6	102.9
Energy Innovation Fund	13	0.0	0.0	0.0	0.0	0.0	0.0	0.0	6.0	0.0	0.0
Global Carbon Capture and Storage Institute	13	0.0	0.0	0.0	0.0	0.0	0.0	0.0	87.7	100.0	100.0

Low Emissions Technology Demonstration Fund	13	0.0	0.0	0.0	0.8	1.5	1.3	54.6	0.0	38.1	76.5
National Clean Coal Initiative	13	0.0	0.0	0.0	0.0	0.0	0.0	0.0	25.2	0.0	0.0
Otway Basin Pilot Project	13	0.0	0.0	0.0	0.0	0.0	0.0	2.0	0.6	0.0	0.0
Renewable Energy Fund	13	0.0	0.0	0.0	0.0	0.0	0.0	0.0	4.9	0.0	0.0
Wind Forecasting Capability	13	0.0	0.0	0.0	0.9	4.5	4.0	3.2	1.3	0.0	0.0
TOTAL		1,151.5	1,117.9	1,343.0	1,280.9	1,773.6	2,074.6	1,857.7	2,086.3	2,505.1	2,630.0

Notes:

a. The financial information has been supplied and confirmed by the departments and agencies responsible for administering the programs listed in the Table. Reference numbers in Column 2 reconcile program expenditures with their respective sector aggregates in Table 1.

b. Departmental expenses attributable to the administration of programs are excluded from the data in accordance with the recommendations of the Frascati Manual (2002, OECD).

c. The R&D expenditures for wool, meat, other rural research, fish, horticulture and grains sectors exclude that component of Australian Government outlays funded from industry levies. Industry Contributions - Rural Research Levies (estimated proportion of levies attributable to research purposes - $m) are presented in the table below:

Industry Contributions

	2001-02	2002-03	2003-04	2004-05	2005-06	2006-07	2007-08	2008-09	2009-10	2010-2011
SECTOR	$m	$m	$m	$m	$m	$m	$m	$m	$m	$m
Wool	56.3	62.6	40.4	40.4	42.0	46.5	45.1	41.7	31.5	32.2
Meat	15.9	19.4	20.5	21.1	21.8	22.1	30.6	34.8	33.7	33.9
Wheat	37.1	39.4	41.4	41.5	41.5	27.6	40.4	31.1	42.3	38.3
Other Grains	24.8	25.6	28.2	25.7	25.9	23.2	36.4	30.8	30.0	24.8
Special Rural	0.0	0.0	0.0	0.0	0.0	0.0	0.0	0.0	0.0	0.0
Fish	4.4	5.0	6.1	2.0	5.7	5.7	0.8	0.2	0.1	0.1
Horticulture	10.4	22.4	25.3	26.5	26.5	16.8	18.8	18.7	20.4	21.0
Other Rural Research										
Chicken Meat	0.9	1.1	1.1	1.1	1.1	1.4	1.0	1.1	1.1	1.1
Cotton	5.0	7.2	3.4	3.5	4.1	4.2	2.0	2.2	3.3	3.4
Dairying	11.5	12.9	16.3	31.0	31.0	31.0	28.0	27.3	28.9	29.2
Dried Fruit n	0.5	0.6	0.0	0.0	0.0	0.0	0.0	0.0	0.0	0.0
Grape & Wine	7.4	7.8	7.7	7.9	7.9	13.2	9.9	12.5	12.1	12.6
Honey	0.2	0.2	0.2	0.2	0.2	0.5	0.3	0.3	0.3	0.3
Pig Industry	11.8	13.3	13.3	13.5	13.5	12.1	3.2	4.0	4.3	4.7
Egg Industry	0.7	0.5	5.3	4.4	4.4	4.1	0.8	0.9	0.8	1.2
Sugar	4.3	5.3	5.5	5.5	5.5	5.1	4.8	4.5	4.4	4.4
Tobacco o	0.6	0.0	0.0	0.0	0.0	0.0	0.0	0.0	0.0	0.0
Forestry	3.0	3.0	3.8	3.8	3.8	3.6	4.6	5.2	4.7	5.3
Rural Industries R&D Corporation	0.0	0.0	0.0	2.6	3.0	4.9	0.8	0.4	1.7	2.0
Total	194.9	226.3	218.5	230.8	237.9	222.0	227.4	215.8	219.4	214.4

d. Funding for this item is not reported in 2009-10 as it does not have a separate funding allocation.

e. The Australian Longitudinal Study on Women's Health was funded from within existing resources of the health portfolio until 2003. From 2004-05, funding for the study was provided by a new measure called Australian Longitudinal Study on Women's Health. The $1.7m in 2003-04 includes $0.8m from the Office for the Status of Women.

f. Includes funding for applied and basic research across health services, public health, clinical and biomedical research. During 2001-02, the NHMRC changed its accounting policy for the recognition of expenditure on research grants, with consequent adjustments to the appropriations, in line with Australian Accounting Standards (AAS 29) and changes to the Minister for Finance Orders. Adjustments have been made to the estimates to expense funds progressively in each year in which research is conducted, rather than in full when multi-year grant commitments are accepted. Thus the adjustments only reflect changes to the timing of the recognition of expenses and do not impact on the aggregate level of multi-year grants able to be approved each year.

g. Only the DIISR component is included here. The bulk of this program is funded by CSIRO.
h. From 1 July 2004, funding for Biotechnology Innovation Fund, R&D Start Grants and part of the IAP - Industry were combined with the new Commercial Ready funding to form a single program.
i. Programs provide support for commercialisation activities, including proof of concept activities.
j. Following the transfer of the science functions to the former Department of Education, Science and Training (DEST) at the end of 2001, the administration of the Innovation Access program (IAP) - International S&T, now called International Science Linkages, was transferred to DEST, while administration of the IAP - Industry component had been retained by the former Department of Industry, Tourism and Resources.

k. The National Collaborative Research Infrastructure Strategy (NCRIS) Program is a successor to the Major National Research Facilities (MNRF).
l. The National Collaborative Research Infrastructure Strategy (NCRIS) Program is a successor to the Systemic Infrastructure Initiative.
m. $200 million has been rephased from 2009-10 to 2013-14.
n. This levy is now combined with the Horticulture levy.
o. This levy has ceased.

TABLE 4. ESTIMATED COSTS OF PROGRAMS AND INCENTIVES PROVIDING SUPPORT FOR SCIENCE, RESEARCH AND INNOVATION THROUGH SPECIAL APPROPRIATIONS AND OTHER MEASURES a, b

	Ref. no. a	2001-02	2002-03	2003-04	2004-05	2005-06	2006-07	2007-08	2008-09	Estimated Actual 2009-10	Budget Estimate 2010-11
PORTFOLIO / PROGRAM		$m	$m	$m	$m	$m	$m	$m	$m	$m	$m
EDUCATION, EMPLOYMENT AND WORKPLACE RELATIONS											
Estimate of Other Research and Research Training Support Sourced from the Australian Government c	9	431.1	434.3	434.7	0.0	0.0	0.0	0.0	0.0	0.0	0.0
National Institutes Program - ANU Component d,e,f	8	157.9	150.7	150.3	154.9	160.7	166.6	167.7	167.5	171.1	174.2
ENVIRONMENT, WATER, HERITAGE AND THE ARTS											
National Oceans Office g	14	2.1	3.9	1.3	2.1	0.0	0.0	0.0	0.0	0.0	0.0
INNOVATION, INDUSTRY, SCIENCE AND RESEARCH											
Australian Research Council h	7	265.8	298.3	399.6	480.9	544.4	570.3	571.8	585.9	652.8	708.7
Clean Energy Initiative	13	0.0	0.0	0.0	0.0	0.0	0.0	0.0	0.0	0.0	100.0
Education Investment Fund - Super Science											
· Super Science - Future Industries	14	0.0	0.0	0.0	0.0	0.0	0.0	0.0	20.0	109.0	119.0
· Super Science - Marine and Climate i	14	0.0	0.0	0.0	0.0	0.0	0.0	0.0	8.0	59.0	66.0
· Super Science - Space Science and Astronomy	14	0.0	0.0	0.0	0.0	0.0	0.0	0.0	0.0	20.0	20.0
Education Investment Fund - Round 1											
· Institute of Photonics	9	0.0	0.0	0.0	0.0	0.0	0.0	0.0	0.2	18.6	9.8

· New Horizons - Monash University Project	9	0.0	0.0	0.0	0.0	0.0	0.0	0.0	0.4	8.0	11.5
Education Investment Fund - Round 2											
· Australian Institute for Innovative Materials	9	0.0	0.0	0.0	0.0	0.0	0.0	0.0	0.0	27.8	16.0
· Building the Sydney Institute of Marine Science	9	0.0	0.0	0.0	0.0	0.0	0.0	0.0	0.0	10.5	6.0
· Centre for Climate Change and Energy Research	9	0.0	0.0	0.0	0.0	0.0	0.0	0.0	0.0	40.0	0.0
· Institute for Marine and Antarctic Studies	9	0.0	0.0	0.0	0.0	0.0	0.0	0.0	0.0	45.0	0.0
· La Trobe Institute for Molecular Sciences	9	0.0	0.0	0.0	0.0	0.0	0.0	0.0	0.0	14.4	34.2
· National Centre for Synchrotron Science	9	0.0	0.0	0.0	0.0	0.0	0.0	0.0	0.0	18.0	15.8
· Smart State Medical Research Centre	14	0.0	0.0	0.0	0.0	0.0	0.0	0.0	0.0	0.0	55.0
· Centre for Neural Engineering	9	0.0	0.0	0.0	0.0	0.0	0.0	0.0	0.0	3.9	10.2
Funding for higher education research promotion j	9	2.5	2.4	2.4	2.5	2.2	2.2	3.5	5.6	5.7	5.3
Funding for research and research training provided under HESA (2003) k											
· Australian Postgraduate Awards Scheme	9	83.2	87.1	89.5	91.2	93.1	94.1	96.6	101.4	151.1	183.0
· Commercialisation Training Scheme	9	0.0	0.0	0.0	0.0	0.4	5.5	5.5	5.5	5.6	5.7
· Institutional Grants Scheme	8	262.9	286.4	285.2	290.6	296.1	302.0	308.1	311.3	157.3	0.0
· International Postgraduate Research Scholarship Scheme	9	14.0	16.7	17.8	18.1	18.5	18.4	19.2	19.4	19.8	20.2
· Joint Research Engagement Program	9	0.0	0.0	0.0	0.0	0.0	0.0	0.0	0.0	160.6	323.7
· Research Infrastructure Block Grants	8	111.2	136.7	160.6	183.0	199.9	203.9	206.0	210.2	214.6	218.5
· Regional Protection Scheme	8	2.0	3.2	5.8	3.0	3.1	6.2	3.2	1.6	0.0	0.0
· Research Training Scheme	8	515.6	528.0	541.9	552.2	562.6	573.9	585.4	591.5	603.9	615.1
· Systemic Infrastructure Initiative	8	23.6	28.4	71.4	39.9	48.7	29.7	0.0	0.0	0.0	0.0
· Sustainable Research Excellence in Universities	9	0.0	0.0	0.0	0.0	0.0	0.0	0.0	0.0	30.0	121.0
Giant Magellan Telescope	14	0.0	0.0	0.0	0.0	0.0	0.0	0.0	0.0	24.6	19.4
Mount Stromlo Observatory Reconstruction	9	0.0	0.0	7.3	0.0	0.0	0.0	0.0	0.0	0.0	0.0
Replacement of Australia's National Marine Facility - CSIRO	2	0.0	0.0	0.0	0.0	0.0	0.0	0.0	0.0	12.0	50.0
Super Science Fellowships - ARC	7	0.0	0.0	0.0	0.0	0.0	0.0	0.0	0.0	2.3	7.1
Support from the Federation Fund											
· Commonwealth Technology Port	6	3.5	8.0	0.0	0.0	0.0	0.0	0.0	0.0	0.0	0.0
· Institute of Molecular Bioscience	9	3.0	0.5	0.0	0.0	0.0	0.0	0.0	0.0	0.0	0.0
· National Marine Science	9	4.5	0.1	0.0	0.0	0.0	0.0	0.0	0.0	0.0	0.0

Centre											
Tax incentives programs l											
· New R&D Tax Incentives m	4	0.0	0.0	0.0	0.0	0.0	0.0	0.0	0.0	0.0	1,470.0
· R&D Tax Concession (125%)	4	280.0	320.0	330.0	370.0	430.0	530.0	620.0	640.0	650.0	170.0
· Premium Tax Concession for Additional R&D (175%)	4	50.0	85.0	100.0	130.0	195.0	320.0	330.0	380.0	350.0	100.0
· R&D Refundable Tax Offset n	4	40.0	182.0	235.0	229.0	242.0	195.0	258.0	349.0	522.0	-135.0
· Research and Development Tax Concession - interim transition measure	4	0.0	0.0	0.0	0.0	0.0	0.0	0.0	0.0	41.7	1.1
· Pooled Development Funds o	6	6.0	7.0	9.0	7.0	9.0	12.0	11.0	10.0	9.0	8.0
· Venture Capital Limited Partnerships p	6	0.0	3.0	35.0	9.0	10.0	10.0	11.0	11.0	11.0	11.0
· Exemption from Early Stage Venture Capital Limited Partnerships	6	0.0	0.0	0.0	0.0	0.0	0.0	1.0	5.0	9.0	15.0
TOTAL		2,258.9	2,581.7	2,876.8	2,563.4	2,815.8	3,039.9	3,198.0	3,423.5	4,178.4	4,555.4

Notes:

a. The financial information has been provided and confirmed by the departments responsible for administering the programs listed in the table. Reference numbers in Column 2 reconcile program expenditures with their respective sector aggregates in Table 1.

b. Departmental expenses attributable to the administration of programs are excluded from the data in accordance with the recommendations of the Frascati Manual (2002, OECD).

c. Following the 2002 Review of Higher Education, the Australian Government announced a package of new higher education policies, to be implemented between 2004 and 2008. The legislation to give effect to the reform package, the Higher Education Support Act 2003 (HESA), was passed by Parliament on 5 December 2003. As a result, this estimate is no longer consistent with the implementation of the new funding arrangements for higher education institutions under the provisions of the HESA and has not been included from 2004-05 onwards.

d. This item refers to funds for research and research training provided to the Institute of Advanced Studies (IAS) of the Australian National University (ANU) through the ANU's operating grant.

e. This was initially referred to as the ANU Institute of Advanced Studies Block Funding. The name has been updated to reflect current DEEWR program name.

f. The estimates for 2010-11 are based on identical breakdown of the National Institutes Program. Actual breakdown has not yet been determined for 2010-11.

g. This program has since 2004-05 been administered as part of the Marine Research program .

h. The ARC was established as an independent statutory authority on 1 July 2001 under the Australian Research Council Act (2001). The funding identified here represents administered funding only.

i. This includes $24m in 2009-10 and 2010-11 for tropical marine research facilities which are the responsibility of the Australian Institute of Marine Science.

j. Includes all supplementary funding to the Learned Academies.

k. The Systemic Infrastructure Initiative has been replaced by the National Collaborative Research Infrastructure Strategy. For an explanation on the disaggregation of the Research Infrastructure Block Grants program and the Research Training Scheme reported in this table, see notes on p.37, Portfolio Budget Statements 2008-09 - Budget Related Paper No. 1.14 - Innovation, Industry, Science & Research Portfolio.

l. This data is based on estimates of revenue forgone as published in the Taxation Expenditures Statement 2009 (TES) and earlier issues. The TES estimates, particularly in later years, are revised each year as more data come to hand. Thus, the series here will be revised in the future. The data relates to the financial year when companies undertake the activity for which they subsequently claim a concession of deduction, i.e. they are the estimated costs to revenue that would have occurred if companies had made the tax claim in the same financial year in which the expenditure was incurred. Thus, the data presented in this table are brought forward by one year with respect to that published in the TES, since the TES data series reports data in the year in which revenue is forgone by the Government (normally, the year after expenditure is undertaken by companies). This will bring the time series into alignment with (1) business expenditure on R&D as reported by the Australian Bureau of Statistics, (2) R&D expenditure data as reported by companies registered for the 125% rate, and (3) times series for R&D program data in Tables 2 and 3 above.

m. Includes the refundable and non-refundable components of the new R&D incentive.

n. The Australian Government Treasury has advised that '...the calculation of the R&D Tax Offset given in the table is the sum of the ATO's administered payments for the Offset and the calculation of the tax expenditure in the 2009 Tax Expenditure Statement produced by the Treasury. This calculation is only a proxy for the benefit provided to taxpayers by this measure rather than an exact representation. An exact calculation cannot be constructed as taxpayers future tax positions cannot be calculated at this point. The future tax positions is integral to calculating the value of deductions forgone by receiving the Offset.'

o. Pooled Development Funds (PDFs) buy shares in Australian companies and their income includes profits made on the sale of these shares and dividends on holding those shares. A PDF could make an investment but it could be several years before any tax benefits are realised. Therefore, caution should be exercised when analysing these figures with investments made by PDFs in any given year.

p. Figures as reported in the 2009 Tax Expenditure Statement, Item B53 Capital gains tax concession for carried interests paid to venture capital managers.

TABLE 5. AUSTRALIAN GOVERNMENT SUPPORT FOR SCIENCE, RESEARCH AND INNOVATION BY SOCIO-ECONOMIC OBJECTIVES a

	2001-02	2002-03	2003-04	2004-05	2005-06	2006-07	2007-08	2008-09	Estimated Actual 2009-10	Budget Estimate 2010-11	% of 2010-11 Expenditure	% of Total Government Expenditure 2010-11
Socio-Economic Objective b, c	$m	$m	$m	$m	$m	$m	$m	$m	$m	$m	%	%
01. Exploration and exploitation of the earth	296.0	299.7	318.1	331.0	354.9	388.3	422.7	438.3	547.9	447.7	5.0	0.13
02. Environment	133.2	141.2	189.0	172.8	185.1	208.6	236.4	234.9	379.6	397.8	4.5	0.12
03. Exploration and exploitation of space	7.1	4.7	13.0	5.1	4.9	4.7	6.3	7.3	76.1	69.6	0.8	0.02
04. Transport, telecommunication and other infrastructures	53.6	72.1	92.3	104.3	120.1	127.4	134.0	149.0	233.5	356.8	4.0	0.10
05. Energy	84.0	121.6	137.0	152.9	194.1	227.9	259.9	402.1	503.3	619.9	6.9	0.18
06. Industrial production and technology	1,058.6	1,089.2	1,246.7	1,234.4	1,351.1	1,480.0	1,693.3	1,649.4	1,957.7	1,868.8	20.9	0.54
07. Health	357.9	419.1	528.2	530.5	829.5	1,124.2	838.1	1,043.4	1,111.7	1,308.8	14.7	0.38
08. Agriculture	355.9	380.1	425.6	434.4	469.0	478.2	497.9	515.4	539.2	539.1	6.0	0.16
09. Education d	9.4	10.9	14.2	16.2	16.8	17.9	19.6	20.4	21.3	26.5	0.3	0.01
10. Culture, recreation, religion and mass media d	73.2	79.3	76.5	73.9	87.8	116.6	131.9	145.7	175.1	92.7	1.0	0.03

11. Political and social systems, structures and processes d	55.6	84.0	104.6	117.4	124.3	134.2	151.0	166.6	208.9	250.1	2.8	0.07
12. General advancement of knowledge: R&D financed from General University Funds (GUF)	1,443.6	1,520.8	1,606.9	1,178.0	1,360.7	1,312.0	1,344.6	1,343.7	1,352.0	1,498.3	16.8	0.43
13. General advancement of knowledge: R&D financed from other sources than GUF	406.4	432.1	579.6	526.5	518.3	550.1	496.8	559.1	793.8	947.4	10.6	0.27
14. Defence	289.7	308.2	322.0	345.3	385.4	447.4	449.8	489.7	509.7	500.0	5.6	0.14
TOTAL	4,624.4	4,962.8	5,653.7	5,222.7	6,002.1	6,617.4	6,682.2	7,165.1	8,409.8	8,923.4	100.0	2.59

Notes:

a. Table 5 represents the total Commonwealth support for science, research and innovation through the Budget and other appropriations allocated by broad socio-economic objective (SEO) categories, classified according to the Nomenclature for the Analysis of Science Budgets (NABS) 2007 SEO classification. The allocation of Budget funds corresponds to the primary intention of the funder. Hence, the allocation according to the SEO categories may vary from that reported in the R&D surveys of the Australian Bureau of Statistics (ABS).

b. The socio-economic objective (SEO) nomenclature is in accordance with the OECD's Nomenclature for the Analysis and Comparison of Scientific Programmes and Budgets (NABS) 2007 for reporting Government Budget Appropriations or Outlays on R&D (GBAORD), and reflects the recommendations of the Frascati Manual (6th edition, 2002, OECD).

c. Figures previously reported against the NABS 1992 SEO category of 'Other civil research' have been allocated across NABS 2007 categories 01-13.

d. Under the NABS 1992 SEO classification, these socio-economic objectives were combined 'Social structures and relationships'.

SELECTED CONTACTS IN THE U.S. AND AUSTRALIA

U.S. GOVERNMENT ORGANIZATIONS

EMBASSY OF THE UNITED STATES OF AMERICA

Moonah Place
Canberra ACT 2600
Tel: 61 2 6214 5600
Fax: 61 2 6214 5970
For mail from the U.S.:
American Embassy Canberra
PSC 277
APO AP 96549

The U.S. Embassy, with its subsidiary Consulates General, is responsible for all of the functions of the U.S. diplomatic mission to Australia. The Ambassador is the senior U.S. government official in Australia. Embassy Officers with primary responsibility for trade policy, trade issues, and trade promotion programs include:

* Commercial Counselor (The Senior U.S. Commercial Service Officer for Australia, who is located at the U.S. Consulate General in Sydney - send inquiries to address below, not to Embassy)
* Economics Counselor
* Agricultural Counselor
* Labor Attache
* Defense Attache

COMMERCIAL SERVICE OFFICES IN AUSTRALIA

The Foreign Commercial Service of the U.S. Department of Commerce has offices at the American Consulates General in Sydney, Melbourne, and Perth. Offices in Sydney and Melbourne are staffed by American Commercial Service Officers, who are part of the Diplomatic Mission to Australia. They manage all aspects of the trade promotion program, with an Australian staff of trade professionals.

The Foreign Commercial Service in Australia works with the U.S. Department of Commerce

District Offices throughout the United States to provide a full range of export facilitation services to U.S. business. The first point of inquiry for an American company needing Commercial Service assistance is its nearest USDOC District Office in the United States.

For general questions concerning trade policy or issues, or industry-specific inquiries:
Senior Commercial Officer for Australia
Commercial Service
U.S. Consulate General
Level 59, MLC Centre,
19-29 Martin Place
Sydney NSW 2000
Tel: 61 2 9373-9200
Fax: 61 2 9221-0573

For inquiries concerning New South Wales, Queensland:
Principal Commercial Officer
Commercial Service
U.S. Consulate General
Level 59, MLC Centre,
19-29 Martin Place
Sydney NSW 2000
Tel: 61 2 9373-9200
Fax: 61 2 9221-0573

For mail from the U.S.:
Principal Commercial Officer
Commercial Service
U.S. Consulate General, Sydney
PSC 280, Unit 11024
APO AP 96554-0002

For information regarding CS programs and services and general inquiries concerning Queensland:
General Manager
American Chamber of Commerce
Level 9, 444 Queen Street
Brisbane QLD 4000
Tel: 61 7 3221 8542
Fax: 61 7 3221 6313

For inquiries concerning Victoria, South Australia, Tasmania and the Northern Territory:
Principal Commercial Officer
Commercial Service
U.S. Consulate General
553 St. Kilda Road, 6th Floor
Melbourne VIC 3004
Tel: 61 3 9526 5900
Fax: 61 3 9510 4660

For mail from the U.S.:
Principal Commercial Officer Commercial Service
U.S. Consulate General, Melbourne
Unit 11011
APO AP 96551-0002

For inquiries concerning Western Australia:
Commercial Specialist
U.S. Consulate General
Commercial Service
16 George's Terrace, 13th Floor
Perth WA 6000
Tel: 61 8 9231 9400
Fax: 61 8 9231 9444

For mail from the U.S.:
Commercial Specialist
Commercial Service
U.S. Consulate General, Perth
APO AP 96530

WASHINGTON-BASED U.S. GOVERNMENT OFFICES DEALING WITH AUSTRALIA

U.S. DEPARTMENT OF AGRICULTURE
Foreign Agricultural Service
Foreign Agricultural Affairs
East Asia Pacific Area Office
Washington DC 20250
Tel: 202 720 2690
Fax: 202 720 6063

U.S. DEPARTMENT OF COMMERCE
Australia Desk Officer
International Trade Administration
Room 2308 HCHB
Washington DC 20230
Tel: 202 482 2471/2955
Fax: 202 482 5330

U.S. DEPARTMENT OF DEFENSE
Defense Security Assistance Agency
East Asia Pacific Division
Office of the Secretary of Defense
Room 4B740
The Pentagon
Washington DC 20301
Fax: 703 604 6541

U.S. DEPARTMENT OF STATE
East Asia Pacific/ANZ Desk
Room 4209
Washington DC 20520/6310
Tel: 703 255-5138
Fax: 202 647 4402

U.S. INFORMATION AGENCY
East Asia Desk
301 4th Street, S.W., Room 766
Washington DC 20547
Tel: 202 619 5847
Fax: 202 619 6684

MULTILATERAL DEVELOPMENT BANK OFFICE
U.S. Department of Commerce
14th and Constitution Avenue, N.W.
Room H-1107
Washington, D.C. 20007

Tel: 202 482 3399
Fax: 202 273-0927

Australia is a donor country to multilateral development banks, not a recipient. There are no MDB offices in Australia. The Australian government liaises with the MDBs through its Embassies in the cities where the banks are located: Asian Development Bank, Manila; World Bank, Washington.

TRADE INFORMATION CENTER (TIC)
Tel: 1-800-USA-TRADE (1 800 872 8723)
202 482 5455 (TPCC Secretariat)
Fax: 202 482 4473
TIC specialists provide basic export counseling and information on export services and programs offered by 19 federal agencies of the Trade Promotion Coordinating Committee (TPCC). The annual report of the TPCC, "The National Export Strategy", designates "the Trade Information Center, situated in Commerce, as the single TPCC-wide information office that will coordinate specialized non-agricultural export information offices".

AMCHAM AND BILATERAL BUSINESS COUNCILS

A. THE AMERICAN CHAMBER OF COMMERCE IN AUSTRALIA (AMCHAM)
AmCham is the premier organization supporting the U.S. - Australian business community. The Chamber has more than 1500 member companies and works very closely with the U.S. Embassy and U.S. Commercial Service in Australia. It has a full program of business information and advisory services, business community networks, business forums, etc. It represents views of the business community to both the Australian and American governments and is active in the Asia-Pacific Association of Chambers and the Asia-Pacific Cooperation Forum (APCAC). It publishes an annual directory of all members.

The American Chamber of Commerce in Australia
Suite 4, Gloucester Walk
88 Cumberland Street
Sydney NSW 2000
Tel: 61 2 9241 1907
Fax: 61 2 9251 5220
Email: nsw@amcham.com.au

B. AUSTRALIAN/AMERICAN CHAMBERS OF COMMERCE (AACC)
These organizations conduct a variety of activities ranging from trade promotion and facilitation, to information programs, to social and cultural activities, depending upon the interests of their members. They also are affiliated loosely with the Australian Embassy and the Australian Trade Commission (AUSTRADE) in the U.S. There are AACCs in the following cities: Atlanta, GA; Chicago, IL; Dallas, TX; Denver, CO; Honolulu, HI; Houston, TX; Los Angeles, CA; Minneapolis, MN; Orlando, FL; Pittsburgh, PA; St. Louis, MO; San Diego, CA; San Francisco, CA. Contact AUSTRADE for further information (see Section 4A for address).

AUSTRALIAN CHAMBERS OF COMMERCE (BY STATE)

Each Australian state has a Chamber of Commerce to promote business relations and investment, including imports and exports, in their state.

NEW SOUTH WALES
State Chamber of Commerce (NSW)
GPO Box 4280
Sydney NSW 2004
Tel: 61 2 9350 8100
Fax: 61 2 9350 8199

QUEENSLAND
Queensland Chamber of Commerce and Industry Limited
Industry House, 375 Wickham Terrace
Brisbane QLD 4000
Tel: 61 7 3831 1699
Tel: 61 7 3832 3195

VICTORIA
Victorian Employers Chamber of Commerce and Industry
50 Burwood Road
Hawthorn VIC 3122
Tel: 61 3 9251 4333
Fax: 61 3 9819 0139

SOUTH AUSTRALIA
South Australian Employers Chamber of Commerce and Industry Inc.
136 Greenhill Road
Unley SA 5061
Tel: 61 8 8300 0000
Fax: 61 8 8300 0001

TASMANIA
Tasmanian Chamber of Commerce and Industry
GPO Box 793H
Hobart TAS 7001
Tel: 61 3 6234 5933
Fax: 61 3 6231 1278

WESTERN AUSTRALIA
Chamber of Commerce and Industry of Western Australia
PO Box 6209
East Perth WA 6892

Tel: 61 8 9365 7555
Fax: 61 8 9365 7550

3. LEADING TRADE OR INDUSTRY ASSOCIATIONS
(Listed by Standard ITA Industry Codes)
Australia, like the U.S., has active trade and industry associations that have various information and industry promotion programs to assist their members.

GENERAL BUSINESS AND TRADE ASSOCIATIONS (ZEC; ZRG; ZSV)

ASEAN-Australia Business Council
PO Box E14
Queen Victoria Terrace
Canberra ACT 2600
Tel: 61 2 6273 2311
Fax: 61 2 6273 3286

Asia Pacific Business Association
PO Box A2163
Sydney South NSW 2000
Tel: 61 2 9235 1222
Fax: 61 2 9221 8109

Association of Consulting Engineers
PO Box 1002
North Sydney NSW 2059
Tel: 61 2 9922 4711
Fax: 61 2 9957 2484

Australian Business Limited of NSW
Private Bag No. 938
North Sydney NSW 2059
Tel: 61 2 9927 7500
Fax: 61 2 9923 1166

Australian Centre for American Studies
Building F18, University of Sydney
Sydney NSW 2006
Tel: 61 2 9351 4815
Fax: 61 2 9351 4817

Australian Chamber of Commerce and Industry
PO Box E14
Queen Victoria Terrace
Canberra ACT 2600
Tel: 61 2 6273 2311
Fax: 61 2 6273 3286

Australian Chamber of Manufactures
GPO Box 1469N
Melbourne VIC 3001
Tel: 61 3 9698 4111
Fax: 61 3 9699 1729

Australian Commercial Disputes Centre
Level 6, 50 Park Street
Sydney NSW 2000
Tel: 61 2 9267 1000
Fax: 61 2 9267 3125

Australian Institute of Management
PO Box 112
St. Kilda VIC 3182
Tel: 61 3 9534 8181
Fax: 61 3 9534 5050

Business Council of Australia (policy advisory group)
PO Box 7225
Melbourne VIC 3004
Tel: 61 3 9274 7777
Fax: 61 3 9274 7744

Customs Brokers Council of Australia (NSW) Inc
PO Box 31
Matraville NSW 2036
Tel: 61 2 9314 1711
Fax: 61 2 9314 2484

Institute of Patent Attorneys of Australia
1st floor, Qantas House
2-6 Railway Parade
Camberwell VIC 3124
Tel: 61 3 9882 8041
Fax: 61 3 9882 8087

Institution of Engineers, Australia
Engineering House, 11 National Circuit
Barton ACT 2600
Tel: 61 2 6270 6555
Fax: 61 2 6273 1488

Market Research Society of Australia Ltd.
PO Box 697
North Sydney NSW 2059
Tel: 61 2 9955 4830
Fax: 61 2 9955 5746

Australia Retailers Association
Level 2, 20 York Street
Sydney NSW 2000
Tel: 61 2 9290 3766
Fax: 61 2 9299 7154

Standards Australia
PO Box 1055
Strathfield NSW 2135
Tel: 61 2 9746 4700
Fax: 61 2 9746 8450

ACCOUNTING FIRMS (ACT)

Australian Society of Certified Practising Accountants
170 Queen Street

Melbourne VIC 3000
Tel: 61 3 9606 9606
Fax: 61 3 9670 8901

The Institute of Chartered Accountants in Australia
GPO Box 3921
Sydney NSW 2004
Tel: 61 2 9290 1344
Fax: 61 2 9262 1512

AGRICULTURAL MACHINERY AND EQUIPMENT (AGM)
Australian Agricultural Machinery Manufacturers Assn
GPO Box 1023
Adelaide SA 5001
Tel: 61 8 8267 4722
Fax: 61 8 8239 1329

AIRCRAFT/PARTS (AIR)
AIRPORT/GROUND SUPPORT EQPT (APG)
AVIATION SERVICES (AVS)

Association of Australian Aerospace Industries
GPO Box 817
Canberra ACT 2601
Tel: 61 2 6247 2233
Fax: 61 2 6248 6157

General Aviation Association (Australia) Inc.
Unit 2, 74 Fullarton Road
Norwood SA 5067
Tel: 61 8 8362 0488
Fax: 61 8 8362 0705

AUTOMOTIVE PARTS/SERVICE EQUIPMENT (APS)
Australian Automobile Dealers Association
PO Box E368
Queen Victoria Terrace
Barton ACT 2600
Tel: 61 2 6273 4333
Fax: 61 2 6273 2738

Australian Automotive Aftermarket Association
26 Sir John Monash Drive
Caulfield East VIC 3145
Tel: 61 3 9572 2686
Fax: 61 3 9572 2956

Auto Parts Recyclers Association of Australia (APRA)
Suite One, 235 Boundary Road
Mordialloc VIC 3195
Tel: 61 3 9587 2194
Fax: 61 3 9587 6556

BIOTECHNOLOGY (BTC)
Australian Biotechnology Association (ABA)
Suite 2, 112a Martin Street
Gardenvale VIC 3185
Tel: 61 3 9596 8879
Fax: 61 3 9596 8874

Australian Institute of Agricultural Science (AIGS)
1st Fl., 91 Rathdowne Street
Carlton VIC 3053
Tel: 61 3 9662 1077
Fax: 61 3 9662 2727

Australian Institute of Food Science & Technology
PO Box 319
Noble Park VIC 3174
Tel: 61 3 9580 6182
Fax: 61 3 9580 6933

Australian Pharmaceutical Manufacturers Association, Inc.
Level 2, 77 Berry Street
North Sydney NSW 2060
Tel: 61 2 9922 2699
Fax: 61 2 9959 4860

Australian Society for Biochemistry and Molecular Biology
c/- Biomolecular Research Institute
343 Royal Parade
Parkville VIC 3052
Tel: 61 3 9662 7299
Fax: 61 3 9662 7266

Environment Management Industry Association of Australia
GPO Box 2231
Brisbane QLD 4001
Tel: 61 7 3229 8522
Fax: 61 7 3229 8577

Medical Industry Association of Australia (MIAA)
PO Box 497
Roseville NSW 2069
Tel: 61 2 9415 1151
Fax: 61 2 9415 2130

Pharmaceutical Society of Australia
44 Thesiger Ct.
Deakin ACT 2600
Tel: 61 2 6281 1366
Fax: 61 2 6285 2869
BOOKS/PERIODICALS (BOK)

Australian Booksellers Association Inc. (ABA)
P.O. Box 1088
Carlton VIC 3053
Tel: 61 3 9663 7888

Fax: 61 3 9663 7557

BUILDING AND CONSTRUCTION (CON)
Australian Constructors Association
PO Box 289
North Sydney NSW 2059
Tel: 61 2 9955 5500
Fax: 61 2 9955 8044

Australian Earthmovers & Road Contractors Federation
74 Burwood Road
Hawthorn VIC 3122
Tel: 61 3 9819 5170
Fax: 61 3 9819 6098

Master Builders Australia Inc.
3rd Floor, 217 Northbourne Avenue
Turner ACT 2612
Tel: 61 2 6249 1433
Fax: 61 2 6249 1373
Process Engineers and Constructors Association
GPO Box 817
Canberra ACT 2601
Tel: 61 2 6247 2233
Fax: 61 2 6248 6157

CHEMICAL PRODUCTION MACHINERY (CHM)

CHEMICALS, INDUSTRIAL (ICH)

Chemical Advisory Service
PO Box 38
Vermont VIC 3133
Tel: 61 3 9335 3208
Fax: 61 3 9335 1750

Plastics and Chemicals Industries Association (PACIA)
GPO Box 1610M
Melbourne VIC 3001
Tel: 61 3 9699 6299
Fax: 61 3 9699 6717

COMPUTERS/PERIPHERALS (CPT)

COMPUTER SOFTWARE (CSF)
COMPUTER SERVICES (CSV)

Australian Computer Society
Ste 1, 200 Riley Street
Darlinghurst NSW 2010
Tel: 61 2 9211 5855
Fax: 61 2 9281 1208

Australian Information Industry Association (AIIA)
12 Campion Street
Deakin ACT 2600
Tel: 61 6 282 4700
Fax: 61 6 285 1408

Australian Internet Industry Association
PO Box 74
Red Hill ACT 2603
Tel: 61 2 6232 6900
Fax: 61 2 6232 6513
email: peterc@iia.net.au

Australian Interactive Multimedia Industry Association (AIMIA)
PO Box N657
Grosvenor Place NSW 1220
Tel: 61 2 9338 0570
Fax: 61 2 9338 1534
email:director@aimia.com.au

Australian Visual Software Distributors Association (AVSDA)
Level 3/160 Rowe Street
Eastwood NSW 2122
Tel: 61 2 9874 9700
Fax: 61 2 9874 9205

(Association represents wholesalers of interactive games and deals with issues such as protection from illegal parallel imports etc.)

DEFENSE INDUSTRY EQUIPMENT (DFN)

Defence Manufacturers Council
GPO Box 817
Canberra ACT 2601
Tel: 61 2 6247 2233
Fax: 61 2 6248 6157

DIRECT MARKETING (DIR)

Australian Direct Marketing Institute
PO Box 464
Kings Cross NSW 2011
Tel: 61 2 9368 0366
Fax: 61 2 9368 0866

EDUCATION/TRAINING (EDS)

Australian Association of Adult & Community Education (AAACE)
PO Box 308
Jamison Centre ACT 2614
Tel: 61 2 6251 7933
Fax: 61 2 6251 7935

Australian Institute of Training & Development (AITD)
PO Box 5452
West Chatswood NSW 2057
Tel: 61 2 9419 4966
Fax: 61 2 9419 4142

Australian National Training Association (ANTA)
GPO Box 3120
Brisbane QLD 400
1 Tel: 61 7 3246 2300
Fax: 61 7 3246 2490

ELECTRICAL POWER SYSTEMS (ELP)

Electricity Industry Ombudsman
GPO Box 469D
Melbourne Victoria 3001
Tel: 61 3 9649 7599
Fax: 61 3 9649 7588

Electricity Supply Association of Australia
Lvl 11, 74 Castlereagh Street
Sydney New South Wales 2000
Tel: 61 2 9233 7222
Fax: 61 2 9233 7244

Office of the Regulator-General, Victoria
Lvl 1 , 35 Spring Street
Melbourne Victoria 3000
Tel: 61 3 9651 0201
Fax: 61 3 9651 3688

Primary Industries and Energy, Department
Core 3, Wing 3, level
Edmund Barton Building
Barton ACT 2600
Tel: 61 2 6272 4492
Fax: 61 2 6271 6612

Sustainable Energy Development Authority
Lvl 6, 45 Clarence Street
Sydney New South Wales 2000
Tel: 61 2 9291 5260
Fax: 61 2 9299 1519

ELECTRONICS (EIP)

Australian Electrical and Electronic Manufacturers Assn
GPO Box 1966
Canberra City ACT 2601
Tel: 61 2 6247 4655
Fax: 61 2 6247 9840

FILM, VIDEOS/OTHER REC. (FLM)

Audio-Visual Copyright Society
PO Box 1248
Neutral Bay NSW 2089
Tel: 61 2 9904 0133
Fax: 61 2 9904 0498

Australian Copyright Council
245 Chalmers Street
Redfern NSW 2016
Tel: 61 2 9318 1788
Fax: 61 2 9698 3536

Australian Council of Film Societies
20 Craithie Avenue
Park Orchards VIC 3114
Tel: 61 3 9876 1128
Fax: 61 3 9808 4714

Australian Film Institute
49 Eastern Road
South Melbourne VIC 3205
Tel: 61 3 9696 1844
Fax: 61 3 9696 7972
Email: afi@vicnet.net.au

Australian Performing Rights Association (APRA)
Locked Bag 3665
St.Leonards NSW 2065
Tel: 61 2 9935 7900
Fax: 61 2 9935 7999
Email: apra@apra.com.au

Australian Record Industry Association (ARIA)
8th Floor, 263 Clarence Street
Sydney NSW 2000
Tel: 61 2 9267 7996
Fax: 61 2 9267 7962
Australian Visual Software Distributors Association (AVSDA)
Level 3/160 Rowe Street
Eastwood NSW 2122
Tel: 61 2 9874 9700
Fax: 61 2 9874 9205

FINANCIAL SERVICES (FNS)

AMBA Credit Services Pty. Ltd.
1 Box Road
Caringbah NSW 2229
Tel: 61 2 9525 3011
Fax: 61 2 9525 8005

Australian Bankers' Association
42nd Floor, 55 Collins Street
Melbourne VIC 3000
Tel: 61 3 9654 5422
Fax: 61 3 9650 1756

Australian Securities Commission (ASC) Business Centre
GPO Box 4866
Sydney, NSW 2000
Tel: 61 2 9911 2000
Fax: 61 2 9911 2030

Dun & Bradstreet (Australia) Pty. Ltd.
19 Havillah Street
Chatswood NSW 2067
Tel: 61 2 9935 2600
Fax: 61 2 9935 2666

Securities Institute of Australia
Level 33, Tower Building, Australia Square
Sydney NSW 2000
Tel: 61 2 9251 6799
Fax: 61 2 9251 6287

FOOD PROCESSING/PACKAGING EQUIPMENT (FPP)

FOODS, PROCESSED (FOD)

Agri-Food Council Secretariat
GPO Box 9839
Department of Industry, Science & Technology
Canberra ACT 2601
Tel: 61 2 6276 1086
Fax: 61 2 6276 2203

Australian Institute of Food Science & Technology (AIFST)
Box 5, Shop 4
James Cook Drive
Kings Langley NSW 2147
Tel: 61 2 9837 1262
Fax: 61 2 9837 3639

Council of Australian Food Technology Association Inc.
12th Floor, The Denison
65 Berry Street
North Sydney NSW 2060
Tel: 61 2 9963 7670
Fax: 61 2 9923 1166

CSIRO Food Science Australia
PO Box 52
North Ryde, NSW 1670
Tel: 61 2 9490 8333
Fax: 61 2 9490 8499

Food and Beverage Importers Association
181 Drummond Street
Carlton VIC 3053
Tel: 61 3 9639 0444
Fax: 61 3 9639 0638

Food Industry Council of Australia (FICA)
PO Box E14, Queen Victoria Terrace
Canberra ACT 2600
Tel: 61 2 6273 2311
Fax: 61 2 6273 3286

Packaging Council of Australia Inc.
GPO Box 1469 N
Melbourne VIC 3001
Tel: 61 3 9698 4278/9
Fax: 61 3 9690 3514

FRANCHISING (FRA)

Franchise Council of Australia Ltd (FCA)
(Formerly FAANZ)
PO Box Q841, QVB Post Office
Sydney NSW 1230
Tel: 61 2 9264 4077
Fax: 61 2 9264 4966

HEALTH CARE SERVICES (HCS)

Australian Institute of Health & Welfare (AIHW)
GPO Box 570
Canberra ACT 2601
Tel: 61 2 6244 1000
Fax: 61 2 6244 1299

Australian Private Hospitals Association
Suite 1, 25 Napier Close
Deakin, ACT 2600
Tel: 61 2 6285 2716
Fax: 61 2 6285 2243
Internet: http://www.apha.org.au
Email: george.neale@apha.org.au

Australian Dental Industry Association
PO Box 536
Strawberry Hills, NSW 2012
Tel: 61 2 9319 5631
Fax: 61 2 9319 5381

INFORMATION SERVICES (INF)

Australian Information Industry Association (AIIA)
PO Box 246
Deakin West ACT 2600
Tel: 61 2 6282 4700

Fax: 61 2 6285 1408

Australian Information Technology Society
PO Box R590
Royal Exchange NSW 2000
Tel: 61 2 9211 9522
Fax: 61 2 9211 6589 I

INVESTMENT SERVICES (INV)

Investment & Financial Services Association
Level 24, 44 Market Street
Sydney NSW 2000
Tel: 61 2 9229 3022
Fax: 61 2 9229 3198
JEWELRY (JLR)

Jewellers Association of Australia (JAA)
PO Box 282
Deakin West ACT 2600
Tel: 61 2 6282 3211
Fax: 61 2 6282 2725

MACHINE TOOLS/METALWORKING EQUIPMENT (MTL)
Metal Trades Industry Association of Australia (MTIA)
PO Box 289
North Sydney NSW 2059
Tel: 61 2 9466 5566
Fax: 61 2 9466 5599

MATERIALS HANDLING MACHINERY (MHM)

Australian Institute of Material Management
PO Box 192
Salisbury, QLD 4107
Tel: 61 7 3241 1800
Fax: 61 7 3274 3670

MEDICAL EQUIPMENT (MED)

Medical Industry Association of Australia (MIAA)
PO Box 497
Roseville NSW 2069
Tel: 61 2 9415 1151
Fax: 61 2 9415 2130

MINING INDUSTRY EQUIPMENT (MIN)
Minerals Council of Australia
PO Box 363
Dickson ACT 2602
Tel: 61 2 6279 3600
Fax: 61 2 6279 3699

OIL & GAS FIELD MACHINERY (OGM)

OIL, GAS, MINERAL PRODUCTION/EXPLORATION SERVICES (OGS)
The Australian Gas Association
3rd Fl. Gas Industry House
7 Moore Street
Canberra ACT 2601
Tel: 61 2 6247 3955
Fax: 61 2 6249 7402
Email: Canberra@ausgas.asn.au

PACKAGING EQUIPMENT (PKG)
Packaging Council of Australia
PO Box 1469 N
Melbourne VIC 3001
Tel: 61 3 9698 4278/9
Fax: 61 3 9690 3514

PLASTIC MATERIALS/RESINS (PMR)
PLASTICS PRODUCTION MACHINERY (PME)

Plastics and Chemicals Industries Association (PACIA)
GPO Box 1610M
Melbourne VIC 3001
Tel: 61 3 9699 6299
Fax: 61 3 9699 6717

PRINTING/GRAPHIC ARTS EQUIPMENT (PGA)
Graphic Arts Services Association of Australia (GASAA)
77 Lithgow Street
St Leonards NSW 2065
Tel: 61 2 9372 1249
Fax: 61 2 9372 1289

Printing Industries Association of Australia
77 Lithgow Street
St Leonards NSW 2065
Tel: 61 2 9372 1222
Fax: 61 2 9372 1288

PROCESS CONTROL INSTRUMENTATION (PCI)
Institute of Instrumentation and Control Australia, Inc
P O Box 82
Balwyn Victoria 3103
Tel: 61 3 9816 3333
Fax: 61 3 9857 5057

SECURITY/SAFETY EQUIPMENT (SEC)
Australian Security Industry Association Limited (ASIAL)
PO Box 1338
Crows Nest NSW 2065

Tel: 61 2 9906 4780
Fax: 61 2 9906 4202

TELECOMMUNICATIONS EQUIPMENT (TEL)

TELECOMMUNICATION SERVICES (TES)
Australasian Teleconferencing Association Inc. (ATA)
PO Box 3151
South Brisbane QLD 4101
Tel/Fax: 61 7 3300 9077

Australian Telecommunications Users Group (ATUG)
PO Box 357
Milsons Point NSW 2061
Tel: 61 2 9957 1333
Fax: 61 2 9925 0880

TEXTILES, CLOTHING AND FOOTWEAR (TXP)

Council of Textiles and Fashion Industries of Australia Limited
GPO Box 1469N
Melbourne VIC 3001
Tel: 61 3 9698 4460
Fax: 61 3 9698 4459

TRAVEL AND TOURISM SERVICES (TRA)

Australian Federation of Travel Agents
Level 3, 309 Pitt Street
Sydney NSW 2000
Tel: 61 2 9264-3299
Fax: 61 2 9264-1085

Australian Tourist Commission
Level 4, 80 William Street
Sydney NSW 2000
Tel: 61 2 9360-1111
Fax: 61 2 9331-6469

Tourism Training Australia
Level 5, 362 Kent Street
Sydney NSW 2000
Tel: 61 2 9290-1055
Fax: 61 2 9290-1011

Tourism Council Australia
Level 3, Tourism House
40 Blackall Street
Barton ACT 2600
Tel: 61 2 6273-1000
Fax: 61 2 6273-4999

Tourism Task Force
Level 9, Westfield Towers
100 William Street
Sydney NSW 2000
Tel: 61 2 9368-1500
Fax: 61 2 9368-0933

Visit USA Committee Australia
PO Box 466
Milsons Point NSW 2061
Tel: 61 2 9954-6040
Fax: 61 2 9955-6042

WATER RESOURCES EQUIPMENT/SERVICES (WRE)

Australian Water & Wastewater Association
PO Box 388
Artarmon NSW 1570
Tel: 61 2 9413 1288
Fax: 61 2 9413 1047

International Association on Water Quality
Australian National Committee
PO Box 388
Artarmon NSW 1570
Tel: 61 2 9413 1288
Fax: 61 2 9413 1047

AUSTRALIAN GOVERNMENT AGENCIES

A. AUSTRALIAN GOVERNMENT OFFICES IN THE UNITED STATES
The Embassy of Australia is responsible for all diplomatic relations between Australia and the United States. Australian Consulates General are located in various U.S. cities and have representational, trade and consular functions.

The Australian Trade Commission (AUSTRADE) is responsible for trade and investment promotion and has offices in the Australian Embassy in Washington, D.C. and at the Australian Consulates General in Los Angeles, San Francisco, Atlanta, Houston, and New York.

Embassy of Australia
1601 Massachusetts Avenue NW
Washington DC 20036
Tel: 202 797 3000
Fax: 202 797 3168
Senior Trade Commissioner

AUSTRADE
c/o Embassy of Australia (as above)
Senior Customs Representative
Embassy of Australia (as above)
Australian Tourist Commission
2049 Century Park East
Suite 1920
Los Angeles CA 90067

Tel: 310 229 4870
Fax: 310 552 1215

KEY AUSTRALIAN FEDERAL GOVERNMENT AGENCIES

Air Services Australia
GPO Box 367
Canberra ACT 2601
Tel: 61 2 6268 4111
Fax: 61 2 6268 5683

Anti-Dumping Authority
20 Allara Street
Canberra City, ACT 2601
Tel: 61 2 6213 6760
Fax: 61 2 6213 6761

AUSTEL (Telecommunications Regulatory Authority)
PO Box 7443
St. Kilda Road
Melbourne VIC 3004
Tel: 61 3 9828 7300
Fax: 61 3 9820 3021

Australian Communications Authority
Purple Building, Benjamin Offices
Chan Street
Belconnen ACT 2617
Tel: 61 2 6256 5555
Fax: 61 2 6256 5566

Australian Competition & Consumer Commission
470 Northbourne Ave
Dickson ACT 2062
Tel: 61 2 6243 1111
Fax: 61 2 6243 1199

Broadcasting Authority, Australian
Level 15, Darling Park
201 Sussex Street
Sydney NSW 2000
Tel: 61 2 9334 7700
Fax: 61 2 9334 7799

Building Codes Board, Australian
20 Allara Street
Canberra ACT 2601
Tel: 61 2 6213 7191
Fax: 61 2 6213 7287

Bureau of Statistics, Australian
PO Box 10
Belconnen ACT 2616
Tel: 61 2 6252 5000
Fax: 61 2 6251 6009

Communications and the Arts, Department of Film and Licensed Broadcasting
GPO Box 2154
Canberra City ACT 2601
Tel: 61 2 6279 1644
Fax: 61 2 6279 1717
Communication and the Arts, Department of Spectrum Management Agency (Radiofrequency Spectrum)
PO Box 78
Belconnen ACT 2616
Tel: 61 2 6256 5555
Fax: 61 2 6256 5200

Communications and the Arts, Department of Telecommunications Industry Division
GPO Box 2154
Canberra City ACT 2601
Tel: 61 2 6279 1894
Fax: 61 2 6279 1890

Construction Forecasting Committee
Department of Industry, Science and Tourism
PO Box 9839
Canberra ACT 2601
Tel: 61 2 6213 6000
Fax: 61 2 6213 7000

Customs Service, Australian
Customs House
5 Constitution Avenue
Canberra City, ACT 2600
Tel: 61 2 6275 6666
Fax: 61 2 6275 6796
Sydney ...... Fax: 61 2 9213 4000 Melbourne ... Fax: 61 3 9244 8220 Brisbane .... Fax: 61 7 3835 3499 Perth .... Fax: 61 8 9430 1771 Adelaide .... Fax: 61 8 8847 9206 Tasmania .... Fax: 61 02 6230 1264 Defence, Department of
Russell Offices

Canberra ACT 2600
Tel: 61 2 6265 9111
Fax: 61 2 6265 2375

Foreign Affairs and Trade, Department of
R G Casey Building
John McEwen Cres.
Barton ACT 2600
Tel: 61 2 6261 9111
Fax: 61 2 6261 3111

Foreign Investment Review Board (FIRB)
c/o Department of the Treasury
Parkes Place
Parkes ACT 2600
Tel: 61 2 6263 3755
Fax: 61 2 6263 2940

Health and Medical Research Council, National
GPO Box 9848
Canberra ACT 2601
Tel: 61 2 6289 7019
Fax: 61 2 6282 8776

Immigration and Multicultural Affairs, Department of
PO Box 25
Belconnen ACT 2616
Tel: 61 2 6264 1111
Fax: 61 2 6264 2670

Industrial Property Organization, Australian
PO Box 200
Woden ACT 2606
Tel: 61 2 6283 2211
Fax: 61 2 6281 1841

Industrial Supplies Office
GPO Box 277
Canberra ACT 2600
Tel: 61 2 6257 1881
Fax: 61 2 6247 0028

Industry, Science and Technology, Department of
51 Allara Street
Canberra ACT 2601
Tel: 61 2 6276 1000
Fax: 61 2 6276 1111

Primary Industries and Energy, Department of
GPO Box 858
Canberra ACT 2601
Tel: 61 2 6272 3933
Fax: 61 2 6272 5161

Quarantine & Inspection Service, Australian
GPO Box 858
Canberra ACT 2601
Tel: 61 2 6272 5455
Fax: 61 2 6272 5753

Steel River Project
PO Box 196B
Newcastle, NSW 2300
Tel: 61 2 4940 7153
Fax: 61 2 4940 7154

Taxation Office, Australian
PO Box 900
Civic Square ACT 2608
Tel: 61 2 6216 1111
Fax: 61 2 6216 2830

Trade Development Zone Authority
PMB 88
Winnellie NT 0821
Tel: 61 8 8947 0133
Fax: 61 8 8984 3417

Transport, Department of
PO Box 594
Canberra City ACT 2601
Tel: 61 2 6274 7111
Fax: 61 2 6257 2505

Treasury, Department of the Parkes Place
Parkes ACT 2600
Tel: 61 2 6263 2111
Fax: 61 2 6273 2614

AUSTRALIAN STATE ECONOMIC DEVELOPMENT AGENCIES

Each Australian state has its own office that provides information on business location, communications and infrastructure, privatization, major projects, work force and skills base, regulations, planning and approval processes, and potential joint-venture opportunities and partners. These offices actively promote foreign investment into their individual states. They have a great deal of information available and offer a variety of business promotion services to corporations interested in establishing a business presence in their state.

AUSTRALIAN CAPITAL TERRITORY
Business Employment and Tourism Bureau
Chief Minister's Department, Warren Dixon
PO Box 1000
Civic Square ACT 2608
Tel: 61 2 6205 0667

Fax: 61 2 6205 0577

NEW SOUTH WALES
Department of State and Regional Development
Level 44, Grosvenor Place
225 George Street

Sydney NSW 2000
Tel: 61 2 9338 6600
Fax: 61 2 9338 6728

NSW Trade and Investment Centre
GPO Box N818
Sydney NSW 1220
Tel: 61 2 9338 6900
Fax: 61 2 9338 6950

Sydney Olympics
NSW Department of Sport Recreation and Racing
PO Box 422
North Sydney NSW 2059
Tel: 61 2 9923 4234
Fax: 61 2 9923 4345

Olympic Coordination Authority
36th F.Governor Mcquarie Tower
1 Farrer Pl.Sydney NSW 2000
Tel: 61 2 9228 3333
Fax: 61 2 9228 5551

Sydney Organizing Committee for the Olympic Games GPO Box 2000
Sydney NSW 2004
Tel: 61 2 9297 2000
Fax: 61 2 9297 2020
Sydney Paralympic Organizing Committee
GPO Box 2000
Sydney NSW 2004
Tel: 61 2 9297 2000
Fax: 61 2 9297 2020

NORTHERN TERRITORY
Department of Industries and Development
GPO Box 4160
Darwin NT 0801
Tel: 61 8 8999 5210
Fax: 61 8 8999 5333

QUEENSLAND
Department of Business, Industry and Regional Development GPO Box 1141
Brisbane QLD 4001
Tel: 61 7 3224 2216
Fax: 61 7 3224 8411

SOUTH AUSTRALIA
Department of Manufacturing Industry, Small Business and Regional Development (MISBARD)
GPO Box 1264 Adelaide SA 5001
Tel: 61 8 8303 2402
Fax: 61 8 8303 2404

TASMANIA
Tasmanian Development and Resources Authority
GPO Box 646
Hobart TAS 7001
Tel: 61 3 6233 5888
Fax: 61 3 6233 5800

VICTORIA
Department of Business and Employment
55 Collins Street, 9th Floor
Melbourne VIC 3000

Tel: 61 3 9651 9999
Fax: 61 3 9651 9770
WESTERN AUSTRALIA

Department of Commerce and Trade
PO Box 7234
Cloisters Square
Perth WA 6850
Tel: 61 8 9327 5666
Fax: 61 8 9327 5481

COMMERCIAL BANKS IN AUSTRALIA

A. AUSTRALIAN BANKS

Advance Bank Australia Limited
PO Box R221, Royal Exchange
Sydney NSW 2000
Tel: 61 2 9964 5000
Fax: 61 2 9236 1999

Australia and New Zealand Banking Group Limited
GPO Box 537E
Melbourne VIC 3001
Tel: 61 3 9273 5555
Fax: 61 3 9273 6142

Bank of Western Australia t/a BankWest
Level 47, BankWest Tower
108 St. Georges Terrace
Perth WA 6000
Tel: 61 8 9449 7000
Fax: 61 8 9449 7050

Commonwealth Bank of Australia

GPO Box 2719
Sydney NSW 2004
Tel: 61 2 9227 7111
Fax: 61 2 9378 4993

National Australia Bank Limited

GPO Box 84A
Melbourne VIC 3001
Tel: 61 3 9641 3500
Fax: 61 3 9641 4916

Westpac Banking Corporation GPO

Box 1 Sydney NSW 2004

Tel: 61 2 9226 3311

Fax: 61 2 9226 4128

AMERICAN BANKS

Bank of America NT & SA - Australia GPO Box 490 Sydney NSW 2004 Tel: 61 2 9931 4200 Fax: 61 2 9221 1023

Bankers Trust Australia Limited PO Box H4 Australia Square Sydney NSW 2000 Tel: 61 2 9259 3555 Fax: 61 2 9259 9800 CS

First Boston Australia Securities Limited Level 31 - Gateway 1 Macquarie Place Sydney NSW 2000 Tel: 61 2 9394 4400 Fax: 61 2 9394 4382

The Chase Manhattan Bank Australia Limited GPO Box 9816 Sydney NSW 2004 Tel: 61 2 9250 4111 Fax: 61 2 9250 4554

Citibank Limited GPO Box 40 Sydney NSW 2004 Tel: 61 2 9239 9100 Fax: 61 2 9239 5856

First Chicago NBD GPO Box N684 Grosvenor Place Sydney NSW 2000 Tel: 61 2 9250 2100 Fax: 61 2 9223 1823

Merrill Lynch International (Australia) Limited Level 49, MLC Centre 19-29 Martin Place Sydney NSW 2000 Tel: 61 2 9225 6500 Fax: 61 2 9225 6655

Morgan Guaranty Trust Company of New York
GPO Box 5248
Sydney NSW 2004
Tel: 61 2 9551 6100
Fax: 61 2 9551 6353

State Street Bank and Trust Company
PO Box 7035
GPO Sydney NSW 2000
Tel: 61 2 9323 6500
Fax: 61 2 9323 6540

NEWSPAPERS

AUSTRALIAN CAPITAL TERRITORY
The Canberra Times
Federal Capital Press of Australia
PO Box 7155
Canberra Mail Centre ACT 2610
Tel: 61 2 6280 2122
Fax: 61 2 6280 4884
INTERNET http://www.canberratimes.com.au

NEW SOUTH WALES
The Australian (national focus)
News Ltd. GPO Box 4245
Sydney NSW 2004
Tel: 61 2 9288 3000
Fax: 61 2 9288 2300
INTERNET http://www.australian.aust.com

The Australian Financial Review (national focus)
John Fairfax Group Ltd.
GPO Box 506
Sydney NSW 2004
Tel: 61 2 9282 2833
Fax: 61 2 9282 3027
INTERNET http://www.afr.com.au/

The Sydney Morning Herald
John Fairfax Group Ltd.
GPO Box 506
Sydney NSW 2004
Tel: 61 2 9282 2833
Fax: 61 2 9282 3027

INTERNET http://www.smh.com.au/

NORTHERN TERRITORY
Northern Territory News
News Ltd.
GPO Box 1300
Darwin NT 0801
Tel: 61 8 8944 9900
Fax: 61 8 8981 6045

QUEENSLAND

The Courier Mail
Queensland Newspapers Ltd.
GPO Box 130
Brisbane QLD 4001
Tel: 61 7 3252 6011
Fax: 61 7 3252 6696

SOUTH AUSTRALIA
The Adelaide Advertiser
Advertiser Newspaper Ltd.
121 King William Street
Adelaide SA 5000
Tel: 61 8 8206 2000
Fax: 61 8 8206 3622

VICTORIA
The Age
PO Box 257C
GPO Melbourne VIC 3001
Tel: 61 3 9600 4211
Fax: 61 3 9601 2327
INTERNET http://www.theage.com.au/

WESTERN AUSTRALIA
The West Australian
WA Newspapers Ltd.
GPO Box D162
Perth WA 6001
Tel: 61 8 9482 3111
Fax: 61 8 9482 3177

TASMANIA
The Mercury
GPO Box 334D
Hobart TAS 7001
Tel: 61 3 6230 0622
Fax: 61 3 6230 0766

NATIONAL PERIODICALS

Business Review Weekly
BRW Media
GPO Box 55A
Melbourne Vic 3001
Tel: 61 3 9603 3888
Fax: 61 3 9670 4328
INTERNET http://www.brw.com.au/

The Bulletin with Newsweek
ACP Publishing Pty. Limited
4th Floor, 54 Park Street
Sydney NSW 2000

Tel: 61 2 9282 8000
Fax: 61 2 9267 2150

The Business Bulletin
National Business Magazines Pty. Ltd.
PO Box 687
Darlinghurst NSW 2010
Tel: 61 2 9212 5588
Fax: 61 2 9212 3709

The Land Newspaper (Agriculture/Country Life focus)
Rural Press Limited
159 Bells Line of Road
North Richmond NSW 2754
Tel: 61 2 4570 4444
Fax: 61 2 4570 4650

BUSINESS DIRECTORIES

Brylar's Australia on Disc
Dependable Database Data
Level 6, 192 Pitt Street
Sydney NSW 2000
Tel: 61 2 9261 8560
Fax: 61 2 9261 8511

The Business Who's Who of Australia
Riddell Information Services Pty. Ltd.
A Dun & Bradstreet company
PO Box 204
Chatswood NSW 2057
Tel: 61 2 9935 2600
Fax: 61 2 9935 2777
Available in CD-ROM or hard copy.
Annual

Directory of Australian Associations
Information Australia
75 Flinders Lane
Melbourne VIC 3000
Tel: 61 3 9654 2800
Fax: 61 3 9639 1548
Quarterly
Kompass
APN Business Publishing Pty. Ltd.
PO Box 172
Prahran VIC 3181
Tel: 61 3 9245 7777
Fax: 61 3 9245 7840
Available in CD-ROM or hard copy
Annual

National Guide to Government
Information Australia
75 Flinders Lane
Melbourne VIC 3000
Tel: 61 3 9654 2800
Fax: 61 3 9639 1548
Quarterly

MARKET RESEARCH MATERIALS

1. INDUSTRY SECTOR MARKET RESEARCH

A. INDUSTRY SUBSECTOR ANALYSES (ISAS) COMPLETED IN FY 1998:
APP CLOTHING, TEXTILE AND FOOTWARE
APS AUTOMOTIVE INDUSTRY
BLD BUILDING PRODUCTS (HARDWARE)
CSV COMPUTER CONSULTING SERVICES
CPT COMPUTERS AND PERIPHERALS (MULTIMEDIA)
DFN DEFENSE INDUSTRY EQUIPMENT (ELECTRONIC WARFARE)
FLM MEDIA (FILM INDUSTRY)
FPP DAIRY PROCESSING EQUIPMENT
HTL HOTEL AND RESTAURANT EQUIPMENT
ICH INDUSTRIAL CHEMICALS
MED MEDICAL EQUIPMENT
MIN MINING EQUIPMENT
PCI PROCESS CONTROL INSTRUMENTATION (FOCUS ON OIL & GAS INDUSTRY)
TEL TELECOMMUNICATIONS SERVICES

B. INDUSTRY SUBSECTOR ANALYSES (ISAS) SCHEDULED FOR FY 1999:
AIR GLOBAL POSITIONING SYSTEMS EQUIPMENT
APS AUTOMOTIVE PART AFTERMARKET
CPT NETWORKING EQUIPMENT
CSF ENTERPRISE RESOURCE PLANNING SOFTWARE
ELP ENERGY EFFICIENCY SERVICES
FRA FRANCHISING
LAB SCIENTIFIC AND LABORATORY EQUIPMENT
OGM GAS TRANSMISSION MACHINERY (COMPRESSORS)
OGM OIL AND GAS FIELD EQUIPMENT
PGA PRINTING MACHINES
POL ENVIRONMENTAL: POLLUTION CONTROL EQUIPMENT
RRE RAILWAY EQUIPMENT
SEC POLICE EQUIPMENT: SPECIAL OPERATIONS
SPT SPORTING GOODS
TEL TELECOMMUNICATIONS EQUIPMENT: CALL CENTER EQUIPMENT
TXF TEXTILE FABRICS

2. U.S. DEPARTMENT OF AGRICULTURE/FOREIGN AGRICULTURAL SERVICE COMMODITY REPORTS AND MARKET BRIEFS AGRICULTURAL COMMODITY REPORTS (FY99)

JANUARY Fresh Deciduous Fruit - annual
Kiwifruit - annual
FEBRUARY Livestock - semi-annual
Tree Nuts - annual
MARCH Grain and Feed - annual
Canned Deciduous Fruit - annual
APRIL Sugar - annual
Dried Fruit - annual
MAY Citrus - annual
Tobacco - annual
Dairy - semi-annual
JUNE Cotton - annual
Wine Competition - annual
AUGUST Livestock - annual
Poultry - annual
SEPTEMBER Fresh Deciduous Fruit - semi-annual
Canned Deciduous Fruit - semi-annual
Agricultural Situation - annual
OCTOBER Sugar - semi-annual
Dried Fruit - semi-annual
Forest Products - annual
Dairy - annual

AUSTRALIA TRADE EVENTS

ACCESS AUSTRALIA - BUILDING PRODUCTS
Location: Sydney, NSW
Aimed at assisting U.S. manufacturers of building products identify potential importers, agents, distributors and direct sales partners in Australia.
Organizer: U.S. Department of Commerce, contact Patricia Matt, USFCS, Sydney
Tel: 61 2 9373 9211
Fax: 61 2 9221 0573

ACCESS AUSTRALIA - INTERNET
Location: Sydney, NSW
Aimed at assisting U.S. developers of I-centric software and hardware identify potential importers, agents, distributors and direct sales partners in Australia.
Organizer: U.S. Department of Commerce, contact Duncan Archibald, USFCS, Sydney
Tel: 61 2 9373 9212
Fax: 61 2 9221 0573

ACCESS AUSTRALIA - RAILWAY EQUIPMENT
Location: Sydney, NSW
Aimed at assisting U.S. manufacturers of railway equipment identify potential importers, agents, distributors and joint venture partners in Australia.
Organizer: U.S. Department of Commerce, contact John Kanawati, USFCS, Sydney
Tel: 61 2 9373 9207
Fax: 61 2 9221 0573

MAJOR AUSTRALIAN EXHIBITIONS (by Industry Sector):
AGRICULTURE (AGM)
Location: Gunnedah, Gunnedah Field Day Site, NSW Exhibition features the latest in farm equipment and technology.
Frequency: Annual
Exhibition Organizer: BAL Marketing
Tel: 61 2 6762 2399
Fax: 61 2 6762 2350

HENTY MACHINERY FIELD DAYS 1999
Location: Henty Field Day Site, NSW
Exhibition features the latest in farm equipment

and technology.
Frequency: Annual
Exhibition Organizer: Henty Machinery Field Days
Tel: 61 2 6929 3305
Fax: 61 2 6929 3180

AEROSPACE (AIR)
AUSTRALIAN INTERNATIONAL AIR SHOW AND AEROSPACE EXPO
Location: Avalon Airport, Melbourne, VIC
Australia's premier air show. Aerospace, defense and technology for the Asia Pacific.
Frequency: Every two years
For information on USDOC Product Literature Center contact:
E. McDonald Tel: 202 482 1237
Phil Keeling, USFCS, Sydney
Tel: 61 2 9373 9209
Fax: 61 2 9221 0573
email: osydney@cs.doc.gov
Exhibition Organizer: Airshows Downunder
Tel: 61 3 5282 4400
Fax: 61 3 5282 4455
email: expo@airshow.net.au
USA contact: Global Tradeshow Services
Tel: 602 671 3919
Fax: 602 671 3922

AVIEX '98
Location: Bankstown Airport, Sydney, NSW
Inaugural general aviation show. Includes defense.
Exhibition Organizer: Aviex Pty Ltd
Tel: 61 2 9791 1174
Fax: 61 2 9791 1073

AUTOMOTIVE PARTS & ACCESSORIES (APS)
23RD AUSTRALIAN AUTOMOTIVE TRADE FAIR
Location: Sydney Exhibition Centre, Darling Harbour, NSW Trade Exhibition featuring all aspects of automotive products, including aftermarket parts and accessories, chemicals, workshop machinery and equipment and crash repair products.
Frequency: Annual (alternating between Melbourne and Sydney)
For information on USDOC Product Literature Center contact:
Bruno Mascitelli, USFCS, Melbourne Tel: 61 3 9526 5927

Fax: 61 3 9510 4660
email: omelbourne@cs.doc.gov
Exhibition Organizer: Trade Fair Australia
Tel: 61 2 9357 7022
Fax: 61 2 9356 3834

AUSTRALIAN TYRE DEALERS AND RETREADERS ASSOCIATION
Location: Adelaide Convention Centre, SA
Conference, also featuring a small trade exhibition for tires and related products.
Frequency: Annual
Exhibition Organizer: MTA-Q
Tel: 61 7 3844 7555
Fax: 61 7 3255 0213

BOOKS (BOK) AUSTRALIAN BOOK FAIR 1999
Location: Sydney Convention and Exhibition Centre, NSW Books, book publishing
Frequency: Annual
Exhibition Organizer: Expertise Events Pty. Ltd.
Tel: 61 2 9977Ð0888
Fax: 61 2 9977Ð0336

COMPUTERS/PERIPHERALS/SOFTWARE SERVCES (CPT,CSF) PC IT '99
The PC Show, held annually in three cities (Sydney, Melbourne and Brisbane), is one of the biggest computer events in Australia, displaying every facet of the personal computing field.
Exhibition Organizer: Australian Exhibition Services Pty Ltd,
Illoura Plaza, 424 St. Kilda Road,
Melbourne VIC 3004
Tel: 61 3 9867 4500
Fax: 61 3 9867 7981

Sydney, NSW
Location: Sydney Convention & Exhibition Centre, Darling Harbour
Brisbane, QLD
Date: May 11-13, 1999
Location: Brisbane Convention & Exhibition Centre
Melbourne, VIC
Date: Aug 31-Sept 3, 1999
Location: Melbourne Exhibition Centre

THE HOME COMPUTER SHOW 1998
Trade show featuring software, education and home entertainment.
Frequency: Three times a year
Exhibition Organizer: Australian Exhibition Services Pty Ltd,
Illoura Plaza, 424 St. Kilda Road,
Melbourne VIC 3004
Tel: 61 3 9867 4500
Fax: 61 3 9867 7981

Sydney
Date: 5-8 June, 1998
Location: Sydney Convention & Exhibition Centre, Darling Harbour, NSW
Brisbane
Location: Brisbane Convention & Exhibition Centre, Brisbane, QLD
Melbourne
Location: Melbourne Exhibition Centre, Melbourne, VIC

INFORMATION ON-LINE AND ON-DISC '99
Location: Sydney Convention Centre, Sydney, NSW
Trade show featuring publicly available data bases for subscription.
Frequency: Biennial
Exhibition Organizer: Australian Convention Management Services
Tel: 61 2 9332 4622
Fax: 61 2 9332 4066

INTERACT ASIA PACIFIC MULTIMEDIA FESTIVAL
Australia's biggest trade show devoted to multimedia services and products. The inaugural 1996 event hosted 32,000 visitors and 128 exhibitors. Particular emphasis is placed on attracting businesses from the Asia Pacific region.
Location: Melbourne Exhibition Centre, Melbourne, Victoria
Frequency: Annual
Exhibition Organizer: Interact Events Pty Ltd
PO Box 273
World Trade Centre
Melbourne VIC 3005
Tel: 61 3 9696 7900
Fax: 61 3 9696 7911
Email: info@interact-events.com.au

INTEROP & NETWORLD
This year's event will cover the following issues: Routing and switching the LAN, Security: joining the Internet safely, network management architectures, ATM - status report, E-commerce, switched internetworks and web server strategies, leading and latest networking products and services.
Location: Sydney Exhibition Centre, Sydney, Australia Frequency: Annual
Exhibition Organizer: Softbank Forum
Tel: 61 2 9369 1242
Fax: 61 2 9387 5482

INTERNET WORLD
Location: Sydney Exhibition Centre, Darling Harbour, NSW Frequency: Annual
Exhibition Organizer: Mecklermedia Tel: 781 237 2050
Fax: 781 237 0062
Contact: Mr Jeff Desrosiers, Director of International Sales

CONSTRUCTION (CON)

The best promotion functions are Field Days, which are outdoor functions sponsored on a State by State basis usually by the Institute of Municipal Engineering Australia. Field Days in each State are attended by Local Government Council and general Government purchasers, engineers and by all major private construction firms. Exhibitors include suppliers of most of the well-known equipment already on the market and newcomers planning to enter the market.

THE ENGINEERS FIELD DAYS
Location: Panthers World of Entertainment, Penrith, NSW Frequency: Annual
Exhibition Organizer: Institute of Municipal Engineering Australia, NSW Division
Tel: 61 2 9267 5231
Fax: 61 2 9283 5255

CIVENEX
Location: Werribee Park, Melbourne, VIC
Frequency: Annual
Exhibition Organizer: WBCM Consultants Ltd.
Tel 61 3 9699 2660
Fax 61 3 9690 9461

LOGOV EXPO

Location: Logan City, Brisbane, QLD
Frequency: Annual
Exhibition Organizer: Logan City Council Tel 61 7 3826 5259

Fax 61 7 3808 0014

EDUCATION/TRAINING (EDS) EDUTECH (Melbourne)
Date: May 23Ð25, 1999
Location: Melbourne Exhibition Centre, VIC
Educational materials and services.
Frequency: Annual
Exhibition Organizer: Australian Trade Exhibitions Pty. Ltd.
Tel: 61 3 9819 0211
Fax: 61 3 9818 8553

EDUTECH (Sydney)
Location: Sydney Convention and Exhibition Centre, Darling Harbour, NSW
Educational materials and services
Frequency: Annual
Exhibition Organizer: Australian Trade Exhibitions Pty. Ltd.
Tel: 61 3 9819 0211
Fax: 61 3 9818 8553

ENVIRONMENTAL (POL)
AWWA 18TH FEDERAL CONVENTION
Location: Adelaide Convention Center, SA
Water and wastewater management and technology.
Frequency: Biennial
Exhibition Organizer: Australian Water & Wastewater Association
Tel: 61 2 9413 1288
Fax: 61 2 9413 1047

FOOD PROCESSING & PACKAGING (FPP)
FOODPRO - 1999

Location: Sydney Convention & Exhibition Centre, Darling Harbour, NSW
This is Australia's premier food processing exhibition and conference, covering processing equipment, raw materials, weighing systems, monitoring, packaging, computers, laboratory, hygiene and testing.
Frequency: Triennial
Exhibition Organizer: Riddell Exhibition Promotions
Tel: 61 3 9429 6088
Fax: 61 3 9427 0829

FINE FOOD AUSTRALIA
Location: Sydney Convention & Exhibition Centre, Darling Harbour, NSW
Food, drink, and equipment exhibition.
Frequency:Annual
Exhibition Organizer: Australian Exhibition Services Pty. Ltd.
Tel: 61 3 9867 4500
Fax: 61 3 9867 7981

FRANCHISING (FRA)
FRANCHISING & BUSINESS OPPORTUNITIES EXPOS 1999
Dates/Locations:
Business opportunities expo for wide range of industries.
Frequency: Annual
Exhibition Organizer: Australian Exhibition Services Pty. Ltd.
Tel: 61 3 9867 4500
Fax: 61 3 9867 7981

HOSPITALITY (HTL)
MELBOURNE'S INTERNATIONAL 12TH FOODSERVICE EXHIBITION
Location: Melbourne Convention Center, VIC
Trade exhibition for the catering and foodservice industry
Frequency: Yearly, alternating Melbourne and Sydney
Exhibition Organizer: Reed Exhibition Companies
Tel: 61 2 9422 2500
Fax: 61 2 9422 2555

AUSTRALIAN HOSPITALITY INDUSTRY EXHIBITION
Location: Sydney Exhibition Center, Darling Harbour, NSW
Hospitality industry trade exhibition.
Frequency: Annual
Exhibition Organizer: Total Concept Exhibitions
Tel: 61 2 9417 8966
Fax: 61 2 9417 8864 LABORATORY & SCIENTIFIC (LAB)
SCIENCE 2000 - 1999
Date: September 7-9, 1999
Location: Sydney
Trade exhibition for scientific instruments and equipment
Frequency: Annual
Exhibition organizers: The Scientific Suppliers Association of Australia, Inc.n
Tel: 61 2 9804 8051
Fax: 61 2 9804 8052n
E-mail: ssaa@enternet.com.aun
Internet: http://www.ssaa.ans.au

MACHINE TOOLS/METALWORKING EQUIPMENT (MTL)n
(AUSTRALIA'S INTERNATIONAL ENGINEERING EXHIBITION)n
Location: Melbourne Exhibition & Convention Centre, VIC.n
General engineering, machine tools, process control, electrical and electronics.n
Frequency: Annualn
For information on USDOC Product Literature Center contact: n
Richard Reise Tel: 202 482 3489 n
John Kanawati, USFCS, Sydneyn
Tel: 61 2 9373 9207n
Fax: 61 2 9221 0573n
email: osydney@cs.doc.govn
Exhibition Organizer: Reed Exhibition Companies
Tel: 61 3 9245 7504n
Fax: 61 3 9245 7520

MEDICAL (MED) ACCESS EXPOn
Disability and Healthcare Solutionsn
Location: Sydney Showgrounds Exhibition Complex, NSWn
Exhibition for products and services for people with disabilities and the frail aged:n
Frequency: Annualn
Exhibition Organizer: Paraplegic and Quadriplegic n
Association of Victorian
Tel: 61 3 9415 1200n
Fax: 61 3 9415 1222n
Email: acccess.expo@paraquad.asn.aun
Internet: http://www.paraquad.asn.au

AUSTRALIAN INTERNATIONAL HOSPITAL AND MEDICAL EXHIBITION
Location: Sydney Showground and Exhibition Complex, NSW
Exhibition Organizer: Total Concept Exhibitionsn
Tel: 61 2 9417 8966n
Fax: 61 2 9417 8864

MINING INDUSTRY EQUIPMENT (MIN) AIMEX '99 (AUSTRALIA'S INTERNATIONAL MINING EXHIBITION)n
Location: Homebush Bay Olympic Site, Sydney, NSW. Australia's largest mining exhibition.n
Frequency: Every four years For information on USDOC Pron
duct Literature Center contact: n
John Kanawati, USFCS, Sydney Tel: 61 2 9373

9207n
Fax: 61 2 9221 0573n
email: osydney@cs.doc.gov n
Exhibition Organizer: Reed Exhibition Companiesn
Tel: 61 2 9318 3893n
Fax: 61 2 9310 5592

OIL AND GAS INDUSTRY AUSTRALASIAN OIL/GAS EXHIBITIONn
Location: Langley Park, Perth, WAn
Trade exhibition and conference for the Australian oil and gas industry.n
For information on USDOC Product Literature Center contact: n
John Shute, USFCS, Perthn
Tel/Fax: 61 8 9231 9410n
email: jshute@cs.doc.govn
Exhibition Organiser: Swan Exhibitionsn
103 Scarborough Beach Roadn
Mt. Hawthorn WA 6016n
Tel: 61 8 9443 3400n
Fax: 61 8 9242 1811

PROCESS CONTROL AND INSTRUMENTATION (PCI) ELENEX/AUTOMATE AUSTRALIAN
Location: Sydney Convention and Exhibition Center, Darling Harbor, NSWn
Trade exhibition with the theme: Process controls, robotics, and electric and electronic equipment for manufacturing.n
Frequency: Annualn
Exhibition Organizer: Australian Exhibition Servicesn
Tel: 61 3 9867 4500n
Fax: 61 3 9867 7931 n
Contact: Noela Cain, U.S. Commercial Service, American Consulate General, Melbournen
Tel: 61 3 9526 5900n
Fax: 61 3 9510 4660

SECURITY (SEC)
SECURITY ANNUAL EXHIBITION AND CONFERENCE
Location: Melbourne Convention Center, VIC
Trade exhibition and conference for the Australian security industry.
Frequency: Annual, alternating Melbourne and Sydney
For information on USDOC Product Literature Center contact: Phil Keeling, USFCS, Sydney
Tel: 61 2 9373 9209
Fax: 61 2 9221 0573
email: osydney@cs.doc.gov
Exhibition Organizer: Australian Security Industry Association
Tel: 61 2 9906 4780
Fax: 61 2 9906 4202

APPTEC POLICE TECHNOLOGY EXHIBITION & CONFERENCE
Location: Showground, Homebush Bay, Sydney
Safety & Security, communications for law enforcement agencies, trade-only show.
Frequency: Bi-annual
Exhibition Organizer: Exhibitor Services
tel: 61 2 9894 8911
fax: 61 2 9894 8533

TELECOMMUNICATIONS EQUIPMENT/SERVICES (TEL, TES) ATUG '99
Location: Sydney Exhibition Centre, Darling Harbour, NSW
Trade exhibition featuring telecommunications products and services.
Frequency: Annual
For information on USDOC Product Literature Center contact:
Bruno Mascitelli, USFCS, Melbourne
Tel: 61 3 9526 5927
Fax: 61 3 9510 4660
email: omelbourne@cs.doc.gov

Exhibition organizer: Riddell exhibition Promotions Pty Ltd
Tel: 61 2 9429 6088
Fax: 61 2 9427 0829
INTEROP & NETWORLD
Date: 22-26 November, 1999v Location: Sydney Exhibition Centre, Darling Harbour, NSW
Trade exhibition featuring the networking aspects of communications and telecommunications. Also featuring a section dedicated to internet products.
Frequency: Annual
Exhibition Organizer: Softbank Form
Tel: 61 2 9369 1242
Fax: 61 2 9387 5482

TEXTILES, APPAREL & FOOTWEAR (TXF, TXP, APP) TCF INTERNATIONAL
Location: Melbourne Exhibition Centre, VIC
Frequency: Annual
Trade exhibition for the textile, clothing, footwear and fashion accessory industries.
Exhibition Organizer: Australian Exhibition Services Pty. Ltd.
Tel: 61 3 9261 4500
Fax: 61 3 9261 4545
E-mail: Shows@ausexhibit.com.au
http://www.ausexhibit.com.au

AUSTEX/GARMENT TECH
Location: Melbourne Exhibition Centre, VIC
Trade exhibition for textiles, clothing, footwear industry machinery & products.
Exhibition Organizer: Exhibitor Services Pty. Ltd.
Tel: 61 2 9894 8911
Fax: 61 2 9894 8533
E-mail: Exhibition@onaustralia.com.au

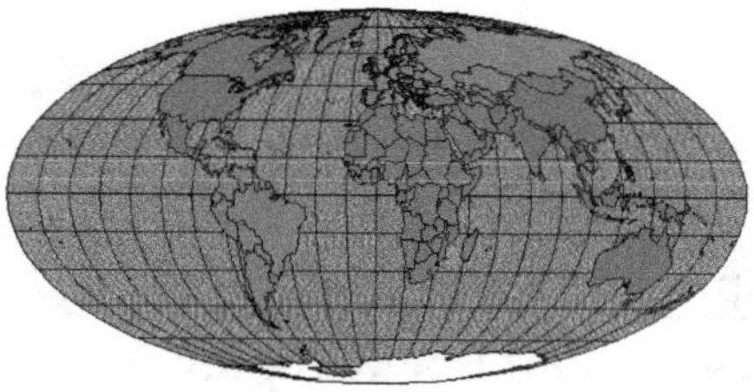

WORLD RESEARCH AND DEVELOPMENT POLICY LIBRARY

Price: $99.95 Each

Australia Research & Development Policy Handbook
Austria Research & Development Policy Handbook
Bangladesh Research & Development Policy Handbook
Belgium Research & Development Policy Handbook
Canada Research & Development Policy Handbook
China Research & Development Policy Handbook
Costa Rica Research & Development Policy Handbook
Cuba Research & Development Policy Handbook
Czech Republic Research & Development Policy Handbook
Egypt Research & Development Policy Handbook
Estonia Research & Development Policy Handbook
Finland Research & Development Policy Handbook
France Research & Development Policy Handbook
Germany Research & Development Policy Handbook
Greece Research & Development Policy Handbook
Hungary Research & Development Policy Handbook
India Research & Development Policy Handbook
Indonesia Research & Development Policy Handbook
Israel Research & Development Policy Handbook
Italy Research & Development Policy Handbook
Japan Research & Development Policy Handbook
Korea, South Research & Development Policy Handbook
Kuwait Research & Development Policy Handbook
Laos Research & Development Policy Handbook
Latvia Research & Development Policy Handbook
Lithuania Research & Development Policy Handbook
Malaysia Research & Development Policy Handbook
Mexico Research & Development Policy Handbook
Myanmar Research & Development Policy Handbook

Pakistan Research & Development Policy Handbook
Palau Research & Development Policy Handbook
Palestine Research & Development Policy Handbook
Philippines Research & Development Policy Handbook
Russia Research & Development Policy Handbook
Singapore Research & Development Policy Handbook
South Africa Research & Development Policy Handbook
Sri Lanka Research & Development Policy Handbook
Sweden Research & Development Policy Handbook
Taiwan Research & Development Policy Handbook
Thailand Research & Development Policy Handbook
Turkey Research & Development Policy Handbook
Ukraine Research & Development Policy Handbook
United Kingdom Research & Development Policy Handbook
United States Research & Development Policy Handbook

www.ingramcontent.com/pod-product-compliance
Lightning Source LLC
LaVergne TN
LVHW080028210926
848481LV00011B/3126